Writers at Work

STRATEGIES FOR COMMUNICATING IN
BUSINESS & PROFESSIONAL SETTINGS

Writers at Work

STRATEGIES FOR COMMUNICATING IN BUSINESS & PROFESSIONAL SETTINGS

Linda Flower
Carnegie Mellon University

John Ackerman
University of Utah

HARCOURT BRACE COLLEGE PUBLISHERS

Fort Worth   Philadelphia   San Diego   New York   Orlando   Austin   San Antonio
Toronto   Montreal   London   Sydney   Tokyo

PUBLISHER	Ted Buchholz
ACQUISITIONS EDITOR	Stephen T. Jordan
DEVELOPMENTAL EDITOR	Tia Black
PROJECT EDITOR	Margaret Allyson
SENIOR PRODUCTION MANAGER	Ken Dunaway
ART DIRECTOR	Peggy Young

Cover Illustration: Bob Lynch, Rep. by Marla Matson, Phoenix, Arizona

Art Program: Marco Ruiz, Dallas, Texas

Address for Editorial Correspondence:
Harcourt Brace College Publishers
301 Commerce Street, Suite 3700
Fort Worth, Texas 76102

Address for Orders:
Harcourt Brace & Company
6277 Sea Harbor Drive
Orlando, Florida 32887
1–800–782–4479 or
1–800–433–0001 (in Florida).

Copyright acknowledgments appear on pages 377 and 378, which constitute a continuation of this page.

Printed in the United States of America

ISBN: 0-15-500007-1

Library of Congress Catalog Card Number: 93-77899

3 4 5 6 7 8 9 0 1 2   016   1 2 3 4 5 6 7 8 9 0

Preface

We decided to write a textbook on business writing and communication because our students and our research taught us the many ways that the world of work was changing. We learned how *business writing* was not confined to large office buildings; it is equally the acts of speaking, writing, reading, and listening in everyday transactions—in professional offices, in not-for-profit agencies, in ad-hoc situations where people plan and act with shared purposes. We wrote a textbook that departs from conventional texts because business communication *is* a specialized kind of writing within a specialized community—while at the same time encompassing the endless variations on communicating in nonacademic settings.

We wrote this book for teachers and students who quite possibly face a common challenge. Often as not, both are newcomers to situations where skill and knowledge about language equate with success. Some teachers may know less about actual business practices but more about language and contexts for communicating. Their challenge will be to teach the strategies, routines, and tools that cross academic, professional, and everyday situations. We wrote this book with teachers in mind who themselves are trying to write and teach for more than one audience.

But, we primarily wrote this book for students—all of us—who either face the challenge of moving from a college environment into a professional one, or from one job site to another. Our goal was to provide students with a repertoire of strategies for adapting: a flexible range of approaches to professional writing that will help with important transitions, in their first jobs away from school and in future positions where they may write in new environments and possibly even in a new career. Throughout this textbook, we assume that students have learned much from their academic, professional, and personal experiences. Learning to write better is largely a process of wisely adapting what you know and can do to new situations: we teach how to assess a social and rhetorical situation, and we teach a process for responding with language to communicative problems.

As we will detail below, our textbook departs in two important ways. First, we made every effort to illustrate and teach the plural contexts, cultures, and communicative problems of business, to convey how language is inseparable from the decisions and actions of people. And second, we make our strategies, procedures, tools, and models as lively and operational as possible, to demonstrate that all writing decisions are relative to a situation. We present writing, typically a mental and private process, as a vibrant and collaborative process of inquiry.

We have based this book on years of research in academic and professional settings, and on the trial and error of our own teaching and the testing of various pieces and drafts of this book in classrooms. We believe we have produced a smart, useful, and interesting textbook on how writers write in the world of work.

Major Features

We included a number of features in this book that we are especially proud of and that distinguish it from other books of its kind. First, we tried not to do everything. We concentrated on our research on planning, collaboration, and community-based writing and on our teaching to select the components of this book.

Strategies for Writing

Each chapter previews and holds a number of key strategies for writing, writing broadly defined as reading, speaking, and composing rhetorically. Read through these strategies to learn the sequence of actions around goals such as reading a situation, planning, drafting, or revising. Each strategy is presented as an activity, often with sub-strategies that help you reach your goal.

Collaboration

We believe collaboration is much more than group work. We present collaboration as part of the context of work, a powerful option in planning and writing, integrated with complex projects, planning, and management. Collaboration also, always, has an ethical dimension.

Scenarios and Situations

In many of our chapters, we present scenarios which go beyond "cases" by presenting the context, players, and texts involved. You may read these scenarios and (briefer) situations to learn the strategies in this text or as problems in themselves for discussion and writing practice. We chose scenarios that demonstrate the decisions and savvy of a range of writers.

Critical Reading We connect reading with writing. We teach how to read for information, ideas and strategies for writing, and to assess the features of a rhetorical situation. For us, "reading a context" is part of "reading to write."

Ethics Ethics permeate every aspect of writing and communicating. Instead of isolating ethics as a unique topic, we have tried to integrate ethics and politics into all areas of this text. We believe that every act of reading, planning, or composing is ethically consequential.

Other Features

- Chapter Previews and Summaries to highlight and review key concepts and strategies.
- Ideas to Action boxes which serve as mental or actual exercises and which prompt the reader or student to pause and make sense of their progress.
- End-of-chapter projects and assignments, often based on real problems and texts, and closely integrated with the chapters, concepts, and strategies introduced. They are also referenced in the Instructor's Manual.
- An Instructor's Manual that includes both a chapter-by-chapter and syllabus approach to teaching with this textbook. It offers a glossary of concepts and terms, suggested readings and resources, and "teaching options" for the various settings for teaching learning business writing.
- A book of supplementary scenarios and cases is available entitled, Writers At Work Casebook for Teachers and Students: Nine Scenarios for Discussion and Practice
- Overhead transparencies are available for instructors from your local sale representatives.

We gratefully acknowledge the following contributors to our textbook, our research, and our teaching.

We first thank the editors and staff at Harcourt Brace College Publishers. We could not have produced this textbook without the patience and support of Tia Black and Margaret Allyson, through development and editing. Stephen T. Jordan was more than our senior editor; he was a partner throughout most of the thinking in this book and offered energy and vision through the final renditions. In addition, Bill McLane argued for years that this book needed to be written.

Next we would like to thank our reviewers: the anonymous ones chosen by Harcourt Brace and those colleagues and friends who offered comments on early versions of our texts: Ann George at Pennsylvania State University and Carolyn Miller at North Carolina State University not only tested our writing in their classrooms, their students wrote us thoughtful critiques and practical letters of advice. As we developed our cases and examples, a number of people showed how unusual "business as usual" can be. We especially thank Pat and Jill Maier, Sandy Yarien, Wayne Peck and the staff and friends at the Community Literacy Center in Pittsburgh, Joann Temple Dennett, Irene Etzkorn, Connie Drury, and Michael Rudick. In addition, we thank the many businesses and writers who allowed us to reproduce their work as examples of business communication and the processes and contexts that give them life (a list of credits concludes this book).

We received valuable and sage advice from Rebecca Burnett, Karen Schriver, Jack Selzer, Jolene Galegher, Paul Anderson, Kitty Locker, Rachel Spilka, and Mary Sue Garay.

Several people contributed directly to the ancillaries with our book. Louise Rehling wrote and compiled the Instructor's Manual and offered advice and support throughout the development of this textbook. Edward Geis, Becky Gesteland, Mark Werner, and Robert Haight contributed scenarios for the accompanying casebook. At the University of Utah, early drafts of this text were excerpted and piloted in Writing 350: Business Writing. Thus, we would like to thank all of the teachers and students connected with this course for their examples, comments, and criticisms.

We would like to thank our associates at Carnegie Mellon and the University of Utah: Kathy Meinzer, Kim Chou, Margaret Olsen.

Finally—and most importantly—we would like to thank Marlia Banning and Tim Flower who contributed love, patience, and many good ideas over the three years of collaboration that led to this publication.

LINDA FLOWER   JOHN ACKERMAN

Contents

6 Working with Others   239

7 Models for Writing   275

8 Tools for Writers   331

Writers at Work

STRATEGIES FOR COMMUNICATING IN
BUSINESS & PROFESSIONAL SETTINGS

1
Contexts and Strategies for Writers at Work

IN THIS CHAPTER we introduce business writers as people who communicate to solve problems in groups and organizations. The writer in our textbook is someone who consciously chooses when and how best to speak, read, write, or even remain silent. Those decisions depend on how well he or she can survey the territory of a rhetorical situation.

We begin with four related concepts:

- Writing well means both *finding* and *solving problems,* with a goal-directed attitude and a repertory of strategies.
- *Problem finders* uncover the multiple goals, agendas, and *conflicts* that define problems.
- Problems are rooted in *rhetorical situations,* a social context, and the reasons or events that prompted you and others to communicate.
- Problems, situations, and the writers who seek solutions are bound by *discourse communities,* people with common language and expectations.

Understanding these four concepts will let you conduct a *rhetorical survey*—a strategy for looking beneath the surface of an assignment and treating your writing as a strategic, social, and rhetorical action.

At the end of the chapter you are invited to conduct your own rhetorical survey of three scenarios, that is, three extended examples of writers and texts in rhetorical situations:

 A CORPORATE SCENARIO. Joining the Digi-Tech proposal team

 AN ACADEMIC SCENARIO. Comparing academic and professional writing

 A NON-PROFIT SCENARIO. Proposal writing at the Community Literacy Center

1
Contexts and Strategies for Writers at Work

THE CONTEXT OF BUSINESS IS THE CONTEXT OF CHANGE

American business is moving into a global economy, and that means that "business as usual" is the business of adapting to change.[1] For example: In the early 1990s General Motors, one of the largest corporations in the world, lost $7 billion, closed 21 plants, and predicted losses of 74,000 jobs over the next five years. As a result, GM reorganized its company and its systems of production, distribution, and marketing. For GM employees the aftershocks of reorganization meant new managers, new peers, shifting responsibilities, and retraining.

Small businesses and entrepreneurs feel the same tides of change. For example, many computer software houses began as small research and development businesses or as individual consultants. But in the face of exponential growth firms such as Novell or Microsoft had to shed the folksy organizational structures of small businesses and learn how to operate efficiently in a corporate setting, while retaining their edge in product development. And consider the impact of Walmart, which has been described as a classic American success story, with a retail and distribution organization that has expertly predicted changes in this country's economy and consumer preferences over the last 30 years. When Walmart grew to over 2000 stores in 1992, its sophisticated merchandising pressured local retail merchants to rethink their marketing strategies, to offer alternative services and products, or be enveloped by Walmart's success. In the next 30 years, the companies that thrive will be the ones that read a changing marketplace and adjust.

In the middle of change, you have to communicate. The people who thrive in the context of business are the ones who can not only analyze problems and communicate their ideas to others, but can enter a new situation and figure out what they need to do—and that often means what they are expected to contribute as a writer or speaker. Consider these two scenarios:

With a degree in finance behind you, you arrive for your first day on the job. The entry-level position for all new bank employees is credit analysis. Your training is in finance, but in this job you will be judged (and placed after six months) primarily on the basis of the skill with which you write the concise two-page credit reports for new loan applications. As your superiors judge your writing, they will not look exclusively for correctness, style, or a detailed summary (skills you may have practiced in school), but for your ability to translate a wealth of information in a way that helps the loan manager make a good decision.

You are beginning your career by entering a computer software company's training program for regional sales representatives. This is the first step toward advancement to account manager with added responsibilities in product development and quality control. Your degree in accounting satisfied the basic job requirement, but your supervisors were also impressed with your coursework in computer science and English. For this job, you were hired because your employer saw in you a blend of business, technical, and communication savvy. Whatever your potential on paper, you now face the task of learning what the sales reps do, how they interact with other departments, and what kind of writing they are expected to produce as they plan for and report on their sales work.

WHAT DOES THIS MEAN FOR YOU?

Whether you expect to work in a major corporation, a smaller company, or as a self-employed professional, the key to success is adaptation and the basic premise of this textbook is that successful writing and speaking depend on how well you *read a social situation and adapt your communication strategies to fit.* This social situation includes not only face-to-face relationships, but the organization you are part of, its standard lines of communication, and its political alignments and history. In school you learned to "consider your audience" when you write or speak. In business you will find that you have many audiences who expect very different kinds of information and communication from you.

If you want to be an effective communicator in business two things must happen. First, beyond learning the standard forms and styles of business writing—such as clear, concise, and correct memos and reports—you have to learn how to solve problems with your writing and speaking. Effective businessmen and women have learned how to assess a situation, define a problem (often in writing), and then use their assessment of the situation to guide their communication. This book will teach you strategies for finding and solving communication problems in business.

Second, in the changing world of business and as your career progresses, you must learn how to *keep* learning how to communicate effectively. New jobs and responsibilities will require that you add new kinds of writing and speaking skills or adjust the old ones. Although the scene may change

apply/adapt comon...skill to new situation

around you, you will have to act as if you know the ropes and operate as if you were a wise member of an organization or social group. We shall introduce to you many familiar forms of business writing and to conventions and strategies for producing the best results; however, we have written this book as much to teach you how to implement these forms and strategies as to address new situations and challenges.

This chapter introduces four key concepts that we shall use throughout the book and that you can apply to any new situation.

- Problem solving
- Problem finding
- Rhetorical situations
- Discourse communities

In a nutshell, we argue that writing is a goal-directed, problem-solving activity. Problem solving, however, starts with problem finding, in which you, the writer, must decide what is at stake in the midst of ill-defined goals, agendas, and conflicts. To solve a communication problem you need to understand how it fits within its larger rhetorical situation. And you need to see how you and the rhetorical situation fit into a larger discourse community.

At the end of this section, all these ideas come together in a technique called the **rhetorical survey** that lets you place each new writing task within its larger rhetorical context. If any of these four concepts are new to you, read this chapter as if you were building a tool kit of concepts for conducting your own survey—for that is exactly what we will do at the end of the chapter.

WRITING AS PROBLEM SOLVING

Throughout our text, when we refer to "the writer," we are thinking of someone who writes, speaks, reads, and listens strategically. We put writing in the foreground in this textbook because, although it appears less frequently in work settings than talk, writing often has the more lasting effect. Indeed, writing has a unique status in our culture: People say it is difficult to produce and respect its permanence. Although we are in the midst of an electronic revolution, writing still is the medium used to formalize decision making.

We also see writers as people who choose wisely when to write, speak, or remain silent, and the writer in our text uses writing and speaking to participate in social transactions, in response to situations that call for action. In some circumstances, the wise decision is no action at all, but even these decisions, to us, are strategic and rhetorical. In this text we are concerned with those situations that call for communicative action and those for which the writer does not know automatically what or how to communicate. Writers become **problem solvers** when they try to figure out the best way to carry out a social transaction; when they:

- Take a goal-directed attitude to shaping meaning, communicating, and interacting with other people; when they
- Use effective strategies to resolve conflicts and to reach their goals.

Effective problem solvers demonstrate two attributes. One is the knowledge, born of experience, that comes only with time on the job. This is the **knowledge** we usually think of as a knowledge of facts, ideas, trends, and relationships that defines advanced skill and experience. The other is **a repertoire of strategies** for planning, drafting, and revising language that can be learned and practiced, just as athletes practice new moves and plays. Some of the strategies presented in this book (designing a technical proposal, for instance) are techniques for special purposes. Others (such as collaborative planning) are more general strategies you can adapt to different situations. These strategies give you a tested, more efficient way to solve problems, often based on research into the problem-solving strategies of experienced writers. However, strategies are not rules or a step-by-step procedure—you have to decide when to use them and how to adapt old strategies to new situations. You must be a strategic thinker, too. In short, good writers and speakers do not depend on luck or a mysterious genius, because they have developed a repertoire of problem-solving strategies. They are not limited to having one "good way" that worked for them in school or on their last work assignment. Instead, they are strategic problem solvers who know how to compensate for limited experience because they can think their way through a new or challenging task. That's the genius we are after.

And it is a power you already possess. From your years in school or your work experience, you already have a substantial collection of strategies for writing and speaking. Many college students survive by developing efficient techniques for condensing and summarizing unfamiliar, technical information in a research paper. Students learn how to skim stacks of texts, find the interesting detail or quote, and produce a paper the night before it is due. Though your instructors may rightly criticize some of these strategies, we think they have many positive attributes, such as the ability to condense information in a hurry. On the other hand, a strategy works best when it fits the task. For example, you also need to know when *not* to summarize, for instance, and when to develop a persuasive argument. When your task isn't formulaic, familiar, or automatic, then preparing the night before on autopilot can be a disaster. We want to broaden your repertoire so you can put both old and new strategies to work in finding and solving professional problems—which includes the "problem" of writing.

FINDING PROBLEMS

a. positive
b. negative

What is a **problem?** Problems arise for all kinds of reasons—when something needs to be done but it is not yet clear how to do it, when you are at point A and need to be at point B, or when two or more goals or agendas come into conflict. Problems arise internally when people have competing goals, such as the desire to contribute to a good cause and maintain a balanced checking account. And, of course, problems arise between people. But don't assume, when two people have a problem, that they are necessarily angry, competitive, or working at cross-purposes. Conflicts are a normal part of professional life because people operate with different goals and agendas. Goals are specific intentions, plans, or aspirations. They grow out of larger agendas that reflect our beliefs, values, and investments that define who we are. Problems in business communication often arise, just as they do in our personal or academic lives, when these goals come into conflict or when one person or party needs something from someone else but those needs are unclear, hidden, or unarticulated. That is why problem solving starts with problem finding, when people

- Define the underlying goals and agendas of others in a situation, and
- Find out where the conflict really lies.

In professional writing, you are likely to find yourself in the middle of a conflict when too many of your own goals come into play at the same time. For example, your specific task may be to write an accurate report to your supervisor in a clear, readable style—*but also* to suggest a plan that will redefine your responsibilities for months to come, *and* to anticipate biases or plans your supervisor already has, and the response of your peers, by whom you want to be seen as a team player. Figure 1-1 presents the ways that people define problems in two common situations: doing a collaborative writing assignment in school and negotiating a contract in business with an outside consultant. In each situation both parties were trying to find a common ground, but their agreement was complicated by conflicting goals and agendas. Problem finding—naming conflicts, goals, and agendas—was the first step toward a solution.

Notice how some conflicts grow out of long-term agendas, such as the way Sam uses the threat of a deadline to motivate his writing, or the consultant's agenda to cover the high costs of developing new workshops. As we said, such agendas are often hidden from view. Frequently, they will not be apparent in a situation or through casual observation, and most people do not habitually

Situations, Tasks	Finding Problems: Naming Conflicts, Goals, & Agendas			Solutions
A collaborative writing task in school	Jean likes to plan ahead; Sam depends on deadlines.	Both writers like to keep their autonomy.	Neither wants to risk a grade and joint work is better.	Write in two sections, but share the planning and editing, to bolster each other's talents.
A contract negotiation with a corporation and a consultant	The corp. wants to pay $X; the consultant wants $Y for services. Both want a contract.	The corp. has to limit expenses & possible losses, i.e., find an acceptable level of risk.	The consultant wants to limit risk by lowering up-front costs or gaining a long term contract.	Set up a cost-per-item scale to consultant.

FIGURE 1–1

Finding and Solving Problems by Naming Conflicts, Goals, and Agendas

share all of their agendas. This means that conflicts are often expressed as two or more solutions that seem to compete with one another: Sam's typical solution to collaborative assignments is to split the task into two parts and hope they fit; Jean prefers to take over and write the whole project because partners tend not to keep up with her scheduling. One advantage of stated conflicts is that it becomes easier to think of ways to reconcile real conflicts than imagined ones. Imagine how different the solution would have been if the corporation and consultant each defined the problem as "the other party is just greedy" instead of as the problem of balancing costs and risks for everyone. Finally, as you can see, the solution to any problem is a tentative one—the best, most informed approach the writer can find at the moment.

READING THE RHETORICAL SITUATION

To find problems, to define them, and to solve them often means knowing how to read a rhetorical situation. A **rhetorical situation** is the immediate social context and the reasons or events that prompted you to speak or write. It also includes the other people involved in this transaction, their goals and agendas, and their attempts at communicating effectively. It is called a *rhetorical* situation because it requires a written or spoken response in which you try to persuade or inform someone else. Walking into a rhetorical situation and responding to it means that you

- Enter into a transaction with an audience, where you
- Choose language to reshape the situation, to establish your own voice or authority, and to anticipate how other people in the situation may respond.

For thousands of years, the art of rhetoric has been the art of reading a situation and choosing the best available means to respond. This definition differs from the popular connotation of the word, as applied to slick sales gimmicks or politicians—that is, to disguise or to twist the truth through fancy language. You enter a rhetorical situation any time you argue an idea with a friend, offer a compliment, or give advice. In everyday transactions people are rhetorical whenever they pay attention and respect their audience and seek an ethical exchange. For example, suppose you are asked to write a straightforward report with the goal of imparting information—but you also design it to convince your supervisor that your information is well documented and complete. You have made a rhetorical decision about the best way to respond to serve your own and your audience's interests. Of course, two people will not always read a rhetorical situation the same way. And this can cause problems.

Consider the following rhetorical situation in which both parties obviously define the situation as problem laden, but each defines the problem differently and assumes his or her message will result in a particular, "appropriate" response. Some time ago, one of us began receiving a magazine to which he had not subscribed. This led to his writing a letter to the editor to cancel the subscription. The solution to the problem at the outset seemed to be straightforward—a short letter must be written that said, "I did not order nor do I want the magazine" with any necessary details (magazine title, dates, etc.). It also seemed clear enough that one would address the communication to an editor or customer service representative, who would simply cancel the subscription.

The rhetorical situation appeared to present no conflicting goals or agendas because the problem was procedural in nature. Or so it seemed. Over time, the situation thickened, because the writer disregarded an earlier request from the publisher to pay the bill, and they in turn apparently did not act on an earlier phone call to cancel the subscription. More recently, the writer was contacted by a bill-collection agency (see Figure 1-2), writing on behalf of the magazine publisher. He in turn responded (Figure 1-3) to reshape the rhetorical situation in his interest. A once-simple situation had grown into a conflict between two parties with related but now competing goals and agendas.

Let's examine the goals and agendas implied by this form letter. Certainly, the "demand for payment due" is an attempt to provoke a payment response. The letter also sends a clear message about the persona and position of a collection agency; it promotes its own authority by invoking legal

SECURITY COLLECTION SYSTEM
A SUBDIVISION OF DATA VERIFICATION, INC.
110 S. CHARLES ST., NEWTON, DE 19800

JUNE 12, 1991

564-77777-AKE46J
MR JOHN M ACKERMAN
1467 EMERSON AVENUE
SALT LAKE CITY, UT 84105

YOUR ACCOUNT: 5629040-7

765900000AKG:2
RE: TODAY'S BACKPACKING MAGAZINE $12.98

DEMAND FOR PAYMENT DUE

YOUR SUBSCRIPTION TO TODAY'S BACKPACKING MAGAZINE REMAINS
UNPAID AND YOUR NAME IS LISTED IN OUR DELINQUENT FILE.

WE HAVE REMINDED YOU SEVERAL TIMES BEFORE THIS OF YOUR
OBLIGATION. YOU SUBSCRIBED TO THIS MAGAZINE AND YOU DID NOT
CANCEL YOUR SUBSCRIPTION. NOW WE HAVE SUSPENDED YOUR
SERVICE BECAUSE OF NONPAYMENT. YOUR ACCOUNT IS LONG PAST
DUE.

INATTENTION TO THIS MATTER WILL RESULT IN SERIOUS DAMAGE TO
YOUR CREDIT RATING. YOU MUST RETURN YOUR PAYMENT TODAY IN
THE ENCLOSED ENVELOPE. MAKE YOUR CHECK PAYABLE TO SECURITY
COLLECTION SYSTEM. WHEN WE RECEIVE YOUR REMITTANCE, WE WILL
REMOVE YOUR NAME FROM THE DELINQUENT FILE.

DETACH HERE ►KPN

DETACH HERE

**TO ASSURE
PROPER CREDIT:**
1. MAKE YOUR
CHECK PAYABLE
TO SECURITY
COLLECTION SYSTEM.
2. PAY THE FULL
AMOUNT.
3. MAIL BOTH YOUR
PAYMENT AND OUR
REMITTANCE STUB.

PAYMENT DUE BY JUN 26, 1991
AMOUNT DUE $12.98
RE: TODAY'S BACKPACKING MAGAZINE
45484AAAAACK33J-001

INFORMATION CONCERNING YOUR RIGHTS
AND OBLIGATIONS APPEARS ON THE BACK
OF THIS LETTER.

YOUR CREDIT RATING: TOO PRECIOUS TO LOSE!

INFORMATION CONCERNING YOUR RIGHTS APPEARS ON THE REVERSE OF THIS LETTER.

FIGURE 1–2

The Bill Collection
Letter

June 15, 1991

Security Collection System
RE: Your harassment based on my assumed account with
    Today's Backpacking Magazine and PC Press . . .

First, the Today's Backpacking subscription con is an
example of a "negative-option" marketing plan, whereby
a vendor provides a sample and starts billing if the
consumer fails to notify that the service or sample is
not desired. Besides the ethical slime in this form of
marketing, it is now being challenged in court. As
reported in my paper (Salt Lake Tribune, June 14)
attorneys general in four states filed lawsuits against
a cable TV firm using this ploy. In my state, the
director of commerce made the negative-option marketing
plan illegal "by applying it to the Utah Consumers
Sales Practices Act." Maybe this applies or maybe not;
the point is people are catching on and doing something
about it.

Second, about three weeks ago I called PC Press and
said that I never received any issues beyond the
promotional hook and that I had no desire, then or now,
to receive their rag. The person with whom I spoke
apologized and said the matter was closed.

Third, if this harassment continues, I will notify the
postal service, the Utah Attorney General's Office or
whomever or whatever is out there to protect people
like me from people like you.

Sincerely,

John M. Ackerman
1467 Emerson Ave.
Salt Lake City, UT 84105

cc: PC Press Inc., 129 North St. Central, PA 18098

FIGURE 1-3
The Heated Reply

and monetary penalties. The agency intends that the fact of the collection letter and the impact of demands and penalties will lead to an expeditious response. However, the recipient reads the letter and the situation differently. The action taken responds to the rhetorical situation created by the collection agency letter, but how did the writer redefine the situation? How would you describe the persona he assumed in this situation and how does this letter imply other goals and agendas?

Similar to the collection agency, the writer used facts, other authorities (newspaper, government agencies), and straightforward wording. By taking a strong position, he selectively responded to the publisher's and collection agency's tactics and policies, defining the problem differently. The writer rejected the role of the "delinquent subscriber," arguing instead for consumer rights based on his understanding of the billing and collection process. In our earlier examples, we presented writing and problem solving as best served through open negotiations of conflicting goals and agendas. This example shows how a rhetorical situation is in the eye of the beholder—people construct rhetorical situations differently.

The message sent, then, is sometimes quite different from the message received. Although the first was a form letter, written for broad (but pointed) application, the writer who received it personalized it into a direct one-to-one correspondence. How would you judge the effectiveness of both letters? The form letter did lead to action, but the responding letter attempted not only to turn the tables but also to advance a position valued by the author. In many circumstances, this being one, writers strategically choose language and even the visual appearance of a text to reshape the rhetorical situation to fit their agenda.

ENTERING NEW DISCOURSE COMMUNITIES

As a business writer, you will not only walk into new rhetorical situations, but into a number of new communities as well. Even if your audience appears to be one person or agency—a bill collector, teacher, or client—that person or group belongs to a community of other readers and writers carrying out the same sorts of transactions. Being a member of an educational community, for instance, shapes what teachers look for and how they respond to your writing. The discourse of school offers some standard ways of communicating between student and teacher. However, the next instant, when either student or teacher opens their mail, they may enter, in part, into the world of a customer or consumer advocate, as with the "heated reply." The longer you stay in school or on a job, the more specialized you become, and the more you begin to write for specific **discourse communities,** groups of like-minded people who share the same interests and responsibilities, if not the same physical context for work. At this point in your schooling, you may still write for teachers, but you are probably also trying to achieve the voice of someone in your field, such as a business major or accountant, financial analyst, or marketing person. When you write and speak in ways that relate to the ongoing affairs of a specialized group, you are communicating to participate in a discourse community.

Joining a new discourse community is a little like walking into a conversation that was going on before you got there. For example, if your employer were to throw a welcoming party for new personnel, before you arrived you would naturally and strategically consider the people who might be present and how you would act given their goals and agendas. As you join the party, you are immediately aware (and probably intimidated by) the number of conversations in progress. You wish you had been present for the earlier discussion to help manage the risks of joining the conversation late. As you speak, you choose your words carefully or perhaps rely on cocktail party chit-chat that you hope will momentarily fit.

Most people find writing and speaking in public situations difficult for the same reasons that they find it difficult to join someone else's conversation. Those who are already part of the conversation make it look easy when it is not. They seem to know what to do; they exhibit that apparent genius of knowing what to say and when to say it. As a writer, you will need to do two things; the first is to

- Recognize the discourse communities you belong to and have just entered, asking "Where am I and what are the expectations and language habits of these communities?"

Secondly, whenever you encounter new discourse, you may have to "enter" it innovatively by

- Learning quickly how to use its language conventions strategically.

Let's take apart that phrase "discourse community." Communities have a history, shared values and turf, and common ways of communicating and carrying on the business at hand. By adding the word "discourse" to "community," we place the power of language to bind people together or to build walls between them in the foreground. Examples of discourse communities are everywhere, and at this point in your life you participate simultaneously in many. You may belong to a discourse community that talks about sports, debates environmental policies, or runs a business—such as a book store, with its OPs (out-of-print), OSs (out-of-stocks), and back orders. Although fluent in the vocabulary of political, recreational, or social groups—such as a computer support group that swaps systems details, the newest software, and application routines—you may have sensed the boundaries of discourse communities that are not quite yours yet. You may have sat at the periphery of a discourse community when you moved from a high school group to a college one, from college to a business setting, or from one job to another.

Words passed you by and you were not always sure what was at issue; you felt these boundaries largely because you appreciated the power of language to decide who can participate, who cannot, and what is appropriate to say.

Your awareness of community boundaries is essential for your writing and problem solving, because if you share the language of a community, you are more able to see the hidden agendas and ill-defined goals we illustrated earlier. A discourse community in a work setting defines itself through a **common language and set of expectations** that are based on:

- shared goals and agendas that come with membership and status;
- active participation in a specialized group, network, or organization;
- specific job requirements shared and understood by others; and
- common language, common topics, and shared ways of presenting ideas or building a case.

Communities tend to overlap, even within a business organization or field. For example, your job as a credit analyst means that you learn how to work with other analysts, people who share common ways of communicating (credit reports, summaries, electronic mail messages, briefing statements). As an employee of a large lending company, you also know how to talk with other departments and personnel, such as investment brokers and managers. With time, you find that you are recognized by credit analysts at other institutions as having a certain know-how. The **knowledge** you have of the discourse community of credit analysts concerns standard forms and procedures and a set of **strategies** for how to transform a file folder bulging with information on a client (credit references, past histories, current plans, assets) into a concise report that speaks to several communities at once.

Learning how to write and speak in a discourse community can get complicated. People already inside the community sometimes think their ways of communicating are accessible or obvious, when they are not. As a newcomer, it is often up to you to figure out the language and expectations of the new discourse. Consider this scenario:

> Your new employer is a small, busy desktop publishing company on West Main Street with a staff of six. On Monday morning, your "training program" as a production coordinator consists of a hearty welcome, a tour of the coffee machine, supply cabinet, and your desk, which holds a pile of projects in process and unanswered mail from local businesses asking for bids. Your "training materials" are the file of correspondence left by your predecessor (requests for information, review of services, proposals, schedules, and follow-up letters), plus the on-the-run advice you get from other people in the office. Few people in your area have time to tell you all they have learned, and you are expected to act as if you not only know your area but the rest of the company as well.

For the newcomer, writing is like performing in any new social situation. You need first to understand the situation as quickly as possible, including its expectations and conventional ways of writing and speaking. And secondly, you need to call up a flexible set of problem-solving strategies—for planning, drafting, evaluating, and collaborating—that lets you translate this understanding into action. This is how we have arranged this book: by beginning with how to read situations, then moving into these strategies.

However, the trials of learning how to operate in a new discourse community do not disappear when the awkward moments in a new job pass by. As you gain experience on the job, that knowledge takes you into new responsibilities, new tasks, new team alliances. As you progress, you will again be expected to figure out community expectations as the language, knowledge, players, conventions, and strategies change—as we see below:

> At this moment, your success as a sales representative in the field has brought you into the office as an accounts manager, where instead of writing field reports, you are using them to help plan the fall sales campaign. This job has in turn given you a seat on the new product development committee, which evaluates proposals from other reps and managers and which makes recommendations to the executive committee. Your discourse community has evolved to include two very distinct audiences—the sales team and the executive committee—who have different but overlapping ways of writing and acting.

Sometimes you have the luxury of growing up within a particular discourse community, and its language and expectations seem like second nature. It is easy to speak like an insider. But what about the times you are asked to enter quickly into a new professional community or to switch hastily to another discourse (and be flexible)—that of the sales force, or management, or product design?

For many people, the most dramatic shift among discourse communities occurs when they leave school. As a student, the standards for writing are relatively stable because there is that community of teachers, scholars, researchers, and other students who share many of the same expectations of what a research report or essay should do and what are the conventions for organization and style. People in an academic discourse community do not always agree on every convention or share all that they know (you have probably had to ask a teacher or a peer to clarify how detailed a paper should be or how to handle assigned readings). But as a member of that community, at least you know which questions to ask. As you move from school to the world of work, many of these academic writing forms and styles will lose their currency. For example, research on new employees in technical fields has shown that new graduates often write long, narrative reports that illuminate their research processes, whereas the senior employees have learned to focus on results and to summarize methods as concisely as possible. On the job, you may have to learn quickly what a firm expects in its quarterly reports, and over time your growth and advancement will depend on how well you learn how to communicate with several discourse communities at once.

CONDUCTING A RHETORICAL SURVEY

In this chapter we have presented some key terms and new ideas. We have said that writing is a problem-solving activity—a response to a rhetorical situation where problems arise out of conflicting goals and agendas. Problem solving, however, starts with problem finding. As a writer you have to define the problem you want to solve by *seeing conflicts,* by *exploring the immediate rhetorical situation,* and by *understanding the expectations of the larger discourse community* you are in.

But how in the world does a writer do that? It is one thing to respond to an explicit task, said face-to-face or given in writing, and it is another to respond to invisible situations and communities. Your first step should be to **conduct a rhetorical survey.** That is, as Figure 1-4 suggests, do a preliminary survey that looks beyond the writing task to the rhetorical situation and a community as a way to define the problem. If you looked up from your computer and saw a *simple* task, you would see something like this:

The Explicit --------> Immediate --------> The Problem --------> The Action
Task, Text, Topic   Audience   At Hand   You Take

Most writing tasks in school and some on the job are like this—the task before you holds most of the important information you need to consider to take action, to write or speak effectively; but writing in work settings is more commonly complicated by the invisible, the situations and communities that reach beyond a writing task or even a primary audience. Inexperienced writers often struggle because they can see no further than the page and immediate context before them.

Complex writing problems are found and solved successfully by surveying the entire landscape before you to give yourself *the big picture*. If you are an old hand, this survey comes as a habit, the knowledge you have through years of experience. If you are new, the survey must be done consciously, explicitly, so that your writing (or speaking or other action) will reshape the rhetorical situation. Notice that your writing is also a part of this event; it is an action that not only responds to the context, but changes it.

Figure 1-4 offers an image of the stance you need to take when conducting a rhetorical survey.

Once you start surveying the landscape to find and define complex problems, the next step is to ask: What are the *key features* I see? Figure 1-4 and

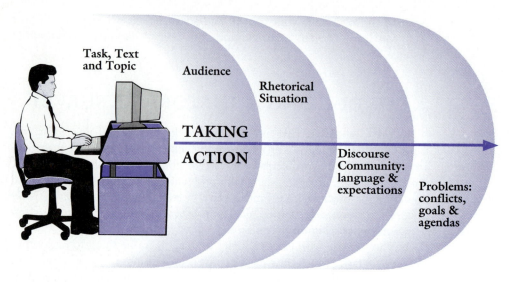

FIGURE 1–4
Conducting a Rhetorical Survey

the following checklist add the four concepts introduced earlier to the more common concepts of tasks and audience in writing. Notice what happens to the problems found and acted upon, and the consequences of those actions. People choose to ignore complexity, to keep things simple sometimes in order to avoid the consequences of situations and communities. We think that conducting a rhetorical survey not only prepares you for writing to serve your own interests but those of the many people around you, as well.

ONCE I HAVE THE BIG PICTURE, WHAT NEXT?

The rest of this book is an answer to the question, "Once I have the big picture, what next?" Our goal is to help you to take *strategic action*. At work, you will often be rewarded for your ability to use multiple strategies, to move through multiple discourses, and to participate in and respect a variety of communities. Here is where your repertoire of strategies for reading, planning, drafting, evaluating, and collaborating can make a difference—if you remain aware of when and how best to use them.

The chapters that follow will show you ways to build on your preliminary rhetorical survey, and help you to develop a greater range of strategies for:

A CHECKLIST FOR CONDUCTING A RHETORICAL SURVEY

THE TASK, TEXT, AND TOPIC

This is where most writers start and inexperienced writers stop. At the outset ask: What am I supposed to produce—what format, organization, or style? What sources should I tap? What information should I cover? Task, text, and topic are useful, but deceptive, pieces, of information because the information is readily available and, on the surface, complete. *ex. Is my task a report? formal/informal? external/internal? organiz? topic?*

THE AUDIENCE

Once writers realize they must not just deliver information in prepacked form, they begin to think seriously about their readers. Writers in business and professional settings compose for three kinds of readers. One is the **primary** audience of decision makers who have to accept, approve, or be persuaded by the text. The other is the **secondary** audience of people who will use the information for other purposes or who need to be informed or included. In work environments, the solitary writer is nearly obsolete, so some of your readers will also be **coauthors.** Organizations often consider the texts their employees write to be another kind of corporate product. Even if one writer signs as primary author, drafts go through editing and review cycles, and larger projects will be delegated to many contributors. Make it a habit to list and prioritize the many people who have given input to what you write.

THE RHETORICAL SITUATION

Experienced writers place tasks and audiences in rhetorical situations. They ask: What event is triggering the need to write? Who are the players involved in this rhetorical act? What are their goals and agendas and how do these interact with mine? Because rhetorical acts have histories, writers ask: What has already occurred? What will happen as a result of my writing? As you survey your audiences' goals, agendas, and conflicts, add to your contribution the variety of purposes attached to their speaking and writing. Can you construct or reconstruct the conversations that defined these previous situations so that your problem definition is tied to action and consequence? The way you

CONTINUED FROM PAGE 19

construct the rhetorical situation will help you choose effective strategies and design your written or spoken response—and it will help you prioritize your alternative solutions.

DISCOURSE COMMUNITIES

You, the people you work with, your audiences, and your rhetorical situation exist within a larger social and cultural context which, like a familiar neighborhood, can go unnoticed or be taken for granted. Look for the language conventions and expectations—the insider talk, patterns of organization, argument strategies, and commonplace ideas—that each community uses and values. Sometimes you want to examine a social, professional, or cultural community in order to act like an insider. At other times, you want to examine it critically, to note how the history and discourse of a community, for instance, has tended to exclude or include members—this ethical move is central to business writing because language has just such power to include or exclude people. Part of the current change in business (referred to earlier) is the rapidly increasing diversity of people in Western business and academic institutions. Your success as a professional will depend on maintaining conversations across these diverse groups and learning to identify the customarily unquestioned habits of language you use that may exclude people because of their gender, sexual orientation, ethnicity, or economic class.

FINDING PROBLEMS

By examining explicit tasks, audiences, social situations, and community expectations you can begin to find the problems and conflicts within this rhetorical situation. Problem finding need not strangle your ability to speak or write. However, the problem you find and then act upon will shape how you act and the consequences that follow. Writers act as problem solvers when they recognize the complexities of personal and interpersonal conflicts, and the solutions they propose are choices from among a number of alternatives. Conflicts rarely boil down to simple choices and often force us to confront old habits and routines. As we demonstrated earlier, the effective writer will try to articulate the goals and agendas that lead to different needs and conflicts among the people involved.

CONTINUED FROM PAGE 20

TAKING ACTION

An action arrow runs through the hypothetical landscape in Figure 1-4 because by speaking or writing you become an active part of the situation. Here is where you need to have a writer's repertory of problem-solving strategies and use the rhetorical survey to consider alternative actions you might take (and where they might take you). Is this the time to write a persuasive report and recommendation or merely to start a discussion? Should you analyze your client's particular problems or just do a dazzling presentation of the new product?

Or take the question of exclusionary language cited earlier: In a diverse professional community, the ethical action of trying to include people who may not fit stereotypes of the mainstream power group is a wise act—you are making an expansive judgment about the potential audience. But bear in mind that you are also making ethical choices when you decide *how* to act, having defined a problem, and when you decide *whose* goals matter. Some people—especially new employees—fear that taking ethical action means that they must condemn the actions of others or insist that what they believe is right. They see ethical action in business as a dangerous, all, or, nothing move. However, ethical action can begin with everyday acts of defining and sharing problems in conversation, at a planning meeting, or in a report; when you decide which problems get mentioned, whose conflicts are discussed, and whose goals and agendas are recognized and valued.

In short, an important part of taking action as a writer is done before you ever put a word on the page, when you survey the rhetorical landscape, interpret the situation, and decide what is important and what is not. The arrow in Figure 1-4 also represents the choices you make about how to act. Once you begin to look at the entire rhetorical landscape from the perspective of a problem solver, you may feel that your status as a newcomer in the hierarchy of a corporation or profession grants you little power or opportunity to think or speak for yourself. However, the more you understand the context at hand and the more strategies you have to call on, the more able you will be to cut a distinctive path through rhetorical situations—even as a newcomer.

- *Reading the Context*   *Chapter Two*
  Building a reflective and critical understanding of situations and problems
- *Strategies for Planning*   *Chapter Three*
  Using alternative strategies to build a rhetorical plan
- *Turning Plans into Drafts*   *Chapter Four*
  Applying your knowledge of conventions and texts
- *Evaluating and Testing As You Revise*   *Chapter Five*
  Anticipating the responses of your readers
- *Working with Others*   *Chapter Six*
  Making collaboration work, especially on complex projects

And for additional help, you can turn to two resource chapters:

- *Models for Writing*   *Chapter Seven*
  Conventional types and uses of business writing
- *Tools for Writers*   *Chapter Eight*
  Techniques for graphic and oral presentations and other tools

Each chapter offers some general, widely applicable problem-solving strategies and other, more situation-specific ones. Some of our strategies will be new to you, but others will simply help you give a name to things you have done before. Our goal here, and throughout, is to help you gain more conscious control over your own strategies. As you read, remember that because this is a book, we present these strategies one by one—as steps in a progression you can follow; but from your own writing experience, you know a strategy's usefulness depends on circumstance: Why wait until you submit an essay to test an idea on a reader, or why limit your planning to the first moments of composing when you know your thinking will continue to evolve?

Ideas to Action

Before you jump into learning new strategies, we suggest that you look at the three scenarios at the end of this chapter, and see for yourself what can turn up when you conduct a rhetorical survey of a real rhetorical event. These scenarios may also help those of you who have little experience in business and professional settings. We will refer to them as examples throughout the text.

Summary

- **Problem solving.** Problem solvers take a goal-directed attitude to shape meaning, to communicate, and to interact with other people. They depend on (and try to develop) a repertory of strong, alternative strategies to reach their goals.
- **Conflict.** Problems arise out of conflict, such as when you are at point A and need to be at point B or when different goals and agendas come into conflict. Notice that the conflict can be in your own mind or between different people.
- **Problem finding.** Problem solving starts with problem finding, that is, with recognizing when the underlying goals and agendas of people in a situation may be in conflict and with trying to define the problem by stating where the conflict really lies.
- **Rhetorical situations.** A rhetorical situation is a situation that requires a written or spoken response in which you try to persuade or inform. It includes the immediate social context, the reasons or event that prompted you to speak, and the circle of people involved in the transaction.
- **Discourse community.** A discourse community is formed when people who share common goals or interests begin to communicate on the basis of a common language, commonplace assumptions, and a set of shared expectations and conventions.
- **Rhetorical survey.** A rhetorical survey is the stance you take in communicating when you want to get the big picture by finding and defining a problem by examining task and audience in light of the rhetorical situation and discourse community before you. Getting this big picture lays the foundation for problem solving and strategic action.

Projects & Assignments

1. What are the multiple goals and (hidden and visible) agendas you face as a writer and problem solver? Draw up a chart similar to Figure 1-1 that describes a rhetorical situation you recently faced in terms of a problem and solution. Try to tease out as many goals, expectations, values, habits, and beliefs as you can that created some form of conflict in this rhetorical situation and write a brief analysis of what they were and what you did. Were any of your conflicts based on hidden agendas or goals you had to infer or figure out? How did you define the problem and what did you do to resolve it?

2. Write your own response to the Bill Collection notice. On a separate page (1) describe how you defined the problem, (2) point out some of the strategies you used in your response, and (3) note the role you are assuming in your letter and the role you are projecting onto your reader—that is, how the two of you are cast in your script for this transaction.

3. If you want to take the experiment in project 2 a step further, exchange letters with another writer and try to guess how he or she defined the problem and the ensuing transaction. (Jot down your prediction for how he or she responded to the three points in assignment 2.) Compare notes: Did either of you perceive the problem, the strategies, or the role the other writer had in mind? Analyze what happened in this exchange and why you think it turned out the way it did.

4. Think of an incident in which you had to enter a new discourse community—or speak or write as if you belonged to one (such as in a course, a sports or social group, a workplace). Write a sketch of this community that would let someone else recognize it—noting the language, the conventions, the ways of making a point or building a case, the expectations, the assumptions that insiders use and that you needed to learn. How did you define your problem at the time and how did you try to solve it? Would you see it differently or act differently now?

5. Before reading through and writing to follow the directions in Task 2 of Scenario 2, take a few minutes to list all that you think is relevant to writing papers in school. Imagine that you are writing a short letter or memo to a schoolmate, perhaps someone transferring in to take many of the classes you have taken. How would you instruct him or her to cope with school and efficiently complete assignments? See if you can generalize about how you have learned to write in school and then compress that information into distinct points such as "Make sure you ask to find out what the directions mean." Use these points to structure your letter or memo (referring to Chapter Seven, Models for Writing).

6. You and some of your classmates may have experience writing and communicating on the job. How would you define the features or characteristics of workplace writing? Use the same search process that we outlined in assignment 5. You may wish to work in groups, to see if you can reach consensus about these qualities. Write a memo, letter, or (in the group exercise), a summary of your conclusions or your group's conclusions to share and to debate further.

How to Read a Scenario

In this section *you* will be rewriting this textbook, by conducting a rhetorical survey of actual writers at work. These three scenarios are based on real people and rhetorical situations in three different discourse communities. Scenarios present the raw material of a complex rhetorical situation—the players, their actions, and the texts. Read the landscapes of these situations as a newcomer would, to conduct a rhetorical survey to build your own interpretation of their key features.

THREE PROBLEM-SOLVING SCENARIOS

A CORPORATE SCENARIO
Joining the Digi-Tech Proposal Team

Request for proposal

AN ACADEMIC SCENARIO
Comparing Academic and Professional Writing

Student paper

A NON-PROFIT SCENARIO
Proposal Writing at the Community Literacy Center

Proposal draft

A CORPORATE SCENARIO

Joining the Digi-Tech Proposal Team

THE SETTING:

Digi-Tech is an international company with a complicated organizational structure having hundreds of employees and where proposal writing is a highly organized and routine process that entails design and delivery of a product.

YOUR ROLE:

Originally, you were hired to manage sales accounts at Digi-Tech, but after six months on the job you were reassigned to the proposal-writing team as a second manager. This team has been overworked and undersized for years, but your "promotion," however logical for the company, has taken *you* by surprise. Your sales supervisor explains that the assignment will give you direct contact with all departments within the corporation and can be a step forward toward further advancement. She explains that you were chosen because of your success as an account manager, but privately you feel the weight not only of learning new responsibilities but of learning to work with new people under constraints familiar to them but not to you. "Confident" and "successful" are not what you feel. Additionally, your new team produces proposals, rather than a service or a company product. Although you consider yourself reasonably good at writing, you have never before had to consider writing to be your end product.

YOUR TASK:

(**a**) As a new member of the Digi-Tech team, conduct a rhetorical survey of the proposal task you have been given. From the information provided in this scenario, how do you interpret the assignment, the audience, the problems, the rhetorical situation, and the expectations of this discourse community? What are the key features that emerge from your survey?

(**b**) Now test your own power to predict a problem. Will all the surveys in your class come up with the same picture? Predict which part of your interpretation is most likely to be shared by everyone in the class. More importantly, on which part do you think people will differ? Why? Write a brief memo to the class explaining your prediction.

WRITING AT DIGI-TECH

For the last 15 years, Digi-Tech has led the field of computer software developers, specializing in architectural and design applications. It has grown from a small, local group of university-based engineers to a privately owned corporation employing nearly 300 people. Digi-Tech has continued to specialize in "intelligent" software programs that condense, organize, and report an immense warehouse of technical information to aid and expedite building design and development. This software is purchased by private and public organizations that are expanding and need assistance in designing buildings and workspaces that accommodate their expanding operations. It is aimed at two kinds of clients: those without much specialized architectural knowledge, such as a city planner, and those who themselves market building and site design. Of late, Digi-Tech has branched into information systems that are specialized for the nonspecialist, to help city planning and zoning offices, transit authorities, and community development organizations.

The company's success results from a good product but also because of a proposal team that has consistently been able to produce solicited proposals that respond effectively to **RFPs** or **Requests for Proposals** and unsolicited proposals to sell and advertise Digi-Tech's products. With the advent of custom computer software, many companies have begun to hunt for computer applications that fit exact technical details yet remain flexible, and that offer complete service in a software installation and maintenance. Other potential customers, of course, only know that they need help with their computer system, and they have heard that Digi-Tech sells a reasonably priced software package that can deliver.

THE STRUCTURE OF THE PROPOSAL TEAM.

The proposal team at Digi-Tech is tiny for a company of this size—only five people (beyond the sales staff), compared with a typical proposal team of up to a dozen people or more elsewhere. One reason why this team has done so well is that they have developed boilerplate material that covers much of the technical and rhetorical information going into their proposals. Boilerplate is preprinted text, such as product descriptions, background information on the company, or organizational charts, that is written well enough and generally enough to distribute to any customer. The team itself consists of a proposal manager, a coordinator, a technical writer, a sales representative, a marketing support person, and others not on the team but who serve as contacts in the other departments: administration, product development, and installation and service. Below is a brief description of the proposal team with some of their agendas and concerns beyond the basics of their job responsibilities.

- Lucia manages and coordinates the proposal process and reports to the executive committee of the corporation. She does not confer directly with salespeople or with clients but does answer questions and delegate responsibilities when answers are not easy to find. Thus, Lucia's roles vary depending on the project at hand, and new, technically sophisticated customers require much more of her attention. Proposal management, however, is only one of Lucia's responsibilities as she also trains new personnel and is being groomed for international marking.

- Eric, the proposal coordinator, compiles most of the answers to a buyer's technical, legal, and procedural questions. Because of his experience, and by using boilerplate information, he helps Lucia expedite the search for new technical information to match a client's needs. Importantly, he also reads and deciphers (with Delia) sales documents and the directions and requirements of the buyer. His computer duties include using a scanner and "configuring" software to transform the client's RFP into a computer text file. This begins the lengthy process of reshaping the customer's requests into Digi-Tech's response. There is another coordinator for especially large projects, but most often Eric works alone and is overworked. Because of his technical expertise, no one else can easily fill his shoes.

- Margaret assists Eric as a technical writer and assists in the final compilation, word-processing interfaces, and document design. Margaret joined the proposal team because Eric needed help delivering the final document to press, although she is often pulled off proposal writing and reassigned to other technical writing projects for the company.

- Delia, the sales representative, engineers the sales bid and is ultimately responsible for the exchange between the customer and Digi-Tech. She knows her competitors and clients well and spends much more time out of the office in the field. This means that Delia must trust the proposal team to deliver a proposal that is not only timely but does not unravel all of her efforts to orchestrate a sale. Delia's salary depends on sales; she generates about six or seven such proposals a year.

- Linda is a member of the sales department and acts as a liaison between Delia and the proposal team, and, in turn, the rest of the company. She gives Eric the information he needs on product development, installation and service, and administration (primarily contractual information). Linda might be the one person who can make Eric's life easier, except that Linda herself wants to move into sales negotiation and is gradually being moved out to do more fieldwork as the market expands.

- Finally there is a wide circle of specialists in other departments who are called upon to provide information needed by the proposal team—answers to the customer's technical questions.

Even within this small team, we can see how goals intermingle and potentially compete. If an RFP comes in that is familiar, Eric can do most of the work (although Eric never tires of sharing that fact). And the technical information sought by Eric and Linda must be written to satisfy a range of audiences in the corporation: product engineers, lawyers, management, and the sales department—in addition to the customer's needs. Lucia's management style is "hands off," which is fine when the proposals are technically easy, when customers are familiar, and when there is enough time; but the corporation's growth has meant an increase in the number of RFPs that has, in turn, taxed everyone's patience. For Lucia, expansion has meant higher productivity (and more visibility) for the proposal team, more pressure to be involved with new clients, and competing responsibilities with her training in international trade. *Your* "advancement" into this proposal team and network has two goals: to relieve some of the pressure on Lucia and to bring someone else up to her level of expertise and involvement.

> **RHETORICAL SURVEY REMINDER**   At this point, you may stop and wonder about all of the social dynamics and territory you must recognize just to fit into this proposal team. As the newcomer, you have noted the high level of skill each team member brings to the team and how it appears to function with a very loose organization. Now, what will you do first to fit in?

THE RHETORICAL SITUATION WITH A PROSPECTIVE CLIENT

On June 15, the Exetor Design Group out of Los Angeles, California, distributed an RFP calling for a specialized software package. The application Exetor wanted to buy would help them create building designs that take into account site specifications, zoning and building codes, and the firm's own guidelines for constructing office and small manufacturing structures. Exetor was introduced to Digi-Tech at trade shows and by word of mouth and expects their software to interface with Exetor's own guidelines for design. The investment in computer software is also a significant step for Exetor, because it would allow the company to expand nationally by turning their design knowledge and processes into a system.

This means that Digi-Tech's proposal to build this software will be closely scrutinized. Although the proposal is written ostensibly for company executives who give the final approval and negotiate with Delia, others at Exetor will read it for their own purposes and make important recommendations. For example, project managers need the software to support the way information already flows within their design teams; accountants are looking for an equitable deal; architects and building construction personnel want the software to complement their design processes. To accommodate these readers, Exetor wrote their RFP by asking each of these groups to write specific questions. Digi-Tech knows the sale depends on how well they satisfy everyone. Digi-Tech must also decide how specific to make their proposal, given the sensitivity of their trade secrets and the desire to hold something in reserve for contract negotiations.

Figure 1-5 shows an abbreviated version of Exetor's RFP, that sets out the scope and guidelines for the proposals that will come from Digi-Tech and other companies.

Digi-Tech had two weeks to decide whether they wanted to make a bid or not and about six weeks to deliver the full proposal—a "comfortable" timetable compared to other product proposals. After delivery, by mid-March, the document would go through an extensive review process by the representatives at Exetor and even their subsidiary contractors. Here is where the larger community of software developers comes into play. Digi-Tech is part of a circle of software vendors, and the company often competes against the same salespeople in the same software companies and even for business with the same clients. These people go to seminars and conferences and read the magazines that list recent sales. Word of a pending deal travels fast through a strong "users group" that is interested in product and professional developments in expert system design. Thus, the proposal team knew that their writing would "leak" into the hands of competitors, since they had little final control of its dissemination. Actually, Digi-Tech depends equally on this community information as unofficial feedback from past clients, peers, and other sales representatives. From the vantage point of a community of software vendors, the process of developing a product or even negotiating a sale begins far in advance and continues far after the actual exchange of RFP and formal proposal. Because this field is growing exponentially and competition for customers is tight, any software company would be foolish not to respect this community dialogue.

Community influences are not limited to the proposing company. Exetor's RFPs have become relatively standardized because design firms such as Exetor have become more routine in their requests and needs. They often hire outside consultants whose only job is to expedite the process of generating an RFP. Though these consultants work with many speciality professions, they bring a uniformity to RFP writing—not in technical details but in style, and thus to contract negotiations themselves. Digi-Tech, in turn,

TITLE PAGE ..../page 1

COVER LETTER OF TRANSMITTAL......................................./ page 2

TABLE OF CONTENTS ..../page 3

INTRODUCTION

Exetor has specialized since 1978 in the design and construction of small urban office and manufacturing structures. Our 128 employees complete on the average of 25 building designs each year, and our business has expanded over the last 20 years to include high-rise and multiple-function structures ..../ to page 5

EXETOR'S SOFTWARE SYSTEM AND SYSTEM NEEDS

Although computers have been used at Exetor as a design tool from the start, we now seek improved linkages among engineers, materials support, and administrative staff. We seek a software system and installation package (to include necessary hardware) that would allow us to link office communication, word processing, and to enhance our architectural and structural design capabilities. This system should incorporate, on demand, site specifications, zoning and building codes, and our specification for building layout and design. We seek a computer network that will, over time, compile and sort our applications of this system to our building projects../ to page 8

DIRECTIONS FOR PROPOSING

We seek a proposal from your company for the design, installation, and support of a computer network and design system that spans and links all our departments. We ask that you respond to all of our questions and, if those responses are pre-printed documents, that they are referenced as such. You may include the names and a brief description of your system package, but for each question and whenever appropriate, we need to know:

a) which of your systems are or are not directly applicable,
b) evidence of success from comparable sites and applications,
c) if other related systems are in development,
d) what questions cannot be addressed in the complete proposal, and
e) the cost breakdown for product packages and extra features.

FIGURE 1–5
Exetor's Request for Proposals (RFP)

Response Deadlines: if you intend to propose   January 28, 1993
                     proposal delivery   March 14, 1993

Correspondence concerning this proposal should be addressed to:

Marlia Banning
Exetor Administration
Box 3390
San Pedro, CA 94060

We require seven copies of your proposal for distribution within our organization. We also need to know the personnel connected with this proposal and representing your company and within your proposal your interim competition and delivery dates for each phase and feature of your software system and service ..../ to page 10
....

QUESTIONS AND TECHNICAL INFORMATION

1. Provide a history of your organization, to focus on the aims of your company and the history of specific product lines and applications...............
....

2. Describe in detail systems which are used to coordinate and facilitate architectural design...

3. Describe a business plan that represents patterns of growth and development over the last 10 years and predicted growth and expansion.......
....

4. Provide a list and organization of personnel association with design systeMs and installations...

27. Describe the system capabilities with regard to three-dimensional design and structural and functional simulation ..../ to page 42
....

CRITERIA FOR ACCEPTANCE

Cost.
Appropriateness and flexibility of computers systems.
Possibility for future expansion and auxiliary products.
Evidence of successful design and installation.
Planning and staffing of support and installation.
Growth profile of your company. ..../ to page 43
Equitable contract terms ....
....

COSTS AND CONTRACT NEGOTIATIONS..
..../ to page 45

FIGURE 1–5,
continued

has begun to recognize consultants who write RFPs that are easy or difficult to read. Although the field is growing, the actual process of writing RFPs and proposals is getting more specialized and competitive, and more people are gaining insider knowledge of both software products and how they are bought and sold.

As you watch the proposal team begin to act, you notice that the rhetorical and economic goals of the team at Digi-Tech are many, especially for the Exetor contract:

- to write a proposal that echoes the format and content of the RFP
- to write to satisfy the various interest groups at Digi-Tech and Exetor
- to write in ways that do not overtax the proposal team
- to write to reflect and respond to the ongoing conversation in the discourse community
- to write to protect and enhance Digi-Tech's corporate image
- and of course, to write to achieve a sale.

With all of these goals—some that overlap nicely, some that compete—familiarity can work against the proposal team, and Exetor may be an especially tough client because their technical staff knows previous Digi-Tech system installations quite well, and their RFP asked for specific product information.

THE PROPOSAL PROCESS

As the rhetorical and economic situation dictates, the process of writing a proposal for Digi-Tech is a process of delegation and collaboration, and the development and review processes happen simultaneously. Proposals are distributed to the proposal team and read first by Delia and Eric, who separate out what is immediately answerable from what needs more detailed information. These unresolved elements are routed to the rest of the company, with the help of the marketing support person, Linda. This first reading is also a step toward reconfiguring the RFP into a proposal. That is, Eric produces a first or working draft by fitting the RFP questions and boilerplate answers he already has into Digi-Tech's time-tested proposal format, customized to reflect a company's RFP. When the tailor-made answers to the more specialized questions are received, Eric creates a second draft that plugs in the new information. This draft goes through a quality control review, which checks the completeness, accuracy, and legality of information provided. With any revision based on this review, and after final revisions and design work at the hands of the technical writer, the proposal returns to the sales representative, Delia, for a final review and delivery. Figure 1-6 shows a graphic representation of this process.

As you join the proposal team, the process for the Exetor contract is well underway. The team has gathered nearly 1000 pages of raw material. The front

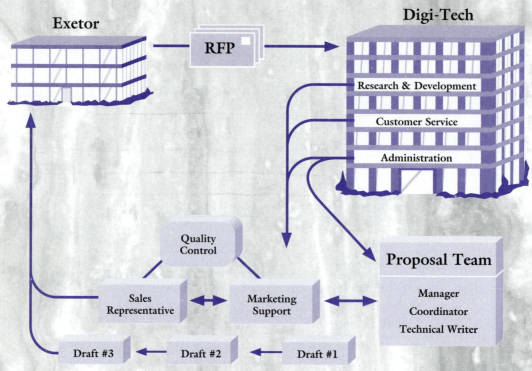

FIGURE 1–6
Digi-Tech's Proposal Process

matter in the proposal will be a cover letter of transmittal, an executive summary, and a short description of Digi-Tech's company profile and software line. Following this introductory material are about 100 pages of condensed and detailed responses to questions and specifics in the RFP. These responses are the most important information in the proposal, as they will be scrutinized by the interest groups at Exetor. Much of the proposal is boilerplate, descriptive material about the company and its products and services. This material, found in the body of the proposal and in the appendices, is far from throwaway. It documents how the company and the product coordinate.

THE PROPOSAL FORMAT

Figure 1-7 shows the proposal format the team is working with, adding the technical detail, boilerplate, and customized responses to needs and expectations at Exetor. The proposal team is quite familiar with this format,

TITLE PAGE

LETTER OF TRANSMITTAL (from sales)

TABLE OF CONTENTS & INTRODUCTION (from proposal manager)

EXECUTIVE SUMMARY

    The customer's problem or stated software needs
    Digi-Tech's solution: existing software packages
                additional features
                service and installation

    Digi-Tech, the company

PRODUCT DESCRIPTION

    Basic operating systems
    Interface capabilities
    Information retrieval and expert systems
    Added features, extensions
    Process of development, installation
    Personnel training and support
    Previous installations, track record

UNIQUE FEATURES for the CUSTOMER'S NEEDS

RESPONSES TO QUESTIONS AND REQUESTS FOR INFORMATION

    [to follow from the RFP, written in a question-answer format, re-printing the customer's questions verbatim]

COMPANY BACKGROUND

    Experience in software design and service
    Sales and service network and record

COSTS AND PAYMENT PROCEDURES

APPENDICES, for example
    Annual reports
    Organizational and staffing charts
    Customer list
    Sample contracts
    Product specifications and use manuals.

FIGURE 1–7
Digi-Tech's Proposal
Format

a model they have developed over the years that seems to respond to most RFPs and allows them to coordinate their search for technical information within the company. To you, this format is daunting: You can see how its structure responds to the rhetorical situation, but the amount of information and the number of people involved are impressive.

Your assignment is generally to assist Lucia in managing the proposal process and to lend a hand wherever you can with this project as part of your retraining. You are also encouraged to find ways to streamline the proposal development process further and to decide how this team—or others, if that is the solution—can adapt to a growing company in a lucrative but competitive market. Where do you begin? One place is to examine where boilerplate can be used and extended, so that the team can focus its attention on truly new technical information for a potential customer and on those places in the proposal where the corporate voice sells the product and services.

RHETORICAL SURVEY REMINDER   At this point, we suggest you complete your rhetorical survey of the Digi-Tech proposal team. With the information you have in this scenario and the two documents that define the transaction between Digi-Tech and Exetor, what stands out to you as the key features in your Survey? Based on the Survey, what will your goals and priorities be? What problems do you see?

AN ACADEMIC SCENARIO

Comparing Academic and Professional Writing

THE SETTING:

In high school and college you probably had courses in which writing was taught or courses in which it was simply assigned and you had to figure out the expectations and conventions of that particular discourse community. Or the setting may be your own previous work experience with writing.

YOUR ROLE:

An expert on your own experience, your role now is to observe and comment on previous writing experience. As a member of a business writing course or employee, you can use these observations to evaluate the academic strategies you have already developed and decide how they adapt to business settings.

YOUR TASK:

1. This is an important section of this book because you write it. We would like you to construct a brief scenario of your experience doing a particular assignment in school. Here's how to start:

A. *Conduct a Self Interview:* Select a typical or recent academic writing situation. If at all possible, use a tape recorder to conduct a 10–15–minute interview with yourself. Otherwise, take notes.

B. *Use Interview Prompts:* Start by conducting a rhetorical survey as you did for Digi-Tech. Review the specific rhetorical situation, the people involved, and the process over time. Try to recreate both the discourse community and the particular goals, problems, and strategies you took into account. For guidance, here are some questions to ask yourself:

- What was written?
- Who initiated the writing? Who received it, responded to it, made use of it?
- Were you trying to *address* a problem? Did you *encounter* a problem or conflict?
- What parts of the rhetorical situation did you find most important to respond to?
- How would you describe the goals and agendas of that problem?
- Can you see any alternative ways you could have responded to the situation?
- Were you always certain about the expectations of this particular discourse community?
- How many stages did your ideas and text go through?
- Did you collaborate with anyone as you planned, wrote, or revised your text?

C. *Write up your own scenario.* Use the prompts above to identify some features to include, but write your scenario to describe the *most interesting features* of the rhetorical situation you faced or observed. You may choose to organize your scenario as a dramatic story, an argument about what writers need to learn, an exposé of some problems or conflicts students encounter, or a comparison of your experience with writing at Digi-Tech or some other professional setting.

YOUR TASK:

2. Read the list of Generalizations and the Myths, Facts, and Research below as points of comparison. Does your experience of writing support the conventional wisdom of the Generalizations or does it qualify them? Does it challenge or support any of the myths? Write a memo to the class that evaluates some of these ideas, based on your own experience

If most of your experience has been with academic writing, comment on the changes you expect you will have to make. If you have had business experience, describe it briefly in your memo and comment on the changes you see in going from college to the workplace.

YOUR TASK:

3. Using your own scenario, compare your experience with academic writing to the experience of writers in the Digi-Tech or CLC scenario which comes next. What do you think are the most revealing points of comparison or difference? Thinking about this comparison, write a commentary on what this could mean for you as a writer. Address your analysis as a letter to either Ben, the CLC Director, or Lucia, the manager at Digi-Tech, who is responsible for training new staff and might find your insights helpful.

SOME POINTS OF COMPARISON

To help you develop your own scenario and compare academic and professional writing, here are some things other people have had to say about the difference.

DO THESE GENERALIZATIONS FIT YOUR EXPERIENCE?

Academic Assignments	Professional Assignments
Teachers give them.	Though specific assignments are given, most of your writing comes with your job.
Teachers primarily evaluate them.	The responsibility and reward for writing goes far beyond a grade.
Your purpose is to learn or to recite information about specific topics and texts.	Producing is more important than learning
You sometimes collaborate with other students, but you still are responsible individually.	What you produce affects and can reflect on many others around you.

Assignment writing becomes a "dead letter" once the course is over; you never touch it once it is handed in.

Assignments often end with little direct carryover to other assignments, and, certainly none to other classes and projects.

What you produce represents a decision by (and may exist as a product owned by) the company.

Texts are judged to be "good" not because they are "cxorrect," but because they function as part of larger, often long-term transactions between readers and writers.

CAN YOU TELL THE MYTHS FROM THE FACTS?

We have heard a number of reasonable but faulty accounts about how people write in today's business and professional settings. There is also a growing body of survey research on who writes to whom, and why, and it often paints a different picture. This is not to say that myths do not describe what could happen to someone, sometime, but the research suggests that chances are it will not happen to you. Can you tell the myths from the more probable facts?[2]

Myth or Fact? *The function of writing is to convey information.*

Research: While all writing in some way conveys information, most writing has multiple functions because writers have multiple purposes. Not only do they write to inform, they write to impress; they write to assure that they are team players; they write to further a conversation.

Myth or Fact? *My degree and professional advancement will isolate and protect me from writing. The higher I progress, the less I will be called upon to write.*

Research: As the business environment changes, upper-level employees do not necessarily write more, but their writing is much more specialized and immediate. Electronic tools have stepped up the pace and improved the quality of communication. This means that people at all levels communicate often and directly in writing.

Myth or Fact? *With my degree and a good position, I can turn my writing responsibilities over to others.*

Research: Managerial writers do delegate their writing tasks, but in doing so they often inherit more responsibility for rewriting the work their staff has produced. The age of the secretarial pool, however, is over.

Myth or Fact?   *In school, I write to complete a teacher's assignment; on the job, I write more independently, for my own goals and agendas.*

Research: Freedom is bound by responsibility, and assignments will follow if not haunt you in many worlds of work. Generally, writing tasks are split between chosen and given assignments. Also, most writing in professional settings is in some way collaborative: People write as a team, and individuals write with the guidance, expertise, and approval of others. Approval is often a key, and a complicated sign-off process is common.

Myth or Fact?   *Writers at work mostly produce short, direct documents such as memoranda and letters and rarely produce longer documents such as reports or proposals.*

Research: There is truth here—writers more frequently write memos and letters, but frequency does not correlate with importance. Memos, letters, phone and electronic mail often lead to the production of longer documents. Proposals and reports and lengthy position statements still define broad policies and actions for businesses.

Myth or Fact?   *If I want to know how to write a memo, letter, or report, I can look it up in a book or style guide. Business writing is (thankfully) formulaic.*

Research: Most people say they learned to write on the job, although they acknowledge how important courses in writing can be. Variation is the norm, and customized proposals, reports, memos, and letters are more common than what books and teachers portray as models. Style guides help with organization and style, but they do not help you think and act.

Myth or Fact?   *Business and professional writing is direct, clear, and brief.*

Research: Writers report that they value clarity, conciseness, organization, correct grammar, and spelling. Most readers would say the same thing, although some research suggests that these standards are relative to situations and organizational cultures. Sometimes writers feel pressure to conform to the styles and habits around them and to use "less-clear" writing styles because of this pressure.

Also, simple, direct writing is more a consequence of preparation than an expression of style. It is made possible through prior communication and networks of spoken and written information.

Myth or Fact?	*Business and professional writers are some of the worst.*
Research:	Actually, research has found examples of ineffective writing in all walks of life; no branch of academic or professional life owns good writing. What business writers report is that they are aware that much of the writing around them is inadequate, and they have little time or strategy to fix it.
Myth or Fact?	*At work, I mostly talk to people, and writing fades in importance.*
Research:	True, speaking is more common than writing, but what is not clear from the research is how speaking interacts with writing. Also, writing consumes on the average one day out of five, and writing appears to be integral to decision making, advancement, and personnel evaluation.
Myth or Fact?	*My job training will teach me how to write.*
Research:	Though writers point to on-the-job training, they do so with some regret. Knowing how to write cannot come quickly enough, and writers spend on the average three hours per page. Writers report difficulty with planning and knowing how and where to start. A constant pressure is knowing how to produce quickly a message that effectively reaches a range of audiences.

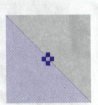

A Nonprofit Scenario

Proposal Writing at the Community Literacy Center

THE SETTING:

In this scenario we see a proposal team that may challenge some popular images about business writing, images which picture a young, (usually) male middle manager striding, briefcase in hand, into his high-rise office in a large corporation. In reality, the demographics of the American workforce has changed to reflect changes in the population as a whole as more women and people of color take on important roles. Moreover, the world of business is not limited to the corporate world of big business. It includes entrepreneurs trying to start and run small businesses, employees such as medical staff or real estate agents who use writing to do their jobs, consultants and technical specialists hired for special purposes, and a great many transactions in professional groups and institutions that are not conducted solely for profit. This proposal team is part of a growing nonprofit organization located in an inner-city neighborhood.

YOUR ROLE:

Thanks to the success of the proposal described below, the CLC has hired you to run the new TREES project and to develop a proposal for the funding to continue it.

YOUR TASK:

1. (a) Conduct a rhetorical survey of the proposal task you have been given. From the limited information you have in this scenario, what are the key features that surface in your survey? (b) Now test your own power to predict a problem. Will all the surveys in your class build the same picture? Predict which part of your interpretation is most likely to be shared by everyone in your class. More important, on which part do you think people will differ? Why? Write a brief memo to the class explaining your prediction.

YOUR TASK:

2. To give yourself an even greater challenge, divide your group in half so that Group 1 does a rhetorical survey of Digi-Tech and Group 2 does the same for the Community Literacy Center. Now write your memo to the class predicting similarities and differences in what each group will see as a key feature. Explain your prediction.

YOUR TASK:

3. In this chapter we have looked at three discourse communities: a corporate community formed around writing a contract proposal; a nonprofit organization proposing an idea and seeking funding; and an academic community formed around college writing. In fact, many people would say the class in business and professional writing, communication, or management you are taking is now itself a specific discourse community. Here, then, are our questions: (a) Do you think the corporate discourse community you saw at Digi-Tech is strikingly similar or importantly different from the community of a nonprofit organization? (b) How

does your academic discourse community differ from these two? What do these differences mean for you? Write a memo that shares your thinking with the rest of the class.

WRITING FOR THE COMMUNITY LITERACY CENTER

For 72 years the Community House had been a landmark social service organization located in a multiracial, inner-city neighborhood, providing recreation, food, shelter, and community support. In 1988 it began to shift from traditional social service activities to a new focus on literacy projects that could enable at-risk teenagers to develop new skills to speak for themselves. We enter the scene as a proposal is being drafted to a public aid foundation which would establish a new Community Literacy Center (CLC) within the Community House by helping to pay salaries for staff and to fund new programs. Through one pilot project, called WRITE, neighborhood teenagers had just published a booklet on teenage pregnancy written from the teens' point of view. Another project, HELP, would involve teens in planning and remodeling inner-city housing.

THE MEMBERS OF THE PROPOSAL TEAM

Unlike the standing Digi-Tech team, this one was created around a need and opportunity. Each member brought not only different expertise, but a slightly different agenda and set of goals.

- Ben (the Community House director) brought an educational vision, administrative experience, and a long-term plan for supporting youth and community literacy in this urban neighborhood.

- Marta (first project leader) brought a strong neighborhood perspective for developing the WRITE program and making changes for young African Americans who needed to find positive role models and an affirmation of their own potential.

- Shirley (second project leader) joined the staff to work on the WRITE project and do research on how teens made decisions, so was more interested in supporting/observing the process than teaching or changing it.

- Chris (the contractor) was part of a community organization to create affordable housing in the area and wanted to involve teens in his remodeling projects (although the CLC saw such reconstruction as a vehicle to teach literacy, rather than the goal of HELP).

- Kate (the professor), a literacy researcher at a nearby university, had helped design WRITE as a way to help at-risk students, and, like the director, wanted to connect teaching and community literacy. Prior projects made her a link between the Community House and the Foundation.

- Edward (the senior foundation officer) was the primary audience for the written proposal. He had long supported alternative approaches to education and understood the CLC's approach to community literacy.

- Dale (second foundation officer) specialized in housing and development issues. She came with a traditional view of literacy as reading and school writing and was generally skeptical about funding academic projects.

THE PROPOSAL PROCESS

Within networks like this, ideas and proposals emerge out of a series of discussions and often build on prior texts and conversations. This writing group exists as a response to a problem or opportunity, not as a professional entity. Figure 1-8 is a November-to-May timeline that reveals some of turning points in this writing process which led to new plans and an evolving series of proposal drafts. We refer to the writers by their names and titles to highlight the different goals and roles they brought to this project. As you read through, look for parallels to or contrasts with writing at Digi-Tech or the ways your own writing projects have developed.

As the timeline and series of drafts suggest, proposals like this emerge out of a sustained conversation marked by a number of revealing decisions and turning points, which include finding a shared purpose, reading, and responding to the context.

FINDING SHARED PURPOSES

Unlike a school assignment, it is hard to say when this project actually started or who was in charge, even though the Center director was ultimately responsible. The plan emerged out of a series of collaborations, driven by an ongoing need to find funding, at a time that seemed ripe to develop a coherent plan and a Center. As a result, the *purpose* of this document is really a mixture of the different things these five people wanted to do. For instance, while the Community House director was most

The CLC Proposal Timeline

November 26 After a successful pilot year with the WRITE project, the Community House staff meets with the senior foundation officer to propose supporting WRITE and the new HELP project by funding the Community Literacy Center. During this informal conversation, the officer poses several questions, such as, "What is your 'concept'?" The writers interpret these questions as an informal RFP--as criteria a successful written proposal would meet. However, in the middle of the discussion, Edward introduces Dale, who specializes in community organizations, and CLC writers gain a new, skeptical audience.

November 30 Chris, the contractor, and Shirley draft a brief description of HELP. However, the director and the professor, with their long-range goals in mind, reorganize and extend their text by placing the description of HELP within a larger proposal for the Cornmunity Literacy Center (CLC).

December 3 Meeting on another project, Kate and Edward (the senior officer) discuss the need to support "diverse literate practices" in the city (which Kate links to the CLC).

Discussing that idea later with Kate, Ben (the director) sees how "diverse literate practices" can become the organizing "concept" requested back in November. He then arranges these practices into the figure of a wheel, which becomes a graphic symbol for the project.

December 21 To prepare for a one-hour meeting with Dale (the foundation officer) the CLC writers hold a three-hour breakfast planning meeting. They use this time to present the HELP plans orally and get feedback before finishing the text. That night, the director drafts a "script" that reviews the points decided on at breakfast.

December 29 At the meeting, the skeptical second officer raises important questions (i.e., Can the teenagers really be in charge of decisions?) and seems unconvinced about the value of linking HELP, a housing project, to literacy. To the CLC staff this is a critical link in the proposal.

January 4 Over the next few weeks the director and professor hold phone conversations with both foundation officers. A third draft is faxed to the foundation as a "talking draft" to ground these conversations. However, when the discussion finally gets to a specific budget and timeline, the foundation officers (who submit projects to their Board for approval) say they want to support the long-range CLC agenda but suggest that the group propose HELP as a one-year pilot project now. This will demonstrate the feasibility of a literacy center, which could then be proposed the next spring.

A fourth draft is written that completely reorganizes draft three. It foregrounds the HELP project and subordinates the plan for the CLC, using it to provide a rationale and long-term goals for HELP.

March-May This version of the HELP proposal goes through a tough internal review in which foundation evaluators raise questions which the Center director answers in writing. This review is positive and HELP is eventually approved by the foundation board.

FIGURE 1–8

The CLC Proposal Timeline

committed to the long-term educational vision of the CLC, the contractor wanted to develop low-cost housing, and the academic project leader wanted opportunities to observe teens making decisions. Although the two foundation officers worked closely together, each had a professional investment in developing a coherent portfolio of projects in their different areas.

Given these different, equally valuable agendas, the process of writing the proposal was a process of creating a set of **shared purposes** on which the members of this group could agree. They had to "read" each other's agendas as well as the requirements and procedures of the foundation as they drafted and redrafted their proposal.

READING THE CONTEXT

Foundations, like other organizations, have their own internal agendas, which can change over time. Historically, the foundation's programming in education had been sharply separated from human services (which involved social work, community organizing, and housing), but there were some signals that it might now want to link these areas. If true, this changing situation was an opportunity, since the HELP project was an ideal bridge. On the other hand, when Dale came on the scene, the writers could no longer assume that the "foundation" understood or supported the CLC's educational agenda. To succeed, the writers decided, they would literally have to educate people to see the value in what they were proposing.

Reading the context meant deciding which concepts and which goals to emphasize and which to pass over quickly. Which discourse community (and set of expectations) within the foundation are you talking to? For instance, readers from the educational community would be looking for a clear plan of instruction, ideas supported by research or evidence, and what could be learned as a result of the project. However, foundation readers in community organizing and human services are often skeptical of schools (institutions in general) and the language of research. They would look instead for projects with grassroots organizations built on community consensus, in which staff "facilitate" rather than "lead" people who are on the margins of the social system. At the same time those members of the foundation from the business community would be certain to argue for projects that build leadership potential and skills in young people and might be leery of the neighborhood politics and in-fighting often associated with community organizing.

RESPONDING TO CHANGES IN THE CONTEXT

Here (see Figures 1-9 and 1-10) are two parallel sections from drafts 2 and 3 of the proposal that talk about goals. Look first at Figure 1-9: Can

Proposal Draft 2

We propose to establish the Center for Community Literacy with the City Foundation as a funding partner for the period of four years plus one pilot year. Specifically we are requesting funding to set up the infrastructure for the Center necessary to implement the HELP program.

We have five goals for the Center for Community Literacy:

1. to provide a safe place with positive role models
2. to teach collaborative learning strategies
3. to produce action documents and products (rehabilitated houses) and provide information regarding these efforts in appropriate community forums
4. to establish learning partnerships with universities
5. to engage in action research that produces models of community literacy to be used in other neighborhoods.

FIGURE 1–9

Draft 2: An in-house working draft of the CLC Proposal

you identify which writers left their mark on this early version of the proposal? Whose goals (Ben's, Marta's, Shirley's, or . . .) do you see? Now look at Figure 1-10 to see how this plan adapted to Dale and the perspective of community organizing. Can you see any traces of the agendas, goals, and language of "community organizing talk" in the text? Where did the five points of Figure 1-9 come from and what happened to them in Figure 1-10?

How could a proposal like this be so fluid and open to change? First, unlike the writer of a school assignment who may have a single point or idea to promote, these writers had a long-term commitment to some general goals for literacy and empowerment—an invested agenda in which they believed. This big picture gave them a willingness to consider and even seek out alternative ways to get where they wanted to be. Secondly, they knew that the best plan was one that would meet their needs by meeting the needs of the foundation at the same time. Reading the context meant choosing what to bring out, which part of the story to tell.

Some of the context these writers were reading was abstract and hard to grasp, like the changing goals and agendas of the different players. Other parts were like red flags. At the December meeting, the foundation officer for community organizing appeared enthusiastic about the idea of HELP, but seemed either skeptical or uncertain of the place literacy had in all of

A Proposal for the Community Literacy Center and H.E.L.P.
The Housing Empowerment and Literacy Program

The Problem: A Literacy Crisis

There is a literacy crisis in our community and around the nation that challenges us to reconsider some of our fundamental assumptions about literacy.

Urban Educating Partners

We need to address this literacy crisis among "at risk" youth by boldly rethinking our ideas about literacy, learning, and schooling in urban communities. Our proposal calls for a two-pronged approach with the following objectives:

1) to influence current educational policy.

2) to develop a new learning dynamic for urban youth that draws from the grassroots expertise of residents, community leaders, and teachers in the city's schools. . .and involves addressing problematic social situations in ways that "at risk" youth work collaboratively with adult mentors to tackle significant community problems. The learning process will be designed to foster literate problem solving and to contribute to the increased self-esteem that follows from achievement. . . .

[Following. . .a discussion of the first prong of the policy. . .]

The Community Literacy Center

A New Learning Dynamic

The second prong of our approach calls for developing new ways for urban youth to take literate action. Committed to the potential of young people who are "at risk" in the system, we want to shape opportunities that do three things:

1) that let urban youth engage in significant literate practices such as organizing support and building consensus, drafting memos of understanding, and composing action plans necessary to rehabilitate vacant houses in struggling neighborhoods.

2) that make the voices and perspectives of not only youth but other silent groups whose voices are rarely listened to heard in community decision making.

3) that help youth develop the leadership, expertise, and self-esteem that follow from achieving tangible success in the community.

The Community Literacy Center

[This paragraph sketches key facts about the Center: location, facilities, history, other sources of support, including a figure that graphically presents its six key activities, including HELP.]

FIGURE 1–10

Draft 3: A talking draft faxed for the January discussions of the proposal

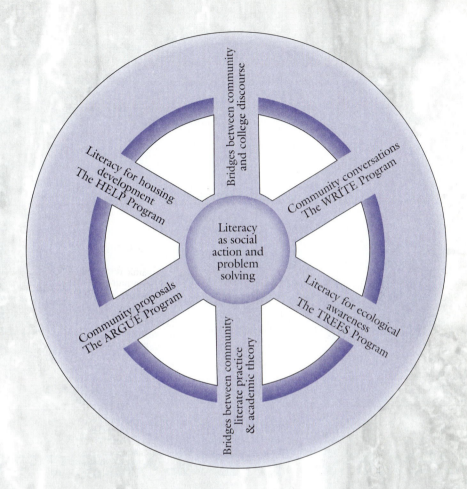

FIGURE 1–10,
continued

this. It was only when she was about to leave that a chance comment revealed that, for her, this talk about literacy meant school writing, that is, teaching students to produce well-written, formal text. The CLC writers suddenly realized that *they* were using "literacy" as a code word. For them it meant using writing to take action, to describe, explain, or argue with assurance; to speak up and operate within a technical discourse, for example, about housing redevelopment or on social issues like teen pregnancy or practical discussions of parenting. However, it was clear that merely talking about their project alone had not created a new image of literacy strong enough to replace the limited and conventional practice the foundation officer was so skeptical about. Do you think draft 3 (beginning on page 48) helps to communicate their intentions?

Ben (Director):	Introduce the notion of the center and the wheel (5-7 minutes).
	Present the HELP program (10-12 minutes).
Chris (contractor):	Describe HELP. Goals of this literacy program mirror those of some community developers, namely *the need for community involvement* (Goal 1).
Shirley (leader):	Our second problem is to find a way to get teens involved so they can actually have ownership of the process. *Develop new leadership in the community* (Goal 2). [She is to elaborate on how the CLC will do this.]
Chris (contractor):	Describe the Memorandum of Understanding that teens working with the developer will have to draft as a way to show the literacy skills involved in development.
	• community input through interviews with key players-- involves active listening • interpreting community views • developing one's own view • developing consensus as a team • reflecting consensus back into the community setting
Marta (leader):	Raise the issue of building trust and the strong track record of Community House as a "safe place."
Ben (Director):	That's where we are. Can you [directed to Foundation Officer as experienced community organizer] advise us how to help keep leadership and members of the community involved?
Kate (professor):	Link between community and school. [Bring this up only if it seems relevant; may be a low priority in this discussion.]

FIGURE 1–11

Informal Script for a
Planning Meeting

PLANNING TO TALK

Another important turning point was the group's three-hour session to plan for a one-hour meeting with Dale. Their goal was to hash out which points *had* to be made—no matter where the conversation went. The notes from this meeting, which the director distributed the next day, took the form of a script in which everyone had a distinctive role and a point to make (see Figure 1-11). The script reflects the writers' image of how a "perfect meeting" would go and the decision path they wanted their audience to follow.

As you might have predicted, the Foundation officer brought her own agenda and questions, and the discussion did not follow this sequence or timetable at all. However, because this plan was organized around the *key points that needed to be made no matter what,* it paid off. In the midst of a lively give-and-take conversation, the writers were able to make their "best case" even though they didn't control the presentation.

VISUALIZING THE WHOLE

Remember the foundation officer's question, "What is your concept?" To write a successful proposal, the CLC needed to transform its multiple goals and agendas into an integrated plan. According to the director, one breakthrough came from a diagram that emerged out of conversations. When Kate told Ben about her argument for "diverse literate practices," he saw in it an "organizing concept for the CLC," which he then visualized as a wheel and turned into a graphic that shows how projects like HELP and WRITE were related to the Center's other goals to bridge school and community. Because the wheel figure and concept made the logic of the Center more visible, it not only went into the proposal, but became the focus of the group's planning meetings and arguments about how to structure the whole.

References
1. See for example, "Big Recall at GM: Exasperated by the giant's slide, the board reshuffles the top brass," *Time,* April 20, 1992 (p. 32), and "The Two Sides of the SAM WALTON Legacy," ibid. (pp. 50 ff.) as well as reports in many other news and business magazines and journals.
2. See Paul Anderson, "What Survey Research Tells Us about Writing at Work." In *Writing In Non-academic Settings,* L. Odell & D. Goswami, Eds. (Guilford, NY: Press 1984), pp. 3–74.

2
Reading the Context

IN THIS CHAPTER we show you how to read further into a rhetorical situation—to find, analyze and state problems for writers. The first strategy helps you conduct a rhetorical survey by teaching you the features that define a rhetorical situation.

 STRATEGY 1. Reconstructing a Rhetorical Situation
Look for these nine features:

The Players	Tasks and Triggering Events	History
Relationships	Constraints	Paper Trail
Investments	Organizational Structures	Ethics

We also show you how to pull these features together and how many of them have real consequences for writers in a final scenario.

 SCENARIO. The Mountain Trails Horse Center
This scenario introduces other strategies that help you act as a problem solver: strategies for reading texts and for analyzing and stating problems.

 STRATEGY 2. Informational and Rhetorical Reading of Texts
Get the facts and the stories behind the facts.

 STRATEGY 3. Finding and Analyzing Problems
Analyze a problem in five steps.
Learn the features of a written problem analysis.

As you read, we may ask you to take on the role of a newcomer, someone who needs to understand a rhetorical situation quickly in order to act.

2
Reading the Context

In Chapter One, we asked you to think of yourself as a problem solver who views writing as a rhetorical action. Simple writing problems are those in which writers can respond with habit or routine, or the task and audience are relatively obvious. Complex problems are common in business and professional settings, where the conflicts underlying them are related to people and social features in rhetorical situations and to the language patterns and expectations in discourse communities.

To respond strategically to either simple or complex problems, writers must be careful readers. In this chapter we first show you how to look for the important features in a rhetorical situation—what we think it means to "read a context." The first strategy is designed to help you conduct a rhetorical survey of any new task or situation, laying the foundation for problem-solving. The second strategy helps you read in the more usual sense; we show you how to read for information and how that is different from reading rhetorically. Both strategies lead to a concrete starting point for writing, finding, analyzing, and stating problems. If you face a task or problem that you think is simple, you may choose to skip Strategies 1 and 2, but do not fall into the trap of misjudging a rhetorical situation. By reading a context and reading texts rhetorically, you are best prepared to state your communication problem and to act.

As you work through this chapter, we will ask you from time to time to take on the role of a newcomer, someone who needs to understand a rhetorical situation quickly in order to act in the way that a business consultant is asked (and paid) to size up a situation quickly and provide a problem analysis and solution. Although a consultant, who is an outsider, works under little of the social pressure in an organization, the successful ones do approach each new contract with their eyes open, reading a rhetorical situation to assess quickly the problem at hand. That is the approach we want you to take from this chapter, as we illustrate in Figure 2–1.

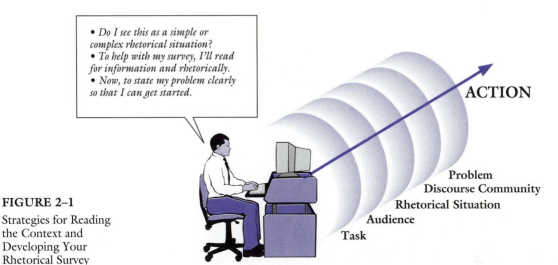

• Do I see this as a simple or complex rhetorical situation?
• To help with my survey, I'll read for information and rhetorically.
• Now, to state my problem clearly so that I can get started.

ACTION

Problem
Discourse Community
Rhetorical Situation
Audience
Task

FIGURE 2–1

Strategies for Reading
the Context and
Developing Your
Rhetorical Survey

STRATEGY 1: RECONSTRUCTING THE RHETORICAL SITUATION

The rhetorical survey you did in Chapter One may have convinced you that the real context for communication often has many layers, some of which are not always apparent. The problem is that you can deal only with those layers—those tasks, audiences, conflicts, or expectations—that you see. As student writers know, a superficial survey of what a teacher wants can lead to wasted efforts or even disastrous results.

This strategy will help you uncover the rhetorical situation by looking closely at nine features. Although it is more accurate to think of social situations as webs of relationships where moving one part of the web affects others, we have turned it into a list of features that invite extra attention and can guide your strategic action. You may be asking, why call this strategy "reconstructing" the situation instead of just "seeing" it? The fact is that when you make sense of a situation, you are always constructing your own image of which features matter and interpreting what they mean. As we saw with the "Bill Collection Letter and Heated Reply," people see things differently. The same situation can look very different to you, depending on which features you emphasize, or on what you choose to analyze. The point is, that *how* you reconstruct and interpret a new situation will determine *what* you do as a writer. That is why, in this discussion, we have sometimes used new names for some of the concepts in the rhetorical survey. For example, if you think of your audience as one of many "players" in an event, you may build a more realistic interpretation of how communication has taken place.

There are **nine features** that comprise rhetorical situations in business, professional, academic, and even everyday settings. The following strategy overview lists the nine features to show you how they fit with the other concepts introduced thus far.

STRATEGY OVERVIEW	
Features in a Rhetorical Situation	**Rhetorical Survey**
The *players:* primary and secondary audiences	Audience
Relationships (professional or social) among players	Situation, Community
Their *investments* in different goals and agendas	Situation, Community
Tasks and triggering events	Task
Constraints: money, time, space, equipment	Situation, Community
Organizational structures	Situation, Community
History of the problem, situation, and people involved	Situation, Community
Paper trail: models, examples, contributing texts	Situation, Community
Ethics: values and the actions that define them	Situation, Community
	⇓
	Problems for Writing
	⇓
	Action

As we emphasized in Chapter One, there is much to see beyond the basics of a task or immediate audience, and many of these features can be traced to the language practice and expectations in discourse communities. Here are definitions and brief examples of these nine features. If you wrote your own scenario in Chapter One, see whether or not you covered these nine details or if you could.

1—The Players

Primary audiences receive your writing and make decisions from it. At Digi-Tech (see Scenario 1, Chapter One), the primary audience in name might be the president of the company, but in function would be an *ad hoc* committee representing the various groups who would use Digi-Tech's products. But like most business communication, there are many others who eventually claim a piece of writing: anyone for whom policies or decisions that stem from your writing matter. Over the history of a piece of writing, secondary audiences are those who use, or are effected by, your communication. In proposal writing, a user's group may eventually read and study a proposal even though they do not directly affect or benefit from a sale. For nonprofit agencies and groups, such as the Community Literacy Center (Scenario 3), foundations fund proposals and act as primary audiences, but the proposal itself can be read by community, private business, and educational audiences as well.

2—Relationships Among Players

Obviously if you can name the players involved in a rhetorical situation, you can probably comment on how they are related. Distinguish between *given relationships*—those that come with a job or role—and *social and political relationships*. In the Digi-Tech scenario, the second manager added to the proposal team was handed, in a sense, six given relationships because of the structure and history of the proposal team. You are functionally related to other managers and to the sales and support staff by the work relationships set forth in the proposal process. Given relationships are sometimes found in job descriptions but rarely do they describe the social relationships that actually take place.

Social and political relationships are the glue and goo of getting along and working with people. Some coworkers develop friendships and loyalties after-hours, and others develop loyalties (or animosities) through years of collaboration. As the new manager, are you walking into a situation where friendships and working alliances are already formed? How might these kinds of relationships confound those already established? Can you look at someone's responsibilities or personal background and predict points of relational conflict? Social and political relationships are very real features of a rhetorical situation and become factors both in how you act and in how your actions are taken.

3—Investments in Different Goals and Agendas

As we suggested in Chapter One, problems are a normal part of human interaction because people have many unstated goals and agendas that lead to conflict. People's investment in a rhetorical situation also depends on how they reconstruct it—how they paint the picture of what is important and needs to happen. And they are invested because of values and activities that precede and follow the rhetorical situation. Personal promotion is a common agenda in business, but people also form attachments to pet projects or may value a particular company culture or routine. Interestingly, many company "mission statements" fail even to acknowledge that employees have personal investments in their identities and work behavior. This may be their purpose—to diminish individual and group personalities in the face of a company-wide ethic or esprit de corps. Some researchers are finding, however, that company statements that effectively exclude personal investment are often ignored or publicly scorned.[1]

Here is a brief scenario that illustrates how players with relationships and investments can complicate a rhetorical situation—even in school:

> Darnell faces a common but often unacknowledged bind for students in that he was given an assignment that must satisfy several critical readers: a teacher with strict standards for evaluation, classmates who function as a support group with considerable peer pressure, and an audience outside of the classroom. In Darnell's business writing course, he and three other students were asked to develop a brochure that introduces international students to the admissions process at their university. The need for this brochure is clear: International students arrive on campus with little knowledge of the ins and outs of attending class and thriving in the university climate.
>
> In researching the rhetorical situation, the students learn that international students have difficulty with the whole process of entering the university, from admissions to finding housing. The Admissions Office, in conjunction with the university's Students Abroad Office, offers a limited budget and has asked students to develop a brief set of procedural guidelines for admission. Darnell's group likes the project because it is seemingly well-defined, is supported by two university offices, and has real consequences for students: They spend time and energy researching and negotiating the project, and at this late hour, have very real investments in what they have so far achieved. At this juncture, the project satisfies the course assignment. However, as it develops, it seems that the players in this rhetorical situation see things differently.
>
> - The project officer in Admissions wants only a half-page set of guidelines for the admissions procedure.
> - Students Abroad sees the brochure as a glossy, promotional tool to attract new students.
> - The instructor sees it as the major project in a course that not only stresses adapting texts to the needs of specific readers, but should include user-friendly instructions that were developed in sufficient detail. Most other projects in the course will be at least five pages long.
> - Within his group, the facade of harmony begins to crumble as Roque, a student whose family migrated from Mexico in the 1950s helps Darnell to rethink this rhetorical situation even further. Roque, as a member of the International Students Association, sees the brochure as an opportunity for international students to have a voice in their own initiation, pushing the project's participation beyond local, native-born students extending their welcome mat. With his urging, Darnell confronts some of his own biases regarding who is in the position to welcome whom to native soil and the American university.

This rhetorical situation has a number of players who, on the surface, can be named and placed according to their given relationships. Students, teachers, and university officials are related by the formal structures and authorities of the university. However, whom we label as primary and secondary audiences depends on how you (or Darnell) reconstruct the rhetorical situation. The offices fund the project and give it a name, but over time, at least for Darnell, the audience he has in mind is made up of international students, who have their own claim to the project.

Moreover, the relationships and investments within their student group are important. Even though Roque had the greatest insights into problems with current guidelines and other proposals, in their meeting with Admissions officers he was reluctant to voice his criticisms, feeling it would be an act of discourtesy. Within the group, Roque tends to avoid conflict by stating his disagreements indirectly and privately. Susan likes to take control of the discussions and does not hear or know how to read Roque's indirection. In Darnell's reading of the situation, the group needs to negotiate with Admissions for more latitude in the project. The final text would be more successful if they could bring out what everyone has to offer and proceed with some sense of consensus, even though he has learned that every investment will not receive equal attention.

4—Tasks and Triggering Events

If every rhetorical situation began and ended with a specific task, life would be simpler. In school, teachers have agendas and goals that are translated into tasks that you complete for a grade and to learn. At work, tasks like a quarterly report may seem routine, but they become rhetorical because someone (you, a peer, your supervisor) made the situation rhetorical. Tasks typically are the "what" of a rhetorical situation, the product, but even that is often subject to someone's interpretation. *Triggering events* are the actions, needs, or consequences that make a task necessary. Some triggering events are obvious, routine, as in "I need a memo outlining your travel requests," and can be traced back to one person. But other tasks are triggered by a wide chain of events. Communication theorists have used the term *exigency* to describe this moment or activity because they wanted a word that referred to a collage of factors that build to an act of communication.

At Digi-Tech, the task was straightforward enough—to propose a product line in response to an RFP. The triggering event was the arrival of the RFP. The definition of the task, because of Digi-Tech's teamwork and experience with the proposal, was mostly predetermined, although we saw that the proposal document itself had to respond to a range of readers and purposes. However, other circumstances triggered the decision to add another team manager: (a) the existing manager needed help; (b) the proposal team was under pressure to produce; (c) another manager would provide long-term stability; (d) you, the new manager, fit the profile; and (e) there were probably political forces at work as well. Someone—a supervisor—decided that, for these reasons, an additional manager would lead to initial and long-term benefit. Triggering events may be traced to a decision or event, but often are more accurately described as a confluence of factors.

5—Constraints

For most communication tasks, there are material constraints that must be addressed: A timeline (deadline); available resources such as products, word-processing, or graphics; personnel, workspaces, and even information are material constraints that at best appear to be resolved or stable when a triggering event puts a rhetorical situation in motion. Once a group of people like the Digi-Tech proposal group becomes a team, many of these constraints are satisfied in advance. Consider, for example, the problem of answering a client's questions about technical information. The proposal team does not have this information and must turn to specialists in the company to find it. Here is an informational constraint: How does a proposal writer quickly answer a question—for example, about the memory capacities in the architectural design software? The writer not only needs to be able to ask the right question, but have the interoffice (and interpersonal) links to find it quickly. Relationships and investments can also become constraints when they interfere with the processes of making decisions and communicating.

6—Organizational Structures

Business communication is traditionally viewed as organizational communication for good reason. Most business transactions involve organized groups of people, whether they represent a company, a corporation or an ad hoc group of people brought together with a shared purpose. The Community Literacy Center proposal team is a group that convened for a specific purpose: They do not have the structures, routines, roles, and titles (much less legal and fiscal ties) that define formal organizations, yet they quickly formed an internal structure for sharing information, purposes, and their writing, as it evolved.

Businesses also typically depend on hierarchical structure for efficiency and control. The average organization may be arranged by title and responsibility—take, for example, the organizational structure of Eastman Kodak, from a 1984 annual report.[2]

    Board of Directors
        Executive Committee
        Audit Committee
    Executive Officers
    Corporate Staff Divisions
        Communications
        Relations
        Finance and Administration

        Legal
        Research
Operating Divisions
        Chemicals
        Photographic and Information Management
        Diversified Technologies
        Photographic Products
        Manufacturing Equipment
        Manufacturing and Support Operations
        Customer and Marketing Support Operations
        International

The organizational structure of a company the size of Eastman Kodak can be staggering. In their yearly report, they announced that the Photographic and Information Management division had been reorganized to increase and expedite product development, decision making, customer service, and functional integrity. Thus, the organizational structure can itself present a problem to be solved as one composes a document that will be read throughout an organization.

Assessing the organizational structure of a corporation, small business, or ad hoc group is important since that organizational structure often shapes the rhetorical situation. Where players are positioned in an organization defines their relationships and at least partly defines their investments and the constraints they work under. Also, the organizational structure will often dictate not only who reads important pieces of writing but in what order.

7—History of the Problem

Even if you, as a consultant and rhetorical problem solver, are able to isolate players and the material situation, you may have missed important factors in why and how people around you act as they do in a rhetorical situation. Communication problems usually have histories that add weight to investments and explain organizational routines and priorities. Problems and solutions tend to run in cycles and knowing the history can afford a decisive advantage. Here is another scenario.

> In the 1970s many large companies like the Western Bank reorganized their divisions into independent profit centers. Although this made sense in areas that could show specific products, such as research and development, it was not well received in other divisions. One autumn Chandera Washington in Accounting had been told to draft the memo that instructed everyone to comply with the new method of internal accounting and to submit their end-of-year data to her for compiling. However, when the time came, she found that many supervisors simply did not comply. The Accounting Department found their first announcement had generated little data and a good deal of ill will, but they still had to produce their report.

Chandera was facing an even more difficult situation in the next memo. Should she demand compliance from supervisors who were just ignoring Accounting's request? An opportunity to read this rhetorical situation a little more accurately came at a writing workshop in which Washington's text was being used to talk about writing at the bank. By chance, a number of supervisors from the affected departments were sitting in to observe this first meeting, and they began to describe their response to this memo. As longstanding members of the company, they were unhappy to see another responsibility pushed off on them—their quarrel was with management and their decision to reorganize, not Accounting. The company's reorganization pressured them to conduct independent audits, when they had few ideas for doing so efficiently. They had no history of keeping appropriate records and, more to the point, were not in the habit of working in a climate of self-inspection. So there was little content to report and no motivation to do it.

By listening to and studying the history of this rhetorical problem, Chandera discovered that her problem was less one of forcing them to abide by new rules and more of acknowledging change, proposing a gradual transition, and showing her reader HOW to do this audit.

8—Paper Trail

Part of a writing problem's history may be contained in the trail of documents that record a series of decisions. If you are new to a situation, a paper trail may give you many important pieces of information: the history of a document type, a model to guide your writing, a record of who has done most of the writing, examples with issues or features to draw upon, and a contributing network of ideas, decisions, or other texts (see Chapter Four for strategies for building drafts). If you were given the task of compiling a quarterly report for your group, your instinct might be to look for past reports—not only to see how they are written but to reconstruct historically the kind of thinking that went into them.

Paper trails may be difficult to trace because of the wide use of electronic communication. But even e-mail can be printed and read as a series of decisions that lead to a final or current document.

9—Ethics

Ethics permeate all of the other eight features of a rhetorical situation. Situations and problems become rhetorical partly because ethics are involved. Today, ethics has been associated with a host of public and sometimes inflammatory issues. The business community is representative of a culture at large that has been trying to open doors for women and minorities who historically have been denied access to positions of power and advancement. The debates of late have centered on equal opportunity and sexual harassment, but ethics has to do with *any* decision that influences the treatment of other people. The problem with deciding what is ethical or not in business is complicated by the competitive nature of commerce, where "getting the job done, no matter the expense" can translate into harmful practices against the less-empowered or even against competitors.

Ethics can be approached at policy level: A company's writing guidelines may discourage sexist language, or a corporation's mission may be to give minorities equal access to education and jobs, or a firm may devote a percentage of its profits to community or environmental causes. The business community, of late, has embraced many of these causes, learning that ethics can promote and not detract from growth. But *micro-ethics* are played out in any rhetorical situation if you accept the fact that a rhetorical action has some consequence for the people involved. Many people want to avoid ethical questions and actions, because they see them only as policy decisions or because they do not want to face the consequences of their actions. We think the vitality of many organizations depends on conscious ethical action, even if it challenges the status quo in an organization, because such action keeps employees involved and invested in the future of an organization or community. For us, conflict is inseparable from positive change.

PUTTING IT ALL TOGETHER

We will conclude this section with another scenario, one that demonstrates how a rhetorical situation can be initially read and then reread. Suppose you were hired as a consultant, as if one of us were actually to put together a series of workshops on technical report writing. Your client is a mid-sized engineering firm specializing in waste management and environmental engineering. Your contact, Connie Hess, defines the problem to you on the phone and in writing this way:

- Designing a training program for managers and technicians
- Establishing good will and attendance (to satisfy the president)
- Addressing, if not correcting, criticism of the quality of their technical reports.

To accommodate the features presented above, this rhetorical situation appeared to be initially comprised of:

Players	The old guard who preferred to leave writing duties to secretaries
	The new guard who were fresh from school and did not like to write
	Managers who wrote often but who delegated much of this work
Triggering Event	Poorly written reports, criticism from customers
	The president's call for a solution—a workshop

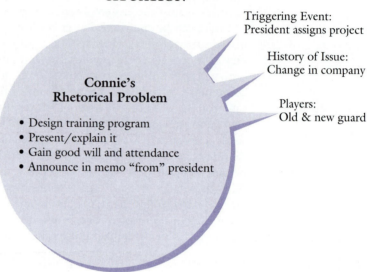

FIGURE 2–2

The Apparent Rhetorical
Situation

> *Task*   A proposal for a series of training meetings, with memos
> encouraging attendance (see Figure 2-2)

This construction of the situation seemed detailed enough until Connie
began to speak further about her situation. For nearly nine years she has
been the administrative assistant to the president, which meant that she had
supported the company through its growth from a small group of engineers
to a full-fledged company of 25 engineers and technical personnel.
Although the firm hired a word-processing pool, much of this writing was
still handled by Connie, until the firm's growth demanded that engineers
and specialists write more and more of their own reports. In addition,
growth had produced two tiers of engineers, the old guard that had established routines and preferred to work independently (without workshops)
and the new guard who had risen to managerial roles and wanted the business to produce more and better research documents. Thus, with more
information, the rhetorical situation began to expand:

> *Investments*   Connie believed in the workshop but wanted an assis-
> tant to provide help when the workshop was over.
> The president supported Connie and thought the
> workshop would solve the problem by placing more
> of the burden on his employees.

The engineers and managers generally supported the idea, but were not looking for more work; most just wanted to hire more secretaries.

Constraints   Engineers are busy; they could meet only late afternoons and after-hours, when most wanted to be at home with their families.

History   Workshops had been tried once before, and attention had flagged quickly because they were boring. The old guard also had little school training in writing.

Paper Trail   Though Connie and the president outlined some general features of the poorly written reports, the exact nature of the problems could not be ascertained without reading back through a number of reports of varying quality.

Organization   You, the consultant, learned that the firm has gained some efficiency by delegating research assignments and writing duties. It became important to understand how the writing and revising process fit into the delegation and research processes of the engineers.

Ethics   We think there are many issues here. How many do you see as this rhetorical situation builds? How would you respond to them if you were working with Connie to set up the workshop series? How would you negotiate this workshop given the slightly different agendas of yourself, Connie, the president, and the workshop participants? (see Figure 2-3.)

Ideas to Action

These nine features of the rhetorical situation play a large role in business and professional settings. In the projects at the end of the chapter we ask you to use these features to "read" the following scenario from the Mountain Trails Horse Center as a consultant would. But before you go on we would like to pose a question only *you* can answer. How many of these features are already familiar to you? Which of these features can you see at work in the writing you have done in your college career? Do relationships, investments, constraints, paper trails, etc., play any part in academic writing?

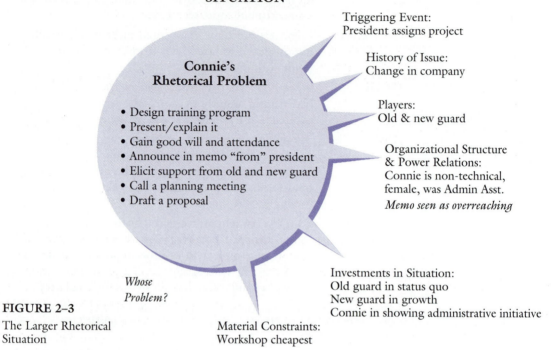

THE LARGER RHETORICAL SITUATION

Triggering Event:
President assigns project

History of Issue:
Change in company

Connie's Rhetorical Problem

Players:
Old & new guard

- Design training program
- Present/explain it
- Gain good will and attendance
- Announce in memo "from" president
- Elicit support from old and new guard
- Call a planning meeting
- Draft a proposal

Organizational Structure & Power Relations:
Connie is non-technical, female, was Admin Asst.
Memo seen as overreaching

Whose Problem?

Investments in Situation:
Old guard in status quo
New guard in growth
Connie in showing administrative initiative

FIGURE 2–3
The Larger Rhetorical Situation

Material Constraints:
Workshop cheapest

SCENARIO

The Mountain Trails Horse Center

The Mountain Trails Case is a real situation. As you read this case, try to use the strategies we have just described to reconstruct this rhetorical situation for yourself, just as we tried to do. At the end of the chapter, we will ask you to act as a business communications consultant to various parties in this case. And to help you do that, we will introduce two additional sets of strategies for rhetorical and informational reading and for analyzing problems.

Pat and Jill Maier run an outfitting business in the mountainous state forests of northern Pennsylvania. For ten years Pat has taken small groups of horseback riders on 1–4 day trips into the mountains using state forest roads, old logging roads, deer trails, and bushwhacking—a mixture designed to have a low impact on the environment. One highlight of his trips is a 2-mile stretch on an abandoned railroad grade above Pine Creek Gorge, followed by a descent into the canyon itself to ride a narrow trail along the banks of the river. Called the Little Grand Canyon of Pennsylvania, Pine Creek offers white water canoeing and fishing and supports herons, eagles, kingfishers, and owls in an area populated by deer, fox, and black bear. It is an area to both preserve and enjoy, but how that is done could support or endanger the survival of a small business like Mountain Trails.

On June 28, the State Senate designated Pine Creek Gorge as a National Landmark and approved a 62-mile recreation trail along the old railroad right of way. However, like many such bills, the decision of how to develop the area and what to allow or disallow was left up to the Department of Environmental Resources (DER) subject to discussions with the community in this rural area whose economy relies heavily on hunters, anglers, and outdoor tourism.

To protect and maybe even improve their own interests, the Maiers knew they had to propose a plan that would (1) fit in with the (still unstated) intentions of the DER, (2) acknowledge or accommodate the other positions in the community, but (3) would, in the face of inevitable points of conflict, make a strong case for their own position. In this community many civic decisions are discussed informally, when people meet on the street or drop by the office of the forest rangers, park commissioners, and so on. But, looking at the size and official nature of this problem, the Maiers felt they needed to support this oral negotiation by offering the DER a balanced and workable plan early on in the decision process—rather than try to change an undesirable decision after it had been announced. Here is a timeline of some of the critical events and attitudes they had to anticipate in their reading of the situation. How would you as a proposal writer read this context? What issues are at stake? Can you predict the proposals the other players in this rhetorical situation are likely to be making to Mr. Davis at the DER?

Timeline

June 28	After months of talk, Senator Roger Madigen's bill passes and the Rails to Trails proposal is officially set in motion.
June 30	Maiers send their plan in a letter to Arthur Davis, Secretary of DER.
July 19	A delay. Conrail won't turn over its right of way as promised unless the state also accepts liability for its use and stipulates that this title can revert to Conrail if it is needed, rather than to landowners.

(continued on page 74)

Dear Editor:

We are writing as Tioga County land owners, taxpayers and voters to protest the Rails to Trails Proposal for Delmar, Shippen and Morris townships.

As property owners along this proposed trail we feel this is an undesirable project and not in the best interest of the majority. This trail would benefit only a few people, mostly a few local businesses and some already financially well off individuals. No one has taken into consideration the plight of the individual property owners involved.

Right of way was given to the railroad company nearly 100 years ago, and the railroad now wishes to abandon this particular line. It is our feeling that this property should all revert to the property owners who have paid taxes on this land for years and continue to do so now. We, as property owners, should have the right to have our land back, and not have taken from us as a recreational project we object to and one which will cause many of us problems.

We live in the country by choice, wishing for our privacy, which this proposal would destroy. We have many financial concerns for our property. We are farmers. We have fences, cattle, sheep, horses, etc. along this proposed trail. Who's going to protect our fences, gates, barns, etc.? Who is protecting our rights as property owners? We DO NOT want this trail across our farms and properties. Who is going to take care of the sanitary conditions of this trail? Or will be asked to give more property to cover this project?

In this day and age of constant problems in the cities with burglaries, muggings, etc., we don't want strangers wandering on our land possibly starting fires, climbing our pastures fences, leaving gates open. We want our rights as property owners, taxpayers and Americans. If this were a project which would bring many jobs to the county, such as a factory, we would not protest the loss of our land so strongly, but this project does not benefit the average person in our county. It will only benefit an elite few.

Please act in our behalf to stop the Rails to Trails project.

Sincerely,

Concerned Property Owners and Taxpayers

FIGURE 2–4

Landowners' Letter to the Editor (July 19)

County organizations back Pine Creek trail project

When Conrail failed to abandon the 62 miles of rail line between Wellsboro Junction and Jersey Shore, many questions were raised over the fate of the rail line. [Since then] the Tioga Association of Recreation and Tourism, . . . the Wellsboro Area [and] . . . the Williamsport-Lycoming County Chambers of Commerce [have gone] on record in support of the trail.

Jim West, owner of the Canyon Motel in Wellsboro and chairman of the tourism committee of the Wellsboro chamber, said he feels the trail will benefit everyone.

"I definitely support the rail-trail project," said West. "DER has made a substantial financial commitment up front to this project. They should be able to do a first-class job of landscaping the trail and providing adequate support like parking and toilet facilities as needed."

"Wherever there are people you can expect some problems such as litter, but on the other hand hikers are usually ecologically minded," West added. "They are more likely to pick up someone else's litter and put it in their pack than to drop something themselves. Also, the trail will clearly benefit the whole area economically."

"I think all businesses, not just tourism-based businesses will benefit," said Margaret Shettel, Colton Point Motel owner. "I don't expect to see any dramatic increase in numbers of new visitors but I do think that people already attracted to the area will be encouraged to extend their stay here. This extra time means they will eat out more, buy more gas, and maybe shop in a local store. This has to have a positive ripple effect on the entire county. I also believe a controlled rail-trail is the only way to protect the abandoned grade from illegal trespassing."

Susan Dillon of Pine Creek Outfitters, Inc. in Ansonia, agrees.

"I believe we need a managed rail-trail," Dillon said. "Both our business and our personal 'quality of life' as residents will suffer if there is nothing positive done with the abandoned Conrail line."

"The entire right-of-way is already attracting illegal users who go around whatever barriers are there," Dillon added. "In the canyon portion, which is a registered National Natural Landmark, we have seen vehicles driving along the railroad grade and even camping. In its abandoned state the grade is an open invitation to litter and dump and trespass. We need the rail-trail project."

FIGURE 2–5

News Story on County Organizations (Oct. 4)

To the Editor:

As an organization active in promoting and leading outdoor outings including hiking, backpacking, bicycling and crosscountry skiing, we, the Otzinachson Chapter of the Sierra Club, strongly support efforts by the Department of Environmental Resources (DER) to turn abandoned rail corridors into recreational trails.

During our many years of involvement with outings activities, we have a need for trail systems suitable for families with children, senior citizens, handicapped people, and others unable to negotiate strenuous trail conditions. A rail-trail provides fulfillment of these needs because of its gentle grade and ready accessibility.

In many communities, a rail-trail system has turned an abandoned rail corridor, regarded as a waste area and an eyesore, into a useful outdoor recreational site. In addition to providing a place for hiking, jogging, and bicycling, rail-trails can provide improved access to adjoining public lands for fishermen, hunters, bird watchers and other outdoor enthusiasts.

Rail-trails can also provide an important "greenbelt" transportation link between populated areas and parks and other recreational sites, such as the open spaces of the countryside. Traffic congestion on roads leading to popular parks and other recreational sites might be reduced, an additional benefit.

While some long abandoned rail corridors may be beyond revitalization, public officials should remain alert for opportunities to create rail-trails especially if contemporary rail corridor abandonments take place.

Our north-central Pennsylvania Otzinachson Chapter remains pleased with DER's efforts to establish a 62-mile long rail-trail in Pine Creek Valley. We fully endorse the concept of this trail as well as two bills designed to further establishment of rail-trails in Pennsylvania. We urge your support of HB967, a liability bill to protect Conrail from possible rail-trail use related lawsuits. The passage of this bill remains critical to the establishment of a rail-trail in Pine Creek Valley and should be passed without amendments. The rail-trail funding bill currently before the conservation committee, HB640, should also be supported.

Rails-to-trails manifests great potential to increase and diversify the recreational opportunities available to people in Pennsylvania. Rails-to-trails progress should be supported by our elected officials.

> Roy Fontaine, group chair
> David Hafer, outings coordinator
> Gregory Merchant, newsletter editor

FIGURE 2–6
Sierra Club Letter to the Editor (Feb. 7)

RD 2, BOX 53, CATLIN HOLLOW RD., WELLSBORO, PA. 16901 (717) 376-5561

June 24, 1989

Mr. Arthur A. Davis, Secretary
Department of Environmental Resources
P.O. Box 63
Harrisburg, PA 17120

A PROPOSAL FOR USE OF THE RAILROAD BED IN PINE CREEK GORGE

Dear Mr. Davis:

You are involved in developing a plan for the use of the railroad bed running through the Pine Creek Gorge, located in Tioga and surrounding counties. The planners envision a usage that would make the Gorge's aesthetic beauties available to more people, including future generations, while preserving the area's natural, unlittered, uncommercialized condition. We realize that these two goals are often in conflict, and we have a proposal that satisfies both objectives.

Our Professional Background

We own and operate Mountain Trail Horse Center, Inc., and have been in business since September, 1982. Pat has been in the outfitting business since 1979, gaining much of his experience in Colorado, where he was foreman for a well-respected outfitter: Mr. Rudy Rudibaugh of Fossil Ridge Guide and Outfitters, in Parlin, CO, 303-641-0666. Pat also has a B.S. in Recreational Development from Slippery Rock State College. Operating Mountain Trail Horse Center is our full-time job and primary source of income.

Currently, Mountain Trail offers half-day and day-long rides, and specializes in overnight trips of one to five or more nights. Our program gives people a unique outdoor experience, one that shows the beauty of North Central Pennsylvania's natural habitats and environment. We utilize the Canyon and our expansive state lands from the upper Asaph area to Cedar Run. We also sponsor a pack trip to Colorado and a late season elk hunt in Colorado.

Mountain Trail Horse Center Plan

- Professionally led horsepack trail rides that traverse Pine Creek
- Horse-drawn carriage, buckboard, and sleigh rides in the railroad bed along Pine Creek
- State-approved outfitter for regulation and control

FIGURE 2–7

The Mountain Trails' Proposal

RD 2, BOX 53, CATLIN HOLLOW RD., WELLSBORO, PA. 16901 (717) 376-5561

Our repertoire presently includes a canyon ride during which we cross Pine Creek on horseback, using a small portion of the railroad bed where there is not enough shoreline. This gives riders the chance to see the Canyon from a new and interesting perspective and opportunities to see exciting wildlife and waterfowl. By traversing Pine Creek we are exposed to more than would be afforded by just traveling down the railroad bed. We become a part of the stream, and can better appreciate delicate flora and fauna.

Maintaining our existing trail ride traversing Pine Creek will allow visitors to see the Gorge from all sides, something not possible from the railroad bed.

There is a broad population that cannot hike or bike; these individuals could enjoy the Gorge in horse-drawn carriage, buckboard, and sleigh rides down the railroad grade. Handicapped individuals, elderly persons, and people of all ages could experience the glories of the Canyon in a nostalgic and nonpolluting fashion. The chance to travel through the Canyon as was done in the early 1900s will recreate an earlier and simpler time. Sleigh rides would allow travelers to experience the beautiful ice formations and wildlife in winter, a time of year that many people wouldn't otherwise appreciate. Our idea includes going from Ansonia to Tiadaghton and back, and from Ansonia to Blackwell or Cedar Run. Traveling to Blackwell or Cedar Run would offer the opportunity for a nice overnight package. It also makes shuttling back to Ansonia practical.

We believe that a designated public-use equestrian track would invite misuse and abuse of the Canyon floor. During our career we have personally witnessed this: other horseback riders tie their horses across spring beds, polluting streams and the creek. Another example of the public's extreme carelessness and lack of regard is the condition of the Tiadaghton picnic area.

We feel that control is important, to preserve the area's natural beauty and habitats. Licensed outfitters are more typical in the west, such as the mule trails in the Arizona Grand Canyon; this works to regulate and control the area. Maintaining our Canyon's sensitive ecosystem must be balanced with the rights of citizens to enjoy its wonders. As experienced, concerned, professional outfitters, we are proposing an approach that achieves that balance.

Mountain Trail Horse Center Responsibilities

- Maintain the environment
- Control numbers
- Cooperate with officials
- Keep routes suitable for bikers and hikers

FIGURE 2–7,
continued

RD 2, BOX 53, CATLIN HOLLOW RD., WELLSBORO, PA. 16901 (717) 376-5561

By providing the right, or selling a concession, to Mountain Trail Horse Center, the state can permit a greater number of people access to the Gorge in a safe, low-impact manner. The number of excursions would be controlled, if they became more popular than the ecosystem could withstand.

Mountain Trail Horse Center has demonstrated that we are responsible and cooperative. We maintain contact with officials operating Colton Point and Harrison State Parks. We have worked with our District Forester, Jack Sherwood, and have also provided excursions for the PFA's Penn's Woods Ramblers, including Norman LaCasse and Pat Lantz. They can vouch for our interest, both professional and personal, in preserving our environment, especially that of the Canyon.

As shown historically in l9th century city streets, it is possible for horse activities to co-exist with other activities, and we are committed to leaving the area suitable for others' use. Currently, our Canyon rides do not interfere with fishermen or rafters. We are courteous to anglers by staying clear of their fishing space, and the frequency of our trips is not a constant disruption to others using the creek. Unlike motorized vehicles, horseback riding does not degrade the experience for others; on the contrary, it contributes to the attractiveness of the area. We feel our plan solves your problem of access versus preservation, and we have the qualifications to carry it out.

We will gladly furnish references, as well as names of our customers, who include bankers, doctors, college professors, PA Conservancy members, and ministers. They could provide first-hand information about our business and professionalism. When deliberations are in committee, we would like you to consider and comment on this plan, and deliver feedback to us. We would welcome the opportunity to discuss any aspect in more detail.

Sincerely,

Patrick and Jill Maier
Mountain Trail Horse Center, Inc.

FIGURE 2-7,
continued

The same issue of the Wellsboro Gazette that carries this news prints an angry letter (see Figure 2-4) from affected landowners.

August 16   Fifty farmers and taxpayers (in an area north of where Mountain Trails rides) sign a petition against Rails to Trails and (with uncertain legality) post NO TRESPASSING signs along their portion of the right of way.

Sept. 23   A town meeting is held on whether right of way land should revert to its owners.

Oct. 4   Conrail officially files to abandon 62 miles of rail lines and a news article reveals more about which groups support the plan and what they envision (see Figure 2-5).

Nov. 15   An article by Susan Dillon documents the history of a similar right of way along the scenic Youghiogheny in another county. Abandoned and dismantled in 1960, it had been vandalized by trespassers until a trail was built five years ago. Although this created congestion in the small town and parking problems, it was the only difficulty they experienced. (*Note,* this is the same Dillon quoted in the October 4 story.)

Jan. 10   As plans are still being debated, the paper announces another extension of the time for DER and Conrail to reach agreement.

Feb. 7   A Sierra Club letter to the editor supports specified uses of the trail (excluding off the road vehicles; see Figure 2-6).

Now consider the proposal the Maiers (Figure 2-7) drafted early in the process (hoping to influence the planning process rather than have to argue against a decision that might exclude horses from the railroad grade trail and river). How well did they read the context of the public discussion? Was their decision to act early able to anticipate all of the issues and goals of the other parties in the discussion?

Ideas to Action

Before you go on, we would like you to perform a small experiment in preparation for the next section. On a sheet of paper, jot down all the key points you can recall from the Mountain Trails proposal. How many of the main categories and arguments can you get?

STRATEGY 2: INFORMATIONAL AND RHETORICAL READING OF TEXTS

Texts are sometimes your best or only source of information about a rhetorical situation. But how do you go about reading a text like the Mountain Trail proposal or the Landowners' letter of July? Informational reading strategies help you summarize key points and get the gist, while rhetorical reading strategies reveal the story behind the information. Each will draw on a number of supporting strategies or techniques.

STRATEGY OVERVIEW

Informational Reading
  a topical issue tree
  summary
  claims and evidence
  points
  response

Rhetorical Reading
  intentions
  conventions
  context

READING FOR INFORMATION

Test your own reading of the Mountain Trails case. What were you able to recall from the proposal? Did you get the main concepts that organized the proposal? How many of the key points within each category did you remember? Could you recall the arguments and evidence supporting those points? On a casual reading, people may recall only the points they found interesting or relevant (even though those points may be mere details in the original text). Sometimes, however, writers must read purposefully to extract all of the important information in a text.

How do you know what is important? Well written texts use a number of cues to signal key ideas and show how they are related to one another. Places to look for these cues (and to locate them in your own writing) include: titles, section divisions, topic sentences (that may come at the end of a paragraph), main clauses (rather than subordinate ones), and key terms that are repeated or highlighted. Also look for graphic cues like white space, bullets, and bold face or italic type.

Sketch a topical tree. A systematic reading strategy is to sketch a topical issue tree like the one shown in Figure 2-8. Like a branching tree turned upside down, it locates all the top-level key points or concepts or categories

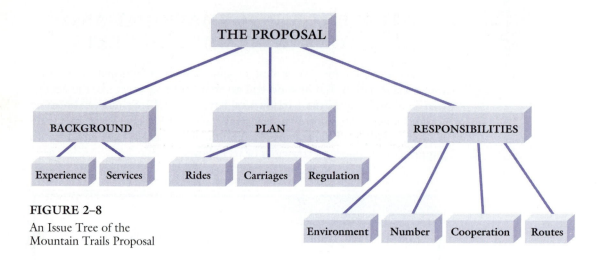

FIGURE 2–8

An Issue Tree of the
Mountain Trails Proposal

at the top of the tree. It then shows the other points, facts, figures, ideas, which make up these larger inclusive concepts. (We will look at techniques for *building* a topical issue tree in more depth in Chapter Three.)

A good informational reading turns a random list of points into a hierarchy or a tree that reveals the structure of ideas. Notice, however, that the most important claim or the most striking fact may appear in the lower parts of this tree, since the hierarchy is designed to show how individual points are part of larger concepts, which in turn make up larger, more inclusive concepts or categories. Reading for the structure of ideas, not just a list of points, also makes it easier to recall a text and separate key points from secondary ones when someone at work asks, "What did that report say?" or when you want to argue with a text.

Summarize   Summarizing is another method of reading for information. When a coworker asks you, "What was the gist of that memo?" your informal summary will report the key point, or what you inferred as the most important point. More formal summaries are constructed with the following techniques:

- *Delete* trivial or redundant points.

- *Substitute* a superordinate term for a list of terms or a superordinate event for a list of events. For example, "hiking, jogging, bicycling," as well as "fishing, hunting, and bird watching" can be summarized as "outdoor recreation."

- *Select* a topic sentence. Well written paragraphs often present their key point in a topic sentence at the beginning or the end of a paragraph. However, for a good summary, select a sentence that not only states the topic (e.g., rail-trails), but make a claim or comment about the topic (e.g., rail-trails link populated and recreational areas). Notice how this example uses both the substitution and deletion technique to turn the long topic sentence from the Sierra Club letter into a short gist.

- *Invent* a topic sentence that summarizes multiple paragraphs. (e.g., The Sierra Club supports rail-trails because they create a "greenbelt" link to recreation for both the outdoor person and the nonathlete. Paragraphs 1–4.) Here is where a good summarizer has to draw inferences and state the unstated idea that links a number of paragraphs. As you begin to name underlying ideas and concepts, summarizing a text will become more like building an issue tree. The longer the text, the more you have to invent in order to produce a concise statement of key points.

Find claims and evidence. The first two strategies emphasize topics and the way ideas are organized within those topics. The third strategy for informational reading attends to the argument that an author uses. With this strategy you build a list or an issue tree focused on the claims and evidence presented in the text. Claims are the primary assertions made by a writer. For example, the Sierra Club letter makes three main claims: (1) rail-trails are good for many kinds of people, (2) they create "greenbelt" links, and (3) the Pine Creek bills should be passed without amendment. Evidence is the basis for support for the claims, necessary because claims rarely stand on their own, and argumentative writing is the practice of joining and supporting claims with evidence. The evidence the Sierra Club presents is partly based on facts—they list ways the trails are used—and partly based on their personal authority—"during our many years of involvement with outings." Look for stated evidence and implied evidence. For example, for some readers, the *fact* that the Sierra Club wrote in support of rail-trails is enough— the implied evidence could be their many years of thoughtful conservation and environmentalism. Obviously evidence that is just implied will work for some audiences and not for others (see Chapter Four for more instruction on claims and evidence).

Find points. A fourth strategy is *point-driven reading*. This strategy lets you read selectively for ideas, positions, or arguments to suit *your* purpose as a writer. It is, therefore, unlike the first three strategies, which remain generally faithful to the ideas, arguments, and organization of the original text. With point-driven reading, you are writing as you read and your writing— your rhetorical purpose—is what guides your reading. In practice, point-driven reading can be an exercise in throwing most of a text away, recognizing what is not useful, and searching for the point that fits your purpose in writing. For example, the Maiers probably read the newspaper articles and letters both to summarize and extract one or two key points or arguments to fit their argument for the rail-trails system.

Respond. Our fifth strategy may seem far removed from business communication, but we believe it is relevant no matter how informative or technical the writing. Your *response or reaction* to a text is also information and is part of the rhetorical situation you seek to uncover. The Maiers probably had a personal response to the Sierra Club letter. For instance they may have responded positively to the Sierra Club as an environmental ally, but have begun to worry whether this powerful organization would develop a competing, hiker-centered vision of the trail. Reactions or responses are part of all reading, because ideas, language, and arguments in a text not only covey information but cue personal values and agendas. You are wise to be aware of your response because responses will color your reading and writing anyway.

Each of these techniques of reading for information will give you a somewhat different account of the text. Summarizing sticks most closely to the text and can produce sharp detail. Issue trees focus on main concepts and their underlying structure and help you recall or present a large discussion at a glance. A claim and evidence summary is critical for understanding and evaluating an argument and the degree to which a writer is being explicit with an audience. Point-driven reading shifts the purpose for reading even closer to your goals as a writer or speaker. And responses acknowledge that people have values and attitudes that surface in any communicative exchange. Sometimes, however, to understand the real "meaning" of a text—as a strategic act in a rhetorical situation—you need to switch from an informational reading to what we call rhetorical reading.

RHETORICAL READING

Reading for information is often a first and necessary step in understanding a text. But sometimes the real point of the text is a meaning you have to infer or construct on top of the literal reading. Rhetorical reading is a strategy that looks at the text as more than words on a page in order also to "read" the intentions, conventions, and context that make up its meaning. In addition to content, readers search for:

- *Intentions:* Who is talking here? Why did they write this text, and why did they write this paragraph or this sentence the way they did? What are the (multiple) rhetorical goals and attitudes behind this text and this way of saying things? The 5Ws of news writing are a handy guide to uncovering intentions: *who, what, when, where* and *why*—with a big emphasis on the *why.*

- *Conventions:* What conventions or rhetorical moves is this writer using to guide my reading? For instance, is this introduction setting up a problem/solution pattern or just giving background information, or why does the writer use italics—to show that a word has a special or technical meaning? (see Chapter Four on building a draft, Chapter Five on revising, and Chapter Seven on models to learn further about a number of these conventions.)

- *Context:* How does this text fit into a larger rhetorical context? How are the voices in the text related as a conversation? Who is it written to and how might they respond? What discourse community is it speaking to, or is it trying to cross communities? What assumptions or belief systems does it buy into?

Now here is how these three forms of rhetorical reading appear, as we return to the Mountain Trails scenario.

Reading for Intentions. Rhetorical reading, in which you focus on intentions, conventions, and context, will give you three significantly different perspectives on what a text means. For instance, look quickly at paragraphs 8 and 9 of the Mountain Trails proposal (Figure 2-7) and do your own rhetorical reading. That is, look at each sentence and ask: What were the authors trying to do here? Why did they raise this point? Why did they put it this way? What did they want the reader to think? Try to predict what the authors would say if you were to ask them to reveal what they were thinking.

Now compare your reading to the meanings Pat Maier reported when we asked him to do a rhetorical reading of his own text.

> Well, the best outcome for me, of course, would be to be the main licensed outfitter for the canyon. I don't know if that is likely, but I'm really trying to ward off another problem down the line when you have open access for horses, and the number of riders increases. I've seen what happens. People come out and find horse shit in their springs, the place is trampled where some idiots tied their horses, and there's trash all around, and since they know you ride the area, they assume it was you. Hikers start finding horse apples on the trail and suddenly there is a big cry to get the horses out of there altogether. I wanted to avoid that, and I know Davis is very aware of the problem up at Tiadaghton. In the next paragraph I'm thinking about the Sierra Club types who are going to oppose the bikes but sometimes oppose horses too. The response to them is the Grand Canyon system, which is a good precedent for balancing preservation and access.

Given these goals behind the text, how much did you see in your rhetorical reading? How well do you think the text accomplishes its purpose?

Reading for Conventions. The first draft of the Mountain Trails plan was a letter from Maier that started with what is now paragraph 2 ("I own and operate Mountain Trails Horse Center . . ."), followed by a request for the DER not to exclude horses or his trips from the canyon. In moving from a letter of personal request to a proposal for a public issue, the Maiers made a number of rhetorical moves that depend on the conventions of proposal writing:

- *Title:* Although not found in personal letters, titles or subject lines are a common feature of letter proposals and reports. This one quickly announces both the topic and the function of the document, cuing Davis how to read it.

- *Problem/Purpose Statement:* Paragraph one defines a shared problem—in light of the goals, values, and needs of the reader—and presents the writer's plan as a reasonable response.

- *Heading:* Since this is background information that Davis may want to skim but others may need to know, the heading signals the function of the section and lets readers adjust.

- *Paragraphs two and three:* This background and self-introduction section is more than just a place to list facts; it is a chance to highlight critical information and to establish the community standing and credibility of the writer. Look closely at how Maiers did this. Why did they select the facts they did? Looking at each sentence as a rhetorical move, what self-image do you think they are trying to project?

Reading for Context. Understanding the overt intentions of a writer is important, but sometimes you want to step back and place the writer and the text in a larger context, *exactly* in the way that we urged you to *reconstruct the rhetorical situation* in which you write. A critical or contextual reading can sometimes reveal how individual texts are merely moves in or are driven by a larger political, social, or historical event and values (like the economic development of a region). It may even reveal motives and assumptions the writers themselves were not aware of or wouldn't talk about if they were.

For example, the speakers quoted in the October 4 "news story" and the landowners writing the July 19 letter both claim to be speaking for the majority. What assumptions are these two groups working from that led to their decisions? Do these two groups hold the same assumptions about the relative importance of property rights versus economic growth or farming versus business? Do they represent the same social/political constituency in the region? Asking about assumptions can uncover some larger issues of politics, power, and values that underlie many texts and most arguments. Finally, this strategy of reading for the context can often reveal conflicts within the writer's own thinking that may be lurking beneath the surface. For instance, look at the values the Maiers bring to being mountain outfitters—from an attachment to wilderness, to experiencing nature in the quiet and nonintrusive ways of camping, fishing, and riding, to a spirit of adventure. Then look at the chamber of commerce interests with which they are necessarily aligning themselves and at the vision of the area as represented in the October 4 article. Are they ultimately the same vision, or is there a conflict that your rhetorical reading could define?

STRATEGY 3: FINDING AND ANALYZING PROBLEMS

At this point in our text, we have already asked you to survey a rhetorical situation, delving deeper into its features and strategically reading texts along the paper trail. Problems can be complex but solvable—through communication—when you have done your homework. The ability to find, define, and state problems is one indication of a successful speaker or writer in business and professional settings, where communication is often a goal-directed transaction between two or more people. Sometimes the purpose of these transactions is primarily to convey information—to describe products or services, to request information or order materials, or to confirm in writing an agreement or contract already made. Such writing may depend heavily on conventions and formats of the purchase order, letter of transmittal, or accounting report to make the transaction predictable to read and efficient to write.

However, as we saw in the scenarios in Chapter One, some of the more interesting and most important transactions in professional life are stimulated not by information and answers, but by uncertainties and problems. Reports are typically written in response to problems and proposals are explicitly designed to solve problems. That much is often obvious; what may be less clear is *how writers first recognize and define problems in order to analyze and solve them.* In this section, we will provide strategies and examples to help and to add to your repertory.

FINDING PROBLEMS

Are you a person who is good at "seeing the underlying problem" within a situation? If so, you are already aware of the difference between a mere situation and a problem. For instance, the fact of pollution in our air and water is merely a situation—it exists. To understand the **problem** we must be able to locate what is at conflict—for whom. Although everyone might agree that pollution is harmful and unpleasant, there was a time in small towns and industrial cities when black smoke from steel mills and the sight of factories expanding along the river were signs of jobs and prosperity. And when car sales go up, so does national prosperity. Pollution is only a problem when you and I want clean air and drive cars that pollute it, or when a society wants both a clean environment and maximum industrial productivity. As a writer, the biggest challenge you will face is not "solving" problems (that is, deciding or stating what to do), but "finding" problems—seeing and defining what is really at issue in a difficult situation.

Problem analysis is a form of detective work. It is the act of discovering the key issues that often lie hidden under the noisy details of a situation. The process of analysis begins when people encounter what is called a **"felt difficulty,"** that is, you feel that something doesn't fit; you feel a conflict. Sometimes the conflict is obvious: Two people disagree, or you discover that you yourself hold two contradictory ideas on a subject such as getting married. Many times both sides of a conflict will have merit: Should we maintain the federally required testing of certain new drugs for long-term dangers while people are dying of AIDS? Sometimes, however, the conflict is harder to pinpoint: You are aware of an unspecified "organizational problem" within your college fraternity or the way work is being scheduled in your office.

The way you define a problem can have large implications. Take a familiar problematic situation—the relationship between landlords and tenants. What is the conflict, and from whose point of view; gouging landlords, irresponsible tenants, a history of assumptions and attitudes that escalates competing needs into battles? What is really at issue here: legal rights or mutual social responsibilities? And will it make any difference if you decide to act on one definition of this problem rather than the other? In the section below we will look at the way an actual group of landlords and tenants we studied went about defining their problem, and at the way a college student analyzed her very different problem doing free-lance work. Of the five mini-strategies we will describe, the first three are the most challenging and have the biggest impact. They also are the strategies that help you decide what to say at the beginning of a written analysis. Figure 2-9 shows how the process of analyzing problems with these five mini-strategies leads to written text.

FIVE STEPS FOR ANALYZING A PROBLEM

1. Define the Conflict or Key Issue

A problem analyst's first job is to discover the critical conflict or key issue that lies at the heart of any felt difficulty. One way to do this is to identify an *A* and a *B* which are in conflict and try to define what is at issue:

> A. I want to quit smoking.
> B. But (however, on the other hand, at the same time), smoking is a long standing habit linked to eating and talking with friends.

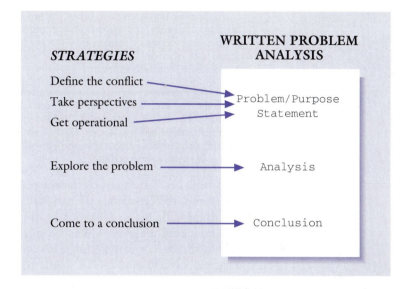

FIGURE 2–9

How Strategies for
Problem Analysis Lead
to Text

What is at issue: deeply ingrained, unthinking habits or habits strongly associated with some personal values?

Now imagine a professional situation: The Neighborhood Redevelopment Commission is deciding whether to target its funds on the Northside
or the Southside. You have been asked to attend the Northside landlord and
tenant discussions and write a brief analysis of the problem(s) revealed. In
this series of discussions (which we observed and documented) the landlords
and tenants were trying to speak for both the low-income renters in their
inner-city neighborhood and for the local owners of those buildings who
had often sunk their slender savings into redeveloping and renting older
houses. Both parties have a clear vision of the conflicts at the heart of their
problem:

> A. Eager to have a tenant in the building and rent coming in to cover
> their own mortgage, tax payments and loans for the building, landlords
> promise they will "fix the place up." It takes both time and money to do
> so, and they spend what seems "reasonable" from their perspective.

> B. Discussing this "fix up" plan, the tenant is reluctant to sound
> pushy for fear she won't get the apartment. But on moving day (tenant
> arrives with a truck, too late to demand more) the repairs are partly
> done. Moreover, the tenant finds she has very different images of what it
> means to "fix" the hole in the wall.

What is at issue here: misrepresentation and broken promises, different
images, unstated expectations? There were other conflicts:

A. The tenant, a single mother, spends most of her September pay on school clothes and expenses—the rent is two weeks late. And to avoid the unpleasant confrontation she assumes would be inevitable, she waits until the landlord demands the rent to admit she can't pay. Besides he never fixed the wall.

B. The landlord, who operates on a narrow margin and has another apartment vacant, has to pay more interest for his own late payment to the bank. He has seen this pattern before and fears the rent will be three weeks late next time. He knows three other small landlords who eventually lost their buildings to the bank. The only option the law allows him is to start eviction proceedings.

What is at issue here: irresponsible tenant behavior, unsympathetic legalistic landlord actions, the economics of marginal incomes, a failure to communicate and compromise before positions become rigid?

In understanding these cases, your problem analysis starts by locating the actions, values, or needs that are really in conflict—late rent matters because the mortgage payment is due. The failure to inform the landlord and set a new payment date creates a conflict because it seems (to the landlord) to predict that the familiar, undependable renter scenario is about to begin. But notice how many ways there are to define these problems even after you have located some of the underlying conflicts. As a writer, your job is to articulate the key conflicts or issues that are at stake. Are you looking at irresponsibility, a shared problem of marginal incomes, or a set of attitudes that keep people from even talking to each other and rule out early negotiation?

2. Look at the Problem from Different Perspectives

Problems do not exist in a vacuum; they are always problems for somebody. That is why different people can define the problem within a problematic situation in radically different ways. In a pure advocacy system, such as a criminal trial, a lawyer may choose to see the problem from only one point of view. But because most business, professional, and interpersonal relations depend on negotiation and cooperation, the best analyst is the person who can talk about the problem from *different perspectives* and define a *shared problem.*

The Landlord/Tenant Problem: Consider some different versions of "the problem" in the landlord/tenant discussion. Tenants describe situations like this: A wage earner is laid off or injured. Although workmen's compensation is available, it may take six months to receive it. This place is indeed more than the family can now afford, yet it takes money to move to a cheaper apartment and to pay the advance and security deposit. Moreover, it's quite possible the present place would go unrented even after they left. From that perspective eviction seems harsh and unnecessary. Nevertheless,

why face the confrontation or the humiliation of discussing the situation with the landlord? The best strategy is just to hold off the inevitable as long as you can.

We also heard some of the problems small landlords face when they too are working at the margin, hoping the furnace in the old house won't break before they can pay for the roof repairs and rent the third apartment. And one reason why there is a hole in the kitchen is because the previous tenants, who left owing three month's rent, also left $600 worth of damage. The low rent this place goes for doesn't provide a profit or cushion big enough to handle all these costs.

Melvin Williams, a cultural anthropologist, heard other perspectives. "For example, I questioned one landlord about his willingness to spend $500 in legal fees to prevent a poor black tenant from residing in his dwelling without paying rent for six months when he would lose only $480 in rent. Thus, by allowing the tenant to remain in the dwelling, he would save $20. His response was that he could not tolerate such behavior in his business because it would damage his reputation and his business relationships with other tenants in the neighborhood. . . . This could lead to a number of maneuverings and strategy concoctions that would eventually destroy his business".[3]

Ideas to Action

Stop for a minute to think about how you are defining this problem to yourself. Jot down what you would say if someone asked you, "What is the central conflict or the key issue here?" Now test your problem definition against the above observations. Could you use your statement of the problem to make sense of the conflicts we have uncovered? Are you able to define a shared problem? Would that definition help you organize a written analysis of this problem for the Neighborhood Redevelopment Commission?

The landlord and tenant group we studied made it clear that both parties come to the situation of low-cost housing in changing neighborhoods with a history of expectations and stereotypes that assign bad intentions and irresponsibility to the other side. Williams speaks for the tenants when he says,

> There is a belief that it is good business for the landlord to scheme and maneuver to earn as much income as possible from his dwellings, usually at the expense of tenants. But it is wrong for the tenants to do the same [e.g., use the Bureau of Building Inspection to let them withhold rent].

However, the landlord and tenant group we observed was also taking the perspective of mediators—as a collaborative planning group they were committed to writing a Memorandum of Understanding that would help both parties. Perhaps that is why they ended up defining this problem not in terms of legal rights and responsibilities, but rather the process of negotiation. When they looked at these conflicts and others, they saw a relationship that had few mechanisms for being clear about expectations (such as checklists that spelled out landlord repairs and completion dates, or statements of the tenant's responsibility for upkeep or preventing cockroaches). And they also saw a pattern of distrust and stereotypes that led both groups immediately to polarize themselves into antagonists when problems appeared: to avoid face-to-face discussion (imputing the worst to the other), which then led to hasty action (e.g., starting the lengthy eviction process), and that in turn generated kinds of retaliation in which neither party would take responsibility for maintaining the house. And both landlord and renter lost. There are two important questions to ask about this definition.

- Do you think this is a shared problem? Will the various members of this situation see their perspectives represented?

- What are the implications of this representation? Compare this way of defining the problem to some of the others suggested above, or the way you were seeing it, and consider the implications of these definitions. What would happen, for instance, if you chose to act on this interpretation or on the one based on legal rights and responsibility? Would the problem definition make a difference in what you did?

The New Employee Problem. We can apply this same strategy for analyzing problems to a corporate situation that may soon affect you. How do managers evaluate their new employees? Is technical competence enough? When we asked two highly successful managers to talk about how they saw the writing of their subordinates, we got two different answers:

Bob Dykstra has a tousled haired, low key style. He loved his years as a chemist, but is now a top ranking manager in charge of New Products Development for his large chemical company. Bob clearly cares about the people under him—but he evaluates them. "You can pick the people who will stay staff people from those who will become line managers," he says, "by how they write a recommendation. One group says 'on this hand, on that hand'; the other makes a decision and says 'why'." Bob talks about trying "to bring his people along," but he uses writing to judge who will make it.

Dick Majors has a different style—expensive suit, diamond ring, and cigars. He heads the office in the state capital of a large accounting firm that handles many government contracts. Their product is reports. He put it this way: "As a manager, I am responsible for bringing people along. For six months I'll take the effort. After that I'll fire him and gamble on getting someone who can write the work up." In financial accounting, the product is a report. "That's want the client gets for the substantial amount of money they spend." But the term "report" may be misleading, since there are many ways to interpret finances and accounting firms don't always bring good news. Yet they want to keep their clients. Accounting depends on writing: "You have to use the report to convince the client that your position is right."

Although Bob Dykstra and Dick Majors recognize that their staffs often have to enter a new discourse, and they do try to help, there are pressures that lead them to expect quick results. Both they and their people are judged by the management and clients on the basis of the reports they send out. And "a report may well make the entire route [through levels of management] whether you planned it or not. It reflects."

You can see the implications of different perspectives and different problem definitions in the actions of these managers. The problem, as Bob Dykstra defined it, was a conflict between the desire to bring his people along and the fact that some writers don't seem to have the management potential he is looking for. For Dick Majors on the other hand, the critical problem was getting the job done right—his priority on high quality reports was often in conflict with the fact that new writers needed some time to learn the ropes. Notice how the problem they defined shaped the problem they solved. The answer to the problem Bob Dykstra posed was to bring some people along in less demanding staff positions. The answer for the impatient Dick Majors, however, was in finding ways to cut his losses by firing earlier or hiring only people who could do both accounting and writing.

But let us say that you can articulate a conflict or key issue for yourself, from your perspective. Then why bother to consider other ways to define the problem? The Community Literacy case in Chapter One offers one answer. The felt difficulty or central problem for all seven participants in that proposal was different. The first foundation officer saw that projects which did not link educational programs to community needs and to existing networks for development were often crippled from the start; while the neighborhood project leader was concerned with children like Shana who lose sight of their own potential as they drift to the margins of school. Yet out of these different perspectives and problems they had to fashion a shared problem and a common understanding. In their more competitive situation the Mountain Trails writers demonstrated another reason to imagine an alternative reading of the problem: To succeed they had to anticipate the problems (and solutions) that others would be arguing for, to make their plan both include and withstand competing proposals.

3. Make Your Problem Definition More Operational

Strategies 1 and 2 help you create a focused but inclusive image of a problem that defines a conflict or key issue and puts it in the larger context of other perspectives. A good problem statement is precise about what is at issue. But what if someone needs to take action based on your analysis of the problem, or what if you want to persuade someone that they should do so? Here you can improve your analysis by making your definition more operational? To be **operational** means to state the problem or your goals as specific operations—as actions or tasks you could actually perform. An operational definition is more useful than an abstract one because it suggests possible courses of action or the features of a good solution. For example, see how we could make the smoker's problem definition more operational by adding information that works as a miniature plan for tackling this problem.

- My problem is cigarettes. (An overly abstract problem definition; no identification of the conflict or key issue.)

- My problem is that I try to cut down on smoking but I can't seem to stick with it. (A more specific statement of a conflict, but it doesn't suggest a way to operate or act on the problem.)

- My real problem is how to break a long-standing habit of smoking at parties or when I am out with friends (more operational), where if I don't smoke I always feel left out or appear unsociable. (An even more operational definition that suggests a number of places for taking action.)

4. Explore the Parts of the Problem

Once you have defined a problem, you are ready to explore the *key subissues* or *subproblems* within the problem. Imagine these as part of a hierarchy with your problem definition at the top; that is, these are the subparts that make up the larger whole of this problem. The landlord and tenant group organized their analysis around four key subissues: the failure to pay rent, landlord responsibilities, responsibilities to the neighborhood, and the process of communication and negotiation. A smoker might decide that the major subissues within the problem of quitting smoking are health, costs, strength of habit, and social pressure. By defining the subproblems, you create an organizing plan for your discussion.

5. Come to an Open-Minded Conclusion

Sometime an analysis of a problem will lead you to a solution. At other times it will lead you to a new, expanded definition of the problem. But you will only know how good your conclusion is if you have considered some other good answers. The chief weakness of most problem solvers is that they leap too quickly to a solution. Upon seeing the first strong alternative they breathe a sigh of relief, say "this is it," and look no further. However, your conclusion will look strong to your readers only if they know you have considered and rejected with reason other logical solutions or ways of viewing the problem. For example, some people feel that smoking should not be viewed as a public health issue at all, but as an example of the exercise of individual rights. Show that you have seriously considered the alternatives.

A good conclusion takes a stand, but it is open-minded in yet another way. It recognizes that any position has its own assumptions and implications. Real problems rarely go away; even the best solutions may only be a temporary fix. And each solution brings its own implications and consequences down the road. Your job as a good analyst is to see down that road and to alert your reader to the implications of your own conclusion. For example, giving up smoking can lead to withdrawal symptoms and an increase in eating.

To write a good conclusion, then, you must do three things: (1) seriously consider alternatives, (2) recognize the implications of your own position, and (3) take a reasoned, open-minded, but solid stand supported by the best evidence you have. It can be uncomfortable to live with the knowledge that no response is absolutely right, but real problems rarely have simple answers.

WRITING A PROBLEM/PURPOSE STATEMENT

Let us assume that you, as a problem-solving consultant, now have a great deal of insight into your problem: How do you write about it? In high school you probably learned some conventions for writing the introduction to an essay or a five-paragraph theme. One convention is to state your topic and three points about it (which you then elaborate with three paragraphs and a conclusion). Another convention for more "creative" essays is to start with an audacious claim, a clever line, or a "good quote." But none of these conventions is valued by readers who need to get to work and who want to know: "What is the problem we need to consider?" and "What is the purpose of this text?" Using a **problem/purpose statement** to introduce a memo, report, or proposal is a widely used convention in business and professional writing because it offers an immediate answer to these questions.

A problem/purpose statement does two things: First, it puts forward the problem, the issue, or the thesis on which you mean to focus. Here is where your analysis pays off, since it lets you come right to the point, defining the problem in terms of its key conflicts; it lets you define it in a way that recognizes multiple perspectives; and it lets you offer the reader an operational definition that he or she might be able to act upon. Secondly, a problem/purpose statement reveals the purpose of this particular text—it tells readers what you intend to do in this memo or report and what they will get out of reading further. A good problem/purpose not only informs, but motivates. It convinces the readers that there is a reason you have written and a reason for them to read on.

Some problem/purpose statements are simple and direct and appear as the first paragraph or first page. They might be labeled "The Problem" or

"Introduction." They could also be embedded within another format, such as a historical review of the situation or a dramatic example. The particular form your problem/purpose statement takes is not important. What is important is that readers will be looking for those two pieces of information very early in the text, and will become impatient if they can't find them or have to wait too long. (See the discussion of the problem/solution pattern as a conventional text move in Chapter Four and examples of different ways problem analyses fit into reports in Chapter Seven.)

In the example below notice how a problem statement differs from two other familiar conventions—topic or theme and a thesis statement. The *topic* or *theme* is what this paper is about—in this case it is about the subject of free-lance designing. The *thesis* is a claim you are making about that topic—in this case that students have a lot of difficulty as beginning free-lancers and need some help. However, if you simply stated your thesis without defining or analyzing the problem or difficulty more fully, you might quickly lose readers. A problem statement may contain a thesis, but it does more by explaining and defining a problem.

The following report by Claudia Benson (Figure 2–10) analyzes a problem she believes is not only important but shared by many design students doing free-lance work for the first time. Before you read on, imagine how you would define the problem. What do you predict will be the key conflict these college students face? And what will be the purpose of this report? As you will see, although Claudia's secondary audience (the users) is made up of students like herself, her primary audience (the decision makers) is the Design Department who will determine what becomes of this report after it is submitted. Claudia had discussed this project with J. Boston, the department head, who said he would be happy to read her report. How could she make this problem which students face a shared problem that the Design Department will want to act upon?

Notice how the Handbook (Figure 2–11) also starts with a Problem/Purpose statement, but embeds much of the problem definition in a personal example that establishes the sense of a shared problem with readers and offers an even more operational definition of what this problem looks like from a student's point of view.

 Summary

- Once you have the big picture a rhetorical survey provides, you can build on that understanding by strategically reading the context around you.
- **Reconstructing a rhetorical situation** focuses on nine features (Strategy 1).

players	tasks and triggering events	history of the problem
relationships	constraints	paper trail
investments in goals	organizational structures	ethics

To: J. M. Boston, Head, Department of Design
From: Claudia Benson
Re: Problems of Beginning Free-lancers in our
Department
Date: April 10,1992

Free-lance designing is a convenient way for students
to make money during the school year, as well as build
their portfolios with printed pieces. Many students,
however, find their first few jobs extremely difficult
because they are inexperienced in the basics of
professional practice. Misinterpretations about the
needs of a client, the constraints of a project, or the
designer's fee are just a few of the problems that
often arise because of the designer's inexperience.
These problems sometimes reflect negatively on both the
student and the Design Department as well. Beginning
free-lancers need something to fall back on--something
to compensate for their inexperience.

Based on my discussions with you and other faculty in
the department, I have designed a Free-Lancer's
Handbook that outlines the free-lance process,
illustrates some problems with examples from the
experience of junior and senior designers in the
department, and suggests guidelines for planning,
estimating a job, and negotiating with a client.
Distributing this Handbook to design majors could, I
believe, help students avoid unnecessary headaches and
see ways to make their business relationships and job
experiences more professional.

Key Conflict

Becomes operational

Shared problem
More operational

Shared purpose

Purpose of this memo

Purpose of the Handbook

FIGURE 2–10
The Problem/Purpose
Statement for the
Decision Maker

Think of your readers as players in this situation who come to it with relationships already established and with investments in some of their own goals and agendas. Look for the event that triggered this task, but look beyond the obvious and uncover some of the constraints on what you do and see how your action fits into the organizational structure. Most problems have a history, and you can uncover much of it, and ideas about what to do from the paper trail of prior discussion. Most problems also involve ethical choices, so be aware of the implications of your own decisions.

- An **informational reading** gives you the gist or a summary of key facts, while a **rhetorical reading** of a text lets you see the meaning and story behind the facts (Strategy 2). They draw on these ministrategies or techniques:

Reading for Information   **Rhetorical Reading**

a topical issue tree   intentions
summary   conventions
claims and evidence   context
points
response

THE FREE-LANCER'S HANDBOOK

By Claudia Benson

Introduction

Free-lance designing is a convenient way for you, the
design student, to make money during the school year as
well as build your portfolio with printed pieces. Many
times though, your first few jobs are extremely
difficult because you are not experienced in the basics
of professional practice.

I got my first job through the Graphics Clearinghouse.
I had never done anything like it before. My contract
in hand, I went to my first meeting with my client. I
was not clear as to what my responsibilities as a free-
lancer were beyond the actual designing (if any at
all), how much I should charge for my services, or how
to make accurate estimates of my time and cost. I had
no idea how or when to talk about money. I was afraid
even to mention the word. As a result I ended up
charging a fee which was set by my client--the money
was definitely not worth the time and effort I put into
the job. I ran into difficulties which could have been
avoided if I had had general guidelines to refer to. Of
course, the job you get will be different from mine in
content, but the problems you encounter may be the
same. This Handbook will not give you the experience
you need or make you a professional, but it can make
your client/designer relationship the professional
business relationship that it should be.

The first section of the Handbook will alert you to
three important points to remember before accepting a
job. Then I will walk you through the three phases of
the design process, looking at problems to avoid and
some guidelines for successful free-lancing.

Conflict

Shared Problem

More Operational
Definition

Conflict

Shared Problem

Purpose of
the Handbook

Purpose
(preview of organization)

FIGURE 2–11.
The Problem/Purpose
Statement for Handbook
Readers

- **Finding problems** starts with uncovering conflicts and felt difficulties (Strategy 3).
- You only solve the problem you define. **Analyzing problems** depends on five strategies:

   1. Define the conflict or key issue
   2. Look at the problem from different perspectives
   3. Make your problem definition more operational
   4. Explore the parts of the problem
   5. Come to an open-minded conclusion

Projects & Assignments

1. This assignment calls for some entrepreneurship and some imagination because you will be taking the role of a *professional business consultant* who has just started his or her own small business. In this role, you are not expected to be an expert in any one organization or its procedures (although you and your team may bring expertise in organizational management, accounting, marketing, or public relations). In practice you are much like any newcomer who has to enter and assess the problems within a new organization, social group, or discourse community. Consultants are common in business today, and the good ones know how to read a situation to move beyond the routine and ordinary. When you start a new job or encounter a new discourse practice on your current job, your task is much the same—people expect you to walk into a new situation, size it up, chart a course, and act. Professional consultants learn to read context quickly (or to draw on past experience) because they are typically hired only after their preliminary analysis has convinced the client to give them a contract.

   Here is the consulting cycle for a typical job. Notice how it parallels the thinking process we described for finding and defining problems, except these are the steps you take first to land a consulting contract and then to deliver a product.

THE CONSULTING CYCLE

Step 1. Define the Problem You Propose to Solve

Before the client is committed you must submit a proposal that is really a definition of the problem you see and think you can solve. An effective problem definition rearranges the facts in a way that teaches the client something new. For example, a company may know it is losing market shares, but you separate the cause from the result by showing them a problem rooted in internal inefficiency. To do this, you may have to dig beneath the surface to see such problems, since the information you get in an initial investigation is usually a distillation of the facts, not the facts themselves.

Your problem definition must propose a preliminary solution; the recommendation about what to do will come later if you land the contract. It should include the steps you will take to analyze the problem and a timetable.

Step 2. Analyze the Problem

If your initial problem analysis was successful and you sign a consulting contract with your client, you begin your research, looking for more information about the problem—and about the context behind the "facts" given to you.

Step 3. Develop a Recommendation or Solution

Your success at analyzing and redefining problems will be measured by two things: Does it lead to a solution or recommendation? And will your client then choose to act upon your recommendations? You must turn your analysis into an action your client could take, making sure your actions directly address the problems you defined.

Step 4. Implement Your Recommendation in a Written Report

Your success as a consultant is not based solely on "good recommendations"—everybody has good ideas. Your recommendation must convince your client to carry them out. The text you write is your product. Your proposal and reports must function rhetorically, to persuade the client by offering a convincing picture and reasons to accept your recommendations. (Clients who pay for clever but useless recommendations rarely come back.) The recommendations you make are typically addressed to a primary audience—the decision maker(s) who will accept or reject your analysis.

To help implement your recommendations, you must also write in clear operational terms to show how others will carry out your recommendation: what to do, how to make it work, how to evaluate whether it is working. These procedures often go to a secondary audience—the staff who carry out the plans and who rely on the quality of your instructions.

Notice what a major role writing plays in the work of business consultants. You must convince a client not only about of the nature of a problem but about the best action to solve it. Consultants must be effective communicators, and that communication begins with a sophisticated interpretation of the problems and working contexts of a client. We present "reading the context" as an early, essential moment in planning but in fact consultants need to read and reread situations all the way through a job.

Because some of your team members work from home, you have set up an e-mail (electronic mail) network that links the group via computer. Therefore, much of your planning and discussion is held through e-mail messages (memos and drafts of texts) sent to the entire group. Everyone joins in the dialogue because they can respond—often minutes after they receive a message—and can see the responses of everyone else.

A typical e-mail message would look like Figure 2–12 (on page 96). (In this example, the parts you actually have to type are in bold.)

Of course, all of your professional correspondence with clients will be on formal letterhead (see the Mountain Trail letter and Chapter Seven). To prepare for the consulting assignments which follow, design a letterhead that includes the name and contact information for your consulting business. Write a short introductory statement on the nature of your services (much like the Mountain Trails "Professional Background" section) which you can insert in all of your letters to prospective clients. This sort of prefab text which you can simply drop into proposals or reports is called "boiler plate" text (see Chapter Four). Since your firm may not have a long history to which to refer, you might choose to concentrate on the services you can offer as problem analysts.

2. Use the nine moves described in Strategy 1 to reconstruct the rhetorical situation as you see it in the Mountain Trails case (or another project you are working on). Some features, such as the triggering event and the players might seem obvious. But once you have sketched your reconstruction, compare it with that of another member of your consulting team (or class). To what extent do writers "construct" their own version of the rhetorical situation?

Write an e-mail memo to the rest of the team that supports or explains your reconstruction in light of theirs.

3. Did the landowners who wrote the July 19 letter get their message across? Remember how the key point information in the Mountain Trail proposal was clearly signalled to the reader. Now construct a tree for the landowners' letter. When you have done so, try to predict four or five key places where your tree might agree or disagree with other people's. Some questions for this discussion might be: When you compare your reading to someone else's, do you notice what signals in the

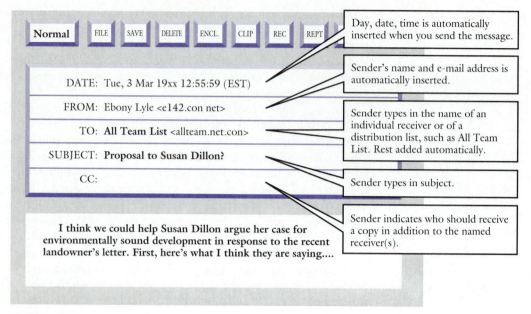

FIGURE 2–12

An e-Mail Message

text lead you to agree? Why did you differ? Did you have any difficulty fitting all the points within a paragraph under a common point or concept? Why or why not?

On the basis of this preliminary testing and analysis, write a polite but highly informational letter from your consulting company to the landowners about how their information was structured and received by some readers and offer to talk with them further if you could be of help. Start the letter with a creative but informative problem/purpose statement and be sure to include your boilerplate paragraph of introduction.

4. Susan Dillon, owner of Pine Creek Outfitters (see the October 4 and November 15 news stories) has expressed some interest in your services to help argue the case for economic development. Having done an *information* reading of the Landowners' letter of July 19, now do a *rhetorical* reading of their letter from as many angles as you can, using the intention, convention, and context strategies. Does this reading give you a different text than your information reading did? Which of the three rhetorical reading strategies was the most revealing with regard to this text? How do you see the problem? Write an e-mail message laying out your reading of the letter to the other members of your consulting team.

Now write your analysis of the landowners' thinking for Ms. Dillon and offer to help her develop her response to their position in an upcoming town meeting. Since she has only recently heard of your small firm, you will have to convince her that you have something to say through the quality of this initial analysis. Following the introduction of your company, get to the point with a problem/purpose statement, followed by your initial analysis of their position. This letter is step one in the consulting cycle.

5. The Maiers heard about you from Susan Dillon and a landowner and have asked you to work as a consultant to Mountain Trails. They have been invited to revise their letter proposal and submit it as a plan for more formal consideration by an internal DER committee. They feel that the first letter needed to raise issues diplomatically, but this second version can speak more directly to the different positions people have taken on solutions. Write a recommendation to Mountain Trails laying out how you are reading this context. Tell the Maiers what kind of changes they could make on page 2 to connect or compare their plan to other alternatives. (Remember, you have to build a polite and convincing case for your suggestions—you are in no position to dictate a decision.) Then, to make this recommendation operational, revise page 2 according to your own guidelines and attach it to your letter. (In practice, you will probably work back and forth between doing your revision and trying to explain your reasons.)

6. As a consultant, you and your team were trying to solve a problem for a particular client. In this assignment your work will be used by your supervisor, Arthur Davis, in order to do his job. You are a new staff member in the Department of Environmental Resources (DER) and Davis has asked you to write a two-page brief that reviews the issues and arguments that have surfaced in public discussions of this question. You have been delegated, in effect, to write a problem analysis that defines a complex problem where multiple goals and values are in conflict with one another.

Present your analysis in a memo. Start with a problem/purpose statement that reminds Davis of what this text is supposed to do. To make your analysis coherent, you will need to find an overall conception for this problem, and then define and describe the key issues you see surfacing in the public discussion. Because the purpose of the memo is to brief Davis, you are not expected to write a recommendation. However, your analysis of the problem will, of course, reflect your interpretation of what matters.

7. Have you been part of a landlord and tenant problem (in an apartment, dormitory or sorority/fraternity house)? Write a background paragraph on the situation to share with the class, then write a memo to the other party (e.g., your landlord or the housing office). Analyze the problem, trying to build an operational, shared vision of the problem.

8. Have you ever done any part-time or free-lance work (from baby sitting or mowing lawns to consulting work) in which you faced problems of the sort Claudia Benson talks about at the end of this chapter? Write analysis of this problem to share with your class, and end with some recommendations for other students who might take such jobs.

9. Use the following checklist to evaluate the problem/purpose statement and the problem analyses you wrote for the above assignments. Look to see if all of these features are present in some form. Remember you can accomplish more than one of your goals with the same statement.

10. This extended free-lance consulting project lets you develop an unsolicited proposal. It involves a number of drafts and kinds of texts and draws on the strategies you will be learning over the next few chapters.

    You are a free-lance communications consultant. Your job is (1) to identify a real-world problem involving communication that you have encountered at school, in an organization, or on a job and (2) to write an analysis and a proposal or recommendation that will help your client understand and deal with this problem. To succeed—to write to make something happen—you will need to design your report around your reader's needs.

    Choose a problem for which you have some special expertise. For instance, as a summer employee you may have a special perspective on management, training or staff problems—from the employee's point of view. And you may have some good ideas to recommend, just as Claudia Benson had for student designers. However, to put your ideas into action, you will have to write a convincing problem analysis and a well-developed, operational recommendation. Here are the steps you will need to take for this assignment:

    (a) Write an initial analysis of the problem (1–2 pages) and a brief statement of what you propose to do in order to study it and develop a proposal. Include a timeline with benchmarks you expect to meet (See Chapter Six for help on scheduling). Give this in the form of a memo report to your supervisor (course instructor) or, if you need their permission and cooperation, to your actual client. Revise your plan on the basis of feedback.

    (b) Once you have identified your problem, begin to collect information and read the situation you are going to be facing. You may want to review this situation in a status report to your supervisor (an early benchmark).

    (c) At your next benchmark, hand in a draft of your completed analysis of the problem and an outline of your recommendations. Use the strategies for planning, and drafting in Chapters Three and Four, and those in Chapter Five for revising on the basis of your feedback.

(d) As you complete the recommendations section of your proposal, consider the needs of your audience. In many communication situations you will have a primary audience that needs to be aware of a problem and willing to act on a recommendation (such as the head of design to whom Claudia wrote). And you will have a secondary audience to whom you will address your actual recommendations in the form of a detailed guide, handbook, or set of instructions (See Chapter Seven). The text you write for this secondary audience may be separate and start with the problem as these readers (rather than the primary audience or decision maker) see it, and be designed around their needs.

As a consultant then, you may need to create two very different texts: one a persuasive, professional analysis and recommendation; the other a usable, inviting, maybe even procedural guide for staff training on your summer job, for being the business manager of an organization you belong to, using and maintaining equipment, or helping other students get professional experience—as Claudia's Free-lancers Handbook did. To plan, design and test this new document, and adapt the strategies in Chapters Two through Six to this new problem.

11. Submit your entire proposal and complete set of recommendations to your supervisor for feedback and approval. Then send it along with a letter of transmittal to your initial client. In choosing your problem and client, think about ways you might use this document as part of your portfolio when you are applying for jobs or as a way to extend your professional experience or make professional contacts. Look at this project within the larger context of your own education and career interests.

References

1. Rogers, Priscilla S., and John M. Swales. "We the People? An Analysis of the Dana Corporation Policies Statement." *The Journal of Business Communication, 27*:3 (Summer, 1990):293–313.
2. Eastman Kodak Company, *Annual Report* (1984).
3. Williams, Melvin. *On the Street Where I Lived* (New York: Holt, Rinehart and Winston, 1981), p. 77.

3
Strategies for Planning

IN THIS CHAPTER we address the challenge of translating your reading of a context into action—plans you make to construct a written or oral text. We begin by distinguishing plans *to say* something from plans *to do* something in writing.

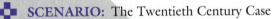 **SCENARIO:** The Twentieth Century Case
Shows how plans *to do* match the complexity of a rhetorical situation.

These five strategies can help you build a rhetorical plan

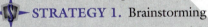 **STRATEGY 1.** Brainstorming

STRATEGY 2. Resting and Incubating

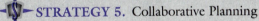 **STRATEGY 3.** Explaining Ideas in a Nutshell

STRATEGY 4. Building a Topical Issue Tree
Develop both supporting details and organizing concepts.

STRATEGY 5. Collaborative Planning
Be a Planner and a Supporter.
Move from a plan *to say* to a plan *to do* with the Planner's Blackboard.
Adapt collaborative planning to resume writing.
Reflect on your own strategies.

Collaborative Planning helps you turn the fruits of the first four strategies into an integrated plan *to do* something through writing and, because you are working with a partner, get live feedback on a reader's needs.

3
Strategies for Planning

TRANSLATING CONTEXT INTO ACTION
TEXTS AND TRANSACTIONS

In school, writing is often identified with *making a text*. The text is the evidence that you have learned the material or can write in a certain style, and the purpose of writing is to display your knowledge and skill. In professional settings, however, the spotlight shifts from texts to **transactions**—that is, to actions among people, and a good text is one that can support transactions. For example, when a company and a client negotiate a deal, that transaction is carried out through proposals and contracts. Within a company, written transactions between people are often designed to exchange or pool expertise: A product designer, for instance, needs to know if an idea is feasible to manufacture, so she exchanges ideas with the production engineer through product development memos. Meanwhile, both the designer and engineer need to read the most recent report from the marketing analyst in order to set their priorities. Another common transaction that depends on writing is getting approval to take action: A project planner submits a budget and budget explanation to the accounting department so they will "sign off" on the plan. In transactional writing, you and your reader each have knowledge and/or decision power that the other person needs.

In making this exchange work, your text will be a rhetorical action—a move in the transaction: It will inform or even teach the reader; it will persuade, document, propose a new line of action, or lay out an issue. And as we saw in Chapter One, in order to be persuasive or useful, writing may also need to fit into an appropriate discourse—to observe the special conventions and expectations that mark a budget proposal, a marketing projection, or a feasibility report. A "well-written" text that merely "displays" how much you know may fail in a professional transaction if it does not respond to the features and conventions in a rhetorical situation. In this chapter we look at how you can transform your rhetorical survey and reading of the context into a usable transactional plan.

Developing strategies for planning can lead to significant changes in your writing and speaking. In our research we have seen that experienced writers not only plan more often, they plan strategically, as well. And survey research reveals that with the little time available in a busy work day, experienced writers make time to plan. Becoming a good planner in writing will also complement the strategic approach you take to your professional work; good planning is a part of wise decisions.

PLANS *TO SAY* AND PLANS *TO DO*

Suppose, after discussing a marketing problem with your department head, he asked you to send him a memo on the problem. Talking to other people and reading the context tell you this is a good time to propose an idea you have long considered. But you are also looking at the paper trail of previous memos and letters on the subject and your rhetorical reading of those texts tells you that other people have a stake in this transaction. They would probably define the problem differently. Now, how can you translate your understanding of this context into an action—into a text that supports a transaction between you, the department head, and other people?

One planning strategy that many writers use in school is to develop a **plan to say,** that is, a plan for the information their text will include. It may be a sketchy list of topics jotted on scratch paper or an elaborate outline with major and minor topics and supporting details. You probably made plans *to say* all through high school whenever you wrote a research paper by shuffling a stack of note cards, or when you wrote a personal essay focused on recollecting your own experience, and *informational reading* strategies often result in plans *to say*, if the reader or writer has no other purpose in mind. A plan *to say* is a useful kind of plan that lets you organize information; however, it is limited because it does not help you see your text as an action you are taking with other people.

A plan to do, on the other hand, helps you think about your text as a set of moves you are making for a purpose, within a rhetorical situation. For instance, in making a plan for what you want *to say* in the first paragraph of your marketing memo, you might focus on providing background information on the marketing problem. But if you went on to make a plan *to do*, you would start thinking: "How do I really want to define that problem? Can I use that initial definition to anticipate the response other people will have to the situation, and lead them at least to consider my eventual suggestion?" Making a plan *to do* lets you embed your plans *to say* within an action-oriented transaction.

In the scenario that follows, we will show you an example of a plan *to do* in which the writers at Twentieth Century translated their reading of the context into an inventive and somewhat daring plan for persuading and educating the readers of their quarterly report. Then, we present five strategies for building effective plans *to do*.

SCENARIO

The Twentieth Century Case

Twentieth Century Investors is a small but well-established mutual fund company that makes money for its shareholders by investing the accumulated capital of many smaller investors in the stock and bond market. Investors in mutual funds range from ordinary individuals who want to earn more than a savings account offers, to companies and institutions investing their entire pension plans. As shareholders in the fund, investors get the price advantage of large purchases and the benefit of professional management to select and to buy and sell stock as needed. But investing is not predictable, and the economy has been far from stable. In the last year, the stock market had taken a series of dives and Twentieth Century's earnings had followed. Over the last six-month period their largest fund, called GROWTH, had declined in value by 13.9 percent. Nevertheless, it was time for a semiannual report that is required by the Federal Securities Commission and mailed to all shareholders. That is the situation. How would you define the *rhetorical* situation?

READING THE RHETORICAL SITUATION

Reports to shareholders are very conventional documents: They usually start with a brief overview or comment on the last quarter's activity (sometimes signed by the president), followed by a financial report of earnings (and losses) that meet federal guidelines for financial disclosure. It would be easy to look at this rhetorical landscape and see no deeper than the task, topic, and text features—to develop a writing plan based on what one needed to *say* that would merely report the decline in the fund's value, following the conventions and guidelines for a concise quarterly report. However, the writers at this imaginative and successful small firm went much further. Figure 3–1 visualizes how the rhetorical survey of these writers (described in Chapter One) went beyond the assigned task and topic as they built a more strategic picture of the audience, the rhetorical situation, problems, the discourse community, and possible actions they as writers could take. We will see them using many of the strategies described in Chapter Two, seeing their audience as players in a transaction with different goals and personal investments (worries and expectations) as well as financial investments in this issue. Also, we will see how a paper trail of glowing reports and history of success became a part of the problem and the ethical decisions these writers faced.

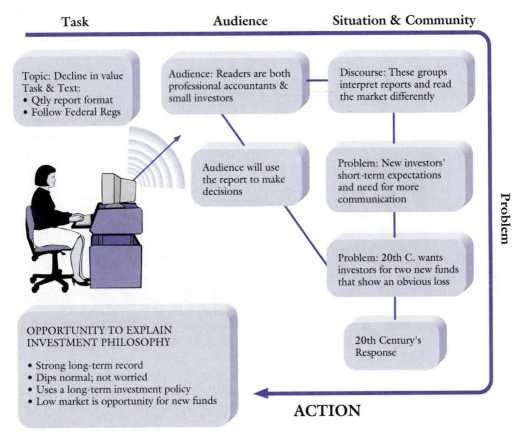

Task   **Audience**   **Situation & Community**

Topic: Decline in value
Task & Text:
• Qtly report format
• Follow Federal Regs

Audience: Readers are both professional accountants & small investors

Discourse: These groups interpret reports and read the market differently

Audience will use the report to make decisions

Problem: New investors' short-term expectations and need for more communication

Problem: 20th C. wants investors for two new funds that show an obvious loss

20th Century's Response

Problem

OPPORTUNITY TO EXPLAIN INVESTMENT PHILOSOPHY

• Strong long-term record
• Dips normal; not worried
• Uses a long-term investment policy
• Low market is opportunity for new funds

ACTION

FIGURE 3–1

Reading the Twentieth
Century Context

For Twentieth Century, the key players in this rhetorical situation were their shareholders. During this period of economic instability, shareholders were especially likely to be concerned about earnings, read the report, and use it to make decisions about future investments. In fact, Twentieth Century had recently introduced two new funds to attract investors, and they wanted this report to convince readers to make additional, new investments. Unfortunately these two new funds had been introduced in November at the beginning of the current decline: Their record for the quarter was a dismal: −14.2 and −20.4 percent losses in value. It appeared that the goals of the company (to keep and attract investment) were in conflict with the goals of the shareholder (for security, return, and growth).

This rhetorical situation is also strongly influenced by the expectations of its discourse community. People who read investment reports belong to a community that expects certain things. Or rather, they belong to two somewhat different discourse communities with different ways of reading. Some readers will be accountants with institutions who invested in the fund—people trained to read figures, analyze financial statements, and evaluate the long-term success of a fund. Others will be small investors who read the synopsis at the front of the report and look for the bottom line—the percent of growth or loss over the current period. They want to know if the value of their investment has increased or actually declined. This was an important part of the problem because Twentieth Century estimated that nearly 50 percent of their clients were small shareholders with investments of $25,000 or less.

In addition to high yields, these small shareholders had also been indicating that they wanted more communication from the company. However, Twentieth Century was a small company and a "no load" fund. This meant that it didn't charge the 8 percent fee on all purchases that the "load" funds did; it didn't maintain a large sales staff, and it didn't even have a public relations office. A big ad campaign to offset weak returns was not the way it did business. This conflict—over how to communicate regarding a loss—was another important problem the writers needed to consider.

When it came time to write the Semiannual Report, these company goals, the organizational constraints, and the readers' multiple expectations were all part of the rhetorical situation, as James Stowers, president of the company, and his investment team saw it. They had already given themselves an image of the problem that went well beyond the formal task—to write a financial report—and beyond the apparent content they had to report. However, it was when they began to plan their own path of action that they saw a way to literally reconstruct this rhetorical situation and reinterpret what it meant.

Most people might have defined the rhetorical problem as how to deal with an awkward failure. Stowers and the investment team defined it, surprisingly, as how to deal with success. For 27 years Twentieth Century had been a small no-load fund chugging along with little or no marketing and low visibility, but a solid, steady performance. As they put it, "Kansas City is not the center of the fund industry." Moreover, it was strongly committed to an investment policy geared to long-term returns—to keeping their assets fully invested and not trying to predict the short-term dips and jumps of the market. Then suddenly, in the last five years, this little company in Kansas City had blossomed into a highly competitive fund. It was on the front page of *Money* magazine and celebrated in *Forbes* and *Fortune*. As a result, many new investors, who had just become aware of mutual funds, had joined when the market was at a peak. They had become used to a steady diet of good news and positive returns.

But many of these small, first-time investors did not understand how the market operates—they expected the fireworks to last. So the problem, as Stowers saw it, was how do you deal with explosive growth and success?

How do you deal with a fundamental conflict between the expectations of some of your investors and the realities of investing, especially given your philosophy of picking investments for their long-term potential rather than their prospects for the next six months? The problem, as they saw it, involved fundamental conflicts between the company's and (some of) the readers' perceptions. This conflict, like the results they had to report and the federal regulations constraining how they did it, was a part of the report writers' task—a part of the goals and constraints they had to work with.

The features sketched in Figure 3–1 are, of course, only a partial record of the audience, situation, problem, and discourse these writers actually considered. But even this sketch makes one point clear—the rhetorical context and problems they responded to depended on an image they as writers had to construct for themselves. To reconstruct this rhetorical situation, they had to review their own goals, imagine their readers' reactions, look for conflicts and constraints, draw inferences, make connections, and develop possible plans. The problem they eventually solved was one they defined out of an insightful reading, that is, a rhetorical *reconstruction*—of the context.

CREATING A PLAN

Given this multifaceted representation of the problem in a rhetorical situation, the investment team at Twentieth Century had to come up with an overall rhetorical plan that addressed the situation—as well as more local plans to carry this out in text. The staff talked over a number of standard options used in the business: Ignore the problem and it will go away (as, in fact, they were confident it would), or resort to generalities about the economy and the market in general. Another option was to take a positive posture in negative times by celebrating past performance ("Fourteen years ago we . . ."), or to shift the focus in the report away from performance to other features of the fund, such as new services or new products. These are all familiar moves used in many annual reports.

The rhetorical plan they chose was somewhat more radical. They decided to face the situation directly and use it as an occasion to explain their investment philosophy, that is, the policy of investing for long-term capital gains and riding out these dips in the market. They decided, in effect, to educate their shareholders—to convince their readers to take the long view, to see this dip as part of the big picture, and even to consider increasing their investments now when stock prices were low.

Making this decision and creating this larger rhetorical plan was a critical first step. It combined an ethical stance on truth in reporting with a plan to persuade worried investors. However, if you were on that investment team, how would you carry out this overall plan in text, even if it sounded brilliant? As a writer, how would you translate this rhetorical plan into text moves? We could imagine the team coming up with a very straightforward

A plan *to say* that Twentieth Century could have used

In reporting the losses for the current period we were concerned that shareholders might misinterpret the results.

- We do not see the current loss picture as a cause for concern.
- Long-term investments ride out the fluctuations of the market.
- The Market operates in this way:
    Point 1
    Point 2 [and so on]

FIGURE 3–2

A Plan to Say

plan for presenting this information in text—a plan organized around what they wanted *to say* (Figure 3–2).

The problem with this plan is that it focuses on the writers' worries not the readers'. It simply recites information like a textbook without adapting it to legitimate concerns of the readers. What the Twentieth Century team actually did illustrates an alternative way to turn these ideas into text. Their text plan was built around a metaphor that the president, James Stowers, had used for years to explain his philosophy: When you invest for the long term, look for the tennis balls that bounce back when the market recovers— and avoid the chicken eggs. They also created a new two-color graph, called a "mountain investment chart," which could graphically show the long-term success of the company's funds and make the quarterly results easier to understand.

The plan they created was based on what they wanted *to do* in text. That is, they saw the text as trying to accomplish something, not just report information. Looking ahead at the excerpt from the final report, notice how it is organized around an issue, not just a topic, and how some ideas are used to develop and support others. And as we will discuss in Chapters Four and Five, notice how the major headings for the report also reflect questions the critical reader is likely to have. We could represent the plan behind this text as in Figure 3–3.

This outline has three layers of detail and highlights two key goals the writers wanted to carry out. When you look at their text, notice how this plan (focused on goals) differs from a more traditional topic outline, a plan *to say,* which would begin as in Figure 3–4.

Both outlines offer a hierarchy of ideas, but a plan *to do* includes language and devices that support the writer's efforts to think and act decisively and rhetorically. It says, "I am using this information to carry out this goal."

anticipate & respond to readers' questions & objection

FIGURE 3–3
A Plan to Do

> **The plan *to do* that Twentieth Century did use**
>
> We need to deal directly with shareholders' expectations for continued growth and/or short-term returns.
>
> So use this loss as an occasion for explaining our philosophy of long-term investment planning.
>
> Use the egg and tennis ball metaphor to show how our policy deals with market fluctuation.
>
> We need to recognize that the reader is also concerned with results and present the report in terms of how those results are achieved.
>
> Point 1. How we Choose Stocks
> Point 2. Characteristics of Twentieth Century funds [and so on]

FIGURE 3–4
An Outline of Ideas

> A. Our Investment Policy
>   1. Choosing
>   2. Characteristics
>   3. Timing
>   4. Long term
>
> B. How We Choose Stocks
>   1. Accelerated earnings
>   2. Stay invested...

Figure 3–5 shows the final version of the earning report delivered to shareholders.

This case illustrates another important feature of how writers translate their survey of a rhetorical situation into a variety of specific plans and into text. Consider all the alternative (and complementary) verbal and visual ways one could present James Stowers' "bounce back" idea. In one part of

A N   O V E R V I E W

While you as a shareholder of Twentieth Century are concerned first of all with the actual results achieved on your behalf, you may also be interested with how those results are achieved. The following comments address four key aspects of the investment policies we pursue on behalf of Twentieth Century.

1. How we choose stocks
2. Characteristics of the Twentieth Century funds
3. How timing affects your investment results
4. The importance of investing for the long-term

How we choose stocks

Twentieth Century is guided by the conviction that *companies demonstrating an acceleration of earnings and revenue growth are likely to appreciate in market value.* Each day our investment team searches for publicly-traded companies with this accelerating growth, using extensive computer hardware and software designed especially for us. Companies that are accelerating are candidates for purchase. Companies that are not accelerating are avoided, or sold if already owned. This process of *active management* allows us to continuously monitor and update the portfolios of Twentieth Century to reflect the latest information available about the companies meeting our criteria.

Another important element of our investment policy is a *commitment to staying fully invested*—a policy that has worked well for us in the past. We do not speculate as to which direction the market is going since we don't know anyone who has consistently outguessed its sporadic moves. While our policy of staying fully invested can produce short-term disappointments, Twentieth Century's record suggests this approach is really more of an opportunity than a risk for serious, long-term shareholders.

Characteristics of the Twentieth Century funds

Perhaps one of the first things you'll notice about your investment in Twentieth Century Investors is that *share prices change almost daily.* The funds do not have a constant value. This is because the common stocks we purchase for the funds represent ownership interests in various companies. As the progress of these companies ebbs and flows, so does the value of the funds' ownership in them. In addition, common stocks as a class of investments are influenced by the relative attractiveness of other investments such as bonds, certificates of deposit, and money market funds.

Shares of Twentieth Century Investors can fall as well as rise in price. Your investment is not immune to corrections in the stock market or disappointments in the companies selected for investment. However, our stock selection policies are designed to help contend with the uncontrollable meanderings of the stock market.

In simple terms, we believe some stocks are like tennis balls, and others are like chicken eggs. A falling market takes them both down. But when the market

Common Stock Investment Team

Jim Stowers III

Dennis von Wauden

Bob Puff

FIGURE 3–5
Twentieth Century's Earning Report

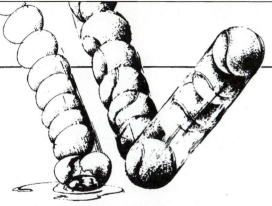

bottoms, tennis balls bounce back. So our goal is simple: find the tennis balls, and avoid the chicken eggs. As a result, Twentieth Century's funds have had the *ability to bounce back strongly in price when the stock market recovers*.

Another characteristic of the Twentieth Century common stock funds is that most of the return they provide is in the form of *capital appreciation*—that is, a higher share price. Their production of *dividend income is relatively low*. The only consistent income provider of our common stock funds is Select Investors. Shareholders who want substantial current income are advised to consider Twentieth Century's U.S. Governments, a bond fund invested in government issues.

How timing affects your investment results

You may be surprised to learn that the single most important factor in your early success with Twentieth Century Investors is the date on which you make your original investment. For example, if you began at a time when the stock market was depressed you probably have had relatively good early investment experience and are quite happy. On the other hand, if you began at a time when the market was peaking, you may be disappointed by your early lack of progress.

The effect of the starting date on your investment results can be overcome by time and effective portfolio management. For example, suppose you had invested $10,000 in Select Investors on Sept. 13, 1978. Early results would have been disappointing because Select and the stock market declined in price shortly after the purchase. The original investment would have declined in value by 14% in eight months.

Thereafter, however, Select staged a strong recovery. Within another eight months, your holding would have bounced back (remember those tennis balls) to a value of $12,900 and by April 30, 1984, to a value of $29,400—almost three times the original investment. Had you redeemed your shares after the initial setback, you would have lost money and would not have had the opportunity to participate in the subsequent growth.

Because of this timing effect, we make the following suggestions:

1. Consider spreading out your investment over time in order to minimize the possibility of making an investment at a market peak.
2. Recognize that the value of your shares will fluctuate up and down.
3. Take advantage of lower prices—buy more shares and average down your cost.
4. Be prepared to give your investment the time necessary to prove its worth.

The importance of investing for the long-term

Twentieth Century recently celebrated its 25th birthday. One of our more important discoveries over the years is the fact that common stock investing is not a short-term proposition. The pursuit of investment excellence requires lots of patience and time—three to five years or more. Shorter periods are chancy because too many events can happen that are beyond the control of investment managers—oil embargos, wars, credit crunches, etc.

The symbol of Twentieth Century Investors is an oak tree, signifying growth, strength and durability. We think the development of a successful long-term investment record is similar to the growth cycle of the oak—neither happens overnight. Yet, with proper care, pruning (as needed) and patience the potential of both the acorn and the well-selected investment can be realized. There are no substitutes for careful management and time.

the text it is carried out visually with a small time-lapse drawing of an egg and a ball falling side by side—one of which breaks while the other bounces up. It is carried out in a different way in the text prose and typography. All those ways of presenting an idea represent alternative visual and text moves open to the writer. Once writers start thinking about what they want the text to do (not just what they might say), they open the door to imagining alternative ways to do it.

Secondly, it is typical of professional writing that this text emerged from a collaborative process that involved not only top management—Stowers and the investment team—but portfolio managers and, in later stages, an advertising company which contributed the visual presentation of Stowers' metaphor. The process of translating plans into text went on at many levels and involved a number of people trying to carry out a coherent, collaborative plan. In the next section we will look as some strategies for generating good ideas and for making the most of formal and informal collaboration with other people.

BUILDING A RHETORICAL PLAN

Good plans are made, not born. Verbs like "exploring" a situation and "building" a plan describe a goal-directed process that may take place over a period of days, weeks, or months and may involve many people. Plans get constructed not only when you sit down to think or start a draft, but in planning meetings and from conversations in the hall. But perhaps the most important thing about plans is that they are easy to *reconstruct*—they are a place to consider alternatives, to play out possibilities, and to compare different ways to make your text do what you want it *to do*. Consider the spectrum of plans writers make, from plans in the head of one person, to collaborative talk, to notes, to drafts, to text for circulation. Each one is a little more expensive to create and more difficult to change. Less-experienced writers often avoid planning because they make an initial investment in text that they take as final. It becomes painful to revise because they do not know how to extend planning through their revising process. Plans can reduce a big problem to its essentials—they let you think with and juggle a handful of ideas and strategies instead of 20 pages of text.

How do you construct an effective plan? Experienced writers use more than one strategy, because some strategies are particularly good at generating ideas, others at organizing, while others help you use the discourse conventions your readers may expect. In this section we will look at five expert strategies: **brainstorming, incubating, nutshelling,** and **using topical issue trees.** The final strategy, **collaborative planning,** is especially good for translating plans *to say* into plans *to do* and for anticipating an audience.

STRATEGY 1: TURN OFF THE EDITOR AND BRAINSTORM.

It seems ironic, but sometimes the best way to deal with a problem is to ignore parts of it. Brainstorming is a strategy for generating ideas in which you focus on an important goal or a key point and ignore the internal critic who says "but that idea isn't good enough," and the internal editor who says, "but you should be writing prose." The idea of a brainstorming session is to let ideas and alternatives flow freely, like a storm of possibilities. If you are in a group, encourage everyone to talk, to suggest even tentative ideas that don't quite "make sense" or that aren't developed yet, or that they cannot support. If you are alone, let yourself jot down ideas as they come to you, even the "half-baked" ones and the intentions you could not quite support out loud.

Brainstorming. Brainstorming works because all your attention is focused on the hard problem—generating good ideas, alternatives, following out intuitions and possibilities. But it works better if you try to observe these rules:

- *Don't censor ideas.* When you come up with an idea or a phrase that isn't quite right, resist the temptation to throw it back and start again. Just talk it out or write it down. You may later discover that with a small change it makes lots of sense. If you are still in the "idea" stage, just jot down variations of an idea as they come to you—storm now, evaluate and eliminate later. If you are working with a partner or group, the cardinal rule of a brainstorming session is that no one can censor, dismiss, or criticize anyone's ideas during the session—the goal is to create, not eliminate.

- *Don't try to write polished prose.* If you are brainstorming in writing, don't stop to perfect spelling, grammar, or even phrasing. Keep yourself working at the level of your key ideas, jotting notes, drawing sketches, or even talking out loud to yourself. If you work at a computer and an argument, sentence, or even phrase doesn't sound right, simply hit the return key, record an alternative version on the next line and go on. When you have written the rest of the argument and return to read your draft and revise, many of those problems will evaporate. The sentence you couldn't write may have been trying to predict the next part of the argument that you hadn't yet written!

- *Keep your eye on your main goals and key points.* When you lose steam or start to drift into free association, come back to the problem you set for yourself and ask: "What else do I need to consider here? What else do I know?"

- *Come prepared*. Brainstorming may sound like lazy planning, but the idea is to generate quickly many more ideas and connections than you have at the outset. Coming to a planning session with two or three opening thoughts will get the process moving and give others something to associate with and amplify.

Freewriting. Another strategy that works by turning off the editor is freewriting. If you have lots of ideas, but feel blocked at the point of producing text, this is a very effective strategy. Simply set aside a period of time and start writing—and no matter what happens, keep writing. Start in the middle; start with what comes to mind. If you feel blocked, then write that down, but keep your pen moving, and keep your thoughts flowing in words (see also "Writers Block" in Chapter Eight). You will be surprised at what starts to come once you turn off the critical internal editors that demand polished prose or perfect beginnings.

Many people find freewriting a good way to begin exploring a topic, even if they aren't blocked, especially in personal writing. Unlike the more goal-directed focus of brainstorming, freewriting depends on the rich associative power of words to lead you to things you may have been thinking, but hadn't said to yourself. The disadvantage of doing your planning in prose (rather than starting with goals, gists, arguments, etc.) is that freewriting texts are often hard to revise or reorganize into the prose adapted to a reader. You must be prepared to start a new draft based on what you learned. That is why in business settings writers often prefer to plan as much as possible before they draft, or they rely on established models and routines.

STRATEGY 2: PLAN OR DRAFT, THEN REST AND INCUBATE.

It is hard to imagine a more productive strategy—and one that comes at a lower cost—then rest and incubation. Giving yourself time between phases of planning and between drafts will almost always lead to better insights and better drafts. But you must use it wisely. At the end of a planning or drafting session, before you stop work, review what you have done, come to some closure and locate the unsolved problem you want to be thinking about. You need to put something in the incubator if you expect it to "hatch." Therefore, **incubation** depends on some initial "problem finding," even if that search only reveals that you do not want to write about a certain topic or that your ideas can only be partly stated.

Why is this strategy of getting time on your side so productive? People used to say that the unconscious mind was at work while you slept. A more modern theory says by the end of a session working on a problem, you have learned a lot that is not reflected in the plan you started with. When you return after a period of rest—it can even be half an hour—you have actually forgotten or are able to abandon your old, inadequate plan and build a new one that reflects more of what you learned.

Like all strategies, even incubation works best if you use it in a purposeful way. Start writing early enough that you leave time to incubate. And as you are doing other ordinary things, like driving the car or falling asleep, keep this unfinished business *actively* simmering at the back of your mind. Look for ideas and connections, and when they come, be ready to *write them down*. Do not expect inspiration to knock twice.

STRATEGY 3: EXPLAIN YOUR IDEAS IN A NUTSHELL.

In business settings, people will rarely stand around waiting for you to get to the point. To get a hearing and be persuasive you need to be able to walk into someone's office and explain your idea in a nutshell. You can use this situation as a powerful strategy for generating and organizing ideas. Imagine your reader as a listener who will give you five minutes of attention. To get your point across, you must be able to reduce it to its **gist** and present it so the main points stand out from all the other information you could (and want to) talk about. To condense your thoughts into a nutshell you may also have to synthesize ideas and create a new concept that organizes or integrates your subpoints. And you have to make sure that at the center of this nutshell is an idea or issue that your reader will see as important.

Perhaps it seems obvious that creating a nutshell is a good way to give a sharper focus and clearer organization to your writing. But, in fact, as people in business often discover, the very act of trying to explain your ideas out loud to another person can give you a whole new perspective on what is important—it's a sense you may not have sitting at a typewriter or keyboard. To use this strategy well, find an occasion to actually teach or explain the gist of your text to a stand-in for your reader—to a peer, a friend, or even (if you think your friends won't worry about you), walk around in the privacy of your room and talk out loud to an imagined reader. Talking out loud, like brainstorming, momentarily sets aside some of the unnecessary constraints imposed by prose. As you construct your nutshell, keep thinking about what you want your listener to know or to do when you are through, and shape your writing to get those results.

STRATEGY 4: BUILD A TOPICAL ISSUE TREE.

When strategies like brainstorming, freewriting, or "creating gists" are successful, writers can end up with a wealth of ideas—and a new problem of how to organize it all into a coherent paper. At this point, trying to start at the beginning and write a text from the top down can be both frustrating and inefficient. It is easy to become confused and overloaded if you are trying to plan the whole organization of your argument and *at the same time* you are trying to write a perfect introduction or the perfect prose of a paragraph. This information overload has given you too many problems to solve at the same time.

Topical Issue trees provide a way to visualize your whole argument at the level of gists or main points (rather than prose) and to see how the parts fit together. An issue tree also has some advantages over a traditional outline, which merely arranges the facts you already know in terms of topics or subject matter. An issue tree focuses on an issue or problem, lays out the hierarchical structure of your ideas, and can help you see gaps in the tree where you need to develop new ideas or information. Issue trees are especially useful at three points in the writing process: when you need to organize the results of brainstorming, develop a paper further, and test the structure of a draft.

USING AN ISSUE TREE TO ORGANIZE BRAINSTORMING

Suppose that you are interested in how writing is used in organizations and in the problems that junior staff may face. You have just read an interesting article about "Writing at Exxon ITD." Figure 3–6 shows some notes from a brainstorming session on ideas that caught your attention and the key words you use (as mental notes) to remember each point. How would you organize these ideas into a paper if your task was to summarize the article? Or if you wanted to use ideas from the article to convince someone?

Clearly, you cannot just shuffle these notes into an outline. An issue tree, like an **outline,** turns ideas into key words to organize them. But it is even more useful than an outline when you need to generate new organizing ideas or to play with alternative organizations. Here is how one writer turned these notes into an issue tree—an upside-down tree that shows how ideas are related. Since she wanted her analysis to be relevant to new staff people, her first step was to come up with a top-level, organizing idea, which for her was: *Some of the critical interactions with your boss revolve around writing.*

Brainstorming & Reading Notes	Key Words (mental notes)
At Exxon, 50% of supervisors' writing-related work was spent on document cycling--doing extensive commenting on technical info, organization and scope of the reports submitted by staff	Comments
Sometimes the cycle of review and revise would be repeated half a dozen times.	Cycle repeats
Supers assigned writing and drafts as a way to manage or schedule projects. The texts then let them monitor staff progress .	Manage/monitor
Junior staff found the document cycle painful and mystifying, but said that it encouraged early planning.	Pain & plan
If you didn't interact with the supervisor in the planning stage, you had trouble at the revising stage.	2 Stages
Later, when staff were evaluated, the super's main source of information was the documents they had written.	Super uses docs
In a competitive setting, documents are a major way to "show what you're doing and also show your competence in doing it."	Docs show you
Supervisors often used staff member documents to establish the standing of their group with their superiors, and said that "confused documents call attention to incompetence."	Establish group

FIGURE 3–6

Turning Brainstorming into Key Concepts

This idea would speak to her readers and would include all the points she wanted to make. (In an issue tree, when an idea is placed above other ideas, it means that that concept *includes* the information placed beneath it (Figure 3–7). Therefore, the ideas at the top-levels of your tree may not be the most important points or claims you intend to make, but they will be your most inclusive, organizing ideas.

However, this writer's creativity did not stop with coming up with a purpose and a main idea. Notice all the terms we placed in bold type: the notions of *Document Cycling* and *Review* as well as *Process, Attitude,* and *Function.* These are all new concepts she had to generate in order to make sense out of her notes and cluster those ideas under her purpose. In essence, the tree says that some of the "critical interactions" between managers and staff are based on the texts people write and that those interactions can be

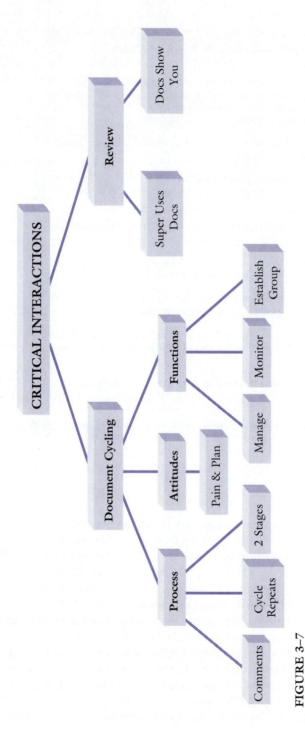

FIGURE 3–7
An Issue Tree on Critical Interactions with Your Supervisor

divided into two clusters—those based on "document cycling" and those based on the staff "review" process. Do you think this is the best way to organize this tree? What structure would you have to create if you decided that "pain and mystery" would be a better top-level organizing idea?

USING AN ISSUE TREE TO DEVELOP DETAILS

Looking back at Figure 3–6, it is clear that the cluster of ideas under "Review" is pretty skimpy for such an important interaction. Many writers like to use visual techniques such as issue trees not only to organize ideas but to extend or develop a line of thinking. If you find you have jotted down a point that seems to need more elaboration, but do not know what else to say, here are seven questions that readers typically want to ask. Try to answer these questions for yourself. They are likely to pull out additional, maybe important, points that were in the back of your mind. These unstated connections and elaborations are part of what makes the idea convincing to you, but they will probably not be apparent to the reader if you do not spell them out.

1. *What do you mean?* This asks for an expanded definition or for key features.

2. *How so?* This asks how something works, or how it came to be, or how you drew that inference. Talk about your idea as an action or a process.

3. *How do you know?* This is a good skeptical reader's request for evidence. What support exists for your claim? For many problems where you cannot appeal to hard evidence or proof, answer this question quite literally by laying out your own reasoning and inferences. Tell the reader how you came to "know" or think what you think.

4. *Such as?* This question is often a reader's response to a vague or overly abstract idea that lacks supporting examples. Abstractions can be powerful when they are followed by an answer to the reader's question of "such as?"

5. *Why?* The question asks for causes, reasons, or background.

6. *Why not?* This may be one of the most important questions you can ask yourself about any claim, even if your reader does not. This is the critical stance that questions your own assumptions and expectations and looks for alternatives—that recognizes that there are always reasons against even a good idea; and it is better to discover them yourself.

7. *So what?* This is maybe the hardest and most important question a writer can ask. It is easy to fall into information telling in writing, but does this information have a real purpose, address a need or problem? Does the paragraph you have just written or the claim you want to make pass the "so what" test?

USING AN ISSUE TREE TO EXTEND A FIRST DRAFT

We have been placing a lot of emphasis in this chapter on working with ideas and gists. But sometimes it is better just to write a draft, to work through a discussion and see where it leads. Writing itself is a powerful way to learn and explore. And yet you want your final draft to reflect a strong, purposeful, hierarchical structure. One good strategy for getting there is to go through your own draft and develop an outline or an issue tree from your draft. Look at each paragraph as a functional unit and try to state the gist. Sketch an issue tree that shows how the main ideas are related and how the text is structured. Developing a tree from your text will often lead you to develop new gists that were implicit but not stated and to see ways your thoughts were structured, but not explicitly signalled in the text. Seeing the tree behind your text helps you make its logic clearer to the reader.

STRATEGY 5: COLLABORATIVE PLANNING

Collaborative planning is a strategy for bringing your ideas, your purpose, and your reading of the situation together into an integrated, rhetorically savvy plan *to do.* As a writer, you may be used to collaborating in everyday, informal ways with friends and teachers. "Collaborative planning" is a particular form of collaboration in which two (or more) partners take on conscious and reflective roles of Planner and Supporter to help the Writer/Planner develop his or her own paper. A collaborative planning session also helps you focus attention on rhetorical questions, because part of the Supporter's job is to prompt you to think not only about what you have to say, but about your purpose and key point, your readers' needs and responses, and the various genre and text conventions you might use to reach your goals. (We will refer to these as the four key areas on the *Planner's Blackboard,* which we will discuss shortly.) You can do collaborative planning with your Supporter at different points in the process: when you are still brainstorming, when you have a tentative plan to share, or when you have a partial draft. However, you will get the biggest results by holding a planning session when (1) your plan is developed enough to talk over, but (2) not so set in stone or text that you will be unwilling to rethink it before you write.

THREE PRINCIPLES OF COLLABORATIVE PLANNING

Although collaborative planning shares some obvious features with other kinds of collaboration you may have done (e.g., peer editing, teacher conferences, and group sessions), it differs from them in some significant ways. In designing your planning sessions, three principles should apply:

- Authority (and the "floor") belongs to the writer as a planner and thinker.

- The aim of this planning process is to help you explore options and build a more elaborated plan *to do* that builds connections among all four key areas on the Planner's Blackboard: Topic Information, Purpose and Key Point, Audience, and Text Conventions.

- The supporter's role is to help you to shape your own purpose and goals, to turn your goals into text, and to reflect on your own writing strategies.

But, you may be asking, "What if I am a team player or don't have such authority over the text of a group project?" Business reports and proposals are often the work of many hands, and your own work may have to reflect the wishes of supervisors or the policy of your company. The answer is that collaborative planning is not the only way writers work together—it is a particular expert strategy for effective planning. If you are a student, these sessions help you develop new skills. If you are an individual writer, asking someone to do collaborative planning with you (and offering to be a Supporter for them) helps each of you do a better job on individual writing and on work you contribute to the group. When your group uses collaborative planning, it means that you make a choice to hold a strategic planning session in which members of the group not only propose their own ideas, but treat one another as Planners and act as deliberate Supporters, prompting each other and the group to consider all the areas of the Planner's Blackboard. In group collaboration someone may even take the role of a moderator, recording ideas on a blackboard and taking the lead in asking supporting questions. Collaborative planning is a strategy for getting the best from everyone.

THE ROLE OF THE PLANNER

As the Planner, you initiate a collaborative planning session by setting a date to meet with your partner and coming prepared to explain and elaborate your plan. At work, you might schedule a formal meeting, or just ask a coworker to give you 15 minutes to talk over something you are working on. In the discussion that follows, we will describe how you in your current situation as a student could use this strategy.

Throughout a planning session, your goal is to make your partner see what you are doing and why. But that does not mean just repeating the content of your paper. As Planner, your job is to convey what your **key points** are, to reveal some of the **reasons and purposes** behind what you are doing, to predict how you think your readers will respond, and to think through some of the **textual conventions** you might use to achieve your purpose or meet your readers' expectations. Because these are key parts of your rhetorical problem, a good plan needs to bring all of these things into the picture. If your partner looks confused, that is probably not a sign that there is something wrong with your partner, but that *your plan* is not yet clear or coherent.

On the other hand, the goal of the session is also to **explore,** to discover something, and to walk away with a better plan. A collaborative session, therefore, is a good place to raise questions and problems and to talk over alternatives and uncertainties that may be at the back of your mind. You may even want to start out talking about how you and your partner understand the assignment or how you read the rhetorical context.

Another part of your role as planner is to set the agenda for this session. What sort of help do you need at this time? Do you need to analyze the situation? Do you need to brainstorm ideas in an open-ended way, or do you want your supporter to play the role of a specific reader and give you feedback on how your argument or presentation will work? As planner, it is up to you to organize this collaborative session to be the most help to you. If it is not working, stop, talk over how the session is going, and consider redesigning the focus of the session.

And finally, as the planner, you get to take the floor. But that also means you must be prepared to talk—you need to come with a plan that is developed enough to discuss, even if you have questions or problems. Your supporter will only help you develop what is already there. On the other hand, if you meet after your ideas are firmly fixed or the text is done, and you have no desire to change it, you will also be wasting your time. Good sessions depend on your ability to explore a rhetorical problem and consider options. As you will find, collaborative talk when you are in an exploratory stage will give you very different help from a session held when you have detailed plans or a draft you want to test. Both kinds of sessions can be useful in different ways. Making a collaborative session work for you is up to you.

THE ROLE OF THE SUPPORTER

The supporter's main job is to help the planner elaborate his or her plan. In doing so, supporters can play different roles that allow them to offer genuine insights and helpful criticism without offending or pressuring their partner.

The Questioning/Reflecting Role. This role is designed to draw out ideas and hold up a mirror to the planner's own thought. Like a good counselor, this kind of partner offers support and encouragement, rather than advice, and reflects back the planner's own ideas, with comments like, "Yes. You seem to be saying . . . [and here the supporter restates what he or she is hearing in his or her own words]." Or "Are you saying that your real purpose here is . . . ?" In the low-effort version of this role, the supporter is merely a laid-back "yes man" who prompts the planner, but does not help extend the discussion. But in the involved version, the supporter is a careful, active listener, on the look-out for connections and implications in the planner's own talk that the planner may not have seen. Reflecting can be a powerful strategy for helping planners explore their own ideas and discover gaps between what they meant and what they said. Notice how, in Figure 3–8, Marta Basker's colleague plays this role in turns 8, 10 and 14.

The Problem-Finder Role. This kind of supporter listens carefully for potential problems—for gaps in the argument, parts he or she cannot understand, or claims that are open to question. The problem-finder also brings up alternative ways of reading the task, other goals that have not been considered, and negative responses readers might have. This supporter helps the writer deal with potential problems early, in the planning stage before the writer is committed to text. In the low-effort version, the partner is a nitpicker or sweeping critic (neither of which writers seem to enjoy). In the involved version, the supporter works to help define what the problem really is and what some possible responses could be. Look at what Marta's supporter does at turns 2, 4 and 6.

The Collaborator Role. This kind of supporter joins in the planner's effort to interpret the task, to develop a plan, to think of alternatives, to anticipate problems, and to evaluate options. This supporter may suggest new ideas or help the planner play around with various ways to organize a section or format a document. Although this may sound contradictory, in the low-effort version the supporter tries to take over and show how he or she would do it—as if this were the supporter's paper. The low-effort supporter simply lectures at or argues with the planner. (It is always easier to say what you would do, than to work with someone's else's ideas and goals.) In the involved version, on the other hand, the supporter listens carefully to the planner's intentions and needs, and works to help the writer do what he or she is trying to accomplish. Notice the supporter's moves at turns 12 and 14.

When you are a supporter, pay attention to which role you are taking. Do you tend to take the same role all of the time? Try to get some feedback from your planner about what he or she finds most useful. If, when you become the planner, your supporter is stuck in one role and you need another, ask your collaborator to switch strategies.

AN EXAMPLE OF COLLABORATIVE PLANNING

The following example illustrates how the give-and-take between planner and supporter not only builds a more developed plan, it also poses rhetorical problems and opens up possibilities. The planner in this excerpt is the young manager of a small branch bank in a "one-horse" town that is fast becoming a rural antique center. This fall Marta Basker's branch won the award for "the fastest growing branch" in First Western bank. Nevertheless, for the past three years she has been unable to get First Western to install an automatic teller machine, which would offer convenience for her regular customers and encourage lucrative after-hours cash withdrawals by tourists. Mick Rawls, the central manager, whose committee allocates the short supply of these machines around the state, does not believe the Valley City branch would produce the required 4000 transactions per month or outperform a new mall. Marta's planning partner is a V.P. at the main office; both are part of an informal network formed by the handful of women in managerial positions in the bank who use each other as sounding boards. (In this transcript their conversational turns are numbered and marginal notes draw attention to some key rhetorical features of this plan). We enter in the middle of their discussion.

Rhetorical Situation

1. **Marta (the Planner):** So I think this is the time to move. At the merchant's meeting two weeks ago I heard the Fidelity (another bank) was in town knocking on doors, shaking hands, telling people they were interested in the town, obviously doing a feasibility survey. One of their questions was: "Do you want an automatic teller machine in town?" Since the President has been in favor of this all along, I left a message on his phone machine as well as on Rawls's (the Central Manager) and Tony's (her boss, a Regional Manager). Told them about the competing bank and said: "If somebody puts a machine in Valley City, I certainly hope it is Western." I got a fast response from the President. He said, "I certainly agree we want it to be First Western. I will be talking to the other members of the Committee in a few days. I'll bring it up."

Audience Response	**2. Chris (acting as a Supporter):** Sounds promising, but where do you think this stands with the others? Will Rawls think you went over his head?
Topic Information	**3. Marta:** He is still clearly lukewarm, and Tony will support me, but he wants to stay clear and will not initiate anything. So what I'm going to do is send a formal proposal to Rawls this week. I have got all the figures on installation costs and placement updated so that part's ready to go.
	4. Chris: Yes. But you've got to frame it right. What's your idea?
Purpose	**5. Marta:** I know I have to make the case on Rawls's terms. This cannot fly just because the President gave the nod. If Rawls isn't actually *happy* with this decision, I would never get anything else from that Committee. My point has got to be financial feasibility—not just the threat of Fidelity.
Text Conventions	**6. Chris:** Right, it's got to be facts without embroidery. But you don't have the figures. They haven't done a study of your area yet.
Topic Information Audience	**7. Marta:** That's my problem. Even the Chamber of Commerce hasn't got good growth figures yet. But what's worse, Rawls has never been here during our busy season. All he saw was a sleepy, level 1 office.
Key Point	**8. Chris:** What do you mean? I don't see your point.
Reader's Expectations	**9. Marta:** Well, I know my customers alone won't make the 4000 transactions, and besides Rawls doesn't care if my customers are happy. He's interested in people using foreign cards (cards from any other bank) cause that's when his operation makes money. (Banks charge each other a fee for each transaction made with the other bank's card.)
Key Point	**10. Chris:** So you're telling me Rawls doesn't appreciate the potential from the tourist traffic? Right? So is that the point you are going to rest this on?
Purpose & Reader	**11. Marta:** Yes, that really is my best argument from Rawls's point of view, from the central office perspective. I've got to lead with that and put the local advantages to my customers as spin-off benefits, I think. The President will pick up on that, but it's Rawls I have to convince.
Text Conventions	**12. Chris:** It's getting the documentation that is the problem, isn't it? What kind of evidence do you have? How about something unconventional?
Topic Information	**13. Marta:** Well, I have feature stories from three different papers about all the village shops on Main Street and why we won the award. You know, over Thanksgiving, I walked around taking over two rolls of film of jam-packed parking lots, shoppers, and visitors

from all over the country. I could do that as an attachment maybe. In fact, the Merchant's Association has given away a quilt for three years now at the annual Valley Festival, and when you look at those raffle stubs, you see more people coming from all over the country.

Text Conventions

14. Chris: Okay, I'm seeing a trend analysis. And that certainly is unconventional evidence!

15. Marta: Yes, but it would be easy to do a little table of the growth in the tourist traffic, or maybe do it like a map with widening circles. I know he will be looking for numbers. I've been collecting my own survey for four years now, and I can show that between 89 and 95 percent of the local businesses bank with me.

FIGURE 3–8
A Planning Dialogue.

USING COLLABORATIVE PLANNING TO MOVE FROM A PLAN *TO SAY* TO A PLAN *TO DO*

Talking and working with other people is a powerful strategy. But collaboration alone will not help you develop a good plan or to move from having a plan *to say,* which we discussed at the beginning of this chapter, towards building a more effective plan *to do*. The Planner's Blackboard is a visual metaphor for this process, which Planners and Supporters use to prompt their discussion.

PLANS *TO SAY*

The first goal of many writers is to develop a plan *to say,* that is, to get a notion or even an outline of words and ideas that could go into a text. As you generate ideas, imagine that you have a mental blackboard in your mind on which you can jot notes, draw connections, sketch maps or outlines, and post ideas, headings, transitions, and wording that will go in your document. Strategies like brainstorming, "nutshelling," and issue trees are good ways to generate ideas and language.

As you work on a plan *to say,* more and more ideas start to fill up what we could call your Topic Information Blackboard (Figure 3–9). The more the better. If the task is simple or your knowledge is already adapted and organized around what the reader needs, then this plan based on topic information can do the job by itself. But sometimes plans dictated by what you know about the topic are not enough, even when you have expert knowledge.

For example, we once tracked the writing process of a group of graduate-

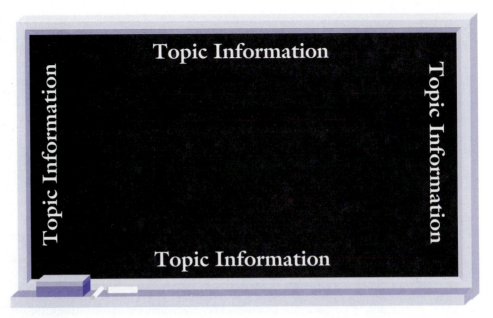

FIGURE 3–9
Planner's Blackboard for a Plan *To Say*.

level public policy students who showed how a plan *to say* can go wrong. They had been asked to evaluate the current F.F.A. guidelines for dealing with wind shear and *to recommend policy guidelines* which would help minimize air crashes caused by this dangerous phenomenon. This task clearly embodied multiple purposes, which included the rhetorical purpose of how to propose new guidelines to Washington in a political climate that supported deregulation of American airlines. Because their recommendation had to speak to a mixed readership of technical experts and policymakers, it required the writers to adapt rather complex technical information, such as details about advanced radar systems, to the needs of that audience. The report they actually turned in, however, was dominated by technical description—it merely reported a mass of complex information—and in doing so it failed to do its job as a piece of transactional writing. Why did this happen? Even though the group had received criticism on just this problem in drafts, and even though only one member of the group was an expert in the area, these writers depended on a knowledge-telling strategy and created a plan *to say* dominated by the technical information they had uncovered in their research. As a result, this text failed in its assigned purpose—to produce an evaluation and guidelines—and it failed to adapt information in light of its purpose and its readers' expectations.

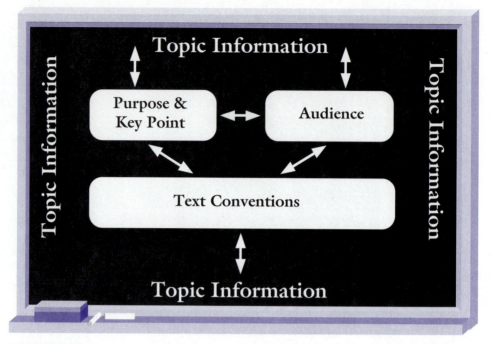

FIGURE 3–10

Planner's Blackboard for a Plan *To Do*.

PLANS *TO DO*

Experienced writers go about planning differently. Like everyone else, they think about what they want to say. But they are not limited to thinking about topic information. First, they *start* with the very goals and constraints the wind shear writers ignored. Experienced collaborative planners, for instance, are likely to start by analyzing and interpreting the rhetorical situation—why was this task assigned; how does it fit in the larger context of a project or a course; who is involved and what are their expectations; what are the features of this kind of discourse?

Secondly, experienced writers go on to build more elaborated plans *to do*. They look at their text as a set of rhetorical moves in a transaction. In order to decide what they need to say, they ask themselves, "What do I want my text to accomplish in this situation—what do I want this sentence, that paragraph, this description, that argument to do?"

Imagine the mental blackboard of an experienced writer, as in Figure 3–10. In addition to the Topic Information Blackboard that is filled with things to say, there are three additional blackboards on which these writers are also posting and revising ideas. These writers spend time thinking and talking about three key areas, which we have sketched as lying on top of the topic information blackboard.

In more detail, here are why these three key areas are so important.

Purpose and/or Key Point. A text may make lots of points, but the key point, the gist, or the main claim is what gives coherence and an organization to the text. But why is the writer making *that* key point, and what is she trying to accomplish with that paragraph, and what is her reason for using an illustration here instead of a list? The answer to all of these questions lies in the author's purpose. Experienced writers cannot only tell you about their general purpose (e.g., to recommend policy guidelines) but about a whole cast of supporting goals and "how to" plans they have for doing something in text as well. They see the different parts of their texts as moves, each of which is designed to accomplish some purpose. And they can tell you the reasons behind these moves.

Even more importantly, these writers recognize that most professional texts have multiple purposes or a number of goals related to different readers. Sometimes these goals come in conflict with one another. Planning is the place to recognize and begin to negotiate these conflicts before they lead to a disjointed text.

Thinking back to the Valley Bank partners, notice how in turns 8 and 10 Marta's supporter keeps probing for her point, reflecting back what she hears Marta saying. At turns 6 and 9 both partners raise some important conflicts—how do you argue from facts and figures when they do not exist, and what do you do when you and your reader care about different things? What sub-goals would you set, what moves would you make if you were Marta?

Audience. As you might predict, the experienced writers also generate ideas about who their readers are, what they know (or do not know), and what they need or expect. In Chapter Two we studied the players and their relationships and investments in rhetorical situations. Experienced writers not only analyze these features of a situation, they role-play and imagine how those readers might respond to the writer's own ideas or text. These writers then post a lot of ideas on their Audience Blackboard that give them direct help in revising their developing plan and shaping their text. Here is where supporters, standing in for the reader, can be especially helpful.

Notice how Marta and her supporter start by reading the rhetorical situation, thinking strategically about how different people stand on this issue and in relation to each other. In fact, in turns 7–11 they lay the foundation for her plan by deciding that it is part of Rawl's image of Valley that this proposal needs to change.

Text Conventions. As every writer knows, setting goals and imagining readers will not write the text for you. Experienced writers spend time thinking about how to translate these more abstract plans into specific text moves. That is, they look at different ways they could carry out their goals in text—ways to emphasize a key point by placing it in a topic sentence or in boldface type; ways to convince a reader by offering evidence or dramatizing the point with a narrative; or ways to make a recommendation more effective by turning it into a procedure the reader can follow.

The term *text conventions* covers a broad range of familiar features or *conventions of written text.* These include features associated with different genres (for example, a problem/purpose statement, list of recommendations, dialogue, a news "lead," executive summary, a graph, an anecdote or case in point, a budget breakdown). Writers also consider alternative, conventional patterns of organization and development (such as, topic sentences, summaries, definitions, comparisons, reasons, examples, transitions). And they may mull over how they could use visual cues to lead the reader (for example, headings, sections, italics, bullets).

When you think about it, many of these conventions are familiar to all of us. The remaining chapters present a number of these useful conventions—many which you will quickly recognize. The difference is that experienced writers talk and think about these features as if they had a tool kit of alternative conventions they could use on this text to carry out their multiple purposes, develop their key points, and adapt to their readers.

Notice how much of their time Marta and her partner spend, once the point and purposes are clear, trying to come up with "how-to" plans for making a factual case. They start by trying to think of different kinds of "documentation" one could use and how to present them (newspaper quotations, photos handled as ancillary materials) and in turn 14 the Supporter even translates Marta's observation into a kind of statistical evidence widely used in business (a trend analysis), which leads them to consider alternative ways to present this "trend" in text.

Making Connections. The small arrows on the Planner's Blackboard in Figure 3–10 visualize another distinctive move experienced writers make. As they plan, they consciously look for ways to come up with ideas that *link* the different parts of their plan. For example, they ask, what text conventions can I use to support my key point? Or, if my reader expects XYZ, what should I do (goals) or say (topic information)?

Notice how in turns 9–11 Marta's goals and her point are shaped by her careful reading of how her readers will respond. Then, given her sensible but problematic goal of making a factual, financial case, both partners begin imagining the text and its features as a response to her larger purpose. If you were to say which blackboard the partners were working on, you would often find these two experienced writers making connections across the blackboards and building an integrated plan *to do.*

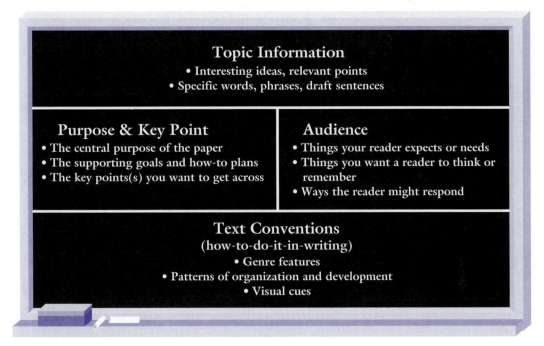

FIGURE 3–11
Using the Blackboard as a Prompt.

USING THE BLACKBOARD TO PROMPT PLANNING

How should you use the Planner's Blackboard? Some writers use it as a kind of outline—actually writing little notes to themselves in the different boxes. You may find that helpful the first time you experiment with this strategy. However, if you turn this metaphor into a simple check list, like a recipe or a short answer test, it could become a straitjacket on your discussion. Many writers prefer the freedom of talking out ideas and taking notes in a normal way. They use the Blackboard as a prompt for things to consider, and as a way to test the plan they have in mind: Have they considered (and posted) some good ideas on all areas of the Blackboard? Figure 3–11 shows some specific prompts.

USING QUESTIONS TO SUPPORT A PLANNER

Supporters have a large impact on the success of a collaborative planning session. Although it can help to talk over a paper with a friend, as a Supporter you play a more complex role. The Supporter is a sort of official memory who always brings the discussion back to matters of purpose, audience, and text. A good Supporter is also able literally to draw good thinking out of a Planner. Here are some questions/comments that let you take different roles as a supporter.

- **Gist.** Listen carefully and reflect the gist of what you heard back: "What I hear you saying is that _____. Am I hearing you right?"

- **Elaborate.** Ask the planner to elaborate. "You just said _____; tell me more about _____ [what you mean or why you said that].

- **Blackboard.** Ask for more information about key parts of the blackboard that the planner has explained only in a sketchy way. "If your purpose is _____ how are you going to do that? What are your other goals?"

- **Connections.** Ask from time to time how different parts of the plan are connected, especially when you see possible links or problems. "If your key point here is _____, how do you think your readers will respond to that?" Or "Is there any link between your purpose and the format you plan to use?"

- **Problems.** Let the writer know when you feel confused or see a problem. You do not need to have a solution; just give feedback about how the plan works for you. "I feel lost at this point; why did you say that?" "I do not know what you mean when you say _____." "Can you tell me how this part of the paper is linked to that part?" Your feedback as a "live reader/listener" (rather than as a critic or advice giver) can help the writer begin to imagine how other readers might respond and start to plan with them in mind.

- **Share.** Share your perception of the task or alternative strategies the writer might consider. "I saw the assignment a little differently; let's talk about what our options are." Or, "You might use an example here." Or "That's an important point you could emphasize."

ADAPTING COLLABORATIVE PLANNING TO A PARTICULAR PROBLEM

As you can see, the Planner's Blackboard is a generic, all-purpose prompt that does not say much about what a specific plan *to do* might look like in a given business or professional setting. Think of the different goals appropriate to credit analysis by a banker, a field report done by a petroleum engineer or a social worker, or a proposal submitted by a business consultant. Because no book (light enough to carry) could cover all of these special contexts and discourses, we have chosen to show you examples of a few and to focus on strategies for *figuring out* what a new discourse expects or a rhetorical situation requires and on general strategies like the Planner's Blackboard which you can *adapt* to your own rhetorical problem.

For example, suppose you needed to write a resumé and letter of application. You could work in conjunction with your instructor, mentor, supervisor or a collaborator, to identify some special context-specific features—within each of the blackboard areas—that you need to consider. Together you could design some tailor-made questions that a Planner and Supporter might want to work on. Figure 3–12 offers a set of starter questions for resumé writing.

THE PLACE OF CONFLICT IN COLLABORATION

Some people go to great lengths to avoid conflict between themselves or others. But in collaborative planning some kinds of conflict are very productive. **Interpersonal conflict**—focused on disagreement between people—is rarely good because it leads to bad feelings and defensive attitudes. A second kind of conflict—**procedural conflict**—is focused on what we should do and how to do it. Groups that spend a lot of time in procedural conflict get bogged down arguing over what road to take rather than getting somewhere. But sometimes, talking over alternative procedures and roads can save a lot of time and get you to a much better place. However, the best kind of conflict is **substantive conflict**—that is, considering different, conflicting ideas people have about the matter at hand (about the best argument to make, how a reader will respond). This kind of conflict—which can be carried on with a warm and supportive attitude among partners—can be highly productive.

When people encourage substantive conflict in a discussion they are willing to delay closure. That is, they do not seek immediate agreement or feel compelled to make a snap decision. Instead they try to consider alternatives, problems, other perspectives. They ask probing questions such as "Why is this NOT the best plan?" and "What else is involved?" When they do come to a decision, they do so with the sense that they have considered some alternatives and have chosen this as the "best" plan, not because it was the "only" plan they came up with.

Collaboration opens up the possibility for productive, substantive conflict, but it does not ensure it will happen. Some partners try to dominate the discussion while others take the role of a passive yes-man. Either move tends to squelch productive conflict. Another problem to look out for

Blackboard Questions Adapted to Writing a Resume And Letter of Application

Topic Information.

1. Start by brainstorming everything you can think of under the general headings of education, work (even part-time jobs that were not "career-related"), honors (awards, recognition, QPA), and activities (extra-curricular, professional societies, volunteer). Use the models in this and other library books and from friends to suggest possibilities.

Purpose and Key Point

2. One of the conventions of a resume is the line called "Objectives" or "Professional Interests." You *could* use it to state what is already obvious to the recipient (e.g., Objective: A position in hotel management), or to state goals that are likely to loom larger in *your* thinking than in the recipient's (e.g., "a cushy, high-paying position with room for quick advancement in hotel management). But you could get more mileage out of this purpose statement if you used it to name some distinctive abilities, values, or goals that reveal something about you your reader might want to know (e.g., A position that uses my management training, practical catering experience, and communication skills in any area of hotel operations that can lead to management responsibility).

3. You tell me your Internship at the University Press was a real learning experience, but what is the point you want to make with it? You worked in Marketing and Production departments, but what skills did you actually develop? What kind of work, decision making did you participate in? Did you develop technical knowledge? Did you develop management or interpersonal skills? Did you take on responsibility for anything ? In other words, if you were asked to talk about what this job did for you (and therefore what you could now do for/bring to your new employer) are there any key points you would make about this job, or this activity? Try to describe those abilities in a few words or phrases.

4. Let's ask this same key point question of all the jobs and activities you list.

One convention of a resume is to list all of your work experience chronologically. But another option is to group various short experiences in different categories, reflecting a point you want to emphasize. Use an issue tree to try out different ways of organizing: for example, Computer Programming Experience (list a series of part-time jobs and small consulting projects) and Work in Sports and Recreation (include life guard, giving tennis lessons at the YWCA etc.)

FIGURE 3–12

Planning a Resume

5. The letter of application that goes with your resume is supposed to accomplish three key goals: 1) to announce your interest in being considered for a job and a set of objectives/needs that you and your reader will share (initial paragraph); 2) to draw attention to some of your key strengths in the more informal and personal prose of a letter (body of letter); and 3) to open the door to a personal meeting (by leaving contact information, requesting an interview, or announcing an intention to call). Some writers waste the body of their letter just repeating the facts about themselves. Given your background and your reader's needs, what are you planning to do in this space?

Audience

6. Imagine your reader as a person with 15 resumes and 25 minutes. Eight applicants have similar degrees and have taken some of the same courses. All have some relevant work experience, but none is an exact fit. Are the facts (schooling, job titles) going to speak for themselves? What does that reader need to make a decision to interview you or to remember who you were after the interview when he or she goes back over the resumes?

a) Readers are looking for (and remember) recognizable people (not a list of facts). Do the different statements in your resume add up in any way to a whole person with goals, training and experience that somehow connect to each other?

b) Resume letter readers have to make lots of inferences, e.g., What should the reader infer from the fact that you spent two summers as a guide at Mountain Trails--that you took an outdoor job to get away from serious work, or that you were responsible for trip planning, for dealing with the unexpected, and for the happiness and safety of 10 people on each trip? (Can you do anything to help the reader make the right inference?)

7. When you look at a statement in your resume about a particular course, a job, or an activity, what would you like your ideal reader to be thinking, saying to him or herself when reading that line? How can you help a reader make some of these inferences about your experience, or about how the different parts connect to form a coherent image of a person?

8. Some writers assume that readers will put a lot of energy into a careful and sympathetic reading, like a teacher willing to dig out and evaluate all their good points. But what if the reader is preoccupied with the job he needs to fill, and his desire to have someone who can learn quickly, does not need a lot of supervision, and fits in with the company's current needs? How could you adapt your resume and letter to the way a pragmatic reader like this might be reading?

FIGURE 3–12,
continued

9. If your letter is tailored to an individual reader or type of employer, what do you know about their strengths or needs that you could use to create a shared goal in the initial paragraph of your letter?

10. Do you see some possible places where your goals and the potential employer's might be in conflict (e.g.,they would probably expect you to travel; you want to have a baby soon)? Can you speak to their goals and still leave room to negotiate if they want to hire you?

11. Ask someone else to read your resume and think aloud about how they are responding, line by line, and how they see the whole picture building up. Where did their response depart from your intentions?

Text Conventions

12. There are many different conventions for formatting a resume. Does your format (the way you cluster and use headings) emphasize your strong points? Would chronology show a pattern of increasing responsibility, or would categories such as Education, Work, Volunteer Roles let you highlight your extensive but unpaid experience managing volunteer projects?

13. Resumes and letters use many conventional words and phrases--which can make them sound stuffy and boring or a lot alike. As you begin to draft key sentences, how can you make your prose sound like a real person talking about distinctive experiences, without violating the expectations for seriousness and formality?

Links Between Blackboards

14. Look at the format you have chosen, the categories you use, and the different pieces of information you highlight. Can you point to each of these and talk about the reason you did it that way, about the purpose behind your words, and about the way you imagine a reader responding to each decision? That is, do your have an integrated plan (in which each Blackboard had something to say) behind all of your major decisions?

FIGURE 3–12,
continued

comes from people's worries about conflict. Sometimes a person's cultural background or upbringing makes him or her feel that expressing conflict is inappropriate. Many women are socialized to be agreeable whatever they are thinking. When this happens in your group, people with good ideas may be reluctant to express a difference of opinion. Try to deal with any of these problems in a direct but tactful way. Expressing different perspectives is both a way to support other people and an important thinking strategy. It may be important for you and your partner or group to look at your own patterns of interaction, acknowledge your different attitudes about conflict, and discuss ways you can use it best.

Adapting Collaborative Planning to Working with a Boss or Client

Collaborative planning works best when both partners understand the role of planner and supporter and are able to focus on all the Planner's Blackboard areas and not just talk about topic information. This means that after this class, you may need to teach a friend or coworker how to use this strategy so you can work as partners with each other. However, in business you may also find yourself writing text that is not your own—text that is for a supervisor who wants to delegate a task, or for a client, or in conjunction with a technical expert. It may be difficult to tell your boss, "let me teach you this planning strategy." Moreover, as the writer in this situation, you need to meet *someone else's* goals and/or express *their knowledge* accurately. And it may be hard to know just what your boss wants or all the political implications he or she knows but you do not. It can be hard to figure out what information your technical expert thought was new or important to include. Asking for a lengthy briefing ("Tell me exactly what I should do") can raise questions of your competence. In these situations writers can go through a frustrating series of drafts that do not quite make it. (Do you recall the description of "pain and mystery" in the document cycling process in the research cited in Strategy 4, Issue Trees?) To make matters worse, your boss, client, or technical expert may not be an "expert at collaboration" and may not be aware of how to share that information with you efficiently.

An adaptation of collaborative planning can be a useful strategy here— not only with your peers, but with the boss, client, or experts themselves. After your first briefing—instead of merely listening, hoping you understand, then writing a trial text—go back to your boss with a ten-minute appointment and a plan. For openers you can ask, "Let me tell you how I understand this" or "let me run my plans by you." Be prepared to give a concise account of your plan—talk out the goals you have set given your understanding of the rhetorical situation, the key points you will use to organize the discussion, the way you expect the audience to respond, and the conventions (genre, organization, or format) you plan to use. Go through your plan for the text in a *brief* but *specific,* section by section way, maybe using an issue tree to lay out the content. This strategy may not turn your boss into a self-conscious and talented supporter—you can do that with your coworkers—but it is a way to make your collaboration focus on some of the critical elements you need to know to develop a good and shared plan. And of course you can also use the Supporters' prompts when you have your initial briefing with these coauthors. Try to turn the briefing session into a planning session and help them to spell our more of the unspoken plans they may have in the backs of their minds.

REFLECTING ON YOUR OWN STRATEGIES

In the assignment section that follows, we ask you to bring a tape recorder and two tapes to all of your collaborative sessions. You may wonder how making a tape of your session would contribute to your planning. It may even make you a little nervous the first time you do it. However, some of the most important things you can learn about planning will not come from this book or an instructor, but from what you teach yourself. You are the one who must figure out ways to adapt general principles and strategies to specific situations. Reflecting on your own successes, problems, discoveries, and strategies is the best way to become a more flexible, strategic thinker. But simply recalling what you think you did in the heat of writing misses a great deal. You are likely to "remember" what you already thought you did and unlikely to discover surprises. However, the tape from a collaborative planning session can give you insight into a telescoped period of focused thinking. It can let you see how you use collaboration—and how you might design it to be more useful. And when the tape, as an independent record, is combined with your own memory, it lets you catch a glimpse of some of your own assumptions, expectations, and effective strategies. It can help you give a name to things you were aware of but did not really control—which can include some of your most problematic but most powerful strategies for writing.

One of the best ways to make use of reflection is to write about it. Listen to your tape and write a brief, personal "observation and reflection" statement. Use the observation part to sketch out an interesting feature of your own planning session—describe in concrete terms something that you found revealing, perplexing, or simply interesting about what you did. Then take a brief space to reflect on what that means, why it happened, or to draw some inferences about what it suggests to you.

Then, in your class (if that is possible) or in your planning group share your observations and reflections. When you share reflections some things to listen for are:

- What problems did people encounter the first time they did collaborative planning? Why?
- How do other people plan to redesign their session next time? What discoveries have they made?
- What did other people see as most successful about their session?
- What did other people discover about being a supporter?

- What specific strategies are other writers using? Are some of these ones you share? If so, what do you think is their source?
- What assumptions or expectations are other people bringing to their writing? If so, what do you think is their source? Is there a reason to question any of these assumptions?

Here is an example of some discoveries a college junior made.

> *My second collaborative session was not nearly as helpful as the first one had been. I arrived with the arguments I had worked on over the weekend fully thought out and presented them in a logical manner. At first, my partner could not find any points that needed clarification, and since I did not think I had any problems left, I did not have any questions. I had a final paper in my mind which made it difficult to accept suggestions. And then she did find a major discrepancy that did not fit neatly into my argument. If my paper had not been so etched in stone in my mind, I would have been more receptive and could have created a far better place for this idea than I did.*
>
> *My reasons for writing a final draft were legitimate, though. We could not meet until Monday and I didn't want to risk starting to write Monday night and not getting it revised to my standards in time. A "real" session would have been better, but in college where five classes are screaming for attention, it boils down to a problem of negotiation. Facing a deadline, I went back to my "tried and true" plan of early draft and revision. On the other hand, comparing these two papers, it seems that when I get collaborating help earlier in the planning stage (as I did on the first one) I produce better finished products.*

Summary

- Writing is a **transaction** between you and your reader
- Making a **plan *to say*** something concentrates on the information you will include, but making **a plan *to do*** something in writing helps let you see your text as an action.
- Use these **strategies** for building a rhetorical plan;
  - **Brainstorming** encourages the free flow of ideas.
  - **Incubation** works when you have already done some planning and are actively resting.
  - Explaining your ideas in a **nutshell** helps you get to the point.
  - **Topical issue trees** let you see the overall structure of your ideas. You can work from the top down to develop details, or from the bottom up to form new organizing ideas.
  - **Collaborative planning** lets you and your partner or group work as planners and supporters to develop a more effective plan.
  - **Supporters** are critical to the success of collaborative planning: They take different roles when they question and reflect, find problems, or collaborate.
  - The **Planner's Blackboard** helps you move from a plan *to say* to a plan *to do* by focusing attention not only on **Topic Information,**

but on your **Key Point** and **Purpose,** on your **Audience,** and on **Text Conventions** you could use to reach your purpose and audience. Also it reminds you to build links among these parts of your plan.

- Conflict can play a valuable role in collaboration when it is **substantive conflict.** Occasional **procedural** conflict can improve your process, but **interpersonal** conflict rarely helps anyone.
- Collaborative planning works best when you adapt it to your particular situation (such as a work situation) or task (such as writing a resumé[1]).
- Reflecting on your own strategies and planning process gives you a new power to understand and manage your own writing and thinking.

Projects & Assignments

1. Hold a brainstorming session with a group on a current paper, trying to observe the rules. Is it difficult for the group to allow the free generation of alternatives without censoring? Later, give yourself 10 minutes to do a brainstorming session alone. It this a strategy you already use or do you find your internal critic often cuts your planning short? Write a memo to your group that shares your observation and reflection.

2. Schedule a collaborative planning session to help you develop a current paper. Remember, timing is important: meet after you have done some preliminary thinking but before you have invested time in a text you will be reluctant to change.

   People often notice the first time they use a new practice like brainstorming, collaborative planning, or peer review, that trying to do the technique itself demands attention and imposes constraints. That is natural, but don't let your session become a rigid Question and Answer session. Use the Planner's Blackboard even if it differs from what you "normally" do, but make the session work for you. Tape-record the session and listen to what you are able to do.

3. Reflect on your own experience as a collaborator, problem solver, and writer. Use the tape of your collaborative planning session to observe what you actually did. Write an observation/reflection memo to your group that succinctly describes your observations—be specific, use examples, details, quotations from your tape, notes and text. Combine this observation with your reflections or inferences about what you learned. Here are some possible topics for the Subject Line of your memo:

   Subject: *An interesting feature of my planning and/or our collaborative process.*
   This open-ended question lets you focus on what this particular experience revealed, given your own interests and curiosity.

Subject: *Using a collaborative process.*

Some questions you might consider: How did my partner carry out the different roles a supporter can take; which of the roles sketched earlier in this chapter would describe us? Did we allow substantive conflict to occur? Was it productive? What was the most/least useful feature of our collaboration? Did the three principles of collaborative planning describe our experience?

Subject: *Building a Rhetorical Plan* To Do.

How far did our session take me toward the goal of building a better rhetorical plan? Did we move from the Topic Info Blackboard to the three rhetorical BBs? Where did we spend most of our attention—on representing the task, or on one of the three BBs? What were the most productive problems we turned up? Did we develop, expand, or improve the planners' initial plan?

Subject: *Designing an Effective Collaborative Session.*

Given this experience, how would I redesign my next collaborative planning session to make it more useful to me? What would I do before meeting? What would I ask my supporter to do?

Subject: *Comparing Sessions.*

Now that I have done collaborative planning two or three times and can make some comparisons, what have I figured out about my planning strategies? What do I do? What surprised me?

4. The rhetorical situation in the Twentieth Century case contained a number of people with different interests/expectations, a number of goals, subgoals and constraints, and a number of possible actions with different outcomes. Moreover, some of these elements came in conflict with each other. Is this situation with its multiple goals and conflicts unusual in business writing situations? Map out the situation you see in another case in this book, or in a problem you are working on. Compare it with Twentieth Century.

5. You have just joined the staff of the Twentieth Century Fund as an Intern analyst as they begin to prepare their next quarterly report. You have been asked to contribute to evaluating and improving on the last one.

   (a) The writers at Twentieth Century had some high expectations for their text. Did it succeed? Write some test questions based on the writers' multiple goals and run your test with readers with business background and readers without. Did both groups get all the main points? Were they persuaded? For instance, how do they interpret the idea of long term investing?

   (b) Plan an extension or revision of the Twentieth Century report for one of your audiences; make it respond to any problems you turned up. (Meet with a collaborative partner who is writing to the other reader and do a tape of your session.) Write the additional or revised copy you think is needed.

(c) As an Intern, you also need to evaluate your own experience. Write a reflection on your planning session. Observe how you used your time, what you accomplished, and where you found problems. Then reflect on what you were able to discover about your own strategies.

(d) Write a memo to Twentieth Century describing your observations from the test you ran and the rationale behind the changes you made. Outline how your plan and text would work as a response to the rhetorical situation. Attach this as a cover memo to Stowers along with your proposed revision.

6. Find two documents that seem to illustrate very different sets of text conventions (you may use documents in this text). Compare them across as many different categories of convention as you can find, in terms of genre, organization, argument technique, style, and formatting. Then for each convention predict what purpose it appears to serve in your document. Are some conventions merely the product of history that no longer seem to serve a function in your document?

7. Test the effect of a convention. Revise one of the texts you looked at in the previous question. Keep information the same, but present it according to a different convention. Get the response of two or three readers and describe the effect of your revision. Did changing the convention you used to present information change how the text functioned?

8. Write a resumé and letter of application for a job you would like to have this summer. Use the adaptation of collaborative planning found at the end of this chapter—but then review the tape of your session looking for other good tailor-made prompts and questions you and your partner had. Write a memo to the instructor of your course about how to improve this set of planning prompts and the models illustrated in this book.

9. Use collaborative planning on a current assignment that has a strong set of conventions (such as procedural instructions, an abstract, or a progress report). Review your tape and develop your own set of collaborative planning prompts tailor-made for this task. Write a diplomatic memo (treat this as an unsolicited proposal) to the instructor of your course suggesting ways to help students plan for this assignment.

A THREE-STEP INTRODUCTION TO COLLABORATIVE PLANNING

To introduce yourself to Collaborative Planning, we suggest you experiment with it in three phases: one focused on making plans *to do,* a second focused on the dynamics of being a collaborator, and a third focused on your own observations and reflections.

MEETING 1. MAKING A PLAN TO DO

Here is your rhetorical task: At the computer company you work for, your group has gained a reputation of being good writers. So the New Products manager has asked you to look over a "before" version of a manual written by one of her experienced computer scientists and the "after" version written by a professional writing student who had served an internship with the company (see Figures 3–13 and 3–14). The New Products manager would like you to compare the two pieces of writing, identify the differences, and write a diplomatic but direct memo (or report or guide—the form is up to you) that would help the computer scientists (the technical experts) write more effective and usable descriptions of their products in the future.

Start by developing a plan for your memo with your entire group or class. Begin with a free-ranging discussion, but use a large blackboard divided into the four areas of the Planner's Blackboard and ask the person recording your ideas on the board to try to place ideas in their appropriate area as they come up. Don't worry if your recorder is uncertain about where an idea fits—keep your attention on generating your plans.

After you have come up with a good set of ideas, however, take time out to reflect on what you did.

- First of all, where have you spent your attention? Do some blackboards have more information, more developed plans than others?

- If you were the one delegated to sit down and write this text right now for the group, is the plan you see adequate or would you like more help in specific areas? For example, do you know what the text would look like; do you know what points should get priority and how you will to do that in the text? Is this a well-developed plan *to do*? How do you know a good plan when you see one?

- Do you see any ideas that really fit in more than one blackboard? That is, did your planning make links across the blackboards with ideas that joined audience and purpose, for instance? Or did you come up with text convention ideas that solved a problem or helped you meet one of your goals? Do you see places you could generate links now if you thought about it?

- How many alternative plans or options did you come up with? Were you, as a group, willing to entertain potentially conflicting ideas? If so, can you track on the blackboard what emerged from those alternative plans or ideas? Or, on looking for them, now do you see any alternatives or generative conflicts in your ideas that might lead to a better plan?

In preparation for your second meeting on collaborative planning, spend 15–20 minutes sketching out your own plan for the memo to the technical

Oil: The Introduction

OIL is yet another text editor. It incorporates features
of many previous editors, but is not quite like any of
them. The goals of the OIL editor are:

- To fit into the Spice environment. In particular
to access the screen through Canvas [Ball 81] and
to take advantage of the large virtual storage
provided by Accent [Rashid 80].

- To be available quickly, at least in skeletal
form. In order for program development under Accent
to be possible there must be some editor available.
The first version of OIL is not meant to be the
last word in editors, but was designed to be
quickly implementable.

- To be smoothly expandable. The first version of
OIL is not the last. Features which are not yet
implemented, but which are anticipated include
programmability as in Emacs [Gosling 81] interface
to MultiScript [Multi 81] and (possibly) multiple
character fonts.

This document concentrates on describing the editor as
it is now, but there is a section near the end on future
plans.

The Basics

OIL is a modeless editor. This means that pressing the
same key will always cause the same effect. This
statement has to be interpreted somewhat liberally. The
ctrl-x key serves as an escape, and changes the meaning
of the next key pressed The ctrl-x and the following key
must be interpreted as a single compound stroke.

FIGURE 3–13

A Portion of a
Computer Manual
Written by a Computer
Scientist: The "Before"

experts. Bring whatever notes, outlines, or text fragments you find useful.
Be prepared to explain to your supporter not only a plan for what you want
to say but your plan to do. Also bring your responses to the survey questions on your collaborative experience (found in Chapter Six) and review the
roles of planner and supporter.

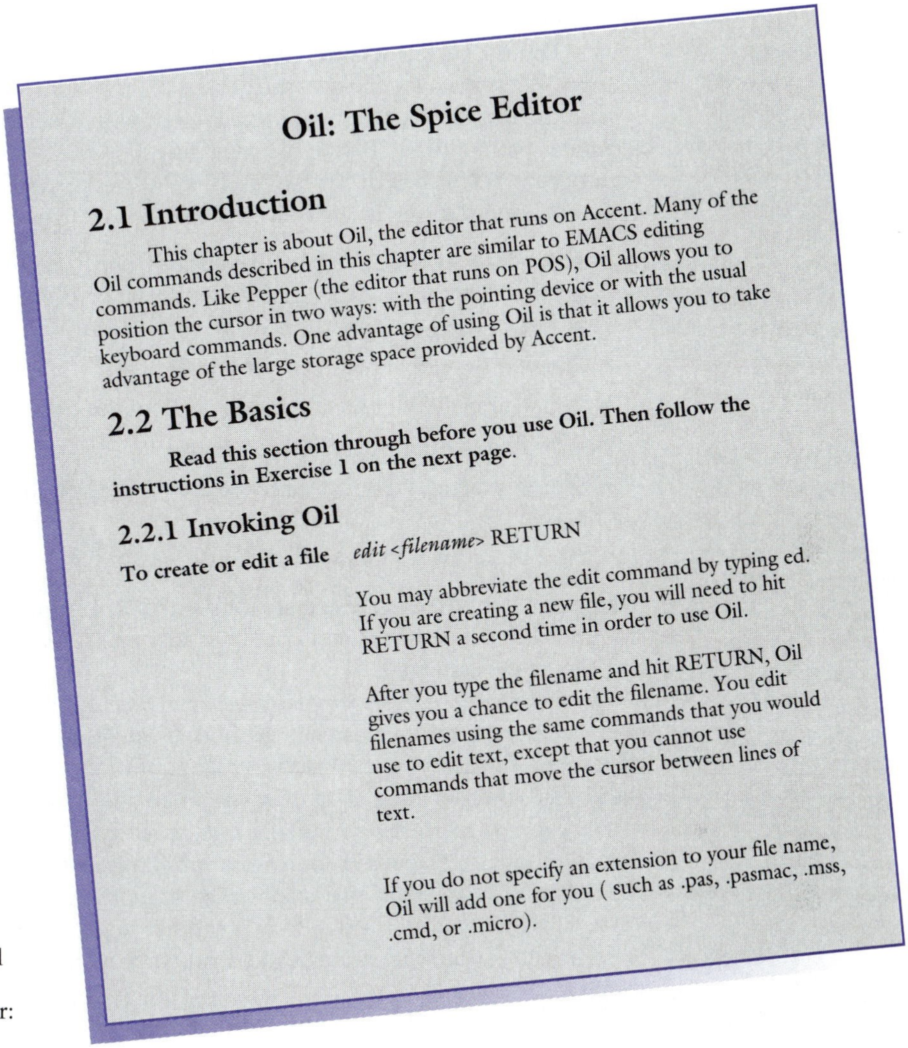

Oil: The Spice Editor

2.1 Introduction

This chapter is about Oil, the editor that runs on Accent. Many of the Oil commands described in this chapter are similar to EMACS editing commands. Like Pepper (the editor that runs on POS), Oil allows you to position the cursor in two ways: with the pointing device or with the usual keyboard commands. One advantage of using Oil is that it allows you to take advantage of the large storage space provided by Accent.

2.2 The Basics

Read this section through before you use Oil. Then follow the instructions in Exercise 1 on the next page.

2.2.1 Invoking Oil

To create or edit a file   *edit <filename>* RETURN

You may abbreviate the edit command by typing ed. If you are creating a new file, you will need to hit RETURN a second time in order to use Oil.

After you type the filename and hit RETURN, Oil gives you a chance to edit the filename. You edit filenames using the same commands that you would use to edit text, except that you cannot use commands that move the cursor between lines of text.

If you do not specify an extension to your file name, Oil will add one for you (such as .pas, .pasmac, .mss, .cmd, or .micro).

FIGURE 3–14

A Portion of a Computer Manual Written by a Professional Writer: The "After"

MEETING 2. COLLABORATING AS PLANNER AND SUPPORTER

Use this meeting to experiment with the roles of planner and supporter and to share your experiences with collaboration. You might start by discussing your own response to the surveys on collaboration in Chapter Six and comparing it to the experience of the group. In particular, do the people in your group or class have similar responses to questions 10 and 11?

Review the different types of supporters discussed above. What do you prefer? Did the people you noted in question 9 differ in their style of collaboration? What makes a good supporter?

Use the rest of this meeting to experiment with and reflect on working as a planner or supporter. Divide up your time so person A works as a planner with person B (for maybe 10 minutes), then break, spend a few minutes to answer these questions about your session:

- How did you organize your discussion? Did you follow an outline, go through the Blackboard Planner areas, or go directly to the key points of the plan or to a problem?
- Did you develop a plan *to do* or a plan *to say?*
- Which area did you most need to concentrate on?
- Who had the floor?
- Which strategies did the supporter use and what effect did he or she have?
- How would you redesign a real session?

Share your responses to these questions with the group. What did you learn from this brief experiment you could use in a real session? Now switch roles and try the process again.

Use Collaborative Planning on your next writing task. Make an appointment to meet with your partner as soon as you have a plan (and probably some notes) which you are ready to talk about. Make sure it is far enough ahead that you have time to rethink your plan and write.

Have a tape recorder and a blank tape for each person at the session. Being nervous about the tape will soon wear off. Try to capture everything, even the informal talk, since that can be an important part of your session. Reviewing the tape later will let you recapture good ideas and let you reflect on your own successful strategies and on ways to guide your collaborative sessions.

MEETING 3. REFLECTING ON YOUR OWN PLANNING

Reflection may be your most important step, since here is your chance to learn from your own experience. Listen to the tape from your collaborative planning session and write a two-page "observation and reflection" statement. (For more suggestions, see the described projects below.) The first time you do this exploration you may want to focus on what you observed about the collaboration itself. But by the second or third time you carry out this reflection, you will probably want to focus on what you can discover about your own writing, assumptions, and strategies. In reflecting on your own strategies, look for things that work for you, but don't be afraid to look at problems, uncertainties, and difficulties too, since those are also important places to learn about writing.

When you present your observation and reflection in class, try to distill the "interesting feature" that will let you and other members of the class share your experiences, problems, and discoveries.

Did you set your own context-sensitive agenda for planning before the meeting? If so, include your prompts and a brief commentary on how they worked and what you would do next time.

Reference

1. Paradis, J., D. Dobrin, & R. Miller. "Writing at Exxon ITD: Notes of the Writing Environment of an R & D Organization." In L. Odell and D. Goswami (eds.), *Writing in Nonacademic Settings* (New York: Guilford Press, 1985).

4

Turning Plans into Drafts

THIS CHAPTER offers you strategies for turning plans into drafts—a process that often operates under time pressure. Therefore, it begins with the decision of whether to write at all and some of the consequences of choosing formal versus informal messages and different media. It asks you to compare six strategies for producing a written or oral draft:

STRATEGY 1. Recycling boilerplate text
Use prior text efficiently.

STRATEGY 2. Imitating a specific text
This is an easy way to begin.

STRATEGY 3. Following models
Evaluate generic or format models versus in-house models.

STRATEGY 4. Designing your own model
Choose options in response to the situation and the paper trail.

STRATEGY 5. Using text moves to develop ideas
Use these six common text moves for shaping ideas and text within a more general model.

Move 1: Organize the text around your key points.
Move 2: Arrange ideas from general to particular.
Move 3: Use a standard rhetorical pattern to connect ideas: Narration, description, comparison, cause/effect, problem-solution.
Move 4: Construct an argument with claims and evidence.
Move 5: Make a rhetorical move within a type of writing or community.
Move 6: Develop prose from graphic ideas.

STRATEGY 6. Finding the gist to develop an oral presentation
Use writing to "draft" a plan for speaking.

4
Turning Plans into Drafts

WRITING WHEN THE PRESSURE IS ON

One clear difference between academic and business communication is the time frame in which one prepares and delivers a message. Compared to business, school offers students the relative luxury of time to invent, research, and prepare to deliver a speech or paper. School assignments are still difficult—because teachers make demands and because students have to juggle the time and effort for one assignment with the rest of their academic and personal lives. Student life is pressured, but in the world of work, the pace, constraints, and consequences related to writing tasks increase to sometimes dramatic proportions.

The goal of this chapter is to give you strategies for efficiently moving from plans to a written draft, and for preparing that draft for public, oral presentation as well. We bring up the pressures of delivery deadlines and demanding audiences not to intimidate but to drive home the importance of three decisions at the juncture of planning and drafting: deciding whether to speak or write, in what form, and with what medium. Consider this scenario:

> At your brokerage firm, you arrive on a Tuesday morning, enter your office and find yourself at "information central." You have seven messages on voice mail, and three on your computer system's electronic mail, including an important query from a prospective international client. You found Post-its on your desk, asking you to stop by to see the sales manager later in the morning and to speak with your company's fundraiser for an AIDS foundation. As you entered your firm, you picked up a handful of letters and flyers from the mailroom, mostly junk mail, and you found some faxed memos from the home office. In your planner are notes that you made to condense last week's sales briefing and to write a summary report to distribute to other brokers in your district. And you are about a week away from an important stockholders' meeting, where you are expected to present sales and marketing reports with projections for the new fiscal year.
>
> Though your job by title is investment planner, it seems to you on this Tuesday—like every other Tuesday and almost every other day— that your job is secretarial in nature. You must wade through a backlog of information—sorting, coding, and responding as quickly and as appropriately as you can. No one else can do it, because most messages

in the various media carry their own significance and have been sent directly to you, with the expectation of a quick response.

Research on communication in business settings illustrates the influence of new communication technology: People can send messages faster and in more ways, but that has meant that the pace of business communication—and thus the pace of business—has quickened. Also the direct, instantaneous quality of electronic media has made many of the traditional roles of secretaries—in which someone would intervene in the drafting process, straighten out the language, and dress it up for public showing—obsolete. Business and professional environments are exploding with information, and the task of sorting and coding this information, and responding by writing and speaking, belongs to you.

DECIDING TO WRITE OR SPEAK

As you survey a rhetorical situation, one of the most important decisions you will make is whether to speak or write. Though countless texts emphasize the differences between the two modes of communication, we prefer to think of them as related. Earlier, we described the *paper trail* as a series of text fragments that will help you reconstruct a rhetorical situation. That paper trail is actually a web of spoken and written communication: When people write, that writing usually is accompanied by speaking as part of its presentation or dissemination. And oral presentations, even casual ones, are either bolstered by written texts or refer to them.

For a stockholder's meeting, you would, of course, speak but probably not without handouts, slides, or overheads to augment your presentation. And your preparation to speak would consist mostly of writing, using many of the planning tools introduced earlier. For example, President Bill Clinton wrote nineteen drafts of his acceptance speech delivered at the 1992 Democratic Convention. Although he delivered the speech seemingly without notes or drafts, he and his advisers depended on writing as a tool to build a lengthy, rhetorically sophisticated text. The text of your presentation at the stockholder's meeting may even achieve a life of its own after you speak, since drafts of speeches sometimes wind up as printed texts or are revised back from oral to written form.

And thanks to electronic tools (fax, e-mail, voice mail) you can carry on conversations with electronic writing and save a spoken message over the phone. Figure 4–1 shows some of the choices you will make in deciding to speak or write and Figure 4–2 presents some of the consequences in making these decisions. But first, let us define some terms.

When we say that people choose a **level of formality** as they speak and write, we mean they choose from among many different types of messages, which vary from highly polished, publishable texts to impromptu, personal,

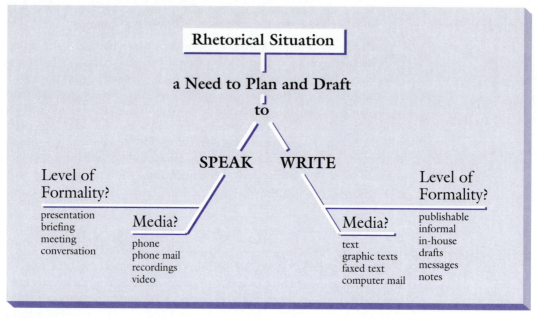

FIGURE 4–1
Decisions in Choosing to Speak or Write.

and informal messages. For example, a proposal can take several forms—a lengthy, polished document, a shorter letter or memo, a computer mail message, or a suggestion set forth in a meeting. Each of these proposals could offer the same solution to a problem, but the packaging will be far different. And the package itself carries important messages. For example, long, highly formatted documents are often taken as complete, serious, and a testimony to hard work. On the other hand, circulating such a text to your colleagues as a "finished" document may also suggest that you are not interested in their input. The shape and style of a message also vary with the **media** chosen, the technology that carries the message. It may be new for you to think of writing as a technology but, like a camera or tape recorder, writing is a tool for recording and representing thinking and speaking. Each medium gives a different stylistic and informational slant to a message, and the decision to speak or write now involves decisions whether to use computers, overheads, photographs, telephones, and/or video communication.

Suppose you are meeting a client for lunch or drafting a short proposal with a follow-up phone call. Figure 4–1 suggests some of the options that surround these events as an instance of writing or speaking. This graphic may also help you see writing and speaking as a web of communication.

The Choice	Possible Rhetorical Advantages	Possible Disadvantages
To write formally: proposals reports formal letters...	Retrievable information Boilerplate, consistency Reproducible information Basis for negotiation, legalities	Time consuming to produce Time consuming to read Stuffy, formal, non-interactive Dominates other communication
To write informally: e-mail notes rough drafts	Fast, reactive Supports dialogue Can lead to formal writing Helps to discover ideas	Elliptical, understated Error-ridden, hard to read Mistaken for formal text Hard to revise to formal text
To speak formally: presentations briefings formal meetings	Condenses writen text A forum for debate, negotiation Presents key points, issues Tests an idea, gathers support	Speakers can dominate Ignores or shadows some ideas Public forum can intimidate Spoken errors can linger
To speak informally: informal meetings office, hallway talk phone messages	Fast, reactive Supports dialogue, collaboration Candid, direct Lowest risk	No record, hard to recapture Translation or restatement needed Excludes others Can be misunderstood

FIGURE 4–2

Advantages and Disadvantages of Various Forms of Speaking and Writing.

Experienced writers have learned how to orchestrate speaking and writing, with varying levels of formality; they learn to think of writing as part of a constellation of phone calls, letters, messages, and meetings—and, of course, formally written texts and oral presentations.

Can you retrace your thinking on a recent transaction in which you had to choose whether (and how) to speak or write? Or can you recapture the talk that surrounds a written text? In school, students may not make as many of these decisions; however, doing an assignment often involves many forms of talk with friends and instructors; notes, drafts, and texts; as well as different media. Or consider the way some students use varied technologies to help them get into college or graduate school. A written statement of purpose is required, but they also arrange for an on-site interview, for which they prepare a strategic conversation. Some even include a videotape as a marketing tool. These students are approaching admissions rhetorically by addressing their audience's needs, mixing oral, written, and visual texts to offer a stronger collective argument for their worthiness.

With choices come consequences. In Figure 4–2, we have listed some of the possible advantages and disadvantages in choosing one form or medium over another, and we have arranged the data around four basic choices—to speak or write formally or informally. As you will see, informality is linked to a casual circumstance and to media technologies that are more spontaneous and reactive. In these cases, not only is a formal style not needed, it may detract from the rhetorical effect on the audience.

After reading through these two figures, you may well remember circumstances when the decision to speak or write went awry. Here is one.

> Suppose that you had hurriedly prepared for a departmental meeting, knowing that a member of the executive committee would be present. Because you are on speaking terms, and because you have heard nothing that suggests that this meeting will differ from other weekly briefings, you gather last week's notes, your yellow legal pad, a sandwich, and the hope that you can recede into someone else's discussion. When you arrive, you find that no one else brought lunch, that an overhead projector is present, and that the meeting room is now oriented to a central speaker—you. Your supervisor expects you to present a summary of the department's activities over the last fiscal quarter, and she remembers mentioning the assignment as you passed in the hallway (but you do not). Of course, you did not choose to come unprepared, but because you misjudged the circumstance and did not plan for a formal oral presentation, you are faced with one of the worst planning-drafting chores—instantly translating your ill-formed ideas and statements into an organized briefing, without the expected media to enhance your presentation and to reach your audience.

Situations such as this will occur from time to time. The next section of this chapter presents strategies to help you translate your plans into a coherent draft based on your reading of a rhetorical situation and decision to write instead of speak. We present five strategies for writing: using **boilerplate, imitating text examples, following models, designing your own model from other sources,** and finally a number of **text moves** for building a draft from the ground up.

BUILDING TEXTS: FOLLOWING EXAMPLES AND DESIGNING FROM SCRATCH

Academic and literary writing is often valued for its originality in form, substance, and style—but business and professional writing is often valued for its consistency and trueness to form. Business writers do not want to reinvent the wheel every time they sit down to write, and, in any case, such originality would probably be judged to be inefficient if not arrogant. Prior texts and models serve important roles in organizations: They meet the expectations of readers, represent part of an organization's culture and product line (in the way that Macintosh computer users now expect and value Mac's style of computer documentation), and models are efficient resources for writers.

Students in school, of course, also look for models and examples for many of the same reasons. If a teacher makes an assignment without a model or format to follow in writing, a first response by many students is to ask for an example—real or hypothetical—to help them build a plan for action. And even if a model or format is provided, students act like writers, and continue to search for examples to draw from and to confirm the rhetorical decisions they are making as they compose. Here are five general strategies that writers use to build their own texts.

STRATEGY 1: RECYCLING BOILERPLATE TEXT

Boilerplate is preprinted text that has been around in an institution's text files or has been written for wide dissemination. Boilerplate has received enough approval that it is acceptable in its present form and can be used in a variety of situations. For example, a school's admissions procedures text is boilerplate text read by students, faculty, and administration. Advertising and marketing materials (i.e., product descriptions) are also often boilerplate. Once a product or service is stable, it is both efficient and rhetorically effective for a company or individual to invest in producing a complete, coherent, and attractive text and leave it alone.

To write with boilerplate sounds easy because someone else has already done the work. You simply lift it from earlier documents and include it in yours. However, its stability is also its weakness, and writers do not use boilerplate casually without considering their readers. Stand-alone boilerplate is almost always accompanied by writing, such as a letter of transmittal or introduction, that makes an explicit link between the boilerplate and the situation at hand. In that statement, the writer could present the boilerplate and explain how it serves the reader's informational needs. The writer could also provide an overview of what is in the boilerplate or explain some ways to read it. Boilerplate is stable and consistent, but writers wisely review it for its accuracy. Even if a product description, for example, is slightly out of date, the boilerplate may work well with a written clarification of the product's new specifications.

If the boilerplate is integrated into longer documents, such as a marketing plan, try to customize the entire text in such a way that it reads, from front to back, as if it were written for the specific audience and situation. For example, a company's history, policies, or values could be written and presented as boilerplate around the organization but not published formally in the way that a product line brochure is published in glossy form. For efficiency and political gain, writers recycle company prose and integrate a company's background (for example) as an introductory paragraph in a variety of documents. The key then is to edit and revise both texts until they match in substance, tone, and even technical language.

The Digi-Tech proposal format (Chapter One) is a good example of the efficient use of boilerplate. If you recall, Digi-Tech's proposal team scrupulously reads a customer's request for proposal (RFP) and even uses the "requests for information" to build their model for a proposal. When they deliver their proposal, which is long and detailed, approximately 90 percent of a proposal is boiler plate. The writers recycle company histories and profiles, product descriptions, service procedures, and contract requirements. They also recycle smaller chunks of information: introductory letters, phrases in their letters of transmittal, and formats for title pages and executive summaries. For their writing task, boilerplate allows them to concentrate on the few but crucial moments when they must write specifically to address the sales situation, set forth in the RFP's statement of purpose and needs.

STRATEGY 2: IMITATING A SPECIFIC TEXT

Many writers, when faced with a problem in a rhetorical situation, will quickly search for a specific example to imitate, such as a friend's term paper in history or the last expense report submitted from a sales team. They would *never* recycle this writing as boilerplate, but they certainly would ask another student or employee for their response to an assignment. The danger in imitating someone else's work too closely is **plagiarism.** In an academic arena, plagiarism means to borrow without approval or acknowledgement, to take someone else's work and call it yours. Most schools have strict policies regarding plagiarizing another student's work or published scholarship. In business, plagiarism is equally unethical, although imitating others' work and recycling boilerplate are common and even advisable. The difference is in the degree of ownership: In school (generally) writers own texts, while in business the organization owns them. Commonly, businesses will treat their writing—from boilerplate to correspondence—as the physical property of that organization.

Working within an organization means working for consistent quality and showing that you are a team player. You may strategically imitate a text as long as you do not plagiarize someone else's ideas or efforts. First find out the status of a text, whether it is copyrighted, under review, or authored by a particular writer or group. What you take from that text can be acknowledged through footnotes, citations, or by receiving spoken or written approval in advance. If you are careful to acknowledge while you imitate, you help to maintain a company's writing history and paper trail and validate its organizational culture.

To build a draft by imitating another text, begin by examining the text's global structure or organization and rhetorical approach. Does it match yours and your rhetorical situation? If the format and organization fit your needs, you may then study the specific text for word and sentence-level strategies. For example, you might admire a writer's tone, or the way he or she defines a problem—but also notice whether this writer uses terminology that you do not understand or cannot use comfortably. Should you think the writer has done something so well that you want to use it, cite and quote as you would in school, or make sure that this recycling is approved.

We encourage you to hunt for specific examples when you compose. The more you work with them and know the people, organization, and community in which you work, the more the process of drafting a new text from another text will become streamlined, and you will learn how not to offend people or violate ownership. As we saw with Digi-Tech, most proposal writing is a process of wisely recycling information, rhetorical strategies, and boilerplate so that the audience receives a text that seems freshly written for them alone, and a company's many voices blend as one. However, to blunder down the paper trail—either missing the opportunity of imitating texts or blithely plagiarizing would be wasteful and politically (and legally) dangerous. In school and in the world of work, specific texts are one of the best places to look for drafting ideas—if you look with the writers' approval and a clear eye toward the rhetorical situation.

STRATEGY 3: FOLLOWING MODELS

A model for writing is an abstract version of an actual text—an example or format that represents "the way things are normally done." Real estate contracts, building codes, a sheet of music, or a tax form are all based on models that people commonly recognize. Readers depend on the features of familiar models to help them do their business. Models are like a road map that show you the best road from Wichita to Abilene—or at least the road most people take. But like a road map, they are also merely an abstraction which you have to turn into the text moves that actually get you there.

This most familiar kind of model is a **generic model** that tries to capture the essential qualities or features of a type of writing. Generic models usually appear in textbooks and styleguides as a **format** that tries to address *all* audiences and situations. And, generic models appear in your mind. If you open a menu or a mystery novel or if you watch a situation comedy on television, you bring a model of what those types of communication and entertainment should contain. You may also have a generic model in mind when a teacher assigns an essay, because you can remember being taught to begin with a thesis or question, to proceed in an orderly fashion through the essay body with supporting details, and to conclude with some restatement of your thesis. In business and professional writing, however, generic models are much more detailed. There are common ways to write a progress report, letter of transmittal, annual report, feasibility study, and so on, and these models are so common that they sometimes generalize across writers, organizations, discourse communities, and even cultures. Chapter Seven offers the characteristics of many of these models and describes how writers strategically vary them for their purposes.

Because models generalize across rhetorical situations, they cannot provide a specific text example—only the format for producing one. Figure 4–3 shows a simple format for a generic model of a business proposal that we then compare (on the right) with the format for writing a social science research proposal.

We offer this comparison to make one important point: Some generic models are truly general (e.g., most people in Western culture can predict the progression of a short story). But even generic models vary from one discourse community to another. You may notice that most of the components of both proposals are roughly the same, but even at this level of detail, we can see important differences that reflect different communities. A business proposal operates around a solution to an agreed-upon problem, whereas a research proposal goes to great length to argue for the existence of a problem or gap in existing research. A business proposal also turns largely on the appropriateness of a solution and how efficiently and cheaply it can be delivered, whereas research proposals carefully describe research methods but may depend less on efficiency and cost as a primary criteria for acceptance. Are there other differences that you can see?

A generic model is different from an **in-house** model. An in-house model is abstracted from *the way things are normally done* in a local organization or discourse community and can be traced to an explicit paper trail. In-house models are sometimes written down as formats, but those formats may vary from the features of a generic model. These variations appear because of the power of discourse communities and organizational cultures to shape the way people speak, read, write, and carry on their work. In a company, writers instinctively search the paper trail for specific models, because these models have earned the approval of readers and writers they value. If they find such a model, they possess a format for composing and probably a series of specific texts that serve as examples.

For example, a local engineering firm in Utah has succeeded in building a business over the last 40 years by writing a certain style of short proposal (see the Bush & Gudgell proposal in Chapter Seven). Their specialty is civil

Business Proposal	Format with Audience Issues
Introduction:	What is being proposed
Problem:	What motivates the proposal
Objectives:	The basis for success
Product:	The solution in detail
Method:	How to implement the solution
Materials Resources Costs	The bill and method of payment

Research Proposal	Format with Audience Issues
Introduction:	Nature of research proposed
Purpose:	Hypothesis, scope of study
Significance:	Potential contribution
Relevant Research:	Related research
Methods:	Collecting and analyzing the data
Resources:	Needed or existing resources

FIGURE 4–3

Comparing a Business Proposal Format with a Research Proposal Format.

engineering, and they have learned how to provide a client with the following information in only a few pages:

- A brief company background,
- A "lump sum" cost for their service,
- Current workload and staffing—their readiness to complete the project requested,
- Office and technical facilities for support,
- Their understanding of the client's project and needs, and
- Resumés of the principal engineers for the proposed service.

If you quickly compare this model format with the generic business proposal format in Figure 4–3, you will see that this company, by habit and preference, deviates from the norm. They created their own in-house model that is familiar to other engineering firms in the intermountain West. In the exercises at the end of this chapter, we refer you to the proposal from this firm for a detailed comparison, but for now we simply want to demonstrate that writers, over time and within an organization or discourse community, effectively depart from generic models, creating their own.

However, writers should not run to these or any other models and cease their survey of the rhetorical landscape. Writers use models effectively mostly as a framework for composing. If you were hired by the engineering firm above as someone who would write proposals, your paper trail would quickly lead you to this proposal and others. It might be handed to you as a specific example, the last and best example. Suppose you were given the twin tasks of generating a proposal for a new bid and, in doing so, reviewing the firm's writing practices. How would you work from generic and specific models to produce a text?

First of all, models tell a writer important information:

- a format or pattern of organization,
- a pattern of reasoning and possible development that meets a reader's expectations, and
- (in some cases) even the language that may be used to launch certain sections.

Models cannot be expected to provide other important information:

- the format or pattern that best fits a reader or a situation,
- specific details and reasoning that fit a situation,
- style, tone, or persona.

Therefore, use these tests when following a model to build a draft:

1. Test the model against any of the text conventions and informational needs apparent in the rhetorical situation and expressed by an audience. Outline or review your goals for writing and the strategies you plan to use to reach this audience. Even though models provide useful information, a survey of the rhetorical landscape may reveal:
   - additional audience needs
   - stylistic preferences
   - or even procedural requirements, such as page layout and number of copies, details that models never reveal. An RFP or guidelines are especially helpful and must be followed closely.

2. If you are working with a specific model, test it against the features of the rhetorical situation and the features of a generic model, if you can find one. Test the model by inspecting each of the components to see whether they speak directly to a reader and seem to carry the rhetorical purpose of a document. You may find that new sections or rhetorical moves need to be added, or that the order in a generic model needs to be changed.

3. Use the model to organize and shape your thoughts, but do not rely on the model to provide explicit detail or to build coherence— it will not. If you translate the format into paragraphs, headings, and subheads, use another technique, such as creating a clear line of topical development (see Chapter Five) that lets you focus on the ways your ideas and argument develop. In other words, don't let the formal pattern of the model make you lose sight of a more important pattern—the logic and structure of your message. Use your purpose and message to help generate all the additional detail you will need to flesh out the skeleton the model provides.

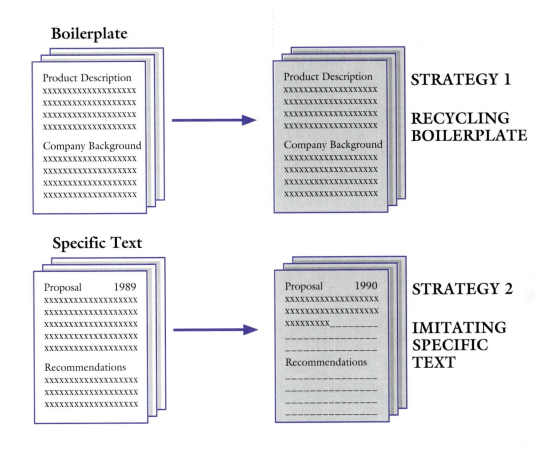

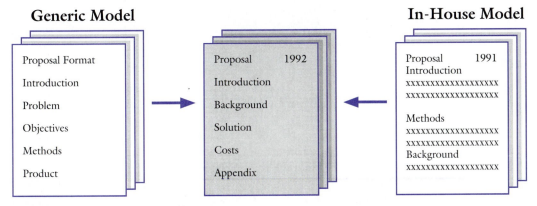

FIGURE 4–4
Five Strategies for Building a Draft.

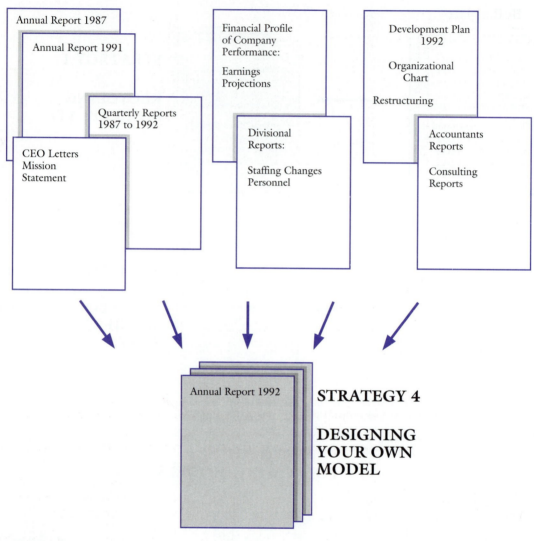

FIGURE 4–4,
continued

4. Test whether the language of the model fits your audience, or does this language introduce unknown terms or an inappropriate style or tone? Models that offer you elaborated examples of text can be easier to work from, but you must use the same caution we urged in imitating a specific text in Strategy 1.

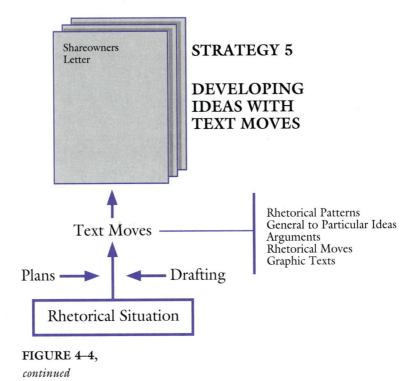

Shareowners Letter

STRATEGY 5

DEVELOPING IDEAS WITH TEXT MOVES

Text Moves — Rhetorical Patterns
General to Particular Ideas
Arguments
Rhetorical Moves
Graphic Texts

Plans → ← Drafting

Rhetorical Situation

FIGURE 4–4,
continued

5. As you fill out the model, make sure you are not creating redundancy. Models offer the illusion of a complete text and additions and revisions can lead to needless repetition because the writer has been relieved of the duty of creating a format on his or her own.

6. When you think your draft is complete, read through it to make sure that the tone and persona, the image you wish to project fit your rhetorical situation.

We would like to end this section by offering a distinction that may help you in school: A model **format** that you find in a textbook is not an **outline,** though the two words—format and outline—seem to mean the same thing for many writers. Formats are a best guess—through common use or your research—as to what readers will look for in a specific type of writing. Formats must be adapted and embellished to fit a specific situation. Outlines are made by writers, to help them plan and to adapt models and other information to their purpose. Outlining allows writers to think in the rawest forms—to sketch. When you can make a clear distinction between the custom-made outline *you* use to plan and revise, and the seductive pattern offered by a model format, you avoid confusing a general model with a specific plan for action.

Figure 4–4 summarizes the three strategies introduced thus far and distinguishes them from the other two to come which will call for even more invention on your part. Strategy 4 still depends on examples, but it uses a number of them to allow you to build your own model. And Strategy 5 takes you back to the building blocks themselves that let you construct a draft from the ground up, calling on an entire repertory of standard text moves. As you have probably already realized, you are likely to call on all five of these strategies to draft any given text.

STRATEGY 4: DESIGNING YOUR OWN MODEL

One of the most common general strategies that writers use is to look for a number of specific examples and from that group choose features they like in order to fabricate their own model. This is a shift in resources—away from what an organization or community decides is *the way things are normally done* to the way you choose to do them. Your originality, however, is still based on a paper trail in that it builds a new conceptual model in response to the work of others. You design your own model in the way that some chefs like to cook—by reading many recipes and by selectively borrowing the best ideas from the lot.

The first activity, as always, is to survey the rhetorical situation, this time gathering as many examples and contributing texts from which your recipe will be created. What texts?

- Specific texts that show what other people have done with the same task

- Specific texts that provide the information and strategies you need

- Generic or in-house models, whose features help you write for a rhetorical situation

Start with Goals. One strategy is to start with your own ideas and goals and comb through other texts, looking for examples, techniques, formats, tricks of the trade that you might borrow or adapt for your purposes. For example, in designing a newsletter for your customers, you find that one of your competitors uses a news story format, a friendly style, and action photos to personalize their staff. But another highlights their research by using a list of bulleted claims on what is working in the field, followed by technical references. Research is your strength, but you want to balance that with a personal voice, so you decide to get the best of both worlds and design your newsletter to include a staff section called, "Let me Introduce . . ." and another technical column with the banner "What Works?" Your job then is to design a new model that integrates these bright ideas, borrowed from other texts, into a coherent text of your own.

Start with Texts. But suppose you were charged with making this year's annual report a more significant document than usual. Here the best strategy might be to start asking around and searching the files for previous texts. You turn up the following:

Current financial profiles and company performance
Past letters from the CEO
Corporate "goals and mission statements"
Organizational charts and descriptions of divisions and personnel
Financial operating data: expenditures, investments, profits and projections
Other reports, annual and quarterly from the past five years
Accountant and other consulting reports

You may feel overwhelmed by how much information must be condensed and organized into one 15-page report that is widely distributed throughout your company and to shareowners. However, looking at these models makes you aware of the "possible" features readers might expect to see in your model of an annual report and certain that none of the "obligatory" ones are left out.

STRATEGY 5: USING TEXT MOVES TO DEVELOP IDEAS

Strategies 1 to 4 all depend on some form of *paper trail: boilerplate, specific texts, models, or contributing texts,* and your general goal as a writer is wisely to write from something you or someone else has written to something new. But some rhetorical situations provide little or no paper trail, or you may decide to start from scratch. You may, as many writers do, need to work primarily from your plans and your survey of the rhetorical situation. Moreover, even if you have models and good examples, they will not tell you how to structure a new approach or create the details that develop it. Here are six **text moves** that help either to generate a reasoned structure for a written statement or to revise and fill out a section in a model. Generally, text moves are patterns of organizing, reasoning, and arguing that build coherence for a reader and develop your ideas. Most of these text moves complement each other, and you will find many at work in one piece of writing, as we will see.

Ideas to Action

Just as most models must be customized for rhetorical situations, these moves do not exist in the abstract. They work because of the text around them. Their effectiveness depends on how they fit into the "global" structure and the rhetorical situation.

To use and even recognize text moves at work in the writing around you will take a little practice in looking at the text as a whole. So, as practice in reading to find text moves, and as a way to ground many of these strategies in an example, look at the "shareowners' letter" (Figure 4–5) that opens the annual report from the Pacific Telesis Group, a growing utility company. Although this sample of writing comes from someone at the top of an organization (and not a newcomer), give this letter a rhetorical reading (as discussed in Chapter Two). Try to see how many of the five text moves listed below you can find woven into this text. How many ways of organizing and connecting the "chairman's" ideas did the writer(s) use? We have numbered the paragraphs for later reference.

Move 1: Organize the text around your key points
Move 2: Arrange ideas from general to particular
Move 3: Use a standard rhetorical pattern to connect ideas
Move 4: Construct an argument with claims and evidence
Move 5: Make a rhetorical move
Move 6: Develop prose from graphic texts

TEXT MOVE 1: ORGANIZE THE TEXT AROUND YOUR KEY POINTS

In Chapter Three, we used a **topical issue tree** to show how writers connect ideas, based both on plans *to say* and plans *to do*. The issue tree places the most important and inclusive ideas at the top and branches other ideas beneath it to show the basic development of thought. This form of outlining, like more traditional kinds, can represent plans for what to say and how to say it and can guide the development of a draft.

Writers, then, can develop their ideas by answering a basic question, *What do I want to say?* and then *arrange their ideas according to their* **key points.** In the shareowners' letter, it looks to us as though the writer began by answering our question as set out on page 172:

Chairman's Letter to Shareowners

Paragraphs	
1	Often the greatest opportunities in life come disguised as insurmountable problems.
2	When the breakup of AT&T was first announced in January 1982, some people said that Pacific Telesis Group was going to have a hard time making it as an independent corporation.
3	We never bought this line of reasoning. Neither did our 1.3 million shareowners.
4	Our strong 1984 results speak for themselves.
5	Pacific Telesis Group earned $829 million on revenues of $7.8 billion. Our earnings per share of $8.46 exceeded our original projection of $8.00 by 5.8 percent. The corporation's 1984 dividend totaled $5.40.
6	What happened? How did the corporation that many observers predicted would be the biggest loser in the AT&T breakup turn out to be one of the biggest winners?
7	To answer that question, you have to go back to 1980, when we developed and began implementing a strategy to modernize our network, reduce our cost and improve our sometimes difficult relationship with our primary state regulator, the California Public Utilities Commission.
8	Our employees mobilized to make it work. And work it did. More specifically:
8a	• Our expenses in 1984 were 5.7 percent below our original projection. Particularly successful were the cost-control efforts of the employees of our Bell Operating Companies. Pacific Bell's expenses per telephone line (we call them "access" lines) improved by 12 percent over 1983.
8b.1	• Second, Pacific and Nevada Bell have invested heavily in the last five years to expand and modernize their core networks. New technologies produce a double bonus for investors. Besides improving efficiency, they increase the range of products and services we have to market.
8b.2	One result of this effort is reflected in the strong 1984 performance of the people in Pacific Bell's marketing organization. Factoring out divestiture-related changes in long distance revenues, the company billed 12 percent more revenues in 1984 than in 1983. The increase in billed business revenues was even higher--nearly 14 percent. These results represent the greatest one year increase since 1974.

Our earnings per share of $8.46 exceeded our original projection of $8.00 by 5.8 percent

8c	• Third and very importantly, we've built a relationship with the California Public Utilities Commission based on mutual respect and

FIGURE 4–5

Pacific Telesis Group
Shareowner's Letter.

trust. The Commission has become a national leader in responsibly addressing the many public issues left unresolved by divestiture--a subject I'll return to later on in this letter.

9   The Commission has been particularly attentive to balancing the legitimate interests of consumers and investors. In 1984, Pacific Bell

---

If you cry "Forward," you'd better make it plain in which direction to go.

---

received a total of $565 million in new rates. At the same time, however, we have worked closely with the Commission to assure that universal access to basic telephone services remains affordable.

10   **Our Road to the Future**
As a result of our efforts over the last five years, Pacific Telesis today enjoys a strong financial and operating position.

11   Most important to investors, however, is not where a corporation has been, but where it's going.

12   But--to paraphrase the playwright Anton Chekhov--if you cry "Forward," you'd better make it plain in which direction to go.

13   Setting our course for the future occupied much of our planning during 1984. We took a hard look at our experience and expertise. We catalogued our strengths and assessed those of our competitors. And we evaluated--critically and carefully--how we could use our strengths to tap the real growth available in today's Information Age marketplace.

14   The result: We now know the road to our future--and we've laid out a clear road map to get us there.

15   The short term prognosis for our core business--our Bell Operating Companies--is good.

16   Our markets continue to grow--not just in absolute numbers--but in the demand for increasingly sophisticated telecommunications services as well.

17   This is the advantage of doing business in California and Nevada.

18   And we're moving aggressively to capitalize on that advantage to increase the value of your investment:

18a.1   • We're moving to bring "equal access" to Californians and Nevadans. Right now, in most locations, if you want to use a long distance company other than AT&T, you must dial as many as 24 numbers to complete your call. That won't be the case much longer. By September 1986, approximately 75 percent of our customer lines will be equipped for equal access to interexchange (long distance) companies. And, under our current modernization program, virtually all customers' lines will be so equipped by 1992.

18a.2   We're not taking this step just because it's a nice thing to do. The interexchange companies currently generate close to one-third of our revenues--it's simply good business to give them what they want when they want it.

FIGURE 4–5,
continued

18b • Over the long term, Pacific and Nevada Bell face ever increasing competition in nearly every aspect of their business. So we're also moving to face the Bell Operating Companies toward the marketplace. To maintain existing markets and create new ones, we've restructured Pacific and Nevada Bell's marketing organization into six segments-- each devoted to analyzing and meeting the technological and service needs of our six key customer groups. We're also developing and marketing a variety of new data and voice services--over 70 in all--to meet market needs.

18c • Finally, we're taking the necessary steps to help ensure the long-term financial health of Pacific Bell. In January 1985, the company filed a rate request with the California Public Utilities Commission. If granted, it will speed up the critical process of capital recovery and increase Pacific Bell's return on equity to a level competitive with other investments with similar risk characteristics.

Why Diversify?

19 One question that I hear from time to time is this. If Pacific and Nevada Bell are doing so well, why are you creating *new* businesses? In other words, why diversify?

20 The breakup of the Bell System gave Pacific Telesis many new options--including the opportunity to enter new lines of business from which we'd been excluded in the past.

21 A lot of critical thinking went into our decision to diversify. We carefully assessed the opportunities and risks in today's rapidly developing Information Age marketplace. And we determined that we had value to bring to this marketplace-- value that could be tapped to help your investment grow.

22 It's important to note here that it's you, our shareowners, who are bearing the risks associated with diversification. California and Nevada ratepayers are not funding these efforts. And, just as importantly, it's you who will reap diversification's rewards. What rewards?

23 Diversification improves our ability to sustain long-term real earnings growth. Our new, diversified businesses have no "authorized" return on equity. Their potential is limited only by the ingenuity and

---

We have no intention of becoming an uncoordinated conglomerate.

---

hard work of the managers who run them. These managers understand that, over time, they're expected to produce a return on your investment dollar that is higher than the authorized return on equity of Pacific or Nevada Bell.

24 Having said that, however, I want to emphasize one very important point. We have no intention of becoming an uncoordinated conglomerate. We intend to operate four or five distinct, major lines of business--and expand each one horizontally and vertically for maximum return to investors.

FIGURE 4–5,
continued

25   Our diversified businesses didn't make a profit in 1984. We didn't expect them to. But we did build shareowner value in these businesses through carefully selected investments.

26   Diversification is an investment in the future of Pacific Telesis--with a payoff for you that will ultimately come in a higher return on equity than those authorized for Pacific and Nevada Bell.

The State of Public Policy

27   Over the past 15 years, a series of decisions--by the Courts, federal regulators, and others--have been made to increase competition in the telecommunications industry. While noble in intent, these decisions have been made in a piecemeal manner with no overall strategy in mind.

28   As a result, consumers and investors, and the corporations like Pacific Telesis who serve them, are faced with an industry that has been deregulated, reregulated and totally restructured.

29   The time has come to address outstanding issues--to forge new policies that serve consumers and investors.

30   We are determined to play a vigorous and responsible role in achieving the consensus necessary for our industry to move ahead. The issues are many and complex; I won't attempt to detail them all here.

31   They include federal regulatory restrictions that prevent the core network from becoming all that it can be. Our telecommuncations network is an enormous asset, and yet we are restricted from providing many sophisticated services that would increase its flexibility and usefulness.

32   Ultimately, that serves neither consumers nor investors. At Pacific Telesis, we believe that any and every corporation ought to be able to enhance its technology to the limit. That way, consumers have the widest possible array of options.

33   Having said that, we realize that public access to local telephone service is viewed as an entitlement in our society. The California Public Utilities Commission and the California Legislature have taken a national leadership role in making sure that subsidized "Lifeline" service is targeted to those who couldn't otherwise afford it.

The time has come to forge new public policies that serve both consumers and investors.

We support them wholeheartedly. And we will continue to work to shape a public policy that guarantees subsidized access to those who need it--without unnecessarily subsidizing those who do not.

34   **The Future of Your Investment**
A corporation, particularly one as new as ours, must operate with a clearly articulated and widely understood vision of its future if its businesses are to succeed and its owners to prosper.

FIGURE 4–5,
continued

35 This simple but critical concept has driven all of our efforts during the past year.

36 We began with one central imperative--to continually increase the value of your investment.

37 In the preceding pages, I've described to you our strategies for deploying technology, marketing technology and diversifying into new lines of business where our skills and experience give us a competitive advantage.

38 I've talked about our determination to help resolve outstanding public policy issues which prevent the core telecommunications network from becoming all that it can be.

39 But there's another, very significant factor I haven't mentioned. I'm talking about the people who work for the Pacific Telesis Group companies. Many have worked here for years. They have the experience and capabilities to make sure we succeed.

40 Others have joined us fairly recently. We've hired some of the most capable people in the country to augment the skills of our existing employees--to give us the right mix of talent to make your investment grow.

41 I can think of no more concrete example of our determination to increase the value of your investment than the stake our employees have in their corporation's future.

42 Like you, most of them are Pacific Telesis shareowners.

43 Even more importantly, starting in 1985, up to 20 percent of the salaries of our nearly 23,000 managers will depend on the financial performance of the Pacific Telesis company they work for.

44 In other words, how well our investors do will directly determine how well our managers do.

45 We're pleased with the results of our first year of independence. We're grateful for your support and intend to spare no effort to justify your continued confidence.

46 But I'm not satisfied yet. And neither is anyone else who works here.

47 The road to our corporate future is bright with opportunity. We know exactly where we're going, and we have the strategy, the skills and the people to make sure we get there.

48 There's a proverb that, to me, captures our determination quite well:

49 "It's not enough to aim--you must hit."

50 Let me assure you of one thing--Pacific Telesis Group doesn't intend to miss.

Donald E. Guinn
Chairman and Chief Executive Officer
February 13, 1985

FIGURE 4–5,
continued

What do I want to say?

¶ 2 (*Who are we?*) PTG as an independent corporation . . .

¶ 4 (*What we have accomplished?*) 1984 results . . .

¶ 7 (*Our history*) Go back to 1980 . . .

¶ 8 (*How we did it*) Our employees mobilized to make it work . . .

¶11 (*Where we're headed*) Not where a corporation has been, but where it's going . . .

The letter continues on to cover diversification, public policy, and introduce the personnel and character of the company. The answers to the question, *What do I want to say?* could simply translate into a **plan to say,** a traditional outline, such as,

I	Introduction	Who are we?
		What have we accomplished?
		Our history
		How we did it
II	Body	Our future investments
		Diversification
		Public policies
III	Closing	Our concept
		Personnel

However, an issue tree is sometimes a better conceptual tool for developing a paper because it presents the relative weight of ideas as well as how they will be developed. And, issue trees tend to reflect **plans to do,** what you want to accomplish as a writer. An issue tree and plan for the same content in the body might look like the plans in Figure 4–6.

The introductory and closing nods to success and personnel are of course important in such a letter, since the purpose of an annual report is to document returns and predict growth. But this second plan reveals what we think is the most important goal in the shareowner's letter, to ask for approval for new direction and policy.

TEXT MOVE 2: ARRANGE IDEAS FROM GENERAL TO PARTICULAR (OR VICE-VERSA)

Some ideas seem to come with a comfortable sense of order, but going from a plan to a draft often asks you to make that relationship much more explicit. One simple but effective relationship is the move from general to particular. Going from general to particular points or vice-versa (from a specific instance to a broader claim) creates a simple but clear relationship. Here are some examples found in the shareowners' letter.

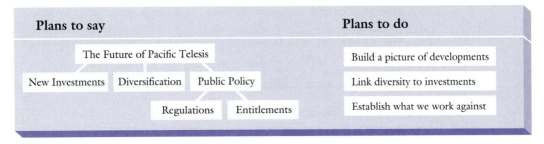

FIGURE 4–6
Alternative Ways to Envision Your Key Points.

Write from **general to particular** to order your details and to support your claims:

General	We're moving aggressively to increase the value of your investment:	(¶18)
Particular	We are moving to bring "equal access" to give interexchange companies what they want	(¶18a)
	to face companies toward the marketplace	(¶18b)
	We are taking the necessary steps to help ensure the long-term financial health of Pacific Bell.	(¶18c)

Write from **particular to general** to lead your reader to a position or conclusion:

Particular	The breakup of the Bell System gave many new options	(¶20)
	A lot of critical thinking went into our decision	(¶21)
	You are bearing the risks	(¶22)
	You will reap diversification's rewards.	
General	Diversification improves our ability to sustain long-term *real-earnings* growth	(¶23)

Another way to think about using the general-particular text move is to represent differing **levels of abstractness** to a reader. Each time you write a new sentence it will either either go up, down, or remain equal in the level of abstractness (or thus concreteness). Language researchers have noticed that paragraphs often follow this pattern:

Topic Sentence	General Statement	High level of abstractness
Detail	Particular	Lower level
Detail	Particular	Same level
Detail	Particular	Same level
Concluding Sentence	General Statement	High level of abstractness

And here is how a paragraph from the shareowner's letter on the topic of "equal access" (18) actually sounds as it move up and down from abstract to concrete and back to abstract.

We're moving to bring equal access to Californians and Nevadans	High
If you want to use a LD company, you must dial as many as 24 numbers	Lower
That won't be the case much longer	Higher
By 1986, approximately 75 percent of customer lines will have equal access	Lower
Virtually all customer lines will be so equipped by 1992	Same
We're not taking this step just because it's a nice thing to do	Higher

Use this strategy to make sure you have developed your discussion at both the high and low levels of abstraction, but without taking the reader on a roller coaster ride. Move from general to particular to explain and support your key points. Move from particular to general in order to make a key point.

TEXT MOVE 3: USE A STANDARD RHETORICAL PATTERN TO CONNECT IDEAS

The effort to develop your thoughts and plans by connecting ideas may lead you to consider other ways to build an argument: Do you want to start by making a controversial claim (e.g., *PTG should diversify!*) and then support it? Or do you want to engage the reader with a vivid description of why the last year was successful? Here is where **rhetorical patterns** come to your aid, suggesting a number of options for reasoning with a reader. Notice that these patterns are not themselves answers to what to write or how, much less how to address a rhetorical situation. Only in school will you be asked, at times, to purposely write with one pattern or another to practice that pattern (as in the infamous "comparison/contrast paper").

Here are five of the most common rhetorical patterns and their key features:

The Pattern	Its Features
Narrative or chronological order	Sequences and drama
Description	Attributes, specific detail, parts to whole, series
Comparison	Differences and similarities
Causality	One event or circumstance leading to another
Problem-solution	A solution to a problem or answer to a question

Ideas to Action

These rhetorical patterns can be used to build a relationship between ideas at a local and global level. To see how they work locally, try to identify some of the key rhetorical patterns used in the shareowners' letter to organize a paragraph or short sequence of paragraphs. We have given you a start.

¶4	Our strong 1984 results speak for themselves	*description*
¶6	What happened? How did the corporation turn out to be one of the biggest winners?	*problem-solution*
¶8	Our expenses were 5.7 percent below our original projection	??
¶8b.2	One result of this effort	??
¶13	Setting our course for the future	??
¶18a.2	We're not taking this step just because	??

Are these the only places a standard rhetorical pattern appears in this document? These rhetorical patterns are often used to develop whole sections or arguments as well at to link individual sentences. What is the smallest and the largest a chunk of text organized by one of these patterns in the shareowners' letter?

Narrative and Chronological Order (sequences and drama)

Chronological order arranges ideas in order of occurrence over time. If you were to tick off daily events in a week, you would be using a chronology. The advantage of this strategy is that it is easily recognized and followed. **Narrative** structure also is chronological—stories unfold as a sequence of events—but readers also expect stories to have a beginning, middle, and end with some sort of drama and a conclusion. Narratives often have the structure outlined below in which the symbol → means *leads to:*

Setting (place, characters)→
   Episode→
     Conflict→
       Development→
         Climax→
           Resolution

Narrative differs from a simple chronology because it contains conflict and drama. Note the uses of chronology and narration in the shareholder letter.

The opening sentences offer a tiny story of the breakup of AT&T with the tension of impending doom as an independent company splits off from a conglomerate. Use narration when drama can make a point or pique interest and use chronology when a transaction or procedure needs to be told in detail.

Description (attributes, specific details, parts to whole, a series)

Any time a detailed illustration of something is needed, writers use description. Rhetorically, **description** teaches by giving a closer, more complete look at something, or by giving an example. Readers respond to description because it enables them to make connections to their experience.

The annual report, because of space, cannot provide a description of every development. But, including an example helps to make the abstract notions of "diversification" and company growth more real. Later in the annual report that follows the shareowners' letter, the writers advertise the goal of "targeting technology for flexibility and profit." They include a description of one such target, an office complex that can provide a host of telecommunications products and services. If, in another piece of writing, it became important to describe this particular complex, we can imagine a lengthy treatment of specific products and services and how they interlock and are made available to the public.

One way to vary descriptive writing is to present a **collection**—a review of the parts that make up a whole or a series of items (i.e., the six necessary ingredients for success). Writers sometimes argue for the complexity or value of an idea simply by showing all of its parts (e.g., an annual report will demonstrate a company's development by listing and describing its network of distribution). Or writers may use description to show the flow of information or even company priorities by describing the organizational structure and how its regions of service are divided along state boundaries, technical levels, or economic profiles.

Comparisons (similarities-differences)

Comparisons are often used to define an idea or as evidence for why something is weak, strong, successful, doomed, etc. Note that many auto ads for American cars involve some sort of comparison with Asian or European products to claim similarities or new improvements. Comparisons can be used to shape entire documents, and political speeches, for instance, are often a comparison of what the present administration has or has not done and what the contender will do or plans to do. Comparisons generally follow two patterns:

1. Compare	All features of A with	All features of B
2. Compare	Feature 1 of A with	Feature 1 of B
	Feature 2 of A with	Feature 2 of B

Both have rhetorical advantages. The first emphasizes the totality of the persons, things, or events compared, and enables the writer to conclude by spending more time and attention on the stronger of the two (or more) for comparison. The second shifts the attention away from the subjects of the comparison and more toward the features by which the comparison is made.

Causality (if-then, antecedent-consequence)

Causality organizes ideas around a pattern of **cause and effect:** because this happened, this will follow. Or, if we we see these events, we can predict the following. Notice how this pattern, unlike description, forces you to make (and support) an inference that one event actually causes another or will cause it. The fact that one event followed another (the rhetorical pattern of chronology), does not prove event A *caused* event B. Politicians use causality when they point out the gloomy past as a reason to support them in a rosy future. Organizations use causality to make cases for investments and reorganization.

In the shareowners' letter, under "Our Road for the Future" (10 and following), the company reports "taking a hard look . . ." by cataloguing the company's and competitor's strengths. Their explicit (stated) claim is that they "enjoy a strong financial and operating position"; the implicit (unstated, implied) claim is that you should continue to invest in us *because:*

A. The short-term prognosis is good (and)
B. Our markets continue to grow (because)
C. We have the advantage of doing business in California and Nevada (and so)
D. We're moving aggressively to capitalize. . . .

The key to using causality is to build a case that supports your claim of cause and effect. Sometimes the case or situation can simply be referred to, such as the breakup of AT&T. But for other audiences, the case must be carefully built so that the reader understands and accepts your reasons for asserting that a cause-and-effect relationship really exists.

Problem-Solution (question-answer)

The problem-solution pattern is a common one in business because it is highly persuasive and can include other patterns of reasoning. With the problem-solution pattern and its variations (such as question-answer), the writer begins with a shared, recognizable problem, situation, or question and progressively moves to a solution supported by evaluation. This makes the problem-solution pattern a basic move in proposals and many reports. In Chapter Two we offered a checklist of things to do in analyzing a problem, moves that could also help you to organize a draft:

1. Start with a *problem/purpose statement* that defines
   - the conflict or key issue
   - as a shared problem
   - in an operational way.

2. *Analyze* the problem in a way that
   - identifies the issues or subproblems and
   - sees alternative ways of responding.

3. *Conclude* in a way that
   - redefines the problem or points to action,
   - recognizes alternative conclusions, and
   - suggests a usable path of action if appropriate.

This pattern for conducting a **problem-analysis** focuses most of the writer's attention on problem finding: on understanding and analyzing what makes a situation so problematic. Compare this to the **problem-solution** pattern (in Figure 4–7) which focuses more attention on arguing for a particular solution. We have illustrated this problem-solution text move with examples from the shareowners' letter (¶19 and following).

A key to this text move is how well the writer establishes the problem and context and how well he or she evaluates them. In the shareowners' letter, the writer assumed a fair amount of agreement, so that the steps to evaluate or even to establish a context are minimal. In other problem-solution texts, such as an unsolicited proposal, these steps require lots of detail.

Read through the shareowners' letter to get a general sense of how this text move works, but then realize that there are endless variations on the five-step progression outlined here. We present evaluation as the fourth step, but you could insert it as soon as you establish a context and problem as criteria a successful solution needs to meet. And the cycle of problem-solution-evaluation could be repeated if a solution had a number of parts to be considered (and accepted) one by one.

TEXT MOVE 4: CONSTRUCT AN ARGUMENT WITH CLAIMS AND EVIDENCE

Businesspeople often write and speak to inform or to persuade. Persuasive writing, such as proposals can be arranged according to a series of claims, with each each claim supported by evidence. **Claims** are statements made as assertions of value, such as *Buying Digi-Tech's software is the best solution to your company's informational needs,* or assertions of fact, such as

1. **Establish a problem** as an opening claim, question, or hypothesis.
   Why Diversify?

2. **Establish the problem's context,** history, features (using other text moves).
   The breakup of the Bell System gave Pacific Telesis many new options...

3. **Make a claim or provide a solution** based on the problem and context.
   Diversification improves our ability to sustain long-term growth...

4. **Evaluate,** with specific criteria, the solution advanced against the problem and context.
   We carefully assessed the risks in today's rapidly developing marketplace...

5. **Conclude** by reaffirming the solution or adding new solutions and questions.
   We have no intention of becoming an uncoordinated conglomerate.

FIGURE 4–7

The Five-step Problem Solution Pattern.

Digi-Tech's software package offers unique features. In persuasive communication, some readers will assume that some of your claims are true some of the time. But important claims always depend on some form of supporting evidence or data that either you or the reader can supply. The types of **evidence** typically used to support claims are:

Authority, testimony	We've been in the business for 40 years . . .
Statistics, data	Only 5 percent of our products need repair . . .
	The majority of our customers return to us . . .
Examples, Cases	We have a number of satisfied customers who say . . .
	The Johnsons are typical and they . . .
Comparison	Let's compare features of the new Alfa Romeos . . .
Definition	The features of our product fit your needs. First, . . .

Warrants are the underlying assumptions or the reasoning that says why the evidence actually supports a claim. In most writing and speaking, these assumptions or warrants go unstated. Sometimes, however, if an audience is new or wary, writers include explicit warrants to go along with claims and evidence. The strength of a claim often rests on the acceptance of warrants as much as on the presence of evidence. In marketing a car, this trio of claim, evidence, warrant could be:

Claim	Ford products are better than GM's.
Evidence	We have a lower rate of return on new vehicles.
Warrant	Our return rate is a reliable indicator of dependability, and dependability is a primary test of a "good" product.

Warrants often operate beneath the explicit surface of texts, leaving much writing based on explicit claims and supporting evidence and *presumed* warrants for accepting their relationship. But would everyone agree with this warrant, that the evidence of lower return rate (strongly) supports the larger claim? Looking at your own unstated warrants as well as your evidence is a way to anticipate places your readers might remain skeptical or even raise rival hypotheses.

Claims, evidence, and warrants can be used to evaluate and organize a text as it develops. If you are building a draft, first choose the major claims you wish to make and arrange them in a reasonable order. (Here you might draw on another text move, such as comparison, or particular to general.) Organizing your claims may show you where you need transitions between claims as you imagine how a reader might respond. Next, decide what evidence you can mount to support your claims, what you need to present, and in what detail. Finally, decide where your warrants or assumption need to be made explicit. Your draft, as an abstract format, could be arranged somewhat like this:

Major claim

Minor claim #1
   Evidence

Minor claim #2
   Evidence
   Warrants

Major claim

Let us see how claims can be used to structure a lengthy piece of writing. For this text move, we refer to a different piece of writing: An architect we know wrote an unsolicited proposal for a recreational water facility in the West. Since he was not responding to an RFP and was writing to a fairly general audience, one that did not necessarily agree with the need for the project, the proposal was constructed mostly as an argument, centering on key claims. In this proposal, the argument for the lake development rested on five claims that, if accepted, collectively supported the main claim—that the project was worthwhile and should be funded. Less important were the methods and resources for fulfilling the proposed development. If the architect cannot gather support, there is no reason to explain how the job will be done.

Figure 4–8 gives an outline extracted from the full proposal, highlighting the claims and evidence used with some of the unstated warrants included in parentheses. Since warrants are supported by beliefs and values as much as reasoning, we will point out that the warrants we list may not be recognized by other readers of this proposal or others close to arguments over the use of natural resources. Our position is that development is not necessarily the

Major claims	Lake Wasatch is good for our state.
	Accept our development proposal (and give us money).
Minor claim #1	Growth for a desert area is tied to water management.
Evidence	We have rationed water in the past.
Evidence	Growth is predicted.
Warrant	*(Water is a key to maintaining the current quality of life, one that all area residents value.)*
Minor claim #2	The lake will open property for development.
Evidence	There are 200,000 acres of shoreline.
Claim #2a	Engineering will stabilize this shoreline.
Evidence	Other developments show success.
Warrant	*(Increased property values are highly desirable.)*
Minor claim #3	The lake will extend recreational possibilities.
Evidence	There are 50,000 registered boats in the area.
Evidence	Other lakes and bays are overcrowded.
Minor claim #4	Recreation and development will promote tourism.
Evidence	4 million visitors come to the area each year.
Claim #4a	They leave after a short visit with nothing else to do
Minor claim #5	The improved lake will also provide waterfowl habitat.
Claim #5a	The improved lake will be compatible with wildlife.
Claim #5b	Sportsmen will enjoy the hunting
Warrant	*(Hunting is the preferred way to enjoy waterfowl.)*

FIGURE 4–8

Major Claims, Evidence, and Warrants in an Architect's Proposal.

best use of natural lands, and that development usually favors those with the money, time, and values to enjoy it.

Lake Wasatch is a proposed freshwater development along the western shores of the Great Salt Lake near Salt Lake City, Utah. We paraphrase to abbreviate the architect's writing.

This proposal is a good example of persuasive writing structured around a list of claims and evidence that could pass easily as a proposal based on reported information. But since water use is a controversial issue in the West, we think the argument could be stronger if some of the warrants were discussed explicitly, given an audience that included those in favor and against additional development of natural resources. This brief outline illustrates how much of the architect's case rested on assumptions about his audience; he presumes that the broad goals to develop natural resources and to promote (and spend money on) a certain life style are uniformly attractive.

Persuasive writing may revolve around one central claim or appear as a series of claims linked through some chain of reasoning. Generally, in business writing, long chains of claims that depend on step-by-step acceptance are not well received for two reasons. People on the job read for specific purposes and are often in a hurry. The most persuasive argument is often a specific response to a specific problem.

TEXT MOVE 5: READ AND WRITE FOR RHETORICAL MOVES

So far, we have described **text moves** as a way to build (and organize) your draft using topics, levels of abstraction, standard patterns of reasoning, and argument. These moves all depend on conventional and rather abstract patterns. But what if you were to see your text as acting out a real conversation with a reader in which each party had a reason to read and to write (which includes trying to understand the other). Then you would start to look at your text as a set of very specific rhetorical moves—moves that depend on a writer's common sense and savvy about the situation. **Rhetorical moves** are a strategic attempt to anticipate the needs, questions, or responses readers in a discourse community will have and to respond to them in the text. This means writers often decide to make this rhetorical move rather than that one by carefully reading the rhetorical situation or listening to the conversation that preceded this paragraph or this text. For example, will the novice reader of this technical manual (or the prospective investor in the company) be looking for some reassurance or an overview, or can you just plunge into a technical discussion?

Another way to imagine a savvy rhetorical move is to ask, *What do readers in this specific community expect?* The term *rhetorical move* is also used by linguists to refer to a pattern of information that has become common in a particular discourse community. For example, biology research reports typically contain a review of literature (i.e., a review of previous research) and one study showed how writers of these reviews normally make four basic rhetorical moves.[1] Figure 4–9 names these four moves and shows where they fit into the format of a typical research report. However, the names are less important than the questions they seek to answer. These rhetorical moves in science writing are designed to answer four basic questions that readers (i.e., other scientists) are likely to be asking. And if a writer fails, for example, to make the rhetorical move that demonstrates a meaningful "gap" in our knowledge, many scientists would see no need to read on.

Where do rhetorical moves come from? They are not found, for the most part, in textbooks or guidelines such as the format model for a research

Research Report Format	Rhetorical Moves	What the Readers Want to Know
Abstract		
Review of literature ————	{Field of Study	*What part of biology does this address?*
	{Previous Research	*What are the related studies?*
	{Gap	*What solution or new information do you provide?*
	{New Research	*How will you accomplish that research?*
Methods		
Findings		
Discussion		
References		

FIGURE 4–9

Rhetorical Moves in Biology Literature Reviews.

report. They can be figured out, however, by doing a close rhetorical reading of a model or specific text example and by asking yourself, "What information does the reader need to participate in this discourse community?" (see Chapter Two).

Our shareowners' letter can be read for its rhetorical moves, stated as questions from the reader. If you took the time to read through the entire letter, you might have heard the conversation between a reader and the writer taking place. Figure 4–10 shows the format for an annual report and some common rhetorical moves found in the letter. It is important to note that these five moves are not an exact fit to the Pacific Telesis Group's CEO's letter, but were extracted from our reading of 30 annual reports.

Rhetorical moves are a powerful strategy for drafting, because you are basically answering the questions that readers want answered. The questions themselves have an order and your response can be further developed using any of the text moves we have introduced. But the catch is *finding* the right rhetorical moves. One way to uncover rhetorical moves is to talk to writers who know a task or discourse community so well they can tell you what readers are looking for. Or you can find them, as we did above, by reading a number of examples to extract the common questions they address.

Rhetorical moves do have a progression to them: The first makes a place for or motivates the second, and so on. The review of literature in scientific reports funnels the reader down, making the best case for new research. The letter to shareholders wins confidence with good news and then elaborates the case for the strength of the company. As you read and search for rhetorical moves, notice how writers purposely vary their moves to fit their purposes and audiences. For example, the shareowners' letter we included began with a piece of philosophy and a false prediction to set the stage.

Annual Report Format	Rhetorical Moves	What the Readers are Looking for
Financial Highlights		
Shareowners' Letter ———	{ The good news, profits	*Did my investments make me money?*
	{ How we pulled it off	*What is their strategy?*
	{ Market developments	*How is the company growing to protect my money?*
	{ Internal developments	*Where and how was the profit reinvested?*
	{ Goals for the future	*What can we expect next year and thereafter?*
Operations, Facilities		
Financial Data		
Discussion, Analysis of Data		
Management and Organization		
Investor Information		

FIGURE 4–10

Rhetorical Moves in Shareowners' Letters in Annual Reports.

Most companies, however, quickly move to the bottom line, their best and clearest statement of their success.

TEXT MOVE 6: DEVELOP PROSE FROM GRAPHIC IDEAS

This last text move is our attempt to recognize that many people like to work graphically before they write or to shuttle back and forth between sketching and writing as they develop a draft. Studies of composing processes in writing have revealed how writers in some rhetorical situations prefer to compose and think in **images.** As their notes and early drafts show, they have "written" their texts by sketching with lines, arrows, trees, boxes and by creating images of what they have to say or how it is organized.

This creative process cannot be detailed here, but we want to encourage those writers who develop their prose by first working graphically. The rhetorical process begins the same, with a close reading of a rhetorical situation, but out of that writers may create an image that predicts or echoes the structure of their eventual written texts. Here is one example. Architects commonly begin with hand-drawn or computer-generated sketches that function as some of the basic conceptual work in composing a building and a written, summary report of the building's "program." In Figure 4–11a and b, we find an architect's "bubble" diagrams that are refined, over time, to the spatial grid found in the main floor space diagram.

In Figure 4–11c, we find further refinements on the building plans in a functional relationship matrix, which organizes the spaces of the building in

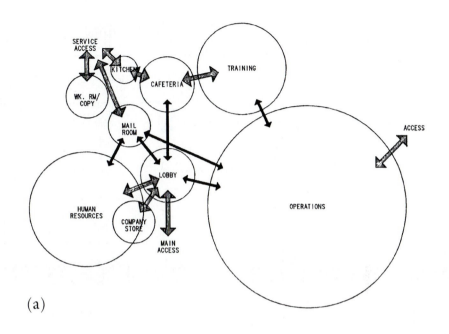

(a)

(b)

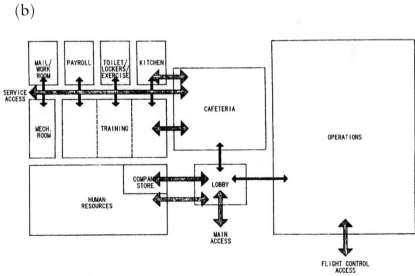

FIGURE 4–11a and b

Bubble and Space
Diagrams in Architecture

MAIN FLOOR SPACE DIAGRAM

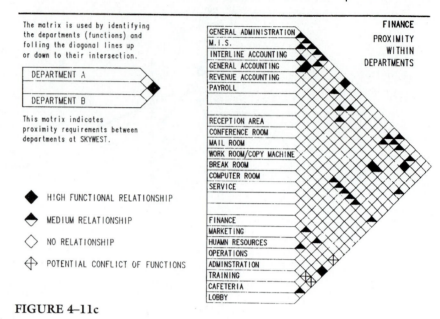

FIGURE 4–11c

list form and by proximity requirements. The composing process will continue to generate different representations of the building requirements, which are finally presented in a summary report (see Figure 4–12). For the architect and for many other writers, composing for a rhetorical situation demands multiple fluencies with images and texts, and one form of composing helps to create and revise the other.

There are endless variations on how writers creatively sketch and model their ideas as they move to create a draft, including outlines and issue trees. These graphic tools also remind us that the strategies we have looked at for developing a draft are not limited to creating a *printed text*.

WHEN A WRITTEN DRAFT INVITES A SPOKEN TEXT

We began this chapter where most people begin in a rhetorical situation—with the decision to speak or write. In this decision process people choose a level of formality and medium. Formality is shaped by the stage at which the draft is published and shared as a written message and by the media chosen. For example, the draft of an idea may be shared as it develops

SUMMARY

FINDINGS: Valentiner Architects has prepared the following document to assist in the design of AirFare Airlines new corporate office building. The purpose of the study was to accomplish the following:

1. To obtain information concerning the present level of personnel, space utilization, functional requirements, equipment use, and functional relationships of the different departments within the existing facility, and;

2. To develop space requirements and functional relationships of all departments based on actual current needs and projected future needs.

To gather information on current conditions, Valentiner Architects met with AirFare and interviewed the various department heads.

The results of this study cover AirFare's estimated space requirements for the next seven years (see chart in space utilization). This study shows a steady increase in space requirements at both the corporate building in downtown St. Louis and at the St. Louis Airport building.

At the corporate office, the finance, marketing, customer service, human resources, and general office spaces were evaluated. Current space requirements account for a total of 21,690 square feet for FY1990. This exeeds the current space available at the building by nearly 4,000 square feet. However, based on space utilization projections for FY1997, this deficiency will amount to nearly 11,000 square feet.

At the airport facilities in St. Louis, the operations and maintenance office space was evaluated. Current space needs account for a total of approximately 9,000 square feet which equals the current space available. Projections for FY1995 show a deficit of approximately 4,000 square feet.

At both of AirFare's operations in St. Louis, there is clearly a growing need for space which will result in major deficiencies within the next five years.

As the first phase of the Space Utilization Program was completed, a major restructuring of the corporate organization was put into effect. The final report that follows incorporates these changes. The following chart shows the corporate administrative structure.

The final phase of the program will be to determine technical requirements for each work area or individual space. Forms used for this analysis are enclosed under Client Data.

FIGURE 4–12

Functional Relationship Matrix and Report Summary

via not only computer mail but by voice mail or in an oral presentation. In that case, the writer becomes a speaker.

Speakers also need models and text moves to work from, and most of what we have presented as strategies in this chapter can be used to plan and draft an oral presentation. We end this chapter by pointing out that most written drafts invite or require companion spoken texts. When you write, the final, delivered text only ceremonially ends the paper trail because writing is usually supported through spoken delivery, negotiation, and collaboration. If you draft a memo, letter, essay, or report, you should also consider how to support it with a spoken message. How, for example, could you preview the purpose, argument, major claims, or key ideas of your formal text in other forms and media that would get the attention of busy readers and help them see how to read it?

Chapter Eight offers some guidelines for how to present your ideas orally in formal and informal settings, for how to use visual aids, and for how to listen and participate in oral presentations and conversations. A key strategy in drafting any of these presentation is knowing what to extract from your written text, which we will look at now.

STRATEGY 6: FINDING THE GIST TO DEVELOP AN ORAL PRESENTATION

Writing and speaking differ in some important ways. First of all, writing is tangible. A written text can be stored, revised, and shared. It can be studied and perfected, and its permanence is the reason why written text solidifies many important decisions and negotiations in the workplace. Writing, however, asks you to spell our your ideas and reasons more fully, to anticipate the needs and biases of your readers. When you speak, this need for explicitness can be balanced, somewhat, by the presence of an audience who can ask questions and nod when they understand or if they do not. The physical connection between speaker and listener makes the text interactive, shared, negotiated.

Therefore, all of a written text need not be presented and Strategy 6 helps you to condense information to the essential ideas for a listening audience. In formal and informal settings, listeners are searching for the **gist** of a communication. As Figure 4–13 illustrates, experienced speakers plan ahead by separating their key points from supporting information and deciding on the gist *they* want the listener to walk away with. This gist is turned into a spoken text and into visual aids that repeat and reinforce the gist.

Here are some of the key steps in this process:

> *Step 1:* Highlight the key problem or question and the key claims that drive your writing. Even in formal presentations, speakers never

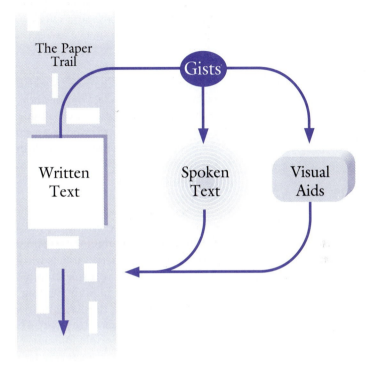

FIGURE 4–13

Using Gists to Turn a
Written Text into a
Spoken Text.

cover as much ground as writers do. So as a speaker your goal is to leave the audience—not with a lot of confusing information, but with your gist, with one or two key points they will remember.

Step 2: Once you have your gist (the issue and your key points), choose an organizational plan that is simple and clearly focused on your gist. In many cases, the rhetorical pattern used in your written text may be too complicated—it will have too many parts and too many details— to work in an oral presentation.

Step 3: Given the time you have to speak, the format, and interest of your listening audience, choose the supporting details that are necessary and appropriate. Delete secondary information which exists in your draft as elaborations, lower levels of abstraction, and extended examples. In fact, one or two good examples or stories, which you take the time to develop, are usually more effective than a number of supporting details that you must rush over or cram into the talk.

Step 4: Select key illustrations and graphics from the text that will help complete your illustration, or develop new ones that simplify and condense information from the text. Handouts that cover key points help listeners follow your talk and remember what you had to say.

See also Chapter Two for strategies for informational and rhetorical reading, to find the key and purposeful ideas in a written text. Rhetorical moves 1 to 4 in Strategy 5 can also help.

Summary

- When you decide **whether to speak or write,** and whether to use a formal or informal mode, consider not only efficiency but the importance of maintaining a record versus dialogue and immediacy.
- **Boilerplate** (text borrowed from prior documents) is an efficient choice for business documents—if it actually fits your situation (Strategy 1).
- **Imitating a specific text**—when it is not confused with plagiarism—lets you take advantage of what can be learned from the paper trail (Strategy 2).
- A **generic model,** such as a format guide, tries to capture the essential features of a type of writing. However, the features of a given type (such as a proposal) may differ considerably from one discourse community to another, so use generic models with a critical eye. An **in-house model** is the format a specific organization has decided to use (Strategy 3).
- For most of the significant writing you do, you will probably need to **design your own model,** borrowing and adapting different features according to your goals (Strategy 4).
- Some of the most flexible building blocks you can use (within a model or to design your own) are **specific text moves** that you can use at both the local and global level of a text to organize, build an argument, and build coherence. Here are some common ones (Strategy 5):

  Move 1:   Organize the text around your key points.
  Move 2:   Arrange ideas from general to particular.
  Move 3:   Use a standard rhetorical pattern to connect ideas.
             Tradition has made these patterns so familiar that readers know what to expect when you start to use one: narration, description, comparison, cause/effect, problem-solution
  Move 4:   Construct an argument with claims and evidence, offering warrants or reasons for the relevance of this evidence, whenever you foresee that it might be questioned.
  Move 5:   Make a rhetorical move.
             A rhetorical move is a strategic attempt to make your text work more like a conversation in which you anticipate what your readers might be expecting next or in which you plan how you want to lead their reading and thinking.
  Move 6:   Develop prose from a graphic idea, using visuals to generate ideas, as well as explain them.

- You can use speaking to support the success of a written document by pulling the gist out of your text to develop a spoken presentation (Strategy 6).

Projects & Assignments

1. Compare samples of business writing to a generic model, one from our collection in Chapter Seven or from other textbooks or sources. A good example to work from is the Bush & Gudgell proposal. It was written by a mid-level engineer at a small civil engineering firm and responds to an RFP distributed by a municipality in Sandy City, Utah. The proposal is typical in content and form of other proposals written over the years at Bush & Gudgell, Inc., an engineering firm. It follows what employees refer to as "informal format," while at the same time adhering to Sandy City's requirements. The writer inherited much of the proposal writing for the firm because he cares about the quality of the writing and knows the growth of the firm depends on it. Like many proposals, it was written hurriedly to meet a deadline.

    Read the Bush & Gudgell proposal against the generic model of a proposal and write a two-page summary report on what you find. Consider:
    - comparative strengths and weaknesses
    - the places where you think the proposal addresses the RFP
    - your experience reading through it, even though you are not the intended audience, and the impressions the proposal gave you about the engineering firm and its rhetorical situation
    - how it might be revised

    Address your report to members of your class who are writing proposals, or to the engineer at Bush & Gudgell Inc., or to another small firm that would like to compete with Bush and Gudgell.

2. Find samples of business and professional writing in a common area. Analyze them for evidence of boilerplate text and as examples from which you could build a model for this type of writing. Even junk mail often has its conventions and you can find places where writers have recycled formats and information. As consultant to the writers in a new company trying to break into this area, write a short memo report that describes places where you think writing is being imitated and recycled and places where writers are "customizing" their writing for their audience. If possible, go back to the original writers and interview them to find out if your reading and their plans and drafting decisions match.

3. As we did with the shareowners' letter, choose a piece of academic or business writing to analyze for the text moves used by the writer(s). Since there are six major text moves that include another five rhetorical patterns, split these moves and patterns up in class and in your groups so that one person is responsible for one feature. In presenting your research, do not be surprised if you find overlap and duplication, since these moves and patterns commonly merge and complement each other.

4. A resumé is both a common business form and an instance of writing that must be tailored specifically to an audience (a potential employer) and a purpose. Sometimes your purpose in writing a resumé is to produce a generic description of your talents and accomplishments that you

will send to many readers. But more often, your purpose is to emphasize your specific attributes and interests in order to fit an employer's job description.

Use the *Text Moves* in this chapter to develop a resumé and a cover letter for the following job description (or another of your choosing). You may wish quickly to build a topical issue tree of your experience and qualifications, but the text moves are important because you will have to choose whether to arrange the text by chronological order, job experience, or some other specific qualification you have.

Financial Services International

Franchise Manager Trainee. To assist in all facets of office operations including front end service, security, accounting policies and procedures, and the training and development of hourly employees. Eventually responsible for all service operations with advancement to Assistant Manager. Excellent advancement opportunities but only from within. FSI is one of the fast growing financial networks, specializing in family and small business financial planning and service.

Experience desired in customer service, sales, accounting, marketing, or financial planning. Send resume and cover letter to Fred Spafford, Personnel, Financial Services International, 5679 Ft. Duquesne Blvd, Pittsburgh, PA 15211.

To structure your resumé, you may refer to the following general format for resumés and to the Document and Visual Design Guidelines offered in Chapter Eight.

Name, address, phone & fax numbers

Objective	[a profile of your abilities and intentions]
Experience	[jobs, positions you have held]
Training	[specific and on-the-job]
Education	[academic, professional]
Achievements	[any accomplishments, awards, promotions]
Personal Information	[hobbies, additional skills, life experience]
References	

If you are choosing your own company (or organization) to work with, make sure you research them as thoroughly as you can, enquiring into the company's history, mission, and as much about the rhetorical situation of the job offered as possible. As you write your cover letter, make sure you use it both to introduce your resumé and present the key points regarding why you should be considered above other job applicants. To do this you will have to pull out the key points from your resumé (and background) and arrange them in a short but convincing argument.

5. Write a letter to an area company or organization inquiring about how they handle boilerplate, models, and guidelines for drafting and revising their formal texts. You will first need to think about the organizational hierarchy of the company, since this information could be relatively hidden from view or purposely not shared. You may find, for example, that some organizations treat their models and guidelines as property. Others may be more forthcoming, especially if you know someone on the inside. See Chapter Eight for guidelines on conducting *Information Gathering Interviews*.

   To write your letter you will have to explain your interest, what use you will make of the information you seek, and the amount of detail that you would find useful.

6. If you work with a number of media (e-mail, voice mail), try to keep a log of either the frequency (e.g., how many times in a day) you use one or the other or the occasions (a specific task or situation). Your log may not be very accurate, but the point is to get some sense of how, when, and why you switch media. Try building a table of frequencies or occasions, plotting the instances or amount of time devoted. Chapter Eight offers some help with graphic tools.

Reference

1. Swales, J. M. *Genre Analysis: English in Academic and Research Settings* (New York: Cambridge University Press, 1990).

5
Evaluating and Testing as You Revise

IN THIS CHAPTER we will help you revise, even though it can seem difficult to step back from your own writing and read it from a reader's point of view. The strategies presented will help you with *local* revisions, that make the text more readable at the word and sentence level, and with *global* revisions, that make it coherent at the level of the whole text.

STRATEGY 1. Look for Writer-Based Prose
Turn writer-based into reader-based prose by looking for an "I" focus, and narrative and survey patterns.

STRATEGY 2. Test for a Reader-Based Structure
Reflect on your plans and use metadiscourse cues that announce plans to a reader.

STRATEGY 3. Check Your Text Against Local and Global Conventions
Use local conventions that improve readability: Old/new patterns, embedded information, coordinate/subordinate patterns, repetition, active/passive sentences
Use global conventions that improve coherence: topical development, rhetorical patterns

STRATEGY 4. Test a Draft with a Reader Review
Design a test to see how readers are actually constructing meaning in a text.

5
Evaluating and Testing as You Revise

IMAGINING A READER'S RESPONSE

Even if you have a model or text to work from, as a writer you will work hard to construct a text: generating and discarding ideas, trying to figure out your point, sketching out alternative organizations, and then trying to signal that point and structure to your reader. But the story does not end there because your various readers have to work equally hard to construct a meaning based on your text. That is, readers want to construct *in their own minds* a coherent text, with a hierarchical organization (like an issue tree) based on key points. And they need to see a purpose for reading. Readers want to know *Why read this? What is the point?* and *How is all of this connected?*—and they want to find answers as quickly as possible.

Readers begin to predict the structure of a text and its meaning as soon as they face a page. They will look for cues that the text might offer about point, purpose, and structure, but if they do not find them, they will go ahead and construct their own version of the text *and assume that is what you intended*. It may be helpful to imagine your readers as needing to *write* your text for themselves. Thus, their own goals and interests will strongly influence what they look for in a text and the meaning they make out of it. Your goal, then, as a writer is to do the best job you can to make sure a reader's process through your text and his or her understanding matches or comes close to what you intended.

Once your ideas are down in a draft of some form, **revision** lets you anticipate how readers will respond and adjust the text to get the response you hope for. **Local revision** involves editing, correcting spelling and grammar, and making local improvements in wording or sentence style. **Global revision** involves looking at the big picture, but that does not mean throwing the draft out and starting again, and it may not even take a lot of time. Global revision, however, does mean looking at the text as a whole—thinking globally about the major rhetorical decisions and plans you made—now that the draft is complete. Global revisions alter the focus, organization, argument, or detail to improve the overall text.

Revision begins with a tricky reading process, a close reading of your own text. You know from your own experience in school that readers can read for different purposes: to skim a text to prepare for class discussion and then to read more carefully for an examination. In business, because writing usually augments a transaction between people, readers look for information but they also look for how well a piece of writing is adapted to their needs. The key to your success as a reviser is your ability to read your own writing critically for different features and purposes. At the simplest level, revision is *re-vision*—the process of stepping back from one's text and seeing it anew. In this chapter we begin with some general strategies for judging your own writing and anticipating a reader's needs. We then provide a number of strategies for tightening your writing at a **local** and **global** level. Finally, we present the **reader review,** which is an active process of finding out how readers make sense out of a piece of writing.

STRATEGY 1: LOOK FOR WRITER-BASED PROSE

Why is it that even experienced writers typically choose to draft and revise rather than write a final text in one pass? Suppose you put time into planning your paper; you followed a good model; you thought about your reader as you chose what to say. Why should your first draft not do the job? One reason is because first drafts often contain large sections of **writer-based prose.** Writer-based prose appears when writers are essentially talking to themselves, talking through a problem, exploring their own knowledge, or trying to get their ideas out. In fact, producing writer-based prose is often a smart problem-solving strategy. Instead of getting blocked or spending hours staring at a blank page trying to write a perfect text the first time through, writers can literally walk through their own memory, talking out on paper what they know. Other concerns, including what the reader needs to hear, are put on temporary hold. Writer-based prose is, in fact, a very effective strategy for searching your memory and for dealing with difficult topics or lots of information. Writer-based prose may also be the best a writer can do in a new situation. A writer facing an unfamiliar task may produce writer-based prose, uncertain of what readers expect.

Whether it is a strategy or consequence, the downside of this strategy is that the text it produces is typically focused on the writer's thinking—not the readers' questions or needs—and it often comes out organized as a narrative or a river of connections. A number of studies of writers new to organizations demonstrate the reasoning behind writer-based prose and its ill-effect. New employees write consciously and unconsciously to report their discovery process or to survey all they know. And their readers impatiently wade through the river looking for the specific ideas and information they need.

Draft 1   Group Progress Report

(1)   Work began on our project with the initial group decision to evaluate the Oskaloosa Brewing Company. Oskaloosa Brewing Company is a regionally located brewery manufacturing several different types of beer, notably River City and Brough Cream Ale. This beer is marketed under various names in Pennsylvania and other neighboring states. As a group, we decided to analyze this organization because two of our group members had had frequent customer contact with the sales department. Also, we were aware that Oskaloosa Brewing had been losing money for the past five years, and we felt we might be able to find some obvious problems in its organizational structure.

(2)   Our first meeting, held February 17th, was with the head of the sales department, Jim Tucker. Generally, he gave us an outline of the organization, from president to worker, and discussed the various departments that we might ultimately decide to analyze. The two that seemed the most promising and more applicable to the project were the sales and production departments. After a few group meetings and discussions with the personnel manager, Susan Harris, and our advisor, Professor Charns, we felt it best suited our needs and Oskaloosa Brewing's needs to evaluate their bottling department.

(3)   During the next week we had a discussion with the superintendent of production, Henry Holt, and made plans for interviewing the supervisors and line workers. Also, we had a tour of the bottling department that gave us a first-hand look at the production process. Before beginning our interviewing, our group met several times to formulate appropriate questions to use in interviewing, for both the supervisors and the workers. We also had a meeting with Professor Charns to discuss this matter.

(4)   The next step was the actual interviewing process. During the weeks of March 14-18 and March 21-25, our group met several times at Oskaloosa Brewing and interviewed ten supervisors and twelve workers. Finally, during this past week, we have had several group meetings to discuss our findings and the potential problem areas within the bottling department. Also, we have spent time organizing the writing of our progress report.

1 of 2

FIGURE 5–1

The Oskaloosa Brewing
Progress Memo, Draft 1

Here is the first draft of a progress report written by four students in an organizational psychology course who were doing a consulting project with a local organization, the Oskaloosa Brewing Company. As a reader, put yourself first in the position of Professor Charns. He is reading the report to answer three questions: As analysts, what assumptions and decisions did

(5) The bottling and packaging division is located in a separate building, adjacent to the brewery, where the beer is actually manufactured. From the brewery the beer is piped into one of five lines (four bottling lines and one canning line) in the bottling house, where the bottles are filled, crowned, pasteurized, labeled, packaged in cases, and either shipped out or stored in the warehouse. The head of this operation, and others, is production manager Phil Smith. Next in line under him in direct control of the bottling house is the superintendent of bottling and packaging, Henry Holt. In addition, there are a total of ten supervisors who report directly to Henry Holt and who oversee the daily operations and coordinate and direct the twenty to thirty union workers who operate the lines.

(6) During production, each supervisor fills out a data sheet to explain what was actually produced during each hour. This form also includes the exact time when a breakdown occurred, what it was caused by, and when production was resumed. Some supervisors' positions are production-staff-oriented. One takes care of supplying the raw material (bottles, caps, labels, and boxes) for production. Another is responsible for the union workers' assignments each day.

These workers are not all permanently assigned to a production-line position. Workers called "floaters" are used, filling in for a sick worker or helping out after a breakdown.

(7) The union employees are generally older than 35, some in their late fifties. Most have been with the company many years and are accustomed to having more workers per a slower moving line....

2of 2

FIGURE 5–1,
continued

these students make in setting up their study? Why did they make them? And where are they in the project now? Then take on the role of the client, the company vice president who follows their progress and wants to know: "O.K. What is the problem (i.e., how did they define it)? And what did they conclude? Would this draft answer these questions for either of its intended readers?

Put yourself in the shoes of the professor. What would you look for in a progress report? According to Charns, he used this report to evaluate the group's progress: Were they on schedule; were they on task; did he need to intervene? However, he didn't need a blow-by-blow story to do that. As an evaluator he wanted to see whether they knew how to analyze an organization: Were they making good decisions (that is, decisions they could justify in this report); had they made any discoveries about this company? His needs as a reader, then, reflected his dual-role as a teacher (supervisor) and an evaluator.

When we showed this draft to a manager (with comparable experience and responsibility to the Oskaloosa VP), we got a very different response. Here was a reader looking quickly for the information she wanted and building an image of the writers' business savvy based on their text. Here is part of her response as she read and thought aloud (the student text she reads is underlined):

> <u>Work began on our project with the initial group decision to evaluate</u> . . . ok. <u>Our project</u> *What project is this? I must have a dozen "projects" I keep tabs on. And who is this group?* <u>This beer is marketed</u> . . . *blah, blah, I'm tempted to skim. This must be a student project. But why am I reading about the fact somebody bought a lot of beer for their frat? Maybe the next paragraph.*
>
> <u>Our first meeting</u> . . . *Ok, they saw Jim and Susan, . . . looked at bottling, . . . wrote their paper. And now they are telling me where my packaging division is located! This is like a shaggy plant tour story. They are just wasting my time. And I suppose I should say that I am also forming an image of them as rather naive, sort of bumbling around the plant, interrupting my staff with questions. I mean, what are they after? Do they have any idea of what they are doing?*

Now put yourself in the shoes of the professor. What would you look for in a progress report? How would you evaluate this group as decision makers? Have they learned anything about analyzing organizations? How would you evaluate their progress at this point? Have they made any discoveries, or are they just going through the steps?

Fortunately, this is not the draft the writers turned in to their professor or the company manager. The revised draft you see below (Figure 5–2) was written after a short conference with a writing instructor who instead of offering advice, asked the writers to predict what each of their readers would be looking for. It took ten minutes to step back from their draft and to rethink it from the perspective of their professor and the Oskaloosa manager. They found that they needed global revision—a revision that kept the substance of their writer-based first draft, but transformed it into reader-based text. As you compare these two drafts, notice the narrative and survey organization in the first draft and the "I did it" focus that are often a tip-off to writer-based prose, and how they improved the second draft.

How would you characterize the differences between drafts one and two? One clear difference is the use of a conventional memo/report format to focus the reader's attention. But beyond the visual display of information, the writers moved away from narrative organization, an "I" focus, and a survey form or "textbook" pattern of organization. Watch for these three patterns as you revise.

Draft 2

MEMORANDUM

TO: Professor Martin Charns

FROM: Nancy Lowenberg, Todd Scott, Rosemary Nisson, Larry Vollen

DATE: March 31, 1987

RE: Progress Report: The Oskaloosa Brewing Company

Why Oskaloosa Brewing?

Oskaloosa Brewing Company is a regionally located brewery manufacturing several different types of beer, notably River City and Brough Cream Ale. As a group, we decided to analyze this organization because two of our group members have frequent contact with the sales department. Also, we were aware that Oskaloosa Brewing had been losing money for the past five years and we felt we might be able to find some obvious problems in its organizational structure.

Initial Steps: Where to Concentrate?

After several interviews with top management and a group discussion, we felt it best suited our needs, and Oskaloosa Brewing's needs, to evaluate the production department. Our first meeting, held February 17, was with the head of the sales department, Jim Tucker. He gave us an outline of the organization and described the two major departments, sales and production. He indicated that there were more obvious problems in the production department, a belief also suggested by Susan Harris, the personnel manager.

Next Step

The next step involved a familiarization with the plant and its employees. First, we toured the plant to gain an understanding of the brewing and bottling processes. Next, during the weeks of March 14-18 and March 21-25, we interviewed ten supervisors and twelve workers. Finally, during the past week we had group meetings to exchange information and discuss potential problems.

The Production Process

Knowledge of the actual production process is imperative in understanding the effects of various problems on efficient production. Therefore, we have included a brief summary of this process.

The bottling and packaging division is located in a separate building, adjacent to the brewery, where the beer is actually manufactured. From the brewery the beer is piped into one of five lines (four bottling lines and one canning line) in the bottling house, where the bottles are filled, crowned, pasteurized, labeled, packaged in cases, and either shipped out or stored in the warehouse.

Problems

Through extensive interviews with supervisors and union employees, we have recognized four apparent problems within the bottling house operations. The first is that the employees' goals do not match those of the company.... This is especially apparent in the union employees, whose loyalty lies with the union instead of the company. This attitude is well-founded, as the union ensures them of job security and benefits....

FIGURE 5–2

The Oskaloosa Brewing Progress Memo, Draft 2

NARRATIVE ORGANIZATION

The first four paragraphs of the first draft are organized as a narrative, starting with the phrase "Work began. . . ." We are given a story of the writers' discovery process. Notice how all of the facts are presented in terms of when they were discovered, not in terms of their implications or logical connections. The writers want to tell us what happened and when; the reader, on the other hand, wants to ask "why?" and "so what?"

A narrative organization is tempting to write because it is a prefabricated order and easy to generate. All of us walk around with stories in our head, and chronology, as we saw in Chapter Four, is a common rhetorical move. Instead of creating a **hierarchical** organization among ideas or worrying about a reader, the writer can simply remember his or her own discovery process and write a story. Remember that in a hierarchical structure, such as an issue tree, the ideas at the top of the structure work as the organizing concepts that include other ideas. The alternative is often a string of ideas simply linked by association or by the order in which the writer thought about them. Papers that start out, "In studying the reasons for the current decline in our return customers,. . . ." are often a dead giveaway. They tell us we are going to watch the writer's mind at work and follow him or her through the process of thinking out conclusions. Following one's own associations makes the text easier to write. But another reason new employees are tempted to write narrative reports is that they were often rewarded for narratives at some point in their career *as students*. They fail to realize that in business the reader is someone who expects to *use* this text (not check off whether or not they did the assignment).

A narrative pattern, of course, has the virtue of any form of drama—it keeps you in suspense by withholding closure. But this drama is an effective strategy only if the audience is willing to wait that long for the point. Most professional and academic readers are impatient, and they tend to interpret such narrative, step-by-step structures either as wandering and confused (Is there a point?) or as a form of hedging. Narrative structures may be read as veiled attempts to hide what really happened or the writers' actual position. Although a progress report naturally involves narrative, how has Draft 2 been able to *use* the narrative to answer readers' questions?

THE "I" FOCUS

The second feature of Draft 1 is that it is a discovery story starring the writers. Its drama, such as it is, is squarely focused on the writer: "I did/I thought/I felt . . ." Of the 14 sentences in the first three paragraphs, 10 are grammatically focused on the writer's thoughts and actions rather than on the issues. For example: "Work began . . . ," "We decided. . . . Also "we were aware . . . and we felt. . . ." Generally speaking, the reader is more interested in issues and ideas than in the fact that the writer thought them.

In pointing out the "I" focus in draft 1, we are not saying that writers cannot refer to themselves or begin a sentence with "I," as many learned in school. Sometimes a specific reference to oneself is exactly the information a reader needs, and a reader may respond to the honesty and directness. Use "I" or "we" to make a claim or when it is an important piece of information, not just as a convenient way to start a sentence. In Draft 2, the students are clearly present as people doing the research, but the focus is on the information the reader wants to hear.

SURVEY FORM OR TEXTBOOK ORGANIZATION

In the fifth paragraph of Draft 1 the writers begin to organize their material in a new way. Instead of a narrative, we are given a survey of what the writers observed. Here, the raw facts of the bottling process dictated the organization of the paragraph. Yet the client-reader already knows this, and the professor probably does not care. In the language of computer science we could say the writers are performing a "memory dump": printing out information in the exact form in which they stored it in memory. Notice how in the revised version the writers try to use their observations to understand production problems.

The problem with a survey or "textbook" pattern is that it ignores the reader's need for a different organization of the information. Suppose, for example, you are writing to model airplane builders about wind resistance. The information you need comes out of a physics text, but that text is organized around the field of physics; it starts with subatomic particles and works up from there. To meet the needs of your reader, you have to adapt that knowledge, not lift it intact from the text. Sometimes writers can simply survey their knowledge, but generally the writer's main task is to use knowledge rather than reprint it.

To sum up, in Draft 2 of the Oskaloosa report, the writers made a real attempt to write for their readers. Among other things, the report is now organized around major questions readers might have, it uses headings to display the overall organization of the report, and it makes better use of topic sentences that tell the reader what each paragraph contains and why to read it. Most important, it focuses more on the crucial information the reader wants to obtain.

Obviously this version could still be improved. But it shows the writers attempting to transform writer-based prose into reader-based prose and change their narrative and survey pattern into a more issue-centered top-to-bottom organization.

STRATEGY 2: TEST YOUR TEXT FOR A READER-BASED STRUCTURE

Reading your text for writer-based prose lets you spot places where you were still exploring ideas or talking to yourself—places that probably call for some sort of global or structural revision to make this text a reader-based document. But that does not tell you how to revise. **Reader-based prose** foregrounds and makes explicit the information a reader needs or expects to find. Reader-based prose tries to anticipate and support an active reader, one who probably will use your writing for some specific end. What do you want your reader to see, think, or do? How will your reader respond? One important approach to global revision is to look at your text as a conversation with the reader, in which you set up some initial agreements and expectations and then fulfill your promises. We offer three ways to test for a reader-based structure: *testing your drafts against your initial plans, using clues that reveal this plan to a reader, and keeping the promises you made in your writing.*

DOES YOUR TEXT REFLECT YOUR PLANS?

Texts have a way of running off by themselves. The more text you produce, the more convinced you are that your prose is complete, readable, even entertaining. This is natural given the commitment it takes to write anything, but because texts often drift away from your intentions, you need a way to keep your text honest or to realize that you have come up with a better approach. So instead of reading your text "as written" and just going with the flow, start by setting up an image of your purpose and plans in your mind's eye, then test your text against that image. Can you find any evidence of your plans in the text?

To get a good image of your plan, return to the Planner's Blackboard or your planning notes to review your plans consciously. In your mind or on paper, restate the plans *to do* and *say* that you produced prior to your current draft, and find the exact places in your text where your writing satisfies (or departs from) your plans to reach a reader. You could set the mental exercise up as a checklist (Figure 5–3).

Holding your draft up against the backdrop of your own plans can help you notice how well the two fit together. Did you have important goals, or good points in your notes that have just not appeared in your text yet? Did you simply forget ideas? Or did you find—as many writers do—that the act of writing was itself an inventive, generative process? Your plans may have changed as a result of writing. If that happened, what should you do? At this point, inexperienced writers often abandon their old plans and follow wherever the text seems to be taking them. However, experienced writers make

My plans for writing, to do and say were...

> The important Goals and Purposes I gave myself...
> My Key Points...
> How I wanted my Reader to respond (and what other responses I anticipated)...
> My choice of Text Conventions...
> How I planned to make all of this work together...

As a checklist, I could evaluate my writing this way:

Plans *to do* and *say*	Draft	Text Reference
Goals...	✓	-------------------------
Key points...	✓	-------------------------
Intended Response...	✓	-------------------------
Text Conventions, Models...	✓	-------------------------
Making it all work together...	????	*oops, gotta work on this!!!*

FIGURE 5–3

Checking Your Text Against Your Plans

another move. They go back into planning and look for possible ways to consolidate their new ideas with other old plans. They try to build a new plan that makes use of the good parts of both ideas. They use this round of planning to guide their global revisions consciously.

This strategy is obviously one you will use more than once—a kind of in-process evaluation that lets you keep checking in with your goals for writing and checking your text against the big picture of what you want it to do.

CUES THAT REVEAL YOUR PLANS TO YOUR READER

Maybe you are satisfied that you have indeed <u>defined</u> a real and shared <u>problem</u> for your reader, and <u>compared</u> some <u>alternative</u> ways to respond to it, <u>supported</u> them with <u>examples</u>, while <u>proposing</u> your favored course of <u>action</u>. But will the reader recognize all of those rhetorical moves? It is possible that you "talked about" this information, but did not make your good rhetorical plan to define, compare, support and propose fully apparent or explicit?

In most pieces of writing there are two conversations going on. One is the information that the reader needs or expects to find: the recommendations that you want to make, the results of your study, the idea you are proposing, the specifics of a solution. As we shall see, this conversation is held together, usually, by a strong chain of topics and an appropriate rhetorical pattern. But the second conversation is explicitly between the writer and the reader, announcing what the reader will find, in what order, and reminding the reader of where he or she is in the text.

This second conversation is often called **metadiscourse.** *Meta-* is a Greek prefix that means "along with" or "among," and the basic strategy is to include explicit statements and cues to the reader that announce and reinforce your intentions along with your content. There are two main ways writers give such cues. One is to talk directly to the reader, inserting metacomments that preview what will come, remind, predict, or summarize. This lets the writer step back, make the plan of the text more visible, and direct traffic, by telling the reader, "In the next section I will argue that . . ." The other kind of cues work more like traffic signals—they are the conventional words and phrases that signal transitions, or logic, or the structure of ideas. Readers often expect to find these metacomments and signalling cues in some standard places. Some common places to insert cues to the reader include:

Title, title page
Table of contents
Abstract
Introduction or first paragraphs
Headings
The beginning and end of paragraphs (i.e., topic sentences)
Entire paragraphs in between long sections

So review your text first (Figure 5–4) to see if you have used enough cues to make your plan clear, and second to see if you have included cues in places readers expect to see some guidance on what to look for and how to read this document.

There is an endless variety of sentences and phrases that can be invented and inserted to announce and reinforce your main ideas and the progression that you want your reader to follow. To show you the power of metadiscourse and how it plays out in a text, here is an excerpt from the shareowners' letter that we referred to in Chapter Four, with the metadiscourse highlighted (Figure 5–5). You may want to turn back and read through the entire letter first. We offer the original paragraph numbers with the cues underlined and the rhetorical purpose of the cues as we read them.

If you read the entire letter, you will see that the metadiscourse accounts for a very small percentage of the writing. But it functions to support a direct conversation between the chairman and the shareowners

Cues that signal your plan and guide the reader:

Cues that lead the reader forward

To show addition:

Again	Moreover,
And	Nor,
And then,	Too,
Besides	Next,
Equally important,	First, second, etc.
Finally	Lastly,
Further,	What's more,
Furthermore,	

To show time:

At length	And then
Immediately thereafter,	Later,
Soon,	Previously,
After a few hours,	Formerly,
Afterwards,	First, second, etc.
Finally,	Next, etc.
Then	

Cues that make the reader stop and compare

But	Notwithstanding,	Although
Yet,	On the other hand,	Although this is true,
And yet,	On the contrary,	While this is true,
However,	After all,	Conversely,
Still	For all that,	Simultaneously,
Nevertheless,	In contrast,	Meanwhile
Nonetheless,	At the same time,	In the meantime,

Cues that develop and summarize

To give examples:

For instance,
For example,
To demonstrate,
To illustrate,
As an illustration,

To emphasize:

Obviously,
In fact,
As a matter of fact,
Indeed,
In any case,
In any event,

To repeat:

In brief,
In short,
As I have said,
As I have noted,
In other words,
That is,

To signal a relationship:

Finally
Because
Yet
For instance,

To introduce conclusions:

Hence,
Therefore,
Accordingly,
Consequently,
Thus,
As a result,

To summarize:

In brief,
On the whole,
Summing up,
To conclude,
In conclusion,

FIGURE 5–4

Giving Cues to the
Reader

> **Metacomment cues that announce and reinforce your intentions**
>
> *To ask a question about your topic or the argument unfolding:*
> What series of events led to event?...
> To answer that question.....
>
> *To preview what will come:*
>
> In the next section, we will see how this formula applies...
> The third paragraph will reveal how...
>
> *To summarize what has been said thus far:*
>
> In the preceding pages, I've described...
> Thus far, I have argued...
>
> *To comment on your writing and thinking as it unfolds:*
>
> I haven't mentioned yet that...
> I'm talking about...
> My main point is...

FIGURE 5–4,
continued

as readers and to help carry along with the actual report and assessment. Notice too in the shareowners letter where in a text the metadiscourse takes place.

DID YOU KEEP YOUR PROMISES?

Your text started out with the best of intentions—a strong rhetorical plan and cues that keep your reader on track. The next test is to see if you followed through on the promises that you made. Read your text as if you were outlining its key points and promises and then look back to see if you have delivered the necessary detail. For instance:

- Your problem/purpose statement promises four main points and an extended example: Does each paragraph keep that promise? By referring back to your announced plan and delivering four main (i.e. well-developed) points in the same order that you promised?

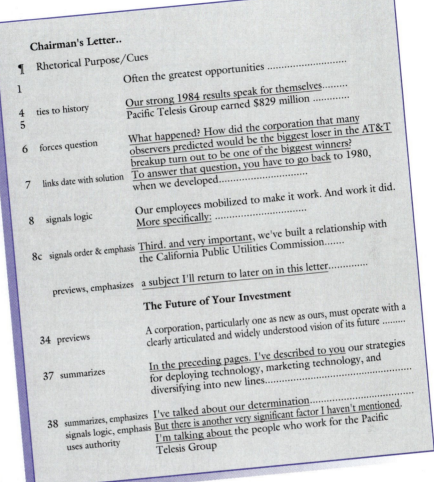

FIGURE 5–5

Metadiscourse in the Chairman's Letter

- Your topic sentence in the seventh paragraph promises the two key instances that support a legal precedent:

Does the paragraph deliver them in the order and detail necessary? The next section of this chapter provides many other devices for making promises to the reader and then keeping them. Strategy 3 presents some conventions that readers enjoy at local and global levels of development, and Strategy 4 shows you how to conduct a reader review.

STRATEGY 3: CHECK YOUR TEXT AGAINST LOCAL AND GLOBAL CONVENTIONS

Text conventions were included in the Planner's Blackboard because writers instinctively try to imagine what their text will look like as a report, letter, essay, etc. There are many, many text conventions that range from ways to link sentences to ways to create an internal logic or progression of ideas to ways to format a text within different generic models. In this chapter, we present a select group of conventions that readers rely on and that writers have used to improve their drafts. As a way to think about these conventions, we distinguish between **local and global conventions.** Local conventions are those devices writers use and readers expect that make words relate to one another, sentences flow, and passages have a "line of thought." Global conventions are those devices that turn a text into a single, working unit; they signal the organization, argument, or a theme running through the entire text.

Your first step in evaluating a draft (yours or someone else's) is to remember that texts depend on these conventions, not because they are "official rules," but because they are a reflection of the expectations of readers in a discourse community. Models, as we discussed in Chapter Four, become conventionalized, not simply because writers have met behind closed doors and decided what a report or proposal should look like. Just as we as consumers have considerable sway over the vehicles we drive and the clothes we wear, readers demonstrate their preferences regarding the written word, and over time those preferences shape the models and conventions we use. Writers try to use these conventions and structures because readers in communities have made their demands on both known over the years.

We began this book by emphasizing the rhetorical and strategic power in reading a situation closely. Here we begin with local conventions, because we assume you either have worked through Chapter Four, which helps you shape a draft globally, or have decided to fine-tune a draft. With each local and then global convention, we offer examples and substrategies for revising.

This section can function as a checklist, to review and revise a draft comprehensively. Or, you may turn to it when specific problems arise, as when you have gotten feedback. The key in either case will be to locate the place and problem in your text that needs revising. Our examples are brief; so make sure that you practice (and share with others) finding, labeling and correcting text problems. With practice, these conventions will become part of your repertory of drafting strategies as well.

Also, remember that readers themselves will work at both local and global levels, depending on their purpose for reading. They read from sentence to sentence to follow a writer's line of thinking, and they seek the big picture, what the text is about and where it is headed. Although readers do both, they sometimes privilege one over the other, depending upon circumstances. In doing a quick read before a committee meeting, readers usually look for the gist of a text, working only at the global level. In judging a technically oriented or argumentative text, however, readers will take the time to examine and question logic and wording at a local level. As you look down our list and plan to revise, make sure you recall the rhetorical situation and how your reader will actually use your writing.

STRATEGY OVERVIEW

Local Conventions
   Old and new information
   Embedded information
   Coordination/Subordination
   Repetition and references
   Active and passive sentences

Global Conventions
   Topical development
   Rhetorical patterns

FIVE LOCAL CONVENTIONS

1. Old and New Information

Traditional grammar describes sentences as having subjects, verbs, and objects. It is also useful to think of them as units of information that have a Topic on the left-hand side, a Verb (or phrase) somewhere in the middle, and another Topic toward the end. Thus, our first sentence in this paragraph could be diagrammed this way:

Subject	Verb	Object
Topic 1		**Topic 2**
Traditional grammar...	describes	*sentences as having subjects, verbs...*

If we think of sentences as offering information about topics, we notice that sentences offer readers both old and new information. Sentences typically begin with familiar, **old information,** by referring back to a topic and information that has been stated in a previous sentence. Notice how our second sentence above ("It is also useful to think of <u>them</u> . . .") refers back to words from the previous sentence. Having made this connection, sentences often close with **new information** or a new topic. Here is an example where this connection falls apart, although we could hardly say the writer is completely off the topic.

Example 1   Construction has begun on the long-planned Regulatory Waste Packaging Facility on the hillside east of the ball diamond. Toxic wastes are an important environmental concern. The baseball diamond was been used by children in my neighborhood for years.

Strategy   When writers are elliptical, skip over ideas, or overload sentences with too many new ideas (at both the beginning and end of sentences), readers note the absence of "flow" or continuity. If you or your readers have to reread to get the gist, *underline noun phrases in both the subject and object position in a passage. Check for how familiar an idea is, meaning how recently it was introduced, and how explicit the reference is to it.*

Below we rewrite the passage. See how the second sentence repeats the idea of a construction location by renaming it as a "site" before it moves to new information about the site. The topics are marked as T-1, T-2 to help you track the old and new information

Example 2   Construction (T-1) has begun on the long-planned Regulatory Waste Packaging Facility (T-2a) on the hillside east of the baseball diamond (T-2b). This site (T-2a/b)) will be used for repackaging medical wastes for shipment to other approved disposal sites (T-3).

Notice how sentence two could have continued to elaborate on *construction* or on the *baseball diamond* that is being lost. But instead, *this site* renames the *Facility* and *baseball diamond* as old information from the previous sentence making "site" the new topic of sentence two. The concluding noun phrase then introduces new information about a new topic, T-3 *repackaging,* linking it to the now familiar, "old" idea of *sites.*

2. Embedded Information

Writers commonly compose complex sentences, which **embed** extra information in clauses and phrases, in order to show the complexity of their ideas. Readers enjoy these embeddings because they make relationships among ideas more apparent, unlike a string of short, simple sentences which sounds choppy or a sequence of phrases within a sentence which sounds like a list. Here is an example that is cluttered with list-like phrases and simple sentences.

Example 1   The computer market is growing. There are expectations *for* the potential *for* more growth *in* the future. *That* has led *to* the decision *by* several venture capital firms to invest *in* the creation *of* new start-ups such as Microware.

Strategy   Look at your draft for list-like sentences which use a number of connecting words (that, which, and, plus) and prepositions (in, of, from, for, by, over, with etc.). *Locate the key words, drop unnecessary words and prepositional phrases. Then write a new sentence which embeds information within a more forceful main point.*

Example 2   The growth of the computer market, *along* with expectations of future growth, has led several venture capital firms to invest in the start-ups of new firms such as Microware.

Embedding phrases and clauses within a sentence helps make relationships clear. However, long clauses or too many phrases can detract from the main clause or idea, since readers try to focus their attention and will remember only part of what they read. Here is another example from a manager who has composed a long complex sentence. The "kernel" sentence is the first clause ("Health Management Systems has gained . . .") which holds the main idea, followed by two embeddings that elaborate on ideas in the previous sentences.

Example 1   Health Management Systems has gained worldwide recognition for its successful corporate quality efforts, *which served* as the model for Managing Total Quality, *a management service* that assists hospitals and other health care organizations in designing and implementing a total quality process that fits and advances their corporate culture.

Strategy   *Any time you resort to longer embedded sentences, locate the main or kernel sentence and see if the embeddings obscure or detract from it.* If you doubt its effectiveness, divide it into simpler sentences.

There is nothing technically wrong with the manager's sentence, unless it were combined with a number of other equally complex, embedded sentences. Then, the reading would probably be tedious. But to be safe, and because it does seem to ramble on, we revised for simplicity.

Example 2   Health Management Systems has gained worldwide recognition for its successful corporate quality efforts. It serves as a model for Managing Total Quality, *a management service* that assists hospitals and other health care organizations in designing and implementing a total quality process. This service and process is designed to fit and advance their corporate culture.

3. Coordinate, Subordinate, and Modifying Patterns

These conventions use a grammatical relationship to point out the logical relationship between your ideas. There are also small words and punctuation marks that conventionally signal these relationships, as we saw in the section on *cues for the reader*. A **coordinate** pattern (signals: *and, but, or, :, ;*) sets up two equal phrases or clauses in parallel to each other. A **subordinate** pattern (signals: *if, although, because, since, when, where, after*) makes one idea depend on or elaborate the other. A **modifying** pattern (signals: *pronouns— who, which, that—and verb phrases ending in "ing" and "ed"*) packs additional information into a modifying phrase or clause. Writers run into trouble when the signals do not match the relationship intended or when the subordination or modification dribbles on. In these examples, the signaling word or phrase is in italics.

Example 1   Video game mania is sweeping the country, *but* many consumers are finding home computers good game machines. Many consumers, *who* bought their home computer for budgeting and education, or *who* bought their home computers for education and imagined better grades for their children, found that a computer, controlled by the kids, is a good game machine.

Strategy   *Locate the words, phrases, and punctuation that signal the three relationships* and make sure you are linking the ideas you want in the relationship you desire.

Example 2   Video game <u>mania is</u> sweeping the country, *and* many <u>con-</u>
Coordinate   <u>sumers are finding</u> home computers good game machines.

Subordinate   *Although* most consumers bought their home computer for budgeting and education, <u>many are using</u> them for game machines, *since* video game mania swept the country.

Modifying   <u>Consumers</u>, *who* bought their home computers for education, imagining better grades for their children, <u>found</u> that a computer, *controlled* by the kids, is a good game machine.

4. Repetition of Words and Pronoun References

Your main topic and related subtopics are developed partly by how much attention they are given, in other words, by how many times they are named. Readers get the message that an idea is important when it is repeated, although blunt repetition can be boring or battering, as in "Management needs more resources . . . Management looks out for you . . . We need a total commitment. . . ." If you are revising technical information or a text where readers need consistent terms, definitions, and applications, be wary of what is called "elegant variation"—changing key terms just for the sake of variety. And remember that a key idea that is mentioned once and dropped will look like a minor idea. However, you can use variation in terms not only to keep readers interested, but to suggest different ways of looking at or labeling your topic. For example, we have often shifted among the terms "draft, manuscript, document, and text" in these chapters. Because these words do not mean the exact same thing, collectively, they help develop the breadth of our topic. Let's return to the example above, this time looking for repeated ideas.

Example 1   Health Management Systems has gained worldwide recognition for its successful corporate *quality* efforts, which served as the model for Managing Total *Quality,* a management service that assists hospitals and other health care organizations in designing and implementing a total *quality* process that fits and advances their corporate culture.

The subject of the kernel sentence is "Health Management Systems." But our impression is that the topic of this passage is really "quality" because it is repeated. Try rewriting this long, embedded sentence as several shorter sentences using pronouns or related nouns to refer to the topic, quality.

Strategy   *Look to see if important ideas can be repeated, possibly inserting a pronoun reference or a synonym.* Blunt repetition of the same word in the same grammatical position can dull a reader's attention.

Example 2   Health Management Systems has gained worldwide recognition for its successful corporate *quality* efforts. *This evaluative program* served as a model for Managing Total *Quality,* a management service that helps hospitals design a *quality*-based process.

5. Active Sentences

Sentences gain momentum when you construct them around agents and actions—that is, when someone is doing something. Business prose often sounds wordy and boring because the action words—the verbs—have been turned into nouns. Here are four strategies you can use to make your style more forceful.

Example 1   In business *communication,* the *effect* of the *overdependence* on *nouns* in *writing* <u>is</u> the *placing* of excessive *strain* upon the inadequate *number* of *verbs* and the resultant *prevention* of the *flow* of *thought.*

Strategies   **1. Lower the *ratio* of nouns to verbs.** For example, the sample sentence contains 12 nouns and only one verb. Rewrite to change that ratio.
2. Avoid weak *linking* verbs. The verb "to be" is a "state-of-being" verb that simply says that something exists (It "is") or that something = something else (X "is" Y). The verb "to be"

can define and point, but it can't act. If you want to get more action in your sentences try to replace these forms of the verb:

be   is   was   been
am   are   were   being

3. Turn *heavy nouns* back into verbs. Heavy, polysyllabic nouns, which make prose hard to read, were often made in the first place by adding a Latin ending to a verb. Turning such nouns back into verbs reveals the actions that are hidden under heavy nouns. Here are five Latin endings to watch for

Remove Latin Endings	From a Noun	To Produce a Verb
-tion	resumption	resume
-ment	announcement	announce
-ing	dealing	deal
-ion	decision	decide
-ance	performance	perform

The following revision has a much better ratio of two action verbs to seven nouns and some of the heavy nouns have simply been eliminated while others have been transformed into verbs (prevents) or verb forms (using).

Example 2   *Using* too many nouns in business writing <u>places</u> a strain on verbs and <u>prevents</u> the flow of thought.

Strategy   **4. Change *passive* sentences into *active* ones.** In an active sentence the grammatical subject of the sentence is an agent who acts. In passive sentences the subject is acted upon and the actor is often buried in a "by" phrase. Passives may sound a little more formal when you first write them down, but that is because we associate them with boring or stuffy prose that most of us are personally unwilling to read. It is possible to sound serious and formal and still be forceful and readable. But as you will see, people often use passives for good (and bad) reasons. To transform a passive sentence to an active one:

- Look for the actor (look for phrases such as "by the manager") and turn that actor into the subject.
- Find the verb (attached to a form of the verb "to be" such as "was decided") and turn it into an action, such as "decided."

The following examples change passive constructions to active ones. Do they improve the writing?

Passive	Active
a. A decision was made by the new manager in which . . .	The new manager decided that . . .
b. It has been concluded that . . .	We concluded that . . .
c. A loss was reported for the 4th quarter.	The company reported a loss for the 4th quarter.
d. It has been announced that a raise was voted for top management at the last board meeting.	Top management voted a raise for themselves at the last board meeting.
e. Your rush order was shipped this morning	We shipped your rush order this morning.

Is the active voice always the best choice? Probably not in example *e,* where the reader is interested in the order, not in who took it to the Post Office. And in example *d,* the <u>writer</u> may have had good reason to keep the agent out of the subject position and to obscure just who it was who voted the raise.

The issue of using an active or passive voice is a tricky one for many writers. The active voice is more forceful, direct, and much easier and more pleasant to read. The passive voice, on the other hand, has been institutionalized as the voice of science, objectivity, and power. Many technical and professional writers learn to write in the passive voice supposedly to place ideas out front and personal identities out of harm's way in the rear of sentences. And indeed, it may make political and rhetorical sense to say, "A decision was made to fire the plant employees," if the firing party does not want to draw attention to itself. On the other hand, many readers will see that move as a way to avoid responsibility when the writer should be taking responsibility. Writers use the passive voice to be diplomatic and to sound objective or detached, but this seemingly simple choice can have an ethical consequence. How we represent ourselves in language is how we act.

Yet other writers cling to the passive voice for more personal or political reasons. Inexperienced writers may choose or slide into a passive voice if they are unsure of their status or the quality of their work. One team of researchers found that employees with uncertain status and position in an organization more often used passive constructions and wordy phrasing. This research revealed that some writers choose a passive voice to protect their identities, even though they have been taught to write with an active voice in school and through on-the-job training.[1]

Use the passive voice to balance out your writing style and rhetorically to place the important idea (or person) at the front and back of a sentence. Watch how the passive or active voice is valued when you move into a new organization or situation.

TWO GLOBAL CONVENTIONS

The local conventions we just examined help make texts clear and coherent at a local, sentence local. They attend to how individual words and phrases are functioning and how individual sentences are tied together. These two sets of global conventions help to give a text a coherent structure.

1. Topical Development

One of the most influential, but often unnoticed, patterns in a text is the pattern that is called its topical development. **Topical development** refers to the way the text moves from one topic to the next. At the sentence level, topics are what a sentence is really about. But how do you find the topic? Sometimes the topic of a sentence is old information and occupies the slot for the grammatical subject. Other times the real topic comes as new information hidden in grammatically unimportant places; it may even be difficult to pick out. You probably can predict one of the problems associated with topical development: Can the reader keep her eye on the ball? Can the reader follow the topical development of a paragraph, section, or entire text? In the example below, track the topical development by locating where the topics are found. Does the text give you good cues for where to find the topic, for what the sentence is about in terms of the important information? Italics mark our reading of the important topics in each sentence.

> (1) In the nineteenth century American business reorganized relationships among people through a new movement to *systematic management*. (2) This movement depended on systematic impersonal *written communication* which subordinated the individual to a rationalized system. (3) It took a complex *system of written communication* in order for managers to oversee widely distributed enterprises, such as railroads, efficiently. (4) *Railroad* management called for large-scale coordination and accurate coordination. (5) For the 10:14 arriving in Chicago, *accuracy* was measured in minutes. (6) More importantly, *systematic or scientific management* broke the power of skilled craftsmen who had built nineteenth-century industry. (7) *Craftsmen* and early trade unions angrily resisted scientific studies and systematic accounts of their work. (8) *Written, permanent descriptions* of skilled jobs made it possible to teach more of such jobs to unskilled (and, of course, lower-paid) workers.

Strategy   One of the best ways to test the coherence of your text at this level is to literally *"track" the topic development*. Especially if a paragraph or a series of paragraphs seems a little confused, if things don't seem to "flow," *go through your draft with a pencil and locate the topic of each sentence—what is that sentence talking about?* Then look at the sequence of topics:

1. Did the topic stay the same? Did you remain focused on your initial topic and develop that idea? (a focused pattern)
2. Did the text jump back and forth among topics? (a switching pattern)
3. Did the topic change with every new sentence, as the "new information" of one sentence became the new topic of the next? (an old/new sequence)

Each of these patterns of topical development can be a useful one. But if your topic keeps shifting or if the topic is literally changing with each sentence, think about the difficulty the reader will have simply following what you are talking about. And then ask yourself, Does my text fully develop my real topic—have I stuck with my point long enough to do it justice?

In our example the paragraph starts out with a clear topical development. Although sentence 2 starts a new topic, *written communication,* it is soon linked in sentence 3 to the original topic: *Written communication* is a part of *systematic management.* But then at sentence 4, we take off in a new direction. Railroads had been introduced as new information at the end sentence 3. Although this new information was only an example, it suddenly seems to capture the writer's attention, to take over and become the dominant topic. What is the reader supposed to think? Has the writer changed the focus to railroads, or did this interesting idea just lead him into a digression? Later we see another surprising shift when sentence 7 follows an old/new sequence to make *craftsmen* the topic of sentence 7.

If we were to lift the topics out of each sentence and array them on a graph, the topical development of this paragraph would look as it does in Figure 5–6.

When the writer went back to her text she realized that her text had "jumped off the track." The topic she really wanted to develop was the role of written communication (within the context of scientific management). Here is how she revised it to keep the topical development clear and still embed interesting information within subordinate clauses and phrases. The topics are again marked by italics.

1   In the nineteenth century American business reorganized relationships among people through the new movement toward *systematic management.*

2   This movement depended on systematic impersonal *written communication* which subordinated the individual to a rationalized system.

2   It took a complex *system of written communication* in order for managers to efficiently oversee widely distributed enterprises such as railroads, which called for large scale coordination and accuracy.

3   *Written accounts* were used, for instance, to break the power of skilled craftsmen who had built nineteenth century industry.

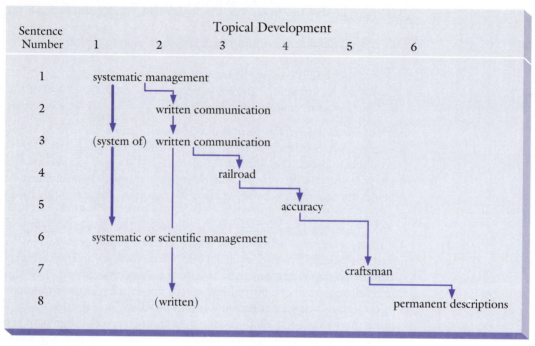

FIGURE 5–6
A Pattern of Topical Development

3 Although the craftsmen and trade unions resisted angrily, *scientific studies and systematic accounts* of their work took away much of their authority.

3 *Written, permanent descriptions* of skilled jobs made it possible to teach more of such jobs to unskilled (and of course lower paid) workers.

2. Rhetorical Patterns

Finally, as you review your text, compare what you have written to some of the **standard rhetorical patterns** we introduced in Chapter Four as aids to drafting your text. Note here that we have lengthened our original list of five by noting narrative and chronological order and "Argument" to include claims and evidence as a general rhetorical pattern.

Narrative:	setting, episode, conflict, development, climax, resolution
Chronological order:	beginning, middle, end
Description:	attributes, specifics, explanations, settings

Comparison: similarities, differences
Causality: if-then, antecedent-consequence
Problem-Solution: problems/issues, solutions/claims, conclusion
Argument: claim, evidence or data, warrant or reason

Notice how each of these patterns can be used as part of another one. The global structure of your text might be set up with a problem-solution pattern; however, in setting up the problem you might start with a description of the current situation and then use a cause-effect pattern to show how that situation is responsible for the current problem. This means that the reader has to read your description, not just as interesting background information, but as a statement of the problem and has to see how the events you describe are the cause of that problem. And then at the end of that section, the reader has to be reminded that you are returning to your global problem-solution pattern. The point is a simple one: Be sure to build in frequent cues to the reader about which conventional pattern you are using.

Another set of global patterns are supplied by familiar generic models, such as:

Five paragraph school theme: introduction, three body paragraphs, conclusion
Letter to the editor
Proposal
Scientific article
News story (who, what, where, when, and why)
Quarterly earnings report

This list is only the beginning, if we consider all the models available to work from in academic and professional settings. As we argued before, none of these generic models or outlines is cast in stone (there are many variations) and none of them is detailed enough to do more than suggest the general structure and format for a written message in a rhetorical situation. But, they are patterns that readers expect to find and will use to make sense of your text.

Strategy   1. *Are you using any of these conventional patterns?* Which ones?
          2. If so, *are you fulfilling the expectations that this pattern creates in the reader's mind?* That is, are you using the pattern consistently rather than off and on? Are you providing all the parts it leads readers to expect, e.g., does your argument have evidence (and reasons) not just a claim?
          3. If your draft does not have any clear global organization, could your ideas be improved or your text made more effective if you *try one of these conventional patterns?*

STRATEGY 4: TEST A DRAFT WITH A READER REVIEW

Our remaining strategy, the reader review, is a direct test of a writer's expectations for a reader and a reader's interpretation and response. But before we present the steps in doing this kind of audience analysis, let us consider why such a procedure is worth your time.

The reader review is derived from the **user edit,** which is an editing and revising technique first used by writers and editors in technical fields. The user edit was invented to test functional documents that teach product users how to do something. The computer industry has significantly improved the manuals accompanying their software and hardware by not only imagining their audiences (computer users with varying levels of experience and technical know-how) but also by taking their composing and revising process one step further. When a draft of a how-to manual is finished, the user testing lab at a company like Microsoft sets up a "scenario" that approximates the situation a user would face and tests their text. At Apple Computers, for example, technical writers have asked first-time computer users to read their manuals, to think aloud, and to act on the procedures in them. The writers witnessed this reading by observing and recording the users' efforts to learn how to use a personal computer aided by a manual. What they found from their user edit was that first-time computers users asked very different questions than experienced users, and that the terminology and directions in the manuals needed to be revised to fit their readers' knowledge base and problem-solving strategies. This was a significant departure from earlier approaches, since technical manuals had a history of being written by specialists steeped in expertise and experience that personal computer users typically lacked. When consultants with Texas Instruments Inc. used this process to revise lengthy manuals for advanced computer technicians, they videotaped technicians completing everyday tasks with a computer and the manual and found that much of the detail in the computer manuals was superfluous to the actual tasks and problems that the system users face on a day-to-day basis. Our point in telling these stories is to highlight the potential value of an actual test of how readers use a piece of writing.

While the user edit was designed for performance-oriented documents, all writing is somehow "used" by readers, who use your text in creative ways to comprehend and interpret your meaning. There is no strategy to anticipate this creativity exactly, but a reader review can provide concrete information that lets you shorten the gap between your intentions and a reader's response.

The **reader review** is adaptable to most types of writing, both when you write and when you work with the writing of others. Unlike a computer manual, which needs to teach a procedure, most business and professional writing needs to inform and persuade. Readers use product proposals to make a decision and status reports to monitor progress, so the review focuses on these functions. While a user edit is typically run in the final stage of a product and documentation review, the reader review can be used to test a draft in-process, depending (as we shall explain) upon the importance of the writing. The word *edit* suggests that a reader review may attend to relatively superficial text decisions such as sentence or word choice. However, a well-designed reader review reveals idea development, style, and the rhetorical approach taken by a writer—any of the text conventions we just presented. Through our steps, we imagine you as the writer seeking a review of your own work. These steps work equally well, however, if you were to consult with other writers, and the reader review can be added to any collaborative writing process.

STEPS FOR DESIGNING AND RUNNING A READER REVIEW

1. Decide What Text Features You Wish to Test

If you could see all that readers are doing as they interpret your draft, you would be inundated with information. Therefore, your first step is to return to your plan, decide on your top priorities, and select the features to test. Your reader review can pursue only a portion of all that went into your text and a portion of the reader's response. For example, you may decide that you want to test

- the clarity of a main idea and certain formatting techniques (and ignore the rest for the moment)
- other claims
- examples included to support an argument
- a rhetorical move or pattern
- graphics
- the voice chosen to reach your readers

Use the reader review to test only prime or problematic features of the draft in question. Deciding which sections can benefit from fine-tuning forces you to rethink and prioritize your plans, your text features, and even criteria, and that alone can guide revision. If a text is primarily designed to convince a reader, then you may structure your review around a main claim or whether a reader accepts the supporting evidence. But you may also prioritize weak features in a text, such as a section you sense is difficult for a reader or was hard to write. Perhaps you are skeptical that you have written your best conclusion; though the conclusion may not be the most important feature of the text, you may decide that a test of that would teach you the most.

2. Choose Your Reader

Like a user edit, a reader review assumes that you are treating your audience's expectations seriously enough to give your text to real readers and honor their feedback. Finding an appropriate reader can be a challenge. An assumed audience might be Joan Q. Public, so that any reader will do for your test. But, what if your text is written for a specialist or someone with unique responsibilities? In selecting your reader(s) for your review, first try to find actual readers who fit the profile you created. If this is impossible or impractical, you will have to adapt by asking a reader to adopt the role of the specialist you have in mind and to read for specific purposes and features that match your plans and expectations.

For practical reasons you may choose classmates or peers to conduct the review, but be explicit about how and why they read. Nonspecialist readers can provide good data for revising, but keep in mind how representative your readers are when you get to Step 4, analyzing your results.

The selection of your reader forces you back into the exercise of constructing a reader profile and seeing how your intended reader will respond to the features you value in your text. As the example below demonstrates, you may set up your review to test the text with a primary and secondary audience, or with multiple readers, or with readers from very different backgrounds. For example, since writers in business organizations commonly write for people above them or below them in the hierarchy, you could select readers with three profiles: upper management, a peer, and subordinates. Thus, you might arrange your review to reflect the primary audience of your supervisor and those in charge and the secondary audiences of a peer with comparable responsibilities and of someone in your charge. By selecting contrasting readers, you learn how to adapt your writing to these three audiences (or whether that goal is realistic).

3. Choose Your Test

With a prioritized list of features and chosen readers, you are now ready to structure your test. Generally in setting up your test, construct a scenario in which your intended reader will read and respond. There are six activities you may use as the basis for this scenario, in order to explore how readers interpret your text.

Think Aloud While Reading Although readers by habit read silently, you may direct them to verbalize their thinking as much as they can. Readers are directed to "say whatever is on your mind" but not to analyze what, how, or why they are reading. This activity will produce an oral version of comprehension and interpretation processes and may illustrate (a) where readers have problems, (b) their strategies for comprehension, and (c) where detail is sufficient or insufficient. The advantage of the think-aloud activity is that it provides a window on the reading process. The disadvantages are that you don't know what the reader will verbalize or to what degree of detail, and you will need a tape recorder and permission to use it.

A useful variation is to have readers proceed silently to certain points marked in the text (section break, paragraph) and then give them a small card that reads, "How do you interpret the text now?" or "What have you been thinking?" This variation loses some of the immediacy of the think-aloud, but it is easier on readers' attention spans and can give you a set of point-by-point interpretations. You also may focus your prompt, asking readers to respond to a feature of the text, as in "At this point in the text, what would you say is the main idea?"

Write a Summary A simple activity for testing your text with a reader is one you may have been assigned in school. Have your readers, at a key juncture (section break, conclusion, etc.) stop and write a summary of what they have learned or come to believe. Not only will this summary provide a rival perspective on what the text is about, readers will volunteer qualitative information as in, "I see the proposal asks for funding, but the authors haven't convinced me that they need it." Summaries are especially useful tools when writers need to test their use of detail and major claims.

Ask, Answer Questions An interactive activity is a short interview, either when readers finish or at various points in the reading. By *interview* we mean questions pertaining to the prioritized list of text features or expectations. A writer could repeat a question such as, "How would you describe the voice in this text?" two or three times through the course of a reading. Or questions could be answered in writing, if readers needed to work alone. Also, writers can simply ask readers, "What questions do you have of the text (or the writer) now that you have read to this point?" The advantage of firsthand questions is that the writer not only hears the answer but is present to ask for clarification and can record nonverbal information (facial, body cues).

Answer Discourse-Based Questions A tool used by language researchers extends interactive questions by basing the questions on specific features of the text. The directions to readers begin with a context and purpose for reading and end with questions based on specific words, phrases, or sections that the writer (or reviewer) deems key or problem-laden. Suppose, for example, that someone wanted to know whether readers appreciated our miniature history of user edits which began this section. Questions could be focused on the examples included, the value of the entire passage, or word and sentence-level decisions.

The value of the discourse-based questioning is that readers' responses will be aligned with a portion of a text—an aid for revising. A discourse cue such as, "Tell me what you were thinking when you read this example," will act as a prompt for the reader that helps jog memories. Open-ended questions such as, "What were you thinking?" or "How did you respond?" may be inviting or nonthreatening, but they often yield vague or fictionalized accounts of why and how readers respond. (See the guidelines for conducting Information Gathering Interviews in Chapter Eight for ways to compose good questions.)

Read for a Special Purpose This tool is also interactive and is based on hypotheses writers have about when, how, and what a reader will perceive in a text. The directions ask for a reader to declare when some text feature (main idea, writer's persona) becomes apparent. Thus the reviewer gives readers a specific purpose for reading, and when the reader feels confident that he or she has achieved that purpose, stops and explains why. For example, a writer may want to know if detail is sufficient and the reader can be asked to stop at the moment when enough is learned to act or solve a problem.

A useful variation is "time-limited scanning," where readers are given the task of reading for meaning or procedures under time constraints, as in, "Read this report for the its key recommendations for a meeting in 10 minutes." This review activity tries to mimic pressures real readers face in the course of their professional or academic lives.

Complete a Procedure Following the example of technical writers and user edits, observe or record how readers make use of task-oriented genres. Many of the other five activities can be used to trace how readers use functional documents. Videotaping with think-alouds provides the most complete trace but is usually expensive or unavailable for classroom reviews.

All of these activities may be revised, combined, and varied depending on the number of readers, the features of texts in question, and the desired time and complexity. We advise students to keep tests simple, as efficient as possible, and purposeful. The trick is to design a test that teaches the writer or reviewer something useful, a result that depends heavily on Steps 1 and 2. Sometimes it helps to cast the reader review as a hypothesis to be tested, or a prediction. Once a text feature or audience expectation is chosen, that feature is treated as a move that is trying to cause something else to happen, as in *This organizational strategy will clarify why my proposal should be accepted.*

One text feature will never dominate a reader's use of a text, but a prediction may help writers focus their reader reviews on specific details for revising.

As a final design criteria, consider whether your text and purpose for revising are best served by a closed versus an open response. If you have read through our list of activities, you see that some are closely structured and limit a reader's response (e.g., answering questions). These allow a closed response. Others turn the reviewer loose (e.g., thinking aloud) and allow an open response. Like interview questions that ask for specific information or invite interviewees to "say what you think," closed or open activities will elicit very different responses from readers.

4. See Whether You Have Learned Anything

The process of designing and running a reader review helps to revise by pulling you back into the planning and drafting process, but the fun comes in when you have data to look at and interpret. How your readers respond (their summaries, think-alouds, and answers) will either confirm your expectations for your writing or will challenge them. The latter may be more interesting and eventually productive because the findings from your test will not only alert you to revision strategies but may help you examine your underlying expectations and purposes for writing in the first place. If you learn that a text feature does not perform, then you can consider another. If a reader becomes confused, or can't answer a question, or gives what you think is a faulty summary, then you are drawn back into your planning and drafting strategies to learn why. Tests will not always tell you what to do to fix a text, but they provide an invaluable service; they will direct you to an area or feature that needs attention. Should you ever reject what a reader does with a text or says about it? Yes, but at least a question has been raised that should not be ignored.

One way to ready yourself for your reader review data is to rethink your design and expectation for the review. Your first step was to limit and prioritize text features and your expectations for your readers. It is helpful to remember that this step is at best an informed guess at both what you need to learn and what readers do in reviewing a draft. Readers may surprise you with their inventiveness, which may also suggest that *you* were also inventing a lot (that readers didn't see) when you read your own draft.

PRACTICAL ADVICE FOR GETTING THE MOST FROM YOUR REVIEWS

Because the reader review is a structured and interactive form of audience analysis, things can and do go wrong. Here are some guidelines for setting up a successful review.

1. Give your reader a context and purpose for reading and clear directions. You may wish even to pilot your directions to "test your test" before asking a busy professional or fellow student to complete the review.

2. If you are working with a specialist or professional person, make sure they are aware of your requirements and approve or accept your methods. For example, some writers and readers are constrained by levels of confidentiality enforced by organizations or maintained through professional standards.

3. Consider your time and your reader's patience. Test only essential portions of a text, so that you do not test your reader's good will or give yourself more data than you have time to interpret.

4. Check your tape recorder and tape for recording sensitivity and make sure all of your materials (photocopies, questions) are clean, legible, and provide enough space for an adequate response.

5. In asking questions, watch your language to avoid leading your reader. A question such as, "We think the main idea here is freedom for gerbils. What do you think?" may end up nudging a reader toward agreement or dissent, rather than toward a response.

6. Avoid specialized terminology. No one will know for sure what a reader review is, much less terms such as problem-solution rhetorical patterns or collaborative planning. If you need to use specialized terms, define them, and make sure your reader understands before proceeding.

EXAMPLES OF TESTS

We have collected some possible tests based on our writing, the writing around you, and familiar projects. We also present three examples of actual student-managed reader reviews. All of these reviews taught the writers (or consultants) something about the texts in questions, though you may see ways to improve the reviews they conducted.

Possible Reviews

1. The last section of the planning chapter tried to sketch different ways collaboration operates in business. Do a close reading of that text (looking at its headings, topic sentences, highlighted information, and conclusions) to predict what the writers wanted people to remember. Ask two students with different backgrounds

and professional goals to read through the chosen section(s) and summarize the main points or what they think is most important to remember and use. Compare their conclusions with the writers' intended main points or purposes in writing that section (as you infer it). Do both readers see the "same" text?

2. You are about to send your final report to a client you have been studying. Your inquiry has turned up a somewhat delicate problem, a situation which you need to describe without appearing to criticize. How will your memo read? Have a reader who understands the situation think aloud as he or she reads and responds to the text, using a tape-recorder to capture the details and development of the response. This is an example of our first reader review activity. Generally, the reader needs to verbalize everything that comes to mind as he or she reads. If there is silence, quietly ask, "What are you thinking now?" Take note of where hesitations, interruptions, digressions, etc., appear. Make sure, as examiner, you have a copy of the text on which to make notes.

3. Twentieth Century (the mutual fund company described in Chapter Three) wants to know if their bold plan to educate the reader—and convince present investors to continue investing—is really working. Ask a reader who is a potential small investor to do a think-aloud, but this time focus his or her reading. Place red dots at the end of key headings, sentences, or paragraphs—places where you want to gauge the reader's reaction. Ask the reader to stop at each of these points—as he or she is reading along—and to think aloud about *how he or she is interpreting the text at this point.* How does that interpretation develop or change over the course of reading? If your reader is doing a rhetorical reading, how does he or she interpret the intentions and message of Twentieth Century?

4. You are working on an unsolicited proposal that will be reviewed by multiple readers. Find readers who have been on the other side of the fence reviewing such proposals before, but who may have only limited time to give you. Do some advance work deciding on what you think are the key issues, strengths, or weaknesses in the document (or glean these from your interview with your client). Ask your reader to look at the text and respond to your specific questions. You may want to speak to each of your multiple readers separately, so that you have a basis upon which to judge consensus or disagreement.

5. Your document is too long to do a detailed reader review, and you want a response to the entire text. Have your reader(s) read

through normally, but interrupt their reading at a few key points to ask what they are thinking or what questions they have. It may help to do this with a tape recorder.

6. You are submitting a job application, and you need feedback on specific features. Give your reader some questions or a problem before they start—tell them to read for specific features or ideas. Questions or problems could include: Who does the audience seem to be? What is the purpose? What is the tone or the persona? What kind of person do you hear behind the text? What is the relationship between writer and intended reader? Who is doing what with (or to) whom? What is the overall impression it leaves? Like test 3, this one allows readers to comment on the purpose and the person they see behind the text. Was that the purpose and person you intended to project?

7. Some people in your group want a spare factual report; others think it needs more background and detail to be usable. What do your readers (quite possibly a teacher) want? Give two or more versions to a reader and have him or her describe which is preferred and why.

8. Suppose you are composing a script for a 20-minute interview and are worrying about dud questions and dead air. Use readers comparable to your interviewee to test the substance and order of your questions.

9. Some readers always look at the pictures first, so test graphic or visual information. You could test to see when readers attend to graphic information and how they interpret it in words, or whether they require any supporting statements, such as how to read the graph, chart, or figure.

10. Create your own reader review, combining these variations.

EXAMPLES FROM STUDENTS

The following three examples illustrate three students working with the reader review in various course projects and show how readers can offer compatible and contrary readings of the same document. Example 1 shows how students investigated a corpus of documents by working through a sequence of reviews. Example 2 shows how student reviews actually affected the priorities and procedures for designing technical manuals at Health Management Systems, and ends with a testimony by technical writers at HMS to the value of reader reviews. The third shows how a review can be set up around two contrasting readers who fit the profile of the intended audience.

Example 1

A group of undergraduate business writing students completed three successive reader reviews as part of a semester-long consulting project with Trans-American Retail, a Fortune 500 retail and distribution corporation. For their project, the students analyzed a series of related documents, consisting of a quarterly report of earnings, a financial analysis, and correspondence. The students' purpose in this analysis was to reconstruct what they called the "web" of communication that informed the quarterly report written to the corporation stockholders as part of a report back to an executive at Trans-American Retail.

To practice conducting a reader review and to chip away at the web of writing surrounding the report, they first reviewed a business letter written by the vice president of investor relations, responding to a request for information on converting preferred to common stock. They asked two classmates to read the letter and give their general impressions, thus beginning with an open-ended review. Prior to the review, this group in particular had debated the importance of a "brief and succinct" business style, especially in short correspondence. The body of the letter follows.

> We are in receipt of your letter requesting information . . . At this time, your Preferred A Stock may be converted at a rate of 1.0782 shares of A Common Stock for each share of Preferred A. If you wish to convert your Preferred A Stock to Common, please sign your certificate exactly as it is registered, without addition or deletion. Have your local bank or a registered member of the stock exchange guarantee your signature. Send your stock certificate to . . .. They will convert your Preferred A Stock into Common Stock and pay you for any fractional shares at a rate equal to the average selling price of the Preferred A Stock as quoted in the Wall Street Journal on the date it is received by them . . . .

This review helped students see how writing can exclude some readers and raised the question of how direct a business writer can or should be when corresponding with stockholders and investors, people who contribute to the company, benefit from its profits, but have little control of operations or management.

Their second review focused on the two and one half page quarterly report written ostensibly for a general audience but one that is also read closely by all levels of management. The reviewer selected was a graduate student in business communication, who the students felt was representative of the common stockholder because she participated in the stock market and was knowledgeable about investments. She was instructed to provide general impressions to the quarterly report, excerpted below.

TRANS-AMERICAN RETAIL ANNOUNCES THIRD QUARTER SALES AND EARNINGS

> Trans-American Retail today announced sales for the thirteen week third quarter of $5,269,984,000, an increase of 6.6 percent over 1988. Sales year-to-date were $15,861,998,000, an increase of 21.2 percent over 1988. Like store sales increased 5.2 percent for the third quarter. . . . The third quarter of 1989 includes earnings of $0.26 per common share for the sale of assets. Furthermore, the company was pleased to report that it suffered only limited damage resulting from the San Francisco earthquake of October 17, resulting in uninsured losses and expenses of only $3,123,000 or only $0.06 per common share. One hundred of our stores, which were temporarily closed, were open and fully operational the morning following the earthquake. . . . As previously reported, Trans-American Retail food stores pre-LIFO operating profit for the year-to-date period in 1989 was impacted by gross margin pressures and advertising costs related to promotional activities in its California stores. Grocery-like store sales increased 5.3 percent in the third quarter of 1989.

Both the letter and the quarterly report were written for the general public, and the graduate student, like the students' classmates, found the language of the quarterly report difficult to read because of technical terms, a confusing organization, long paragraphs, and abbreviations. The students were surprised that their representative reviewer attended to surface and structural details, so they sought a reviewer with even more expertise, though further from the primary audience intended for the report. They decided to test the report on a stockbroker and this time specifically questioned the report's style, technical information, and organization. The stockbroker gave a completely different reading than the previous two reviewers and said:

> *The report provides exactly what I need to be informed . . . the report is boring but exact, with all the meat and potatoes of the corporation's progress . . . it is appropriately brief telling me the type of company, the sales from year to year, and an account of any losses . . . this report is written according to the protocol . . . the way it is done. . . .*

The students came away with a mixed lesson on audience. On the one hand, they learned that business documents are written for different audiences, and that they include some and exclude others. On the other, they became even more interested and suspicious of announced versus intended audiences in business writing. The quarterly report, though written primarily for stockholders in the general public, was more accessible to a small pool of specialists with background and authority similar to the writer.

Example 2

Several students in an undergraduate technical writing course were working with Health Management Systems, an area health service company, and decided, as part of their course project, to help a team of technical writers review a new piece of software and its manual. This software, an in-office product that helps physicians to determine and optimize insurance and medical reimbursements for diagnoses, would typically be used by a receptionist or secretary. Users are expected to learn how to use the product in one to two hours, and the manual includes walk-throughs, examples, and a reference guide.

The students, working with the team of technical writers, structured their review around two readers, an office manager who had coded diagnoses, and a receptionist who had used a similar piece of software. The test consisted of the problem of quickly learning a new piece of software, and students used observation and questioning activities.

The review came at the end of the document cycle; the technical writers hoped that their manual provided all the training necessary for someone with at least some experience with health information software. Likewise, the students were impressed by the time and resources committed to the manual and assumed initially that this hard work, planning, and expertise yielded a perfect end product. A few months later, in an account published in a local newsletter for technical writers, the Health Management Systems writers described the results of the reader review and its value to their collaborative composing process.

> *Even though the tests were simple, we discovered many things that will help us with future writing assignments. Both users felt that the tutorials were easy to follow, informative, and fun. They also felt that the product itself was easy to work with and very sophisticated . . . We also found a few lapses in the documentation, most of which could be characterized as misplaced information. For example, one user felt that a certain explanation should be closer to the related (computer) screen and not buried in a paragraph half a page away . . . The most interesting discovery was how we had been assuming the knowledge of the audience of this book. . . . We also assumed that users understood the parts of the books. Both users seemed unaware of the usefulness of the index or glossary . . . The most important thing we accomplished (with the review), however, was political—we now have support from management to conduct more sophisticated usability testing in the future, and we are beginning to fit it into our current processes.*

Example 3

Students in an undergraduate business writing class decided to test two memos written by a manager at Canyon Recreation Spa, a local tennis and ski club, affiliated with Glacier Peak Ski Resort. The memos targeted memberships and season passes as ways to drum up more business for the club and were written for two specific readers, one an employee of the company who would sell memberships and the other an outsider from whom the manager sought additional help in marketing. The students were intrigued by how the manager altered his style for each audience. Portions of the two memos follow.

#1 (to the outsider)

Following our conversations regarding your participation in the sale of CRS club memberships, it is my opinion that this work could start as a part-time activity which could prove mutually beneficial to both parties. Your getting involved in activities related to Glacier Peak, and having your name appear in inter-office correspondence in some positive marketing-related way, could only help later, if other opportunities at Glacier Peak become available. . . . The policy in the past has been to pay a 25% commission. . . . My proposal to you is to pay you a minimum of $100 on both single and couples memberships, $135 on family memberships, and $165 on tennis and ski combinations . . . Please give this some thought. Believe me, I understand completely no matter how you decide. If it works for you—great; if you want to experiment to see how it goes—great. . . .

#2 (to the insider)

One of the big hooks I am going to be leaning on heavily to raise our membership numbers at CRS is the fact that we have a mountain and our other tennis-club competitors do not. The membership perk of being able to purchase a season pass at Glacier Peak is very attractive to some of our existing members and should be the extra incentive to move some new people to CRC as well . . . it is a perk that Racket Arena cannot match, unless they get in bed with Snow-West, and that is another reason to make it a real bargain. Make it tough for them to match it . . .

The first review was conducted with a sales manager within the company. The manager read both memos and was then interviewed with questions directed at introductory and concluding paragraphs, readability, format, and general strengths and weaknesses. The second review was conducted with a marketing representative with experience in recreational marketing but with no affiliation with the parent company. Some of the questions asked of the two reviewers were:

- Do the opening paragraphs explain the purpose of the memos?
- What do you think the writer wants you (as the intended reader) to do?
- How easy or difficult were the memos to read?
- What do you remember from the memos, now that you are finished?
- From your experience, would you attend to one memo over the other?
- What would you change if you were the author?

The two reviewers concurred in both cases that the memos began with weak opening paragraphs that did not indicate the writer's purpose or the direct request to the reader. Much information was buried, and the writer's informal tone and style worked for an in-house audience but failed as a strategy to attract outside assistance with the membership project. The reader reviews helped these students understand how easy it is to miss the mark when soliciting a busy client or associate.

To conclude this chapter, we want to underscore what we consider are some of the best ways to improve a writer's ability to reach an audience. The reader review, like collaborative planning, aims to make the evaluation process visible. Besides giving you a procedure for learning how readers respond (as opposed to imagining it), the exercise of designing and running a review helps you attend to the evaluation process itself. Both collaborative planning and the reader review invite you into an explicit planning, drafting, and revising process. It is through explicitness that writers are able to benefit from what they do well, adapt what they know to new situations, and ready themselves to learn new strategies and procedures for writing.

You see now that the reader review is an involved strategy for revising that includes other people and a considerable time investment. As you collect strategies for revising and become more familiar and flexible with the procedures, the reader review will serve purposes similar to focus groups in marketing, which are used to test a product on a sample audience. The idea is the same—if you really want to know if your product works, try it out and watch what happens.

The reader review is time-consuming, and we recommend that you eventually use it for documents with multiple audiences, large audiences, or documents that are reissued periodically. In all of these cases, writers presumably seek an efficient and effective process and result. For example, at Health Management Systems supervisors in six divisions write a monthly status report for both their division associates and for the operations committee consisting of the supervisors and the regional vice president. Continually revising these reports constitutes a nightmare that could be avoided with initial reader reviews. Once the report is tested and refined, portions, formats, or organizational patterns can be turned into a boilerplate, that is, a reusable model that significantly reduces the time invested while maintaining the quality of the report.

We propose the reader review and collaborative planning as two general strategies, among others, that can add to your academic training and experience and remain as strategies for business and professional writing as well.

Summary

- Revision lets you test your text at both a **local** level of words and sentences and at the **global** level of argument and organization, and adapt it to the needs of your reader.
- **Writer-based** prose can be a good way to get ideas down, but its "I" focus and narrative or survey organization often mean that, as the writer, you are speaking to yourself instead of a reader (Strategy 1).
- **Reader-based** prose anticipates readers' questions and needs and organizes the text around them. It carries on a conversation called **metadiscourse** with a reader, offering a variety of **cues** for guiding the reader through the text (Strategy 2).

- One way to test your text is to see how well you have used some of the **conventions** readers have learned to expect (Strategy 3).

Local Conventions That Improve Readability	Global Conventions That Improve Coherence
old/new patterns	topical development
embedded information	rhetorical patterns
coordinate/subordinate patterns	
repetition	
active/passive sentences	

- A **reader review** can give you a surprising new perspective on your text by showing you how readers are actually interpreting it. **Design** a reader review by choosing the features you need to test, a stand-in reader, and the kind of test you want to use, ranging from a detailed think-aloud to a discourse-based interview to focused questions or special purpose reading. Then interpret what this response says about your text.

Projects & Assignments

1. How good are your powers of prediction? Analyze the first draft of a current assignment looking for patches of writer-based prose. Mark places where you predict the reader will want more detail or a different order. Read it through for those places where you made promises to the reader and ask if the reader will have trouble connecting what you promised to what you delivered. You may also test your predictions against the responses of other readers, perhaps following some of the guidelines for conducting a reader review.

2. Find in your files a paper written for another class or prior assignment. You are looking for a sample of writing that is no longer being scrutinized and that you no longer care about. See if you are able to spot moments of writer-based prose and survey the strategies in this chapter to draft a revision.

3. Find a sample of writing around school or outside that is targeted to a wide and varied audience, something that will be distributed to a number of people. Interview the writers to try to find out their intentions and the degree to which they researched their audience. Conduct a reader review based on the audience profile they present.

4. Exchange papers in class and write a memo to the writer that highlights and discusses three key features for possible revision. First learn about the writer's intentions and rhetorical plan, if they are not obvious. Next, assess the draft with as many of the revision strategies as you can apply. If you are working in groups, you may divide the three main strategies (beside the reader review) or substrategies within them. Then compare your findings. The key will be to select the troublespots and strategies that will best serve the writer.

5. Extract, as we did with the shareowners' letter, the cues that announce and reinforce the metadiscourse in a sample of writing. Then decide whether or not the writer has include the right number of each kind of cue.
6. Underline all the topics in a section or paragraph, at the front and back of each sentence. Then chart the topic chain by arranging the topics in this manner:

	Topic 1	Verb	Topic 2	Status T-1 T-2
Sentence 1	Divesting capital ...	leads to ...	commodities	N N
Sentence 2	These commodities	support	the infrastructure ...	O N

This analysis can be done very simply by using a colored pen and marking the topics on a photocopy. The topic chain can include the "old and new" status of each topic to help you see how topic development works through a passage and to look for gaps in coherence.

1. Brown, R., & C. Herndl, "An Ethnographic Study of Corporate Writing: Job Status as Reflected in Written Text." In B. Couture (Ed.), *Functional Approaches to Writing* (pp. 12–28). Norwood, NJ: Ablex.

6
Working with Others

IN THIS CHAPTER we extend your work with collaborative planning and building a draft, to focus on collaboration, a common goal and situation in business. We present five strategies to help you work with others in groups and to plan and follow through on complex, collaborative projects.

We begin by asking you to take stock of your own experience working with others (in school or at work) and to review the attitudes you have about collaboration. Then we turn to five strategies for making collaboration work for you.

STRATEGY 1. Decide on Roles for Your Group and Yourself
Adopt roles that emphasize task and group interaction.

STRATEGY 2. Set an Agenda and Link Communication with Decision Making
Utilize goals, activities, plans: Standard Agenda and Delphi methods.

STRATEGY 3. Participate Flexibly and Strategically in a Working Group
Learn the ground rules.

STRATEGY 4. Use the Tools of Strategic Planning and Project Management
Focus on tasks, delegation, timelines.

STRATEGY 5. Reflect and Act on Your Progress, Conflicts, and Ethics

We end this chapter with a discussion of ethics and ethical action, to remind that every action we take, in writing or otherwise, has a social and ethical consequence.

6
Working with Others

Learning how to write for business and professional contexts means learning how to work and communicate with others. In earlier chapters, we described writing as a process of working through problems in rhetorical situations and as participating in discourse communities. Writing activities—and speaking, reading, and listening activities—are always group activities: whether you are writing to deliver a product to someone, writing to submit a draft for an editing cycle, writing to prepare for an event such as a planning meeting, or writing to collaborate directly through team or committee work.

In this chapter, we examine more closely how writers work with others, beginning with a survey of your experience. If you have practiced our strategies for collaborative planning or turned to our guidelines for conversation (in Chapter Eight), you are already thinking about and practicing ways to work with people. With collaborative planning, we defined the helpful roles and procedures available when one person is trying to help another to generate and revise a piece of writing, by actively asking questions and monitoring progress. Collaborative planning is a process and strategy that often produces conflict, as disagreements and rival solutions are negotiated. Conflict is a natural consequence of problem finding and solving, and if handled well, can lead to creative solutions and insights. Like collaborative planning, everyday conversation is marked by roles and patterns of communication that, if recognized, can promote understanding, collaboration, and social good will. In this chapter, we present strategies for working with others and for managing complex projects over time. These strategies focus on roles and procedures available to you and on conflicts that mark many of the ethical decisions in working with others.

TAKING STOCK OF YOUR COLLABORATIVE EXPERIENCE

First we want you to reflect on your experience working with others. In school, the basic social relationship is between you and an instructor, although many of you have experienced the added challenge of group projects, group assignments, or possibly even peer review. We know that all students do not enjoy all group activities at all times. Most students recognize what teachers are trying to do—involve students in a collaborative process of learning, produce more by sharing the load, and anticipate collaborative settings outside of school. But students also recognize and avoid the headaches: dysfunctional groups, increased—not lessened—workloads, and complicated, if not unfair, group evaluation and grading.

As an employee in a company or organization you are likely to be assigned to a committee, work group, quality circle, project team, or management task force. Group work and collaboration in the workplace, interestingly enough, have received the same mixed review as in school. Since the famous Hawthorne studies at Western Electric in the 1920s, groups have been celebrated as

> . . . devices for improving the implementation of decisions and to increase human commitment and motivation. They are now loved because they are also creative and innovative. They often make better quality decisions than individuals, and because they make organizational life more livable for people.

But group work is not a bed of roses.

> [Groups] can, for example, waste time and energy of members, rather than use them well. They can enforce norms of low rather than high productivity. They sometimes make notoriously bad decisions. Patterns of destructive conflict can arise, both within and among groups. And groups can exploit, stress, and frustrate their members—sometimes all at the same time.[1]

What marks the difference between creative, productive, satisfying groups and the opposite? First, the surrounding organizational structure can strongly influence how groups define their tasks, respond to them, and are rewarded. Second, individuals can have considerable sway with their skills, attitudes, and personalities. But how you structure and carry out group work is also important—and that is the part you can do the most about. To learn more about what you can do to make groups run smoothly, take stock of your experiences, working with others, in and out of school. We will start with an interesting finding from research: *Many people do not realize how much they collaborate when they write.*

DO WRITERS COLLABORATE IN PROFESSIONAL SETTINGS?

Do people who write on the job write alone or with others? When Lunsford and Ede asked 1400 professionals, many said "alone" because (it seems) they thought of **collaboration** as two people working together drafting the sentences of a coauthored text.[2] But when their surveys and later case studies went deeper, asking just what these professionals were doing, it turned out that 87 percent of the engineers, chemists, psychologists, city planners, academics, managers, and technical communicators depended on collaboration in their writing. Their short sketches show some of the varied forms this "hidden" collaboration takes:

- Bill Qualls is a city planner. His team for a recent project included a project manager [Qualls], project engineer, hydrology and sanitary engineer, mechanical engineer, architect, telecommunications engineer, electrical engineer, cartographer, planner, and secretary. They post on the wall a big multicolor critical path chart that maps who is doing what for every stage of the process from the original contract plan, through information-gathering and technical stages (including maps and graphics), through pencil, preliminary and final drafts of their end product—a master plan report. This wall map also orchestrates who is in on what part of the collaborative process, from drafting the proposal to the client, to the team visit to the project site, to contract negotiations, through the research, to drafting the plan (which team members do individually, according to area of expertise), and through the series of revisions, deadlines, and submittals. *By the time the team leader—usually Qualls—[fills in] the blocks for the executive summary and the letter of transmittal (which he always writes), [the critical path chart] looks like a Klee painting—its bars ablaze with color. The [chart] provides a visual representation of collaboration, a vivid picture of a job well done.* (Lunsford & Ede, p. 25)
- Albert Bernstein is a clinical psychologist who took responsibility for writing a long-needed brochure for a statewide organization he is active in. He does not have a Pollyanna attitude about group writing. *This particular brochure took me four months to write, and it is not because I am a slow writer. It was because I had to go to board meetings and hear "Well, I don't know about using this word, and this sentence might offend somebody."* Before it was completed, each committee in the organization had to approve the brochure *and they each wanted to add more information about their committee. I wanted the shortest, most direct brochure possible. It was a battle.* (p. 28) And yet, when asked about his "pride in ownership" for writing more generally, Bernstein gave a surprising answer: *When I work with other people, one or two other people, I feel I do a much better job than I would have done alone. I extend myself further and I think I have a clearer idea of what we are trying to do. It brings more out of me so I think it is more mine.* I don't mind sharing the credit. (emphasis added by Lunsford and Ede, p. 29)
- Glenna Johnston is the executive secretary in a small city management office in Oregon. The manager of the office relies on her not just for editing but substantive comments on documents he and others write. Because an office like this often puts out multi-sectioned documents, Johnston often coordinates the team's efforts or writes parts *such as environmental statements that draw heavily upon research or boilerplate materials. She put [many documents] together except the engineering and financial data; she gets this from Bill or Gary. . . .*

She also does a lot of resolution writing (p. 37). Johnston's manager sees collaboration and "listening" as central to his success. At the same time this interview raised a familiar problem: does Johnston's title of executive secretary adequately reflect her real responsibilities?

- As a program administrator with the Department of Education in Washington, Eleanor Chiogioji was in only the second year of her job, but she had responsibility for developing the specs for a multi-million dollar grants competition that would fund research in reading and literacy. On the basis of an initial conceptualization, Chiogioji invited a panel of reading experts to Washington to help chart the relevant issues. Together with her division director and two other research associates, Chiogioji met to "distill the panel discussion." They wrote an analysis of the panel's conclusions and drafted a memo of their own recommendations to the assistant secretary of education. *We came in and we worked ten to twelve hours a day, including Saturdays and Sundays—just constantly. . . . We fed each other ideas. Anne, who is a reading person, would do some sort of writing draft, Xerox it, and we'd all discuss it. We'd take what the panel of reading experts said and our own ideas and through that—just that constant going back and forth—we came out with a fairly good research agenda for the new reading center. . . . [and a] grants competition.* (p. 39)

WHAT IS YOUR COLLABORATIVE EXPERIENCE?

Collaboration in work settings appears to take many shapes, and with those examples, you may recall instances of collaboration outside of school. The work you do in school, and much of the writing, involves groups and collaboration as well. We have adapted the Lunsford and Ede survey to let you see the forms of collaboration they saw and to compare this to an inventory of your own experience and that of your writing group or class.

Ideas to Action

Use the inventory in Figure 6–1 as the basis for evaluating your own collaboration and for considering new options within your groups in school. We structured our inventory around two kinds of collaboration, group-authored texts and single-authored texts. The figures in parentheses let you see how often the bulk of Lunsford and Ede's professionals organized their collaboration in that way.

Fill out the inventory for yourself first, then in class tally the results to see which activities have been used by the bulk (50+%) of your group. Do you differ from the professionals?

Activity	You	Your group
1. Group plans. You draft a part. Group compiles and revises. (45% Occasionally; 33% Never)		
2. Group plans and outlines. One member writes entire draft. Group revises. (21% Often; 40% Occasionally; 34% Never)		
3. One member plans and writes draft. Group revises. (23% Often; 40% Occasionally; 29% Never)		
4. You plan and write draft. You submit it to others who revise it without consulting you. (Occasionally 20%; Never 70%)		
5. The group plans and writes draft. It is submitted to others who revise it without consulting the group. (Occasionally 16%; Never 81%)		
6. One member assigns writing tasks. You carry out your task. One member compiles and revises the whole. (Often 25%; Occasionally 40%; Never 39%)		
7. One person dictates. Another transcribes and revises. (Occasionally, 17%; Never 75%)		

FIGURE 6–1
Survey on Group-Author Collaboration

GROUP-AUTHORED TEXTS

Check off an activity if you have done it in collaboration with someone else at least once. Then, in the next column, compare your tally to that of your group or class by noting what percent of those writers share your experience.

SINGLE-AUTHORED TEXTS

The Lunsford and Ede survey asked about "group writing" of coauthored texts. The survey in Figure 6–2 concerns the role collaboration might play in your own single-authored texts for school or other organizations for which you have written. Check off an activity if you have done it in collaboration with someone else at least two or three times. Then compare your tally to that of your group or class noting what percentage of those writers share your experience. Items 9 to 11 ask you to begin to think about some of the reasons behind your experience.

Activity	You	Your group
1. Interpreting an assignment or analyzing the rhetorical situation with someone.		
2. "Talking over" or "trying out" your plans and ideas for a text in informal conversation before writing.		
3. Meeting for a deliberate planning session with an advisor, group leader, friend.		
4. Submitting a written proposal for comments before you begin a writing project.		
5. Engaging as you write in a sustained mental "dialogue" with the author of another text or an imagined reader, who gets to "speak back" in your imagination.		
6. Getting feedback on a text from your peers or co-workers.		
7. Getting feedback on a text from a mentor, instructor, group leader, or manager.		
8. Negotiating with advisors, editors, readers, peers etc. about the plan or text you want to write.		

9. With whom do you typically collaborate?
      Friends
      Family
      Classmates/Co-workers
      Instructors/Supervisors		

10. What are the problems you have encountered in collaborating?		
11. Did the people you noted in question 9 differ as collaborators? What makes a good supporter?		

FIGURE 6–2
Survey on Single-Author Collaboration

MAKING COLLABORATION WORK FOR YOU

If you are writing in an organization, collaboration in one form or other is a fact of life. But collaboration is not always efficient or easy to manage. Peer reviews, for instance, often produce advice that is either superficial (*You need a comma. Your writing is wonderful!*) or full of sweeping suggestions (*This is how I would have done it.*) that seem off-base given the writer's intentions or would call for major rewriting at a later date. The problem is how to make these dialogues and other forms of negotiation work. This section presents five strategies for:

- Deciding on the roles for your group and yourself
- Setting an agenda and linking communication with decision making
- Participating flexibly and strategically in a working group
- Using the tools of strategic planning and project management
- Reflecting and acting on your progress, conflicts, and ethics

STRATEGY 1: DECIDE ON THE ROLES FOR YOUR GROUP AND YOURSELF

People form groups to solve all kinds of problems and with all kinds of purposes. Groups offer advice, make executive decisions, and serve as ongoing sources of information and communication. Generally, groups are **standing** or **ad hoc,** meaning they meet regularly or they are formed once for a specific purpose. When *ad hoc* groups, such as a task force, are finished, the members disband.

Groups have two basic functions, to complete a task and to build social networks. By name, most groups in business and school are formed or sustained to complete tasks, such as recommending promotions, planning for the future, or evaluating a product. Yet, the announced task of a group often masks the social function. Groups that have standing or regular agendas and members take on their own social characteristics and become subcultures within a company or organization. Groups can be important mechanisms for creating and preserving norms and values such as organizational ethics or the motivation to see a job through to the end. Groups called quality circles, for instance, do not merely monitor progress in an organization and invent new ideas; they are an attempt to build good will and break down boundaries in communication that come with traditional company hierarchies.

In practice, a group's task and social roles may be already determined by the organization they work in or strongly influenced by senior members or leaders. However, you can control the roles you take as a group member. You may choose to adopt a **task-conscious role,** that is, to be someone who initiates an assignment (or reminds others about it), and who seeks out information on the task or criticism of the product. Performing a task-conscious role means always to keep the assignment centerstage by monitoring the progress of the group and pointing out breakthroughs and points of agreement. Or you may prefer to adopt an **interactive role,** looking for ways to encourage members, praise success, and arbitrate conflict. The interactive role uses many of the strategies for good conversation—listening for ideas and values, watching how turns are taken, and repeating ideas to make sure of their accuracy. If you strive for an interactive role, you try to include as many people and ideas in the group's discussion and agenda as you can.

Obviously, a good group leader is both task-conscious and skilled at interaction, and anyone can adopt one or both of these roles. Disharmony and ill will often creep into group work when people adopt a third role, self-promotion. Most of us have suffered wasted collaborative time when someone withdraws from discussion or prematurely rejects an opinion. Self-promotion can also take the form of a dominating, aggressive, or pompous conversational style.

We think it is wise to assign explicit roles in your group. Sometimes people become a group "leader" because they talk the most or like to take over decision making, or are the most motivated to get things done. However, you may wish to assign roles that carry specific responsibilities. Here are some specific roles you may choose to assume or may recognize in the actions of others.

A **group leader** may take on the role of liaison with outside sources or authorities and have the right to make certain decisions and speak for the group. This role is important in committees which must take frequent action.

A **planning coordinator** can play a critical role within a writing group by directing discussion: He or she can act as a planning supporter to the group, keeping track of ideas and positions on a board, asking people to support one another or to consider new issues, or by calling for consolidations, or sketching issue trees of the developing text plan. A text coordinator can be charged with trying to provide an overview of how all the tasks and pieces of writing fit together. A work coordinator may work on a day-to-day basis seeing that people are keeping to schedules and agreements.

A **recorder** is another form of coordinator who can have a great influence on what the group does (and how efficiently it does it). The *recorder* consolidates discussion and decisions into an organized plan, a set of tasks, or a draft text that is given to everyone after the meeting. This becomes the organized memory of the group.

Some groups appoint a **devil's advocate** for each meeting (it is good to rotate this role) who is specifically charged with coming up with rival hypotheses, asking "why not," and arguing for alternative or opposing positions. This role does not call for a personal style of being disagreeable or critical, but of carefully trying to consider and speak for possible different perspectives.

Finally, be aware of the *interactive role* you give yourself in a working group. In social groups, people are often eager to establish their personalities—to show they are interesting, independent, brainy, or entertaining. It is easy to slide from interactive to self-promoting, as Dale found out:

At our first meeting I got into a hot debate over the Mets—I knew I was showing off a bit, but I thought I looked good. Later I found out that half the group was bored and annoyed and labeled me as a dumb jock. And the next meeting I noticed that some people didn't even seem to hear me and no one followed up on my ideas.

In working groups, try to impress people with your good judgment, preparation, and fairness first. Let your personality and special abilities emerge later and in sync with the group's personality and agenda.

Self-promotion is typically the outward result of *hidden agendas.* As we discussed in Chapter One, hidden agendas belong to everyone, in that we all have needs and beliefs that lurk beneath the surface of communication. Group work tends to expose hidden agendas: The personal investments necessary to work with others can bring out the need for personal advancement, affection, or approval. People sometimes exercise the force of their own personality in group settings, and in the process dominate the will and style of others. We do not advise using work-related groups as therapy sessions, but do not be surprised if collaboration brings you and your collaborators closer to hidden agendas tied to issues of security, confidence, and self-identity.

STRATEGY 2: SET AN AGENDA AND LINK COMMUNICATION WITH DECISION MAKING

How can you hold meetings with the least wasted effort? The most efficient meetings (and this usually means the most pleasant ones) have a set agenda. A public **agenda** consists of practical details, such as the times you can usually meet, a functional room, and ways to make contact easily (such as a phone chain, computer mail, a drop off person or place, a way to leave messages). It involves a plan for how you will update each other, when you will check in with your coordinator, and how you will share the products you produce, such as drafts and evaluative comments.

An agenda is also conceptual in that it contains the goals you and other group members have for your meeting and a plan for carrying out your business. The ways that you enter group participation vary depending on whether the group is *standing* or *ad hoc.* Standing groups typically have their own histories with established leaders and roles, and their own routines for when, where, and how they meet. If you join such a group, research the larger organization to make sure you know how this group fits in with others. Prepare by knowing the announced task, but temper your own project goals with those of others. Obviously, some of these goals are hidden agendas, the values and beliefs that drive behavior but are rarely spoken of directly. Joining a standing committee requires extra preparation—you should be as familiar as you can be with patterns of conversation and communication (stories, briefing statements, overheads, etc.). You may find that your goals and agendas will have to adapt to group will or habit or to a leader's style of interaction.

Groups in school are usually *ad hoc;* they are formed for a specific purpose over a specific time period. One challenge in working in ad hoc groups is the inertia challenge, building a shared commitment and a working plan to involve everyone. To get a group moving—as you often must do in school— *set your project goals and make and carry out a plan that includes a decision process.* This decision process, as we will describe, includes techniques for group interaction and the roles writing can play in sharing and shaping ideas.

SET PROJECT GOALS

If your group is just forming, your first meeting will be a planning meeting that established goals, agendas, and plans for action.

1. *Survey the rhetorical situation.* As we urged in Chapters One and Two, get everyone to talk about how they interpret the assignment and to survey the rhetorical landscape as they see it. Encourage different perspectives, and work together to reconstruct a larger sense of the context than anyone alone would have seen. Another reason to encourage everyone to speak now is to avoid unacknowledged differences later in how members of the group see the task.

2. *Set some challenging but achievable goals.* By the end of the meeting try to arrive at an initial consensus about your goals: What are the top priorities everyone agrees on; who are you writing to and how will they use or evaluate it? What if you are not yet sure or need more information? Don't be afraid to come up with alternative plans that you agree to leave on the table. Just be sure you leave the meeting with some clear sense of your options.

   Keep a Record: here is where writing can keep you from reinventing the wheel every time the group meets. Do your brainstorming and planning on a blackboard or large sketch pad, if possible, so everyone is looking at and talking about the same thing and so you can go back to your decisions later.

3. *Turn goals into activities.* Get operational. For example, you want your *Handbook for International Students* to address real needs, not just offer standard information. That means someone has to find out what those needs are; someone has to do something. What? Interview current students? Contact those about to come? Test current documents on an intended reader? Try to turn each goal into a set of real tasks or "how-to" plans.

You may come to early agreement on your goals. But creating operational plans is where you as a group will need to be creative and willing to talk out and listen to alternative plans. At the same time, you want to get so specific that you could imagine everyone walking out the door and going right to work on their tasks. Do you know what to do as you leave the group?

MAKE AND CARRY OUT A PLAN

Do not walk out of this first meeting until you have turned all your talk into a concrete plan.

1. *Assign tasks.* Everybody's job is nobody's job. Draft a *to do* schedule. Decide on the tasks that need to be done, and then decide how to split them or who will do them. The motivation and productivity of individuals in a group is often tied to how clear they are about what needs to be done and who is responsible. Before you leave the meeting, go around the group and let everyone review what they understand they are going to be doing. (Note: here is where a *recorder* taking notes can be really valuable. These notes (especially when they are done on a computer and subject to on-the-spot revision) become an informal contract among members of the group as well as a helpful reminder and schedule.

    Some people love to take on work. Other people go passive in groups, leaving decisions to others, and do not leap forward to take on responsibility. Here is where it helps to have already assigned someone as *coordinator* whose job is to review the tasks, see that they are equitably distributed, and that people are keeping to their promises. This can sometimes be harder to handle as an interpersonal negotiation if no one is officially charged to review the distribution of responsibility.

2. *Set up milestones.* Here is where you take the long view. A milestone is a technical term in business planning that is an important marker of the progress your group has made (e.g., completed all the interviews; collected cost figures; received a first draft from everyone, etc.). A task timeline (or Gantt chart, as we introduce in Strategy 4) will help you create a detailed plan, but here are three important decisions you need to make:

    • What are the major milestones that will mark progress on this project?
    • What are the tasks that need to be done—when—in order to reach each milestone?
    • How will you schedule these tasks in order to meet your deadlines?

This sounds like a lot to accomplish in a first meeting, but look on these decisions as tentative ones, waiting to be improved as you learn more. And remember, any plan is better than no plan. Many of the planning strategies introduced in Chapter Three, such as brainstorming and supporting can also help your group move from a survey of the rhetorical situation toward a plan *to do*.

DECIDE ON A COMMUNICATION LOOP AND PROCESS FOR MAKING DECISIONS

Research on group decision making has revealed a basic pattern of human interaction with four general phases: *orientation, conflict, emergence,* and *reinforcement.* In this subsection, we define these four phases to give you a conceptual tool for monitoring your group's progress. Adapting Goodall's treatment of group decision making,[3] we then describe two common processes found in business, the Standard Agenda and the Delphi methods, as they apply to groups involved with writing.

The first four phases are common to how people solve problems together in a host of situations. Consider a recent project of yours and see whether you can recognize all or parts of these phases.

Orientation	People meet one another, decide upon or hear their purposes and the nature of their tasks.
Conflict	People argue their positions and contest rival claims and evidence. The conflict phase produces useful information and criteria for deciding the best solution or result.
Emergence	The debate gives way to a best choice for a recommendation, solution, or result by applying criteria and the force of will and argument.
Reinforcement	Even though everyone may not totally subscribe to the best-choice solution, enough agreement is present to conclude the process. The unity of the group is represented by its efforts to deliver its result.

The Standard Agenda and Delphi methods offer two distinct procedures for sharing information, relating groups members, and making decisions. The **Standard Agenda** essentially makes decision making public, by deliberately sharing goals, agendas, and the responsibility for insuring productivity, as we have encouraged thus far. The **Delphi** method responds to the practical and conceptual dilemma of holding actual meetings and achieving group consensus by giving far more authority to the leader. The Delphi method, as you will see, also directly involves writing as memos are used to share ideas and feedback.

Ideas to Action

Figures 6–3 and 6–4 offer two methods, presented as basic techniques and processes for making decisions in groups where writing is the intended outcome, such as proposal writing or a final report of a decision or deliberation. Read these methods as prototype procedures since decision processes evolve for most groups, based on their tasks, work environment, and personalities. If you are currently working with a group in class, or if you are just now convening a group, decide which of the two methods you generally favor and discuss the strengths and weaknesses with your collaborators. Compare your preferences for roles, sharing information, and making decisions with the way these are handled in each model, and design a customized decision process. Your method, when made explicit, can augment your planning, collaboration, and project management (as we will discuss).

The Standard Agenda may be a smooth way to move a group toward consensus, but writing—as a product or process—will complicate this method. The Delphi technique (Figure 6–4) seeks to limit the amount of interpersonal negotiation, using writing as a tool for arguing a position.

The Delphi method may strike you as far less collaborative, but it is commonly used in business when time and the will to meet are missing or when there is little debate over the nature of the task or acceptable solutions. In school or at work, you can construct your own method for communicating information and making decisions, one that includes not only direct meeting and negotiation, but the use of media that build distance and efficiency into the process.

STRATEGY 3: PARTICIPATE FLEXIBLY AND STRATEGICALLY IN A WORKING GROUP

Establish the ground rules for group work. Working groups work best when everyone agrees to a common public agenda for how this working group is supposed to operate, as Larry complains.

We spent the first meeting shooting the bull, talking about ourselves, and getting to know one another and I thought this will be a great group. But then by the second and third meeting, when I was feeling pressure from another project, two people still wanted to socialize and we would spend two hours to do 20 minutes of work. What was worse, you could never count on everyone being prepared to work at the same time.

Standard Agenda	As a Decision Process
1. The group learns its goals and purposes and the practical details for meeting to include a time-frame.	*Orientation:* The group established its roles by surveying the rhetorical situation and refining its sense of the problem. Goals lead to activities and tasks, and plans are developed with milestones.
2. The group phrases the question or task that it faces so that all understand and agree	
3. The group collects as much useful information. The group also considers the quality and quantity of this information and whether it challenges its stated goals and tasks.	*Conflict:* Conflict evolves when specific research tasks are delegated and individuals conduct their research. This personal investment can influence a person's sense of goals and specific tasks. In collaborative research, you may need to re-phrase the question and refocus the group's attention.
4. The group writes out the criteria that will be used to judge whether the goals and tasks have been successfully completed. The criteria should represent both the ideal solution and the constraints the group faces in achieving this idea.	
5. The group produces alternative solutions, now that information and criteria have been produced.	*Emergence:* As facts turn into specific writing tasks, either the process of writing or specific sections will need to be delegated. Processes, such as editing or drafting, will help the written product emerge, but they may also produce conflict and the need for continued negotiation.
6. The best solution of the lot is chosen by applying the criteria, especially by deciding not only if a solution is ideal but whether it is attainable.	Choosing the best model, format, and content may not mean that everyone agrees on style or the amount of detail. The writing process continues to challenge the group's constitution long after everyone agrees on a goal.
7. The group presents its final solution--in writing, spoken, or graphic form--with supporting arguments and evidence.	*Resolution:* A written product may represent a conclusive decision making process or it may be an actual product.

FIGURE 6–3
The Standard Agenda Decision Process

Here are some **ground rules** for participation you might consider that distinguish a working group from a social group. But whatever norms you use, strive for a consensus about your group's ground rules and monitor their appropriateness as you proceed.

- Each meeting will accomplish some specific goals. Decide at the beginning what you need to do and review at the end where you

Delphi Technique	As a Decision Process in Writing
1. An authority selects a group and defines the tasks and issues at stake. Only this person (or group) knows the other identities.	*Orientation:* Here the delegation is done quickly, up front and each member is given a task in writing.
2. The problem and task are defined in writing by the authority. Each member writes a position or response, with no interaction among group members.	*Conflict:* The conflict is essentially an exercise in summarizing and interpreting the written statements of the group.
3. The authority details the positions taken by the group members. With this second writing, the members may modify their original position, including their reasons.	*Emergence:* This phase comes when everyone has completed their research, responded to the tasks and ideas circulated by the authority, and produced their written responses. The authority serves as writer and editor.
4. The authority continues the cycle until agreement is reached. The group members remain anonymous throughout the process.	*Reinforcement:* Completion is the reinforcement, and group members may never see the results of their individual labor.

FIGURE 6–4

The Delphi Decision Process

are. Take notes to summarize the group's accomplishments and diversions.

- In between each meeting everyone is expected to *do* something, to bring new information or text to the next meeting. You may choose to begin each meeting by reviewing progress.

- At the meeting everyone should be prepared to share what they have done—to bring typed-up info, make a copy for everyone, or talk about their contribution in a cogent way from notes they have prepared.

- During the meeting, everyone needs to be an active contributor in three ways: (1) by listening carefully to what others say (taking notes on key points); (2) by responding to what others say (this response may be silent since part of the goal is simply active listening. However, the group needs to make sure everyone knows they are heard and understood, which is often done by giving people a thoughtful response; and (3) by contributing alternatives and new suggestions or by helping to develop current topic.

- Maintain standards for conducting the discussion and building arguments. Even though some people in the group are friends or may want an informal atmosphere, relate to each other as working partners.

Here are Julie's comments on this matter:

> *When I first joined the group, I had done a lot of debating and I also felt, because I had more experience with the topic, I was justified in winning the argument over our recommendations by any means possible. When I dismissed a couple of people in the group as nontechnical and naive, I thought all was fair in love and argument. But pretty soon I realized I couldn't get them to agree with me on the time of day. You have to argue differently when you expect to keep working with people.*

In proposing alternatives, building arguments, or engaging in conflict, here are some rules of thumb for participation.

- The goal is fair consideration of possibilities and the methods in an exchange of ideas.
- Do not treat someone who opposes your ideas as a fool or the enemy, or they will do the same in return.
- Be courteous and professional—listen to opposing points before commenting; don't interrupt.
- Respond to people's ideas, not to them, their background, or their motives.
- Build your case briefly (do not monopolize the floor) and base it on reasons (not on the strength of your personality or feelings).
- Try to build a reputation for good judgment and fairness.
- Know when you have lost an argument. Do not labor a point or set up a continuing pattern of opposition.
- Recognize that your upbringing and/or cultural background may make other very certain styles of argument seem "natural"— whether that style is heated, energetic assertion, quiet, almost indirect suggestion designed to avoid conflict, or sarcastic "put downs" to establish your authority. You may have to work at developing this new style of argument which focuses on ideas, offers reasons, and makes balanced judgments.

STRATEGY 4: USE THE TOOLS OF STRATEGIC PLANNING AND PROJECT MANAGEMENT

Since writing tasks often involve other people and are riddled by multiple audiences, varied purposes, a range of information, and complex format requirements, it can help to approach collaborative writing and extended writing tasks the same way managers approach complex projects. Projects are a way of life in business and can be distinguished from on-going management in four ways. **Projects** are defined by *specific objectives,* such as delivery of a product or report and they are limited to a *specific time frame.* Projects also are typically *limited in resources,* such as materials or work space, and they are *completed by an ad-hoc team.* Thus, management projects in general carry the same characteristics as collaborative research and writing assignments: Both face the constraints of specific objectives, time and resource limitations, and the challenge of organizing and delegating responsibility in a working group.

The parallel between management and collaborative writing projects goes further when we consider success. Management specialists and researchers have isolated the basics of successful project management. Teams begin with a **management philosophy,** an agreed-upon agenda, communication process, and decision-making method. Teamwork and goodwill are difficult to legislate, and this is why certain behaviors central to a management philosophy, such as planning and review, are so important. They stand as relatively democratic procedures to help balance out personalities, idiosyncrasies, and the numerous surprises encountered along the way. A sound, articulated philosophy also can offset strengths and weaknesses in a group because those characteristics, if they are stated and discussed, can become the basis for forming a philosophy.

The key is to think of your management philosophy in terms of things you and your group can do. Articulate everyone's expectations concerning deadlines and protected time. Discuss meeting availability and the ground rules for punctuality and preparation, and try to anticipate real costs in terms of travel or photocopying. And most important, discuss the various leadership roles that certain people thrive in at the expense of others. Your goal is to *not* rest on your assumptions about what works best for anyone else or secretly to bear the burden of guilt of completing the projects or to maintain and foster hidden agendas.

This strategy turns many of the ideas for working with others, such as making and carrying out a plan, into tools for managing a complex project. Complex projects are successfully completed when group members develop and act upon plans that clarify:

- Milestones, tasks, and subtasks to be completed
- The order and relationship of these tasks
- Delegated responsibilities and resources that link people to tasks
- A time frame with start-up and completion dates and the durations for each task

Milestones, as we noted earlier, are the major project deadlines which serve as a skeleton for the project. Milestones usually correspond with goals, but they are always concrete—what the group expects to produce by a certain time. If you are involved in a collaborative writing project, a first complete draft would be a common milestone. Milestones are good signposts for review because they are comprised of a number of delegated tasks and subtasks. *Tasks* and *subtasks* are the specific behaviors and procedures that lead to a milestone.

Milestones and tasks may be *delegated* to the group, to a subgroup, or to an individual. The point here is that tasks and milestones must be linked together and delegated to push the efficiency of the group. As a project planner, begin by defining and naming each task and milestone individually and then arrange them in a linear succession. You may wish to begin with a simple list of "to-do's" but work toward a *task table,* a specific and organized list of activities. For each task and milestone, state the *time frame* allotted and when a task (or milestone) starts and finishes. It is important in complex projects to distinguish the time available (earliest start, latest finish) in hours or days from the time required (duration). When more time is available than is needed, *slack time* (also referred to as "float" or a "buffer") is created for each task. This slack time may prove invaluable down the line, when unforeseen events complicate project completion. Many project planners or managers build it in explicitly.

A number of software tools are now available to aid planning, and most of them follow the same logic and ask for the information we have specified. Typically, a planning program will ask for (and use the terms) milestones, tasks, duration, start and finish dates, and resources (the people available for each or entire sets of tasks). The programs often will ask you to build a schedule chart that may take the form of a list, as we suggested, or a critical path chart of related tasks. With the proper and completed information loaded in, the program takes over and reconfigures the information into any number of charts or tables. The task timeline, or Gantt chart, is an established planning tool in business and is essentially a bar graph that uses the vertical axis to list tasks and the horizontal axis to display the time increments over the entire course of the project (see Chapter Eight for more information on graphic tools). These charts are powerful planning and monitoring tools because they condense and visually contrast all of the information necessary for project planning: specific tasks, start-finish times, durations, resources, and a composite calendar.

To illusrate how this information can aid planning, Figures 6–5, 6–6, and 6–7 show the results of the plans for a common problem, making a formal presentation to a committee. Suppose that you have been charged with selecting a new site for an office building and you have one week to gather your notes and research into a coordinated slide show and briefing. You start by analyzing your tasks and gathering the information, which you enter into the task table in Figure 6–5. The tasks in bold are considered milestones. Slack time is the buffer we discussed and "days" refers to the actual duration of time assigned to each task.

Name	Earliest Start	Latest Finish	Slack	Actual Start	Days
Begin preparation for presentation	2/1/92	2/3/92	0	2/1/92	0
Location	2/1/92	2/6/92	3	2/1/92	0
Materials	2/1/92	2/3/92	0	2/1/92	0
Arrange for conference room	2/3/92	2/6/92	3	2/3/92	1
Send out announcements	2/3/92	2/7/92	4	2/3/92	1
Prepare schedule of events	2/3/92	2/7/92	3	2/3/92	2
Prepare analysis	2/3/92	2/7/92	0	2/3/92	5
Create presentation slides	2/3/92	2/7/92	3	2/3/92	2
Deliver presentation hardware to room	2/4/92	2/7/92	3	2/4/92	1
Location ready	2/4/92	2/10/92	3	2/4/92	0
Materials ready	2/7/92	2/10/92	0	2/7/92	0
Give presentation to committee	2/10/92	2/10/92	0	2/10/92	1

FIGURE 6–5
The New Site Presentation Task Table

This table is useful for gathering and arranging information, but timelines and critical path charts illustrate the dynamics of your project and allow a manager to monitor several activities and people at once. As we see in Figure 6–6, a critical path chart of this same information separates the planning and activities for "materials" from those for the "location" of the presentation, demonstrating visually that you will be doing several things at once. Then, in Figure 6–7, we see the same information arrayed along a task timeline. The Gantt chart remains a popular planning and management tool because the tasks are clearly itemized and oriented to a calendar. The task timeline also visually enhances the slack time built into the project. This planner has given herself plenty of leeway as she prepares for the committee presentation on the 10th of February. One way to compare the power of these three representations of the same information is to study how the milestones are noted on each of the three versions.

Planning for the New Site presentation was relatively simple because you worked alone, but project planning more often involves many people and may dictate organizational behavior for months at a time. Look for examples of project planning and management around you. For example, universities and many other organizations often generate "strategic plans" which break all of the resources of a larger organization down into goals, tasks, and assignments over a specific time period.

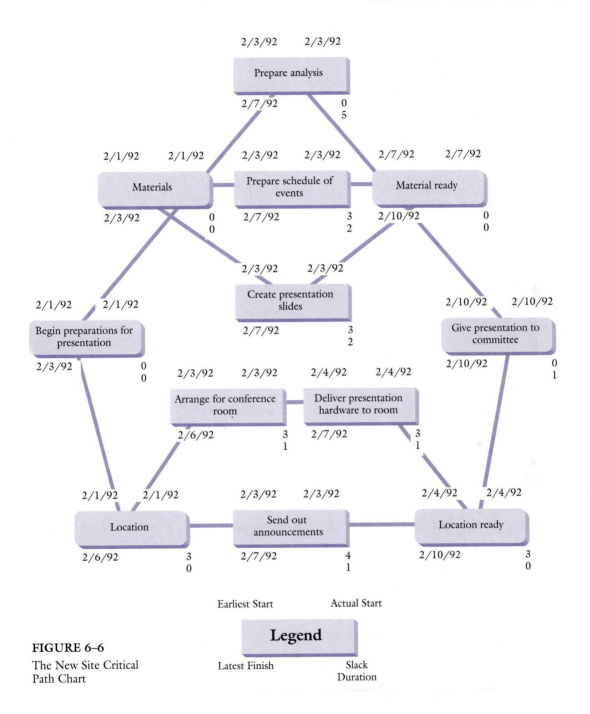

FIGURE 6–6

The New Site Critical
Path Chart

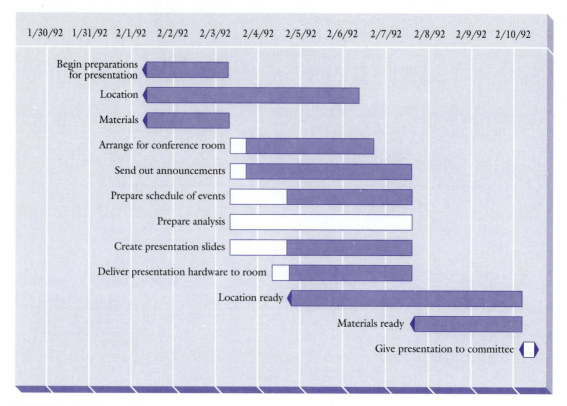

FIGURE 6–7

The New Site Task
Timeline

Here is another example project. Suppose your writing group has decided to develop a brochure for the local Board of Realty. You noticed that when new people arrive in your area, they have a difficult time orienting themselves to the city and county and to options for acquiring housing even though there are a number of inexpensive homes in the city. Here are the same three planning tools, the result of your group's commitment to developing and delivering the brochure. Figures 6–8 and 6–9 presents the task table and critical path chart for the project.

In the task timeline (Figure 6–10), the timeline has been broken down according to individual responsibilities, allowing individuals to monitor their own progress and for the project manager to chart everyone's progress.

These figures may make planning and delegation look easy. Many organizations have noted how difficult it is to plan but how important it is when complex projects are tightly scheduled. If you are just getting started with your group and your immediate goal is to begin planning your research project, consider these steps in launching a project, drawn from an experienced consultant to a technology-based company.[4] Note how these 14 steps draw from the many planning strategies and steps that we have introduced as individual and collaborative planning.

1. Establish a realistic project objective, the goals your group or team must accomplish.

2. Appoint a competent manager or have a plan and philosophy for making group decisions.

3. Define your group or ad-hoc team with appropriate communication links.

4. Staff with the technical and administrative skill necessary.

5. Identify key milestones that will demonstrate definite progress.

6. Identify the project in detail, isolating the specific tasks which support each milestone.

7. Assign each task to an individual or subgroup so that responsibility is clear.

8. Estimate the time or duration required to complete each task and thus to complete each milestone, including the start and finish dates for each task.

9. Estimate, if appropriate, the costs and resources required to complete the project, including their acquisition and refinement as part of your plan.

10. Produce a project schedule using the critical-path method or any of a number of planning tools such as a Gantt or task timeline.

11. Distribute for preliminary review the project schedule and revise with feedback from all participants.

12. Share the revised plan to confirm the group's consensus and ownership of the project.

13. Periodically review progress, expecting variation but with every effort to keep to the assigned schedule. Milestones often work as calls for group meetings and provide the foci for review.

14. Through the completion of the project take notes on the accuracy of task and milestone assignment, resource allocations, budgets, etc. This knowledge is priceless in planning the next project.

Finally, a review process is critical for success, and many groups and project teams begin with lofty goals and cheery attitudes and proceed to lose themselves in their individual accomplishments and personal setbacks.

Project Table　　　Bold alerts writer to idiosyncratic deadline.

Name	Earliest Start	Latest Finish	Actual Start	Resource	Resource	Resource
Phone/Visit Research	2/25/93	3/1/93	2/25/93	Johnson	Freeman	
Library Research	2/25/93	3/1/93	2/25/93	Williams		
Write Subsets	3/4/93	3/11/93	3/4/93	Johnson	Freeman	Williams
Make Initial Contact	2/25/93	3/8/93	2/25/93			
Consolidate Basic Goals	3/12/93	3/15/93	3/12/93	Johnson	Freeman	Williams
Cut and Paste Layout	3/11/93	3/15/93	3/11/93	Williams		
Scope/Pre-test Formats	3/11/93	3/15/93	3/11/93	Johnson		
Write First Draft	3/18/93	3/25/93	3/18/93	Johnson	Freeman	Williams
Present Formal Proposal	3/15/93	3/18/93	3/16/93	Johnson	Freeman	Williams
Format on Computer	3/25/93	3/28/93	3/25/93	Johnson		
Establish Test	3/26/93	4/29/93	3/30/93	Freeman	Freeman	
Test Documents	4/1/93	4/8/93	4/2/93	Johnson	Freeman	
Evaluate Results	4/5/93	4/10/93	4/9/93	Johnson	Freeman	
Revise Both Versions	4/8/93	4/15/93	4/14/93	Johnson	Freeman	Williams
Reformat Both Versions	4/15/93	4/18/93	4/21/93	Williams		
Prepare Compiled Report	4/18/93	4/29/93	4/26/93	Johnson	Freeman	Williams
Present Documents to Clients	4/22/93	5/1/93	4/26/93	Johnson	Freeman	Williams

FIGURE 6–8

The Board of Realtors Brochure Task Table

A plan is only as good as the follow-through, and regular planning and review meetings will help ensure success. Before your next meeting, consider some of the reasons why projects get off-track.

- Project objectives are poorly defined or poorly understood by those responsible. Overly ambitious objectives may stretch team members beyond their capabilities or stamina. Treat objectives as goals but also as learning. Immersing oneself in a given task may clarify the original objective and lead to a proposal for revision of what is actually expected by an individual or team.

- Project deadlines are compromised by unanticipated events or are unrealistic in the first place. Solid plans cannot anticipate every constraint or hurdle, and it is human nature to promise more than one can deliver. The real danger comes when individuals or the group

Board of Realtors Brochure Critical Path Chart

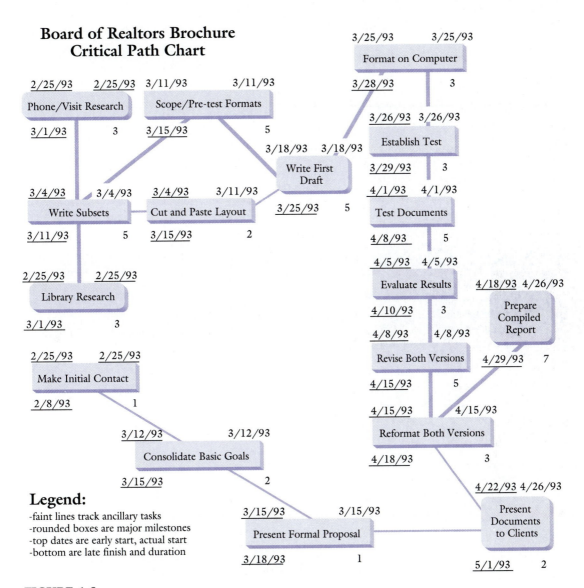

Legend:
- faint lines track ancillary tasks
- rounded boxes are major milestones
- top dates are early start, actual start
- bottom are late finish and duration

FIGURE 6–9

The Board of Realtors Brochure Critical-Path Chart

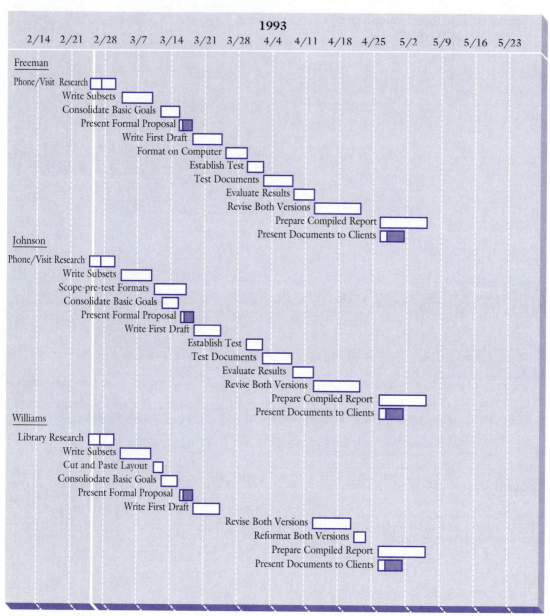

FIGURE 6–10

The Board of Realtors Brochure Task Timeline

begin to "cheat" because the schedule is unreasonable, and no one is willing to admit it.

• Project staffing is determined by availability more so than ability, or, within an organization, the authority and coordination between various factions is murky. Collaborative projects often begin with a spirit of volunteerism and shared duty, but the course of the project may reveal that certain people have hidden talents and interests that can benefit the entire project team. In this light, learning what a person or group can handle is essential for the long-term sustenance of the group.

• Someone by role, personal fiat, or insensitivity dominates the ability and drive of someone else. People may not even be aware of the tendency to assess someone else's worth prematurely. Here again is why territorial and procedural guidelines should be built consciously into a management philosophy.

These four situations are common and should not be seen as a recipe for failure. Rather, when recognized and confronted, they are the bases for continued planning, evaluation, and revision—the bases for success. To prepare for a review session, refamiliarize yourself with the group's planning chart and your individual assignments. Prepare an oral or written summary of your work to date. Do not come only to vent your frustrations but rather to propose alternative deadlines, procedures, and staff assignments.

STRATEGY 5: REFLECT AND ACT ON YOUR PROGRESS, CONFLICTS, AND ETHICS

1. *Review/Revise the Plan.* One important way to give everyone a feeling of ownership in a project is to review periodically, reconsider, and update your plan. What have you learned? What has changed since you initially reconstructed the context? Have you come up with better ways to achieve your goals, new tasks? Does the schedule need to be revised to reflect reality?

2. *Review Your Progress.* Where do you stand on your schedule? What do you need to do to meet the next milestone. Schedules must often be changed; but when that happens, make it a group decision—do not just let deadlines go by.

   Remember too, as students, a part of what your group members may be learning is how to work with a group and keep on schedule. Be tactful, be understanding, and be clear and straightforward in your expectations that everyone do his or her share. The alternative of silence usually leads to resentment and lowered motivation.

Reviewing progress is also an act of quality control. People have very different standards for their first drafts, from rough notes to ready-to-print. So use these progress reviews to help your partners keep moving by giving them supportive, good-natured feedback that suggests "what to do next."

3. *Reflect on the Dynamics of Your Own Collaboration.* Remember, as students, one of your top priorities is to learn from a collaborative situation. Being a good collaborator—one who can make a group succeed—is a real skill that takes more than being a sociable person. Take time to reflect as a group on how this group is working. We do not just mean to evaluate yourselves as good or bad, but to observe how the group is making decisions, solving problems, working as a social unit. A good way to start these reflections is by describing "an interesting feature" of the process as you see it. Listening to a tape of a group meeting is a good preparation for this reflection.

THE ETHICS OF CONFLICT

In Chapter Three we talked about the value of **substantive conflict** in which people propose alternative ideas, play devil's advocate, or raise questions and see problems. **Procedural conflict** (over how to go about doing the project) can improve efficiency, as long as it does not drag on and become a substitute for doing something. **Interpersonal conflict** focused on individuals or relationships, however, usually leads to bad feelings and bad decisions. Conflict is valuable but risky and is also threatening to some people. Is your group a place that encourages substantive conflict? Try to focus your reflection on specific instances. How did different people in the group react to those conflicts? You may find that some group members who were part of the conflict were quite comfortable, while others felt reluctant to disagree, fearing it would be taken as an attack. Would there be a way to make such conflict more productive?

You might set aside some time to ask everyone to reflect on their own **participation:** Do they fear they talk too much (while everyone else wishes they would speak up more)? Do they see themselves as fulfilling a particular role in the group? Do some people have difficulty speaking even in small groups? What is going on in their minds that makes it difficult?

There are two good reasons to care about participation. One is practical: Silent or more passive people are often untapped resources that could improve the quality of the group. As teachers, we have been surprised over and over again by students who sat silent in class but opened up in writing or conferences with good ideas and incisive responses to the questions raised in class. It is to your advantage as a group to get everyone's input, even if you have to use more formal means such as taking turns, or regularly asking for input from those more reserved.

The second reason is ethical. Our democratic ideals assert the worth and significance of every person regardless of their race, gender, creed, sexual orientation, or background. But to act on those ideals, we may have to counteract some strong forces in our society which work to silence or exclude certain people. Sometimes those forces reside in the situation. Businesses, for instance, have found that women and African Americans only enter an institution on equal footing after there is a critical mass of like people in the organization. Being a lone and visible minority turns people into outsiders. Does your group operate according to the norms of the dominant group (in terms of the places you meet, the social topics you discuss, the ways you relate) that are not the norm for everyone? Don't ignore practical details: Can a single mother returning to school come to your evening meetings? Can everyone afford to meet over dinner? Is there an equivalent to the "men's locker room" where some of the group carry on business and others are excluded?

Sometimes the forces that silence operate within the minds of the silenced. If you have never felt the force of racism or sexual discrimination, it may be hard to imagine the uncertainty it can foster: Am I being dismissed or ignored because I am black, or female, or gay? Because minorities have been in situations where the answer to this question was "yes"—often time after time—there are good reasons they may feel cautious or critical about entering a new group. For many, this history of lowered expectations, or being dismissed leads to feeling unnecessarily self-critical, or to assuming one must be a super achiever just to be accepted as competent. Given this state of affairs in our society, your working group may need actively to counteract these assumptions and concerns, take responsibility for sending a clear message to someone in the group that his or her participation is valued.

Finally, sometimes the forces that silence others are in ourselves. As well-meaning members of a group, we carry assumptions and habits within us that slip out unawares. Two members of our group begin to speak at the same time, one with an assertive male voice, the other with a soft, even somewhat timid female speech pattern: To whom do we turn to listen? How did we pick our group in the first place? What markers do we use to size up someone's ability or acceptability?

When groups are governed by democratic and ethical ideals, the groups thrive and the quality of work increases. But perhaps even more importantly, groups are a small version of the larger institutions in which most of us work. Reflecting on, and using school to learn about how we function in groups, is a good preparation for deciding where we stand in the larger circle of our profession and society.

GROUPTHINK AND ETHICAL ACTION

Groups have social roles, and one stated purpose (found in many company mission statements) is to achieve team spirit—a feeling of commitment and shared purposes tied to a consensus. But the downside of team spirit is another spirit called **groupthink.** There is security in numbers, and the desire to fit in, jump on the bandwagon, or go with the flow leads individuals to cave in to group pressures, avoid dissent, and silence their own thoughts and opinions. When groupthink takes over, the desire for uniformity and consensus is stronger than a desire for accuracy or effectiveness; outside opinions are ignored, reality testing disappears, and moral judgment is silenced. Does your group pass the test of encouraging *dis*sensus (as opposed to wanting immediate *con*sensus), or generating cooperative conflict, and of allowing for diversity even when you come to a consensus on actions to take?

We need to be realistic about the pressures groups can create. But that is only half the story. If you know how to carry out the balanced argument we talked about above, your working group in the business world will become one of the best places to act on your values, to speak for neglected or even unpopular views, and to take ethical action while still maintaining professional, cooperative relations with your colleagues and employer.

In the situations we sketched at Digi-Tech, the Community Literacy Center, Mountain Trails, and Connie's engineering firm (Chapters One and Two), people were making decisions that could help or hurt customers, the environment, the cities they lived in, as well as affect the happiness, self-esteem, or careers of coworkers and business competitors. Daily business decisions are often ethical decisions if you look deeply into the consequences. American business has a reputation for subordinating everything to the profit motive and for endorsing an ethic of competition, self-interest, and survival. If that is true, how could you possibly fit in, join a professional discourse community, or be a team worker and still speak for just action? There is a pressing need to speak for justice in business and the professions and there are many people who share these concerns. There are also some good ways to do so—and still be a "success."

Ethical action *begins,* not in great gestures of blowing the whistle or even in certainty about what is right and what is wrong. It begins in the way you analyze situations and define problems in the texts you write or in the issues you raise in a group. Think back to *conducting a rhetorical survey* in Chapter One and the more specific strategies for reconstructing the context and finding and defining problems that followed. Did you consider all the people who actually have a stake in the situation as you saw it and who will be affected by the problem you defined and the decision your group comes to? This is the first place for team players to speak up for justice—by recognizing *all* the stakeholders in a rhetorical situation (the consumers, the community, coworkers, or the environment, as well as corporate shareholders), and by bringing the values, needs, and consequences to these stakeholders into the picture and into the discussion. Speaking up for justice can happen simply by raising questions (What are the environmental consequences of substituting this material in our product?); by observing assumptions (Are we assuming that this increase in our profit margin is the only goal?); and by making ethical decisions a natural, necessary part of the problem as we define it (We cannot assume we speak for the minority contractors until we consult them). Movies and TV like to paint ethical action as black-and-white decisions, to deceive someone or quit your job. The price of success is to give in, put up, or shut up. And sometimes people do need to take dramatic and courageous stands. But the rhetorical strategies that we bring forward in this text put issues on the table in a collegial way. They not only give you a way to make ethical decisions and take ethical actions, but to make such thinking a visible part of your professional life and maybe even to change some corporate notions of "business as usual."[5]

Summary

- Collaboration involves trade-offs. It can take more time but lead to better work, if you know how to make the most of a group.
- Collaboration can take different forms, from coauthored writing to sharing tasks, to sharing ideas.

Making Collaboration Work for You

- Decide on **roles** people need to play (Strategy 1). Do you want to take a task-conscious role, keeping the assignment centerstage? Or do you prefer an interactive role, focused on supporting the members of the group? Does your group want a leader or coordinator? Would a formal recorder or devil's advocate help?
- Setting up an **agenda** gives you a plan for how to proceed and a way to test your progress. Make your agenda include some challenging but achievable, and operational goals (Strategy 2).
- To carry out a plan, assign tasks and set up **milestones**—the events or products that mark visible steps in your progress.
- A **communication loop** makes it easy to share information and make decisions, even if you cannot meet as a group.
- A **standard agenda** depends on a shared decision process that lets goals and decisions evolve as the group works together. The **Delphi** method gives more authority to the leader to decide how to make use of everyone's input.

- The time you spend talking over **ground rules** for working together can save time and prevent frustration later (Strategy 3).
- Business **projects,** like writing projects, are defined by specific objectives and a specific time frame. Tools developed for strategic planning and project management can help you manage your collaborative writing groups (Strategy 4).
- Tools like a **critical path** chart and a timeline or **Gantt** chart ask you to decide on milestones, the relationships between tasks, resources, responsibilities, and a time frame.
- **Reflecting** on your progress and the choices you made lets you monitor and control your group work at the time and learn from it for the future (Strategy 5).
- How good is your group at encouraging **participation** for everyone, including people who are not personally assertive?
- Does your group foster the kind of substantive conflict that tends to counteract **groupthink?**

Projects & Assignments

1. Look back at your responses to the survey on group work. How well has your experience as a student writer (or on the job) prepared you for these patterns? Write a brief assessment of your own experience.
2. Here is an outline for a "biosketch" that you can use to survey your experience and background in school and out and as an additional resource for collaboration. When each group or class member has completed the biosketch, they can serve as notes for introductions or profiles to distribute.

Biosketch

a. Name, address, phone:
b. Major, year in school:
c. Interests, career goals:
d. Work experience, responsibilities:
e. Past writing courses, training:
f. Computer skills (operating system, graphics and access):
g. Other skills (graphic, editing, interviewing, public speaking):
h. How do you view your writing ability? What have you recently written?
i. Are there topics, projects, tasks, or skills that you particularly want to pursue?
j. Do you have preferences in working with others?
k. Do you like to lead groups, play a supporting role, or avoid them?
l. How might members and leaders resolve conflicts in a group? What has been your experience?

3. Interview and observe an agency or department where collaboration is commonly used to make decisions and complete tasks. Refer to our

material in "Tools," Chapter Eight, on how to conduct an information-gathering interview, and make sure you have permission to take someone's time. Conduct a short interview that explores:

How groups are formed, sustained, evaluated, dispersed
How individuals in groups view their roles and responsibilities
How groups or teams collaborate
How they plan and monitor their progress

4. Some people think doing group work in school is a good preparation for the social reality of writing in business. Others say that it is unfair when grades are involved. Write a memo of recommendation to your instructor outlining some of the strengths and weaknesses of single-authored and group-authored collaboration, based on your experience. Given the Lunsford-Ede survey, what would you recommend instructors teaching business and professional writing should do?

5. Strategy 2 lists some specific steps you can take to manage your group work. Assign someone in your group to be the Monitor. The Monitor is responsible for (1) checking off which of those moves you make, (2) jotting down (very briefly) what you did or decided, and (3) reminding the group which of these moves you have yet to make. At the end of the planning session, take 10 minutes to evaluate your success as a group at using Strategy 2, and write a brief memo on what you did, what worked and didn't, and what you want to try next time.

6. The Standard Agenda and the Delphi methods of decision making represent two very structured—and very different—ways to handle group decisions. Experiment with one technique or the other and write a memo to your instructor that (1) evaluates how it worked and then (2) makes a case for how you would modify it for your situation. As you outline your proposed modification comment on: Who are we? What roles do we prefer (and why)? What must we accomplish and when?

7. Strategy 5 suggests some ways you can reflect on your own group performance. It is a good idea to include a 10-minute review session at the end of each session. Make a tape of your group sessions, just as you do with collaborative planning. Review the tape (so you can base your comments on observations) not just memory, and prepare a short report to make to your class about the progress, conflicts, and ethical issues you observed working in your group. (And just to test your powers of prediction, note down the feature of your process that you think will distinguish you most from the other groups.)

8. Most discussions of ethical choices in school writing focus on only two things: the decision to cheat on exams or to plagiarize on papers. Do you think the more complex kinds of ethical problems and decisions sketched in this chapter come up in any of the writing or group work you have done in school or not? Write a brief problem analysis of this issue for instructors from your point of view as a student.

9. The Community Literacy Center scenario at the end of Chapter One,

offers an interesting description of people working together to achieve numerous goals. Although we might say that the proposal team acted "ethically" by working to acquire funding for a not-for-profit, community program, study the scenario for *micro*-ethical decisions. These are the everyday decisions that people make as they work and write in rhetorical situations. For each decision that you find, who gave ground, who benefited, and whose agenda carried through?

10. The Community Literacy Center scenario also offers a timeline of events. Use these events to construct a critical path chart and task timeline to allow you to practice the planning tools (and planning software) introduced as project management.

11. Strategy 2 (on setting an agenda) and Strategy 4 (on strategic project management) describe a rational process, an ideal version of group work. The Community Literacy Center Scenario in Chapter One described the real process of proposal writing at a nonprofit organization. As you reread the scenario, sketch out an agenda for the group (goals, activities and roles for different people) and a critical path chart (with milestones and responsibilities) that includes all of the unexpected things that did occur. How does this real path differ from the ideal one they might have planned in advance? Turn your observations into a small set of guidelines that might help a project group like yours be flexible and anticipate what can happen (the problems and the opportunities). Write these guidelines as a memo to your own project group, showing how they apply to your group's experience wherever you can.

12. The Digi-Tech team you read about in the Corporate Scenario in Chapter One is holding a meeting to discuss adding new features to the Digi-Tech software. Such changes would help the architects at Exetor take these new features and specifications (such as a building's affect on the existing neighborhood) into account in their planning when they design office buildings and small manufacturing structures. When you think of the various stakeholders involved in development projects—people who are affected by development of the site or who work in office or manufacturing buildings—do you see any voices or concerns that are typically ignored in this planning process? Do the features which these stakeholders would find important have a place in the architects' and contractors' deliberations? Write a memo for this meeting that will make your ethical concern a practical concern at the meeting.

References

1. Hackman, J. R. "The Design of Work Teams." In J. W. Lorsch (Ed.), *Handbook of Organizational Behavior*. Englewood Cliffs, NJ: Prentice-Hall, 1983 (315–342).

2. Lunsford, A, & L. Ede. *Singular Texts/Plural Authors: Perspectives on Collaborative Writing*. Carbondale, IL: Southern Illinois University Press, 1990.

3. Goodall, L. H. *Small Group Communication in Organizations* (2nd Ed.). Dubuque, IA: Wm. C. Brown Publishers, 1990.
4. Glaser, G. "Managing Projects in the Computer Industry." *IEEE,* October, 1984.
5. Anderson, P. "Individual, Moral Agency, and Communicative Responsibility in the Teaching of Technical Writing." Conference on College Composition and Communication, 1991, Boston, MA.

7
Models for Writing

WRITERS NATURALLY seek models to work with and from, and this chapter offers many of the standard types of writing found in businesses and professions. Each model is described with a general format, a set of guidelines for adapting the format to situations, and examples. As we presented in Chapter Four, these models are, at best, approximations of the writing you will do. Therefore, use them only as a basis from which to write. Chapters One through Six will help you to adapt these models to the situations you face and to plan, draft, evaluate, and revise strategically.

FORM 1. Short Correspondence
Memoranda
Letters

FORM 2. Reports
Technical
Feasibility
Progress: informal, quarterly
Annual

FORM 3. Proposals
Request for Proposals; A Long, External, Solicited Proposal
Short Internal
Short External

FORM 4. Directions, Procedures, and Handbooks

This review begins by asking *What are the common forms of business writing?* and *How do you choose one form over another?*

7
Models for Writing

This chapter presents formats and guidelines for standard written forms in business. We have arranged the chapter around broad categories of writing: *short correspondence, reports, proposals,* and *other specialized forms.* The chapter assumes that you have turned to it because you need a picture or image to work from, a starting point. In Chapter Four, we began our discussion of drafting with boilerplate and models because it is natural and wise (rhetorically, politically) for writers to look for examples to guide their way.

Therefore, this chapter should be a resource for you, but it will not take the place of a careful survey of your situation or of planning and drafting to reach an audience. The forms that we present here have little, if any, of the rhetorical, social, or political information that makes writing so important in business and professional settings.

WHAT ARE THE COMMON FORMS?

For many years, researchers have surveyed businesses and professional settings to learn what is written, how often, and with what importance. Figure 7–1 summarizes general trends from two such studies,[1] illustrating that time spent does not always equal importance.

Of course, this figure does not accurately represent all businesses and organizations; for example, external proposals (rated moderate) could be the lifeblood for many companies and consume most of the time for some writers. Other trends are noteworthy: Writers spend much of their time cranking out letters and memos (along with phone calls and electronic mail), the ongoing conversation in most organizations or discourse communities. This correspondence, however, is not rated as important as internal proposals and progress reports. This may be true for two important reasons: Proposals and reports *inside* a company formalize and make public this conversation, and (especially with proposals) they capture the distilled ideas and arguments for change. People want to look good when their ideas are on the line, and these forms illustrate their good ideas and productivity.

Scholarly writing and consulting reports are ranked the lowest in importance and time spent, with little surprise. These kinds of written forms

	Importance	Time Spent
Internal proposals	high	high
Progress reports	high	high
Final reports	moderate	high
Miscellaneous memoranda & letters	moderate	high
External proposals	moderate	moderate
Internal reports (design, expense, travel)	low	moderate
Directions, specifications, procedures	low	moderate
Consulting reports	low	low
Journal articles, speeches	low	low

FIGURE 7–1

Common Business Forms, Their Importance to Writers and Cost in Time

attempt to share information with a much wider audience, often outside of a specific organization but within a discourse community. The Digi-Tech scenario illustrated how important this kind of information can be, but it is not valued in the same way as internal, organizational writing or writing for specific deadlines and shared purposes.

WHY DO PEOPLE CHOOSE ONE FORM OVER ANOTHER?

People choose from the above list of forms (and many others) because they are writing for specific purposes and because their writing precedes and follows specific documents. Throughout this book, we have presented the *paper trail* as an important part of the rhetorical situation and a potential tool for writers to survey a situation and to plan to write. If you are looking for example formats and guidelines, you are trying to recreate that paper trail. Here is a hypothetical paper trail, another way to think of the range of business forms. We have arranged in a flow chart most of the standard business forms as they might appear in a complex but ordinary business transaction.

Suppose your business traded communication software, and you wanted to sell your product to a new client in town. They have heard about you through trade shows, journals, and through positive reference from other venders. Here is how most of the standard forms for writing would come into play, supported also by oral communication (Figure 7–2).

In Phase 1, much of the correspondence is relatively informal, relying on phone calls, electronic mail, and letters to sketch out need, availability, and interest. Letters follow less formal, oral communication to start a public

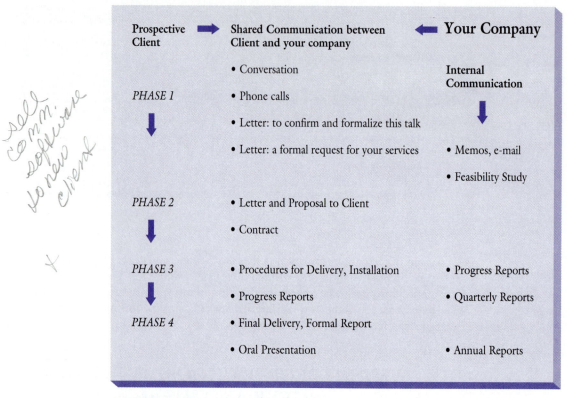

FIGURE 7–2
A Progression of Standard Business Forms

record and to send a formal request for proposal. Of course, within your company, the possibility of a new client triggers internal correspondence, and in this case a feasibility study to learn whether your software house can meet the client's needs on time.

In Phase 2, an external proposal is sent, with a contract following closely behind. We can imagine other informal correspondence taking place to announce the proposal and to expedite its assessment. In Phase 3, with the acceptance of the contract and proposal, progress reports play an important role: reporting on-time development of the software to the client, and weekly developments (good or bad) to various teams within your company. These internal reports are compiled to help write your company's quarterly report as well and eventually the annual report to shareowners.

Phase 4 is the delivery of the product—in this case software, installation service, and a sizable report that accompanies the product itself. This report not only explains and teaches, with directions and procedures, how to install and maintain the software, it reports the research involved and presents a trouble-shooting guide for future use. Products and reports are usually accompanied by direct person-to-person presentations; so your business deal ends, in a way, where it started, with less formal, oral communication.

As you use our models for classroom exercises or as models for writing, make sure you survey closely the rhetorical situation in which you write and the trail of papers and talk around you. The danger, lurking in all examples and formats, is taking something at face value. To guard against this, many larger organizations are publishing their own style guides, which list their models, formats, and written preferences. As you leave school or approach a new job, the best guidelines are those that help you adapt examples, models, and formats to specific audiences and purposes.

Following are four general types of business forms—*short correspondence, reports, proposals,* and *specialized forms.* Each type is arranged with a brief description of use, guidelines for developing and varying these forms, and examples that we think illustrate how to use and adapt generic models and formats for their purposes.

FORM 1: SHORT CORRESPONDENCE

Memos and letters are used to maintain the "conversation" in business: memos are typically used within an organization and letters to divisions or departments or to associates outside of the organization. Letters are preferable to memos for informal and formal circumstances. A letter could add a personal touch, and letters of transmittal commonly accompany long reports or proposals. Letter formats are also used for short correspondence that needs to set a formal, businesslike tone. Promotions and reprimands, for example, may be announced with a letter.

MEMORANDA

As Figure 7–1 illustrated, memos and letters take up much of a writer's time; memos are effectively written when they

- present a clear design, a well formatted message
- remind or make explicit the problem, issue, or solution at hand
- provide an appropriate level of detail
- support the message with the right word choice and tone.

The first six chapters of this book should help you prepare your message by assessing a situation and deciding how to draft a piece of writing. Since most memos (and letters) are in response to some other piece of communication, your awareness of the situation is critical.

The appearance of a memo is easier. Figure 7–3 shows the **format for a standard business memo** with flush-left margins. This memo, like most, begins with a standard heading for routing the memo and to recognize its intent quickly.

Guidelines for Writing Memos

- Memos may or may not incorporate company logos, titles, or letterhead. Preprinted forms will often have the heading blocked out for consistency.

- Check the conventions in your organization carefully; sometimes it is customary to include titles or positions next to names. Some writers sign their memo with their initials over their name to give a touch of respect.

- "Subject" (which is sometimes replaced by "Re") tags the memo and can be used to label a series of memos.

- Some memos may vary this standard form, by adding the date flush right, but do not mix letter formats (below, for example salutations) with memos.

- Memos are usually limited to a page or two at the most. Begin with either a greeting or short introduction that quickly announces the purpose of the memo.

- Memos are assumed to be brief and written to those who need no introduction or extensive background information in order to respond.

LETTERS

Letters are usually recognized as being more formal than memos, but they follow the same four criteria for effectiveness we presented for memos. Letters need to be visually appealing and written to address specific issues with appropriate detail and tone. Figure 7–4 shows the **format for a standard business letter.**

Guidelines for Writing Letters

- Avoid abbreviations for anything but obvious titles, such as *Mr., Ms.,* or *Dr.* or post office abbreviations (P.O. Box, PA for Pennsylvania).

- Most letter correspondence is with letterhead stationery; do not repeat address information.

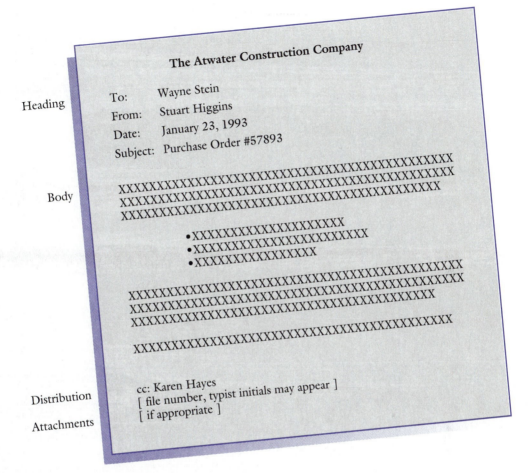

FIGURE 7–3
Standard Memo Format for Internal Correspondence

- If you do not know actual addressee, you may substitute an office or organization's name, as in *Central Distribution. To whom it may concern* is too vague for most correspondence and the general reference *Dear Sir* or *Gentlemen* is both sexist and often inaccurate.

- Salutations are usually kept formal, avoiding *Dear Stuart,* which is more common for personal correspondence. You may write a first name in pen over the formal salutation, if the correspondent is well-known.

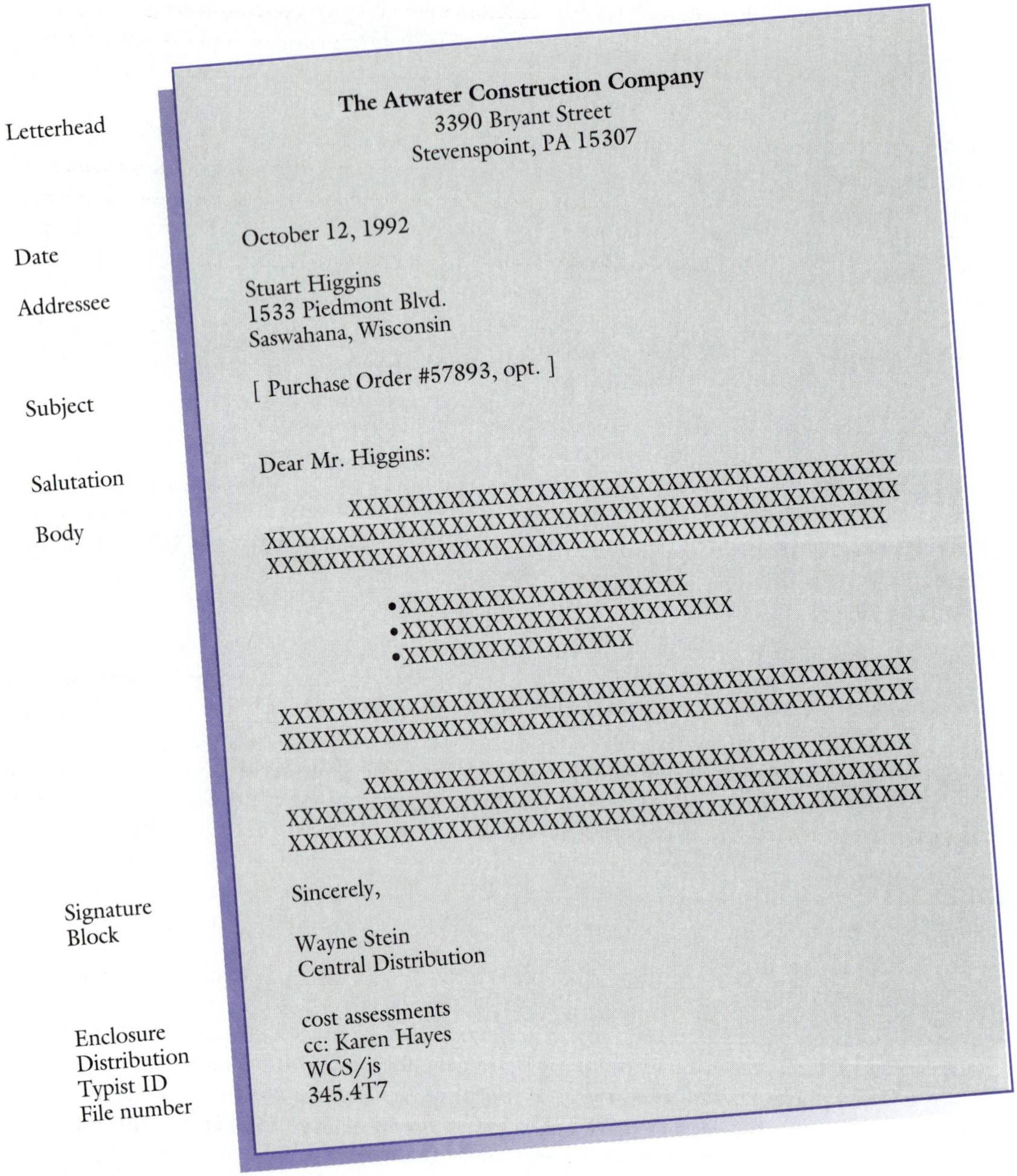

Letterhead

Date

Addressee

Subject

Salutation

Body

Signature
Block

Enclosure
Distribution
Typist ID
File number

The Atwater Construction Company
3390 Bryant Street
Stevenspoint, PA 15307

October 12, 1992

Stuart Higgins
1533 Piedmont Blvd.
Saswahana, Wisconsin

[Purchase Order #57893, opt.]

Dear Mr. Higgins:

XXXXXXXXXXXXXXXXXXXXXXXXXXXXXXXXXXXXX
XXXXXXXXXXXXXXXXXXXXXXXXXXXXXXXXXXXXX
XXXXXXXXXXXXXXXXXXXXXXXXXXXXXXXXXXXXX
XXXXXXXXXXXXXXXXXXXXXXXXXXXXXXXXX

• XXXXXXXXXXXXXXXXXXX
• XXXXXXXXXXXXXXXXXXXXX
• XXXXXXXXXXXXXXX

XXXXXXXXXXXXXXXXXXXXXXXXXXXXXXXXXXXXXXX
XXXXXXXXXXXXXXXXXXXXXXXXXXXXXXXXXXXXXXX
XXXXXXXXXXXXXXXXXXXXXXXXXXXXXXXX

XXXXXXXXXXXXXXXXXXXXXXXXXXXXXXXXXXXXX
XXXXXXXXXXXXXXXXXXXXXXXXXXXXXXXXXXXXXXX
XXXXXXXXXXXXXXXXXXXXXXXXXXXXXXXXXXXXXXX

Sincerely,

Wayne Stein
Central Distribution

cost assessments
cc: Karen Hayes
WCS/js
345.4T7

FIGURE 7–4
Standard Letter Format for External Correspondence

- Subject lines are sometimes added when coded information (such as a purchase order number) is involved and the letter is one of many that must be tracked for other uses. As with memos, the wording should be short and consistent.

- The body of letters varies with writers, their readers, and their situations. Letters tend to have a central message that is sandwiched between opening and closing paragraphs. Try for short sentences and paragraphs and use document design techniques (Chapter Eight) to make your letter as visually appealing as possible and blocked into functional units.

- Postscripts may be added to the notations that follow the signature block, and marketing and sales letters add them for emphasis and to add a personal touch. Most "postscripts" are afterthoughts and probably should be integrated into the letter.

- If a letter continues beyond the first page, print the second on good quality non-letterhead paper. You may add a heading that includes name of recipient, page number, and date. (See Example 3, "Letter of Confirmation and Contract," on page 287.)

Example Memos and Letters

To demonstrate how letters and memos create a chain of correspondence between organizations and clients and to illustrate how writers effectively vary standard formats, here is the file of correspondence between an engineering firm and a university program. The firm, Rogers and Associates Engineering Corp. (RAE), wanted a short course on writing technical reports and contacted the University Writing Program (UWP) for help. The letters and memo that follow illustrate how closely one message follows another, and how these writers used short correspondence to carry on formal business negotiations. Included in the series are Examples 1-6:

RAE to UWP	Confirmation letter, a brief RFP for a short course	May 3
UWP to RAE	Letter outlining a tentative proposal	May 10
RAE to UWP	Letter of confirmation and contract	June 9
UWP (internal)	Memo to university budget office	June 9
University to RAE	Letter acknowledging and accepting the contract	June 20
RAE to UWP	Letter of thanks, completion	Sept. 21

As you read though these letters, notice how the writers vary their style but, for the most part, keep their message up front for the reader.

R
A   **Rogers & Associates Engineering Corporation**
E   Post Office Box 330
         Salt Lake City, Utah 84110
         (801) 263-1600

May 3, 1989

Mr. Michael Rudick
Director of Writing Programs
University of Utah
Salt Lake City, Utah 84112

Dear Mr. Rudick:

This is to confirm our telephone conversation of last week regarding a short course in technical writing to be given at Rogers and Associates offices. As we discussed, most of our professional people have had technical writing classes in the course of obtaining their degrees. However, we feel that a brush-up course would greatly improve the quality of our technical reports.

We are of the opinion that a 1 to 1-1/2 hour class once a week for six to eight weeks would probably be the most beneficial course of action; approximately 12 employees would be in attendance at each class. Specific writing problems we would like included in the course are:

- Organization of the technical report
- Principles of outlining
- General rules of grammar (verb tenses, etc)
- How to clearly state technical objectives and results
- Orienting technical writing to intended audiences
- How to discuss and where to locate technical tables
- Writing summary chapters.

Thank you for your help. If further clarification is needed, or if you have any questions, please call.

Sincerely yours,

Connie S. Drury
Administrative Assistant

csd
cc: Dr. Vern Rogers

415 East 4500 South • Salt Lake City Utah 84107

Restate shared
information

Outlines basics for
further discussion.

Bulleted list of
concerns.

The author noted
that she did her
own typing

EXAMPLE 1

Confirmation Letter, a Brief RFP for a Short Course

THE
UNIVERSITY
OF UTAH

10 May 1989

Ms. Connie S. Drury, Admin. Asst.
Rogers & Associates Engineering Corp.
P. O. Box 330
Salt Lake City, Utah 84110

Dear Ms. Drury:

Since we last spoke on the phone, I've discussed your firm's instructional needs with colleagues. The specific items you listed in your letter as needing attention are the sorts of things we deal with in our technical writing courses, and we should be able to adapt our materials and teaching techniques to the needs of your on-the-job writers. Provisionally, I would expect to assign one or two qualified instructors to this project and place them under the supervision of Prof. John Ackerman, who coordinates technical writing in our Program. They would then draw up a formal proposal for your consideration.

The proposal would probably shape itself into three phases: (1) preparation, in which our instructors would study samples of the documents writers produce in your company, with the aim of identifying specific issues to emphasize; (2) the instructional program, which includes workshops for the writers and commentary on what they produce; and (3) evaluation of the results and the appropriate follow-up. I believe we can accommodate the time schedule you suggest, and, throughout, we would nearly always be using the actual documents your writers are working on. I assume that many or most of these documents are collaborative projects, and we would attend to the processes involved in that kind of work.

I mentioned to you the alternative ways in which we could manage the contracting. Either your company could hire the personnel as private consultants or could engage the University Writing Program as the contractor. I would, personally, prefer the latter, as I would like to have the Program identified as contributing to extramural professional writing; clearly, our teaching benefits from experience with what goes on in the world we prepare our students to enter, and we would welcome the opportunity to show our qualifications. We must, however, be sensitive to the frequently levelled charge that University agencies compete unfairly with private firms offering comparable services. I'm discussing this issue now with some administrators, in the hope of convincing them that the benefits outweigh the disadvantages.

This summarizes where we're at to the moment. Please call if I can clarify anything or if you have any new information that would help us prepare the proposal.

Sincerely yours,

Michael Rudick
Director

University Writing Program
345 Orson Spencer Hall
Salt Lake City, Utah 84112
(801) 581-7090

Flush-left letter design.

Reminder of prior correspondence. Recognition and attention to specific items in past letter.

A three-part proposal

The new issue of how to set up the contract.

Sharing the behind-the-scenes activity to keep the reader informed.

EXAMPLE 2
Letter Outlining a Tentative Proposal

R
A   **Rogers & Associates Engineering Corporation**
E   Post Office Box 330
                    Salt Lake City, Utah 84110
                      (801) 263-1600

Vern C. Rogers
   President

June 9, 1989   G-1-U

Mr. Michael Rudick
Director of Writing Programs
University of Utah
Salt Lake City, Utah 84112

Dear Mr. Rudick:

This letter will serve as formal confirmation of our agreement to the terms outlined below for the University of Utah to provide a Technical Writing Workshop at the offices of Rogers and Associates Engineering Corporation (RAE).

_____

TERMS OF AGREEMENT

A technical writing workshop will be conducted at the offices of RAE. The workshop will begin as soon as possible and will be conducted in three phases:

Phase 1. Preparation

This phase will involve a "site visit" by instructor(s) which will acquaint instructor(s) with how work is accomplished and allow meeting members of the RAE staff prior to the workshops. Also during this phase, a study will be conducted of RAE reports. Instructors will become familiar with RAE style and the type of information contained in reports. The document study will also enable instructors to determine areas of strength and weakness.

Phase 2. Instruction

The workshop portion of the plan is based on a once-per-week session of 1-1/2 hours for approximately six weeks. It is possible that one or two more weeks may be needed depending on the material needing to be covered. There will be two instructors at each session; a supervisor

415 East 4500 South • Salt Lake City Utah 84107

The tone shifts to procedures and legal concerns, since money is now at stake.

The contract, echoing the earlier proposal, is presented.

EXAMPLE 3
Letter of Confirmation and Contract

Mr. Michael Rudick
June 9, 1989
page 2

G-1-U

will also be used but will not necessarily be at every session. RAE documents will nearly always be used in order to illustrate particular problems and facilitate pertinent suggestions for improving writing skills.

Phase 3. Evaluation and Follow-Up

An evaluation of the workshops, including any follow-up suggestions, will be made. If desired by RAE, a report containing recommendations and comments will be written.

The agreed price will be $3,000.00, payable in two equal payments of $1,500.00. The first payment will be due upon commencement of Phase 1 of the workshop play, with the final payment due upon satisfactory completion of the workshop. All invoices should be directed to:

Mrs. Geri Wood
Accounting Supervisor
Rogers and Associates Engineering Corporation
P.O. Box 330
Salt Lake City, Utah 84110-0330

We would like to thank you for all your help in arranging this workshop, and with all your efforts on our behalf in communications with the University. We are looking forward to a successful program which we know will greatly benefit our employees as well as Rogers and Associates.

Sincerely yours,

Vern C. Rogers

Vern C. Rogers

VCR:csd

cc: G. Wood

515 East 4500 South • Salt Lake City Utah 84107

A new contact person is announced.

Cordial closing

EXAMPLE 3,
continued

A variation
on the
standard
heading.

University Writing Program

DATE: 9 June 1989

TO: Vice-President James Brophy

FROM: Michael Rudick. Director

RE: Request for waiver of indirect costs

The University Writing Program is contracting for a short in-service course in technical writing with Rogers and Associates of Salt Lake City. In order to meet that firm's price limit, we are requesting that the University waive the customary indirect costs.

A brief context,
and a strategy for
keeping the cost
of the short course
low.

The total contract is for $3,000. This is a small amount, and, we think, relatively cheap for the services being offered. But we are willing to contract at that price for three reasons:

- we gain experience in the professional world we are training our students to enter, and we can then use this experience to improve our technical writing courses;

- since we will do a good job at this, it could lead to further requests for similar services, which we would feel entitled to contract at a more realistic price;

Key arguments for
"waiving direct
costs" are
presented in
bulleted form.

- our Program, and the University through it, should benefit from increased visibility in the local professional community.

The personnel to be involved are instructors in our Program's technical writing course, and the project is to be supervised by Prof. John Ackerman, the coordinator of that course. The experience they gain will have quite direct effects on the course's design and teaching. Students in that course (largely from the College of Engineering) are qualifying themselves for jobs in companies like Rogers & Associates; they stand to benefit from exposure to what we can learn about how writing is produced (and improved) in professional situations.

An attempt to
address potential
arguments against
the request for
waiver of costs.

I do not anticipate that the University Writing Program would ever be in the business of extramural instruction in a big way, because we haven't a large enough staff to do so. But I can imagine our doing this sort of thing from time to time. It could benefit the Program financially, it would contribute to our teaching, and it would give us some recognition in the professional community, all of which are advantageous to the University. So, your granting our request this time would enable us to get started.

Thank you for your consideration.

EXAMPLE 4

Memo to University
Budget Office

THE
UNIVERSITY
OF UTAH

20 June 1989

MR. VERN C. ROGERS, PRESIDENT
ROGERS AND ASSOCIATES ENGINEERING CORPORATION
P.O. BOX 330
SALT LAKE CITY UT 84110

SUBJECT: Award-Fully Executed
U of U PID #8906049

Dear Mr. Rogers:

We wish to acknowledge receipt of your letter award dated 9 June 1989 for the project entitled "TECHNICAL WRITING WORKSHOP" under the direction of Dr. John Ackerman, University Writing Program.

The amount of the award is $3,000. The period of performance is 9 June 1989 through 15 August 1989.

We appreciate your support of this project.

Sincerely,

Richard H. Timpson, Director
Sponsored Projects

smr

cc: Dr John Ackerman

Office of Sponsored Projects
309 Park Building
Salt Lake City, Utah 84112
(801) 581-6903
Fax Machine (801) 581-3007

Uppercase print for a formal tone.

Subject line to help track this letter.

Formula used to accept and acknowledge the contract, restating key items.

EXAMPLE 5
Letter Acknowledging and Accepting the Contract

R
A   **Rogers & Associates Engineering Corporation**
E   Post Office Box 330
                        Salt Lake City, Utah 84110
                          (801) 263-1600

Vern C. Rogers
   President

September 21, 1989

Dr. Michael Rudick
Director, Writing Program
University of Utah
Salt Lake City, Utah 84112

Dear Dr. Rudick:

On behalf of all the participants of the Technical Writing Workshop series at Rogers and Associates, I would like to offer our sincere thanks and hearty congratulations on an excellent program. Many of the ideas and techniques presented have already been implemented and the results are beginning to show.

We would offer special plaudits to Dr. John Ackerman and Mr. Tom Hazuka for their roles in the workshops. Their willingness to incorporate our ideas and wishes helped *"personalize"* our program, allowing special emphasis on particular technical writing problems. The enthusiastic approach employed by Dr. Ackerman and Mr. Hazuka made the lessons interesting and thought-provoking, and their innovative *"homework"* assignments, using samples of Rogers and Associates reports, gave us the opportunity to see our problems first-hand. The success of the workshop is clearly a reflection of their hard work and planning.

Once again let me express our thanks for your efforts setting up the workshops through the University — we realize that without your help the workshops might never have taken place. We appreciate the time you spent developing the structure for the workshop series and your foresight in selecting Dr. Ackerman as the Workshop Supervisor. The University of Utah is indeed fortunate to have such well qualified, innovative, and responsive people in its writing program.

Sincerely yours,

Vern C. Rogers

VCR:csd

cc: Dr. J. Ackerman
    Mr. T. Hazuka

515 East 4500 South • Salt Lake City Utah 84107

EXAMPLE 6
Letter of Thanks,
Completion

FORM 2: REPORTS

Since business people are routinely accountable for their actions, and because their actions usually have a significant consequence—such as a sale, reorganization, or a promotion—much writing in business takes the form of a report. Reports are common in business also because information is as much a product as hardware or services. Most reporting is relatively brief, because the information is used within an organization (and thus needs no extra explanation), or it is written for a specific problem or situation (such as a consulting report). Longer reports accompany substantial research or as the basis for important decisions with complex ramifications.

note X
repts as decision making tools — a means to end it not

Figure 7–5 offers a list of common business reports and their uses. Generally, shorter reports have a simple format, made simple because the writer shares a high degree of information with the reader. Short reports tend to respond to a specific need for information, and therefore they should feature that information, getting it said as quickly and clearly as possible. Other background information (history, methods, extensive interpretation, lengthy examples, etc.) is usually far less relevant because it is shared information or beside the point of the report.

Brief reports generally follow a simple format, one that may be integrated into a memo or letter form. Reports have two key features:

Introduction	They review the problem, question or topic of the report:
	What will the reader find?
	How does it connect with prior correspondence?
	What problem or need is addressed?
The Facts	They present findings, answers to questions or relevant information:
	What information does the reader need?
	Is it presented in the order and manner expected?
	Is the detail appropriate?
	Have I shared the information with all who care?

The Problem/Purpose Statement and Problem Analysis format described in Chapter Two are specific examples of this pattern. You will succeed as a report writer if your writing carries these two features, and as long as you present your information in an orderly, readable manner. Below are formats, guidelines, and examples of some of the common business reports.

TECHNICAL REPORTS

Technical reports may be about technical information, such as financial or engineering data, but the format for a technical report has features common

Shorter Reports	Uses
Task force or Committee	Reports that present the results of a specific group or team that meets for a specific purpose or routinely for a common goal.
Minutes or Summary	Reports that reduce and distribute key events or aspects, to create a public record or archive.
Expenses or Travel	Reports of expenditures or performance that are essential for accounting or monitoring of activity.
Periodic	Reports of a regular basis (weekly, monthly, quarterly) that illustrate and summarize progress to date and whether project goals have been met.
Progress or Status	Reports linked closely to goals, tasks and objectives--often as part of lengthy projects with many people involved.
Longer Reports	**Uses**
Feasibility	Reports that support or lead to a decision or a choice between two alternatives.
Technical	Reports that present the results of a lengthy research process where extensive data gathering has occurred.
Annual	Reports that summarize and positively characterize an organization's development and productivity.

FIGURE 7–5

The Uses of Common Business Reports

to many longer reports. As Figure 7–6 illustrates, the *front matter* contains the necessary information to route the document, present it visually, summarize it, and offer a organizing plan for the reader. Then the *body* of the actual report begins with a carefully organized argument: why the research was necessary, how data was gathered, what was found, and what it all means. In the *closing matter,* the report provides less essential information, which is usually read by secondary readers.

Guidelines for Writing Technical Reports

- *Covers* and *Title Pages* usually serve the function of helping to route a document, protecting it, and giving it a polished appearance. Title pages should include the names and affiliations of the contributors and any referencing information (file numbers, copyright information, or restrictions on distribution or photocopy-

Front Matter	*Cover* or bound jacket *Letter of Transmittal* announcing the report *Title Page* *Executive Summary* which reduces the entire report and presents findings *Table of Contents* *List of Figures* for readers who want to move quickly to tables and graphs *Glossary* of key terms
Body	*Introduction* An overview of the report content and structure Provide or remind the reader why the report (and research) is needed. *Method* How the information or report was prepared Convince the reader that the best, most reliable steps were taken. *Facts* What was found, what is delivered Link the data directly to the problem or situation at hand. *Discussion* How the facts fit the problem Explain how to make sense of the facts, how and how not to interpret. *Conclusions* The overall significance of the research results Make clear for the reader how the results fit the larger picture. *Recommendations* Future actions, the next step Leave the reader with a clear plan for action.
Closing Matter	*Appendices* with supporting material of secondary importance *Notes* explaining complex points or provide references.

FIGURE 7–6
Standard Format for a Long, Technical Report

ing). Title pages usually center and enlarge this information for easy reading.

- *Letters* (or memos) *of Transmittal* are important statements, announcing the arrival of a report and completing the social negotiation between a writer (as in a proposal team) and a reader (a client). Letters of transmittal rarely introduce new information: They mention the title or substance of the report; they may say something about the features, content, or arrangement of the report; they may express appreciation for hard work or contributions, and they importantly share an avenue for continued correspondence (such as a contact person or the invitation to speak or write).

- *Executive Summaries* follow or sometimes replace a table of contents. These summaries are included because reports are often read for the recommendations or key findings from the research. Therefore, they should present the key information to support the decisions and actions of the reader and this information should be presented in the same order as the reader will find in the full text. Never add new information, introduce new terms, or present any inconsistencies with the longer report.

- *Tables of Contents, Lists of Figures (or Tables),* and *Glossaries* all help to itemize the key features in a text and make them accessible. The table of contents should exactly match headings that divide and organize the text, with clear numbering. They should have enough detail so that readers can scan to find the information and location they want. Lists of figures summarize and make accessible all of the graphic information in a text, a useful reference for those readers who want to skip the discussion and pursue the data. Glossaries can be arranged alphabetically, like a dictionary, or by location (by chapters). They provide brief definitions and may include cross references. Consider including a glossary if your readers need extra instructions in your terminology.

- The report itself is usually arranged around the standard format for the body, illustrated in Figure 7–6. Writers vary these sections, when the situation or reader warrants it. Consult Chapter Four for strategies for developing these sections and include "metadiscourse" (Chapter Five) to cue the reader to movement from one section to another.

    Use document design techniques (Chapter Eight) to separate sections visually. Especially if a report is lengthy, start sections on a new page, and use clear headings to announce the progression of information.

- *Closing Matter* usually consists of an appendix, which presents in list form detailed information that would otherwise clog a report. Writers often move numerical data, examples, and product descriptions or other boilerplate to the appendix so that readers can reference it if they choose. An appendix is a resource file, so the references in the text (i.e., see appendix C) must be clear and accurate. Sometimes business writers are bound by contract or law to include documents in an appendix—in the case, their physical appearance is all that is necessary, or they will be read by secondary or specialized readers such as accountants or lawyers.

Other closing matter such as *Endnotes* or a *Bibliography,* may be included if an organization or community require them. An *Index* would accompany only a very long report, in which readers will cross reference information. In building an index, identify the words or terms that readers will need or question, list the words that refer to these key words or terms, arrange them alphabetically or with headwords in the way a cookbook lists recipes under "Entrees."

Example Financial Committee Report

Examples 7a and 7b are presented to show a lengthy technical report in two forms. School districts are accountable to the Board of Education, with capital outlays established by the state legislature. Jordan School District's finance committee met and researched their expenditures for six months, concentrating on expenses, income, and recent and projected growth and development. After summarizing their financial status, they presented recommendations to fund their district appropriately. Therefore, this finance committee report condenses months of research and makes a proposal in the form of recommended funding.

First is an outline of the report to give you a sense of how they organized the information and arranged it, adapting the standard report format to fit their needs. The body of the report begins with the Financial Committee Mission and Background. Methods ("Procedures") and findings are combined in section III, followed by a section that outlines policy for expenditures and a section that presents funding alternatives. The excerpted version of the actual report below shows how that staggering array of features and goals noted in the outline was turned into a concise report.

FEASIBILITY REPORTS

Feasibility reports are necessary when important decisions need further study. Maybe your firm needs research to decide how to diversify, or your school needs research to know whether a new admissions plan will work more efficiently. Generally, feasibility reports are arranged around this general format. See Figure 7-7 on page 306.

The form of the report may include many of the features of a longer technical report, such as a title page, letter or memo of transmittal, table of contents, appendix, etc. Usually, readers will expect if not predict one alternative in a feasibility study; therefore, present the bottom line in a letter or executive summary.

OUTLINE

Jordan School District
Finance Committee Report

Cover Letter

Presentation of the report to the Utah State Board of Education
Explanation of the activities of the Finance Committee and purpose of report
Expression of gratitude to Board, other committees who helped

Executive Summary

Recommendations are based on the following:
- The need for building improvements, program expansion, equipment additions in order to meet safety codes
- School Construction is needed to provide for enrollment growth and to replace buildings with serious problems

Recommendations
1. In five years provide $172 million to fund the projects outlined
   to be provided as follows:
   a. Sell $115 million in voter-approved general obligation bonds to build six schools
   b. Provide $57 million to complete pay-as-you go capital improvements
2. Adopt a balanced funding approach by levying tax rates
   Impact
- Tax increase on homes

I. Finance Committee Mission

To develop a multi-year financial plan for Jordan School District
Deal with capital outlay needs
Identify funding options
Establish financial priorities

Goals:
A. Review district's financial status
B. Review financial needs of all aspects of School District
C. Review revenue options
D. Review priorities
E. Prepare and submit a report to the Board of Education

EXAMPLE 7a

Finance Committee
Report Outline

II. Background of the Problem

    A. Tax History
        1. Decline in business and industry tax base
        2. Population growth
    B. Changing Demographics
        1. Increased student population
            a. New housing in South and West
    C. Buildings
        1. Average building age is 22
            a. Seismic and other code upgrades are due

    D. Summary

III. Procedures and Findings

    A. Mission and Goals
        Review of mission and goals assigned

    B. Outside Consulting Firm
        Dougherty, Dawkins, Strand & Bigelow Inc. serve as advisors

    C. Enrollment Growth
        Enrollment projections studied to determine future needs

    D. Status of District Buildings
        Buildings reviewed, seismic and general maintenance criteria

    E. Current Budget Status
        Capital Outlay and debt service reviewed

    F. Project Funding Capability
        Revenue determined insufficient for upkeep and growth needs

    G. Revenue Options
        General obligation bonds determined most feasible

    H. Committee Reports and Funding Requests
        All project priorities and costs evaluated

    I. Interim Report

    J. Foundation Principals and Priority Guidelines
        Subcommittee organized to develop principals

    K. Sifting Subcommitee--Removal of Project Duplication
        Funding requests integrated

EXAMPLE 7a,
continued

L. Establishing Project Priorities

M. Project Rankings and Funding Allocations
same as previous

N. Funding Recommendations
Money requested for high priority projects

O. Tax Rate Proposal
Combined property tax rate best approach

IV. Foundation Principals Governing Capital Expenditures

A. Public Schools to provide quality experiences in safe environment

B. Teachers are the true educators; facilities etc. support teachers

C. Schools do not function in isolation. They require support of family,
community etc.

D. All "stakeholders" in education process hold responsibility for cost

E. Funding for capital expenditures limited, resources should be
assigned to priorities, which are:
1. Meet requirements of legislation or regulation.
2. Keep education environment safe.
3. Provide facilities, materials, services necessary for learning.
4. Consolidate facilities and programs where possible.
5. Provide maintenance.
6. Provide facilities adequate for future growth.
7. Replace facilities that are not cost effective.
8. Meet the needs of supplemental programs.

F. Maintain an appropriate capital outlay ratio between all priorities
• tax rate of .0020 annually devoted to maintenance and
upgrading
• tax rate of .0020 annually to meet debt service and capital
outlay

G. Alternative housing and distribution of students used to maximize
capacity

H. Planning should maximize opportunities for the use of state
resources

EXAMPLE 7a,
continued

I. Facilities should be shared between schools and community when possible

J. Schools supplement, not supplant roles of home and community

V. Examination of Funding Alternatives

   A. Pay as you go: Ability of the Board of Education to pay for capital projects with cash available.
      1. Constraints; existing debt payments and property tax rate
      2. Can't generate enough money

   B. Lease/Purchase Financing: leases can be entered as long as they are subject to annual approbation
      1. Recommended for vehicles and computers only.

   C. General Obligation Bonds
      1. Least costly of the alternatives
      2. Must be approved by simple majority in general election
      3. Bonds would be retired in fifteen years

   D. Miscellaneous Sources of revenue
      1. "Robin Hood" bill
      2. Interest on investments
         a. Neither are predictable

Appendix

A. Committee Members listed

B. Enrollment Projections (Graphs)

C. Capital Outlay Project Requests—List of Duplications

D. Synopsis of Capital Outlay Planning Cornmittee Reports
      1. Alternative Housing Report
      2. Seismic Committee Report
      3. Transportation Committee Report
      4. Ongoing Maintenance Report
      5. Technology Committee Report
      6. Remodeling/Renovating Committee Report
      7. Jordan Technical Center Master Plan

EXAMPLE 7a,
continued

Jordan School District

Critical Issues
in Capital Outlay Planning

FINANCE COMMITTEE REPORT
June 9, 1992

EXAMPLE 7b
Finance Committee
Report Excerpts

Board of Education

Jordan School District

Dr. Raymond W. Whittenburg — Superintendent of Schools
9361 SOUTH 300 EAST • SANDY, UTAH 84070-2998
Phone (801) 565-7100 • FAX (801) 565-7136

June 9, 1992

Board of Education
Jordan School District
9361 South 300 East
Sandy, Utah 84070

Dear Board Members:

The Finance Committee is pleased to submit its final report according to the charge given it by the Board of Education.

This report summarizes the efforts of the Finance Committee. which held over twenty (20) meetings from December through May. Throughout the process, the committee conducted a number of activities and discussions that provided understanding and built consensus among committee members. That consensus is reflected in the recommendations presented in the final report.

The committee wishes to express gratitude for the many hours of work by the other Critical Issues in Capital Outlay Planning committees in making initial recommendations. Their clear and insightful information was invaluable to us.

As we conclude our task, we thank you for the opportunity to be of service to you and to the patrons of the Jordan School District.

Sincerely,

Clark Stringham, Chairperson
Finance Committee

EXAMPLE 7b,
continued

Jordan School District
Critical Issues in Capital Outlay Planning
Finance Committee Report
June 9, 1992

1

EXECUTIVE SUMMARY

The Finance Committee's recommendations are based on the following observations:

- An increase in the current tax rate is necessary if Jordan District is to make the building improvements, program expansion, and equipment additions required to meet life/safety codes, keep buildings in an adequate state of repair, and maintain quality education programs.
- Additional revenue is required to fund the school construction necessary to provide for enrollment growth and to replace those schools with such serious problems that upgrade and retrofit are not economically feasible.

Finance Committee Recommendations:

1. In the next five years, provide $172 million to fund the projects outlined in this report.
   Capital funds should be provided as follows:

   a. Sell $115 million in voter-approved general obligation bonds to build six schools (three replacement and three additional). Retire the bonds 15 years from the date of issue.

   b. Provide $57 million (about $11.4 million annually) to complete pay-as-you-go capital improvement projects in existing buildings.

2. Adopt a balanced funding approach by levying the following tax rates:

   Debt Service...0.0020 (10 mills)
   (To fund bond payments for school construction and major renovations)

   Capital Outlay..0.0020 (10 mills)
   (To fund pay-as-you-go improvements in existing buildings)

   Total..0.0040 (20 mills)

Impact:

- Estimated annual tax increase on a $75,000 home assessed at $50.200....$58.00

EXAMPLE 7b,
continued

Jordan School District
Critical Issues in Capital Outlay Planning
Finance Committee Report
June 9, 1992

2

I. FINANCE COMMITTEE MISSION

The Finance Committee was charged by the Board of Education to develop a multi-year financial plan for Jordan School District that deals with capital outlay needs, identifies funding options, and establishes priorities.

Goals:

A. Review the District's financial status.

B. Review the capital outlay needs related to enrollment growth, building maintenance, building refurbishing/remodeling, transportation, seismic retrofit, and technology.

C. Review the capital outlay revenue options.

D. Review the capital outlay priorities recommended by other Critical Issues Committees.

E. Prepare a report for the Board of Education which includes a multi-year financial plan for addressing capital outlay needs.

EXAMPLE 7b,
continued

II. BACKGROUND OF THE PROBLEM

A. Tax History

Jordan School District prior to the late 1970s was considered one of the most wealthy school districts in Utah. With the combination of a reduced growth rate in porperty tax revenue from industry due to a decline in the copper market and rapid growth in student population, Jordan School District went from one of the highest to one of the lowest school districts in property tax revenue per student. The problem stems from the fact that Jordan School District is made up of bedroom communities with very little of its tax base coming from business and industry. Most of the wage earners commute out of the district to their employment. Hence, the majority of the tax burden for Jordan School District falls upon the homeowner as contrasted to other districts in the valley where more of the tax burden is borne by business and industry.

B. Changing Demographics

Another aspect to the problem is Jordan District's changing demographics. The district is experiencing an increasing student population as a result of increased new home construction and higher occupancy levels of existing homes. The district is divided into three administrative areas—North, South, and West. The increasing student population is particularly pronounced in the South and West Areas, while the maturing population of the North Area is experiencing minor population declines. (See Enrollment Projections—Nov. 26, 1991, in Appendix B, pages 20-21.) Another interesting and difficult aspect of the problem is rapid expansion of the middle school and high school populations.

C. Buildings

The final aspect of the problem is the aging of the district's buildings upgrades. The average building age is now 22 years buildings is rapidly increasing. The cooling systems ne up

EXAMPLE 7b,
continued

PROGRESS REPORTS

Progress or status reports brief people on the competition of tasks. The readers of progress reports usually have received some kind of proposal or plan, and they want to know if you or your team are proceeding according to schedule. Progress reports also can initiate change, and you can use them to report departures or glitches in planned actions, how you will deal with those changes, and your suggestions for a successful and eventual comple-

Jordan School District
Critical Issues in Capital Outlay Planning
Finance Committee Report
June 9, 1992

5

III. PROCEDURES and FINDINGS

The Finance committee met bimonthly from mid-December, 1991, through March, 1992 in two-and three-hour work sessions at the District Office. Beginning in April, the full committee or subcommittees met weekly or as frequently as necessary to complete the work on schedule. Following is a list of tasks completed, findings, and resulting decisions:

A. **Mission and Goals**
The committee became familiar with the scope of the Critical Issues in Capital Outlay Planning Project by reviewing the missions and goals assigned to the Finance Committee and the six other project committees.

B. **Outside Consulting Firm**
The board of Education selected the firm of Dougherty, Dawkins, Strand & Bigelow, Inc. to serve as advisors to the Finance Committee and provide such profesional services as financial projections, feasibility studies relat funds, legal requirements, etc.

C. **Enrollment Growth**

EXAMPLE 7b,
continued

tion of the project or task. In Chapter Six, we concluded our discussion of managing complex projects with examples of graphic tools for planning and monitoring progress. If your group or team developed a task time-line, you could use progress reports to announce the completion of tasks along that timeline. Figure 7–8 on page 306 shows a general format for a progress report.

Example Informal Progress Report

Look back at the discussion of the Oskaloosa Brewing case in Chapter Five. Notice that the final version of this report was designed to satisfy two audiences, the faculty supervisor who wanted to monitor the decision-making process of the group, and the company official who wanted to see what, if anything, they were finding. This example (considered Example 8) uses headings to let readers locate the answers to their questions.

Introduction
  Identify the problem, question, or task at hand.
  Present an overview of the alternatives addressed (with recommendations) or
  Present the process that led to the selection of these alternatives.

Research Methods
  Introduce the criteria applied or
  Introduce the research conducted and why the methods are appropriate.

Findings and Evaluation
  Present the results of your research by judging each alternative against the criteria.
  Explain why and how the criteria distinguished one choice from another.

Recommendations
  Present a detailed account of why one alternative is better or why one choice is better.

Conclusion
  Present a plan for acting on the chosen alternative or
  Discuss how a choice or alternative can be implemented.

FIGURE 7–7

Format for a
Feasibility Report

Introduction
  Identify the project or task that your report addresses.
  Briefly summarize the need, background, problem.

Your Progress or Status
  Report work completed, following the organization of a proposal or earlier correspondence.
  Report work left to complete.
  Report changes or revisions in the plan, proposal, or timeline.

Conclusion
  Place the work completed and the work to do in the larger picture of the project or task.
  Comment on variables which could affect your work, the work of others, the project.

FIGURE 7–8

Format for a Progress Report

Example Formal Quarterly Report

When the authors of the following report submitted their 500-page proposal to the Federal Office of Education, proposing to establish a Center for the Study of Writing and Literacy and a five-year program of research, they also submitted a five-year timeline. This timeline specified what would be accomplished at the end of each quarter in each research project and whether any "deliverables" (that is, interim or final reports) would be due.

Here is the report from one of these projects (Example 9). Notice that it starts with boilerplate text. The original timeline has been literally copied from the computer version of the proposal and turned into a form which is sent to every Project Director three weeks before the quarterly report is due in Washington. The Project Director uses the report to show that he or she is on schedule and has met the contractual obligations, or to explain any changes or delays.

ANNUAL REPORTS

These reports, like progress and status reports, are periodic in that they routinely report the status of an organization. Annual reports have become highly specialized in larger companies because they must condense huge amounts of information and because they are used to maintain the company image and culture. Consultants are hired to produce well designed and illustrated reports. These reports, then, have a political value far beyond their factual basis. Figure 7–9 illustrates a standard format for an annual report.

Example Quarterly and Annual Reports

The Twentieth Century report (Chapter Two) and the chairman's Letter to Shareholders (Chapter Four) let you compare two versions of this report form. Financial reports to stockholders have to meet certain federal guidelines (which we will not cover here) and have a number of typical features: a letter from the President giving a (relatively) plain language summary of events and earnings for the past quarter, often accompanied by a line graph showing growth of earning, a pie graph showing the distribution of investments, followed by the financial report itself. However, we included these reports (Example 10) to let you see how even a conventional form is adapted by writers and used for specific rhetorical purposes.

FORM 3: PROPOSALS

Any time you argue for an idea or offer a solution to a problem, you are writing a proposal. Proposals, as we saw in Figure 7–1 take much time from

Quarterly Report to the Office of Educational Research and Improvement
Year 2, Quarter 3
(June - July - August, 1992)

NATIONAL CENTER FOR THE STUDY OF WRITING AND LITERACY YEAR 2: THIRD QUARTERLY REPORT

Research and Development

THE WRITING OF ARGUMENTS ACROSS DIVERSE CONTEXTS.

Project Director: *Linda Flower*, Carnegie Mellon University.

Flower's project focuses on the transitions that college and adult writers from diverse backgrounds must make as they learn to write persuasive arguments in situations that demand new rhetorical skills. The project will track how writers in three settings understand the process of constructing arguments (the diverse backgrounds and kinds of knowledge they bring to the process of writing, the ways they plan and revise, the strategies they employ to produce texts) and how they make the transition to a new context (with its specific expectations, assignments, and criteria of "good" writing).

Schedule:

Quarter 3	Study 1	Begin analysis of conflict data.
	Study 2	Transcribe and prepare data.
	Study 3	Adapt materials from Studies 1 and 2 for Community Center

Study 1 is on schedule. Study 2 is ahead of schedule. Study 3 is on schedule. (See the following for details of each Study.)

Study 1:

As we begin the analysis of the conflicts found in our data on students' planning, this study is starting to show why students have difficulty constructing the kinds of argumentative texts they are being taught to create....

In this analysis we are constructing a matrix of "actively negotiated conflicts" for each student (interrater reliability identifying conflicts in transcripts is approximately 80%)....

This analysis will give us a much more operational understanding of how students interpret instruction in specific argument strategies. And it will let us document some of the questions and conflicts that students may also be negotiating--which are not part of the explicit curriculum.

Study 2:

Study 2 is ahead of schedule and is beginning to produce some preliminary results. In contrast to expectations often held for non-traditional students, these writers . . .

Study 3:

Because a Landlords and Tenants project at the Community Literacy Center offered the ideal opportunity for studying negotiation in a community context as we proposed, we pushed this project somewhat ahead of schedule to take advantage of this event, and moved into the collection of data. We were able, as planned, to gather data from this community argument that closely parallels the design for studying academic argument outlined in Study 1.

EXAMPLE 9

Format for a Quarterly Report

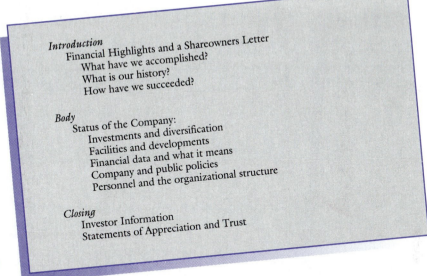

Introduction
   Financial Highlights and a Shareowners Letter
   What have we accomplished?
   What is our history?
   How have we succeeded?

Body
   Status of the Company:
      Investments and diversification
      Facilities and developments
      Financial data and what it means
      Company and public policies
      Personnel and the organizational structure

Closing
   Investor Information
   Statements of Appreciation and Trust

FIGURE 7–9

Format for an Annual Report

writers and are valued highly, especially when they are internal proposals within an organization. Besides distinguishing internal from external proposals, we can separate solicited from unsolicited proposals. Most proposals are **solicited** in that someone states a problem and asks you or someone else to solve it. Requests for proposals (RFPs) are common in business and now are a specialized form for soliciting competitive bids and plans. Other solicited proposal are less formal: Your boss asks for your thinking on a new sales tactic, or your writing group needs to define its process of delegation. You could, as many writers do, briefly propose a solution.

Unsolicited proposals are those in which the writer, the proposer, defines and initiates the solution to a problem. Suppose you have noticed that people waste time in a cafeteria line and you propose a reorganization to the dining staff. Your unsolicited proposal has to work even harder to establish a problem, since your readers will not consider your solution until they are convinced that a problem exits. You might think that few proposals in business are unsolicited, but most consulting and service companies depend on unsolicited proposals because they can use them to market their products effectively.

Generally, all proposals follow a simple but effective rhetorical plan. They link problem to solution with three basic steps:

Introduction
    Introduce the company, person, or agency: purposes, goals, tasks
    Provide a history or background as is needed

Problem or Need
    State the problem or need in language and detail that is accessible to a
    number of readers
    Introduce all of the key features or variables

Directions for Proposing
    Provide the procedural details in submitting a proposal
    Explain all technical or legal requirements
    Offer criteria for acceptance

Specific Information
    Present all of the technical questions that must be answered

Costs and Contracts
    Describe all financial requirements and procedures.

FIGURE 7–10

Format for a Request
for Proposals

Problem Statement	Writers pose, state, or acknowledge a problem
Objectives	Writers state the purpose or value of their solution, linking it directly to the problem
Product	They present a detailed account of a solution and how they will deliver it

You can see that whether a proposal is solicited or unsolicited will affect this simple plan. Sometimes writers will not have to work to establish the original problem or even define their solution. In some cases, the effort goes toward explaining how the proposed solution—the product—will be developed and delivered.

In writing proposals, it makes sense first to focus on the problem and how it is best stated. In Chapter Three, we provided strategies for writing problem statements. Solicited proposals often are preceded by an RFP, which has its own general format and pattern of reasoning (Figure 7–10).

Internally, proposals may be written in a memo or letter format. Longer or external proposals, however, often have the front and closing matter that encase longer technical reports. Just as when you present a formal report, take care with the title page, letter of transmittal, table of contents, and

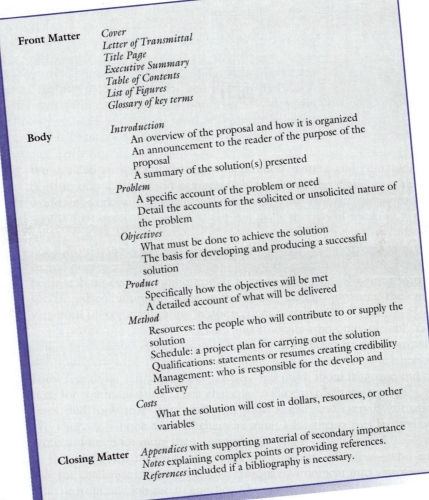

Front Matter
Cover
Letter of Transmittal
Title Page
Executive Summary
Table of Contents
List of Figures
Glossary of key terms

Body
Introduction
An overview of the proposal and how it is organized
An announcement to the reader of the purpose of the proposal
A summary of the solution(s) presented
Problem
A specific account of the problem or need
Detail the accounts for the solicited or unsolicited nature of the problem
Objectives
What must be done to achieve the solution
The basis for developing and producing a successful solution
Product
Specifically how the objectives will be met
A detailed account of what will be delivered
Method
Resources: the people who will contribute to or supply the solution
Schedule: a project plan for carrying out the solution
Qualifications: statements or resumes creating credibility
Management: who is responsible for the develop and delivery
Costs
What the solution will cost in dollars, resources, or other variables

Closing Matter
Appendices with supporting material of secondary importance
Notes explaining complex points or providing references.
References included if a bibliography is necessary.

FIGURE 7–11

Standard Format for Proposals

other front matter. Figure 7–11 shows a format for the body of a proposal, elaborating on the three steps mentioned above.

As we shall see, organizations and writers will vary this format, at times collapsing objectives and problems into one section or linking the product to its delivery ("method"). Here are three examples of proposals to study and draw from.

In Chapter One we introduced proposal writing at Digi-Tech to illustrate the amount of collaboration that goes on in an organization and the complexity of rhetorical situations that span a number of people. In that scenario, we present Exetor's RFP that details their needs for an expert software system. Digi-Tech then responded by producing a lengthy proposal, but one that had very little custom writing. Instead, Digi-Tech used boilerplate writing and extensive appendices to address most of Exetor's technical needs. The heart of the Digi-Tech proposal (Example 11), as you can see if you review the outline we included, is its item-by-item response to Exetor's technical question. This proposal is a good example of a writing team that studied the RFP and tailored their written response to the information and form of the RFP.

If you read through the letters and memo sequence between Rogers and Associates Engineering and the University Writing Program, you have a sense of the developing proposal of the short course on technical writing. In fact, both parties made informal and formal oral and written proposals back and forth, until an agreed-upon plan was developed.

Here is a brief internal, unsolicited proposal, written by Michael Rudick. It was unsolicited in that he was not required to produce one, and his earlier letter presented the three basic points to his plan. However, he wrote this proposal because he wanted one to circulate and to have on file, anticipating the need for a written proposal from his desk.

Next, on page 315, is a proposal from an engineering firm that we mentioned in Chapter Four. You will see that it varies from the standard format, moving the costs for the project up front. As you read through, try to imagine why the proposal was written in this manner.

PROPOSAL
for
A SHORT, IN-SERVICE COURSE IN TECHNICAL
COMMUNICATION SKILLS
FOR EMPLOYEES OF ROGERS & ASSOCIATES,
SALT LAKE CITY

Submitted by
THE UNIVERSITY WRITING PROGRAM,
University of Utah,
May, 1989

Michael Rudick
Director

AIMS AND CONTENTS

The University Writing Program (UWP) proposes a short, in-service course in technical communication skills for personnel at Rogers and Associates. Persons engaged in producing reports at Rogers are college graduates, most of whom took technical writing courses as part of their degree programs, but need some further work in improving their abilities.

Administrators at Rogers have identified several areas in which they would like to see improvements: audience accommodation, organization, clarity in exposition, summary techniques, placement and documentation of tables, grammar and usage. University Writing Program courses in technical writing include instruction in these areas, among others, and we propose to adapt our pedagogy and materials to the needs of writers at Rogers and Associates.

We will assign a team of three persons to this project. Two of our instructors, experienced in teaching technical writing, will conduct workshops at the Rogers headquarters, working under the supervision of Prof. John Ackerman, coordinator of technical writing courses in our Program, who will design the instruction according to the plan described in the next section.

EXAMPLE 12

A Short Internal
Proposal

PLAN

1. Preparation

   a. *Site visit*. The UWP team will visit Rogers and Associates to speak with administrators and writers in order to learn the company's procedures and the conditions under which technical documents are produced.

   b. *Document study*. Rogers and Associates will make available to the UWP team samples of the range of documents the company produces, together with their judgments on the quality of these documents. The team will study the documents in order to identify problems to emphasize during the instruction.

2. Instruction

   Instruction will be carried out in six weekly workshops, each about 90 minutes long. The workshops will include presentations by the instructors on the topics to be covered, discussions of on-going work relating to those topics, study of samples, exercises, editing sessions, and the like. In nearly all cases, work will focus on the documents writers are currently producing for Rogers. Participants may expect to submit work each week to the instructors and to their peers for comment and critique.

3. Evaluation and follow-up

   After the instructional phase, the UWP team will submit to Rogers and Associates a memorandum consisting of:

   a. A self-evaluation of their work. detailing what has been accomplished and what problems were encountered, as well as an evaluation of the writers who participated in the workshops.

   b. A set of recommendations to Rogers and Associates for establishing or maintaining in-house procedures conducive to producing writing up to the standards the company wishes to maintain.

   The contents of the memorandum will be based on the UWP team's assessment of its work and on an evaluative instrument given to the workshop participants. After receiving the memorandum, Rogers and Associates administrators may meet once more with the UWP team to discuss any issues raised.

COSTS

Preparation	$ 400
Instruction	1,280
Evaluation and follow-up	620
Materials and other expenses	275
UWP overhead (10%)	240
TOTAL CONTRACT	$2,875

The UWP will request a waiver of University of Utah indirect costs for this project. If the waiver is disapproved, the percentage of indirect costs is determined by University's Research Administration unit; therefore, the total contract cost may have to be increased by whatever percentage is agreed on.

EXAMPLE 12,
continued

PROPOSAL FOR
PROFESSIONAL ENGINEERING SERVICES

WATER SYSTEM MASTER PLAN
AND
ANALYSIS

PREPARED FOR:
SANDY CITY

FEBRUARY 1991

EXAMPLE 13
A Short External
Solicited Proposal

BACKGROUND

Bush & Gudgell is an interdisciplinary planning, surveying and engineering firm wish corporate headquarters located in Salt Lake City, Utah, and branch offices in St. George, Utah; Page, Arizona; and Las Vegas, Nevada. Established in 1948, the firm has 40 engineers, planners, landscape architects, surveyors and technicians dedicated to serving clients in a professional manner from project initiation and technical studies to management services during project construction. This experienced staff has varied and diverse backgrounds, affording a client the benefit of broad-based expertise. Organized primarily to facilitate the interaction between engineering skills and the needs of the client, Bush & Gudgell can thus provide a personalized service that reflects the sensitivity and understanding required for each project and client.

Professional services and capabilities are offered in many aspects of civil engineering, planning and surveying. These services include: water systems and storage, water rights, environmental and sanitary engineering, hydraulic analysis and hydrological studies, landscape architecture, urban and regional planning, economic and feasibility studies, transportation engineering and design, construction management and inspection, and project management. In-house computer facilities, word processing and reproduction capabilities aid the staff in providing a full complement of services.

LUMP SUM PROPOSAL

The total lump sum charges for this project will be $39,900.

WORK LOAD

The staff work loads at Bush & Gudgell are at a low point right now, enabling the firm to begin the Sandy Study immediately upon a notice to proceed. While the scope of the study is extensive and it is apparent that several months will be necessary to evaluate all of the alternatives desired, the large staff available for this project will assure timely completion prior to the end of July, 1991.

Frequent coordination meetings with the Sandy City Water Staff and or the City Engineer will be a key part of the study as Bush & Gudgell perforrns the services. In this manner, local information and ideas will have a better chance of being evaluated and put into place, at an early time.

1

EXAMPLE 13,
continued

TEAM MEMBERS

Mr. John L. Probasco, P.E., President of Bush & Gudgell, Inc., will be the Principal in Charge of this Sandy City Study. Short resumes for Mr. Probasco and the rest of the project team members for the Sandy City Study are included in one of the following sections.

SIMILAR PROJECTS

The Salt Lake City office of Bush & Gudgell was established over 40 years ago. Since that time, the firm has engineered over 41,000 projects for several hundred clients. Clients have ranged from small cities, districts, individuals and companies to large metropolitan areas. Typical projects include environmental studies, water and sewer master plans and studies, wastewater facility plans, water and sewer pipelines, water reservoir designs, water and wastewater treatment plant designs, construction and cadastral surveys and development projects. In addition, Bush & Gudgell acts as Engineer for several cities and districts.

PARK CITY City Engineers

In 1964, Bush & Gudgell was retained by Park City Corporation to do a network study of the water system and recommend design improvements. Because of the success of this service, from 1964 to May, 1985, Bush & Gudgell served as City Engineers. Master plans for water facilities were developed to provide service to a population of 20,000. Various ordinances were developed, construction standards prepared and adopted, and all utility, grading and storm drainage plans developed by other engineers and architects were reviewed by Bush & Gudgell. John Probasco, who is presently President of Bush & Gudgell, served in the capacity of City Engineer until 1982, at which time Eric DeHaan was assigned that responsibility. When development subsided in 1986, Mr. DeHaan was hired by Park City to continue the work that he had been providing as an employee of Bush & Gudgell.

DELTA CITY Water Study

Bush & Gudgell performed a complete Water Study and Network Analysis for Delta City at the beginning of a huge population increase caused by the construction of the IPP power plant. Delta is located in the western part of the Great Basin desert. Several topics covered in this study are the same as those requested in the Sandy study (i.e. water storage requirements, well improvements, alternate water storage methods, etc). The recommendations from the study are being implemented as additional developments and changes in the system occur. A supplemental study was completed in December, 1989, to address a large annexation to the City.

2

EXAMPLE 13,
continued

<u>SANDY CITY</u> Alternate Irrigation System Study

Bush & Gudgell completed this study to determine the feasibility of using an old abandoned portable water storage reservoir for storing irrigation water for three City parks. Ditches and pipelines flowing into and near the reservoir were analyzed along wirh the storage requirements of the reservoir itself. Many years of previous usage records and flow data in rhe ditches were reviewed. The unbiased recommendation that was adopted actually eliminated a major design fee from lhe Bush & Gudgell contract with the City.

<u>BRIAN HEAD</u> Water Facilities Study

Bush & Gudgell completed this study and network analysis for this tourist-intensive community and addressed several issues, including emergency water availability during a water shortage. Current and future water usage were determined. Wells, springs and multiple storage alternatives were evaluated. Costs of each alternative were determined to allow the elected officials to determine phasing and funding possibilities. Many of rhe proposed solutions are already in place. A new reservoir is also planned for this year.

<u>COALVILLE</u> Master Water and Facilities Plan

Bush & Gudgell performed a similar study for this community, which experienced a large population increase as a result of an oil field east of the city. A key part of the study was emphasis on several storage alternatives.

<u>SMITH'S FORK PROJECT</u> Level II Study Final Report

This srudy for the Wyoming Water Development Commission focused on surface storage reservoir alternatives. It also included a cost-effective operating plan and discussions about water quality and improvements.

CAPABILITY OF THE CONSULTANT

FACILITIES

<u>Office Facilities</u>

Corporate headquarters of Rush & Gudgell are maintained in Salt Lake City, Utah, with an office building containing more than 12,000 square feet of space. A branch office containing approximately 4,000 square feet of space was established in St. George, Utah, in 1966. In 1988, a branch office was

EXAMPLE 13,
continued

established in Page, Arizona. In 1990, a small branch office was established in Las Vegas, Nevada. Modern printing and graphics reproduction equipment are maintained at the Salt Lake City and St. George offices to insure high quality preparation and reproduction of report, plans and plats. Up-to-date electronic data processing makes it possible to analyze many alternatives to determine the best and most cost-effective alternatives. Word processing equipment facilitates the processing and printing of reports and publications in a high-speed, quality operation.

Electronic Data Processing

In house computer capabilities include the following:

1. Northstar Dimension with Novell Network:

   A. Seven monochrome work stations, each with 512 K RAM
   B. One color work station, with 512 K RAM and 8087 math coprocessor
   C. 60 MB (megabytes) hard disk storage
   D. Uninterruptible power supply

2. Eight stand-alone computers:

   A. Kaypro 286i, IBM-compatible AT, 640 K RAM, 20 MB hard disk, 80287 Math coprocessor chip, color monitor
   B. 4 Everex 386/20, 4 MB RAM, 40 MB hard disk, NEC Multisync Plus high resolution color monitor, 80387 math coprocessor. Also equipped with an uninterruptible power supply and a separate Hercules monochrome monitor for dual screen operation
   C. 2 Everex 486/20, 8Mb RAM, 40 MB hard disk, NEC 3d monitor. Also equipped with uninterruptible power supply
   D. Joy Systems 386/25, 3 Mb RAM, 40 MB hard disk, NEC 3d monitor, 80387 math coprocessor

3. Three Hewlett Packard 85A microcomputers with two 5-1/4" floppy disk drives

4. One HP Draftmaster plotter and one 7580A plotter

5. One 9-track tape drive capable of storing 17.6 megabytes of data on one tape

6. One Hayes 1200 baud phone modem

4

EXAMPLE 13,
continued

7. Printers:
   A. 2 Hewlett Packard LaserJet II
   B. 1 extra wide carriage printer (C-ltoh M-1550)
   C. 3 standard dot matrix printers

8. Eight Summagraphics 12 x 12 digitizers

Software

The most up-to-date versions of the following software are maintained in Bush & Gudgell's library to enhance production capabilities: KPipes, Autocad, D.C.A. Engineering Software, WordPerfect, Revelation Database Management, Jacs, Supercale 5, Civilsoft (COGO), Sierra Cybemetics (COGO), Super project Expert, Storm, Water, Earthwork, Autoword, Basic A, Mega Basic, Turbo Pascal, Term, the Army Corps HEC Series, SLC Drain, Smart Plot, Autoplot and Slick. The following programs are used for small utility routines: Popcorn, Auto menu, Pfs:write, Boardroom Graphics, PC Write, PC Deskteam, Filease, LeMenu, and Desq View. Miscellaneous software developed by Bush & Gudgell include the following: Hydraulic Flow, Bid Schedule, Hydraulic Grade Line, Detention Pond, Task Schedule, Cross Section, Quantity and Tabulation.

The firm's in-house computers are also linked to several nationwide mainframe computer systems that provide access to several other engineering programs.

QUALIFICATIONS OF STAFF

Resumes of key staff members assigned to this Sandy City Study and Network Analysis follow on the next pages.

UNDERSTANDING OF THE PROJECT

The project consists of an evaluation and study of Sandy City's existing and future sources of potable water, along with storage, pumping and piping systems to determine the long range best course of actions for the City to follow.

Finally, this study will address the long term best locations for future storage facilities and the associated pipe trunk lines. All these various features will be presented as cost-effective ways to assist the City in meeting its water requirements.

5

EXAMPLE 13,
continued

THE RECENT COLLEGE GRADUATE'S HANDBOOK OF FINANCIAL INFORMATION

With Special Reference to the Concerns of Single Women
Irene Etzkorn

To the Reader

Test yourself with this quiz adapted from one which appeared in *Working Woman* magazine. If you can answer all of the following questions correctly, this handbook has little to offer you. However, if you are unsure of the right answers, you may find this handbook helpful. Take a few minutes to quiz yourself by answering tue or false to the questions.

1. Tracking down the credit bureau that has your records is not easy without legal assistance, because under the law, credit records must be kept confidential.

2. Credit bureaus routinely swap information about your bill-paying habits.

3. You can lose your credit without even knowing it when you marry.

4. The fastest way to build a credit history is to take out a small loan even if you don't need it and put it in a savings account so the interest will help to pay the loan interest.

5. Your "discretionary income" is 10 percent of your savings.

6. Bankers suggest you have ten months' salary in savings before you consider investing.

7. "Growth funds" are riskier than "income funds."

EXAMPLE 14
An Informative
Guide

FORM 4: DIRECTIONS, PROCEDURES AND HANDBOOKS

In business, good ideas are rewarded when they become "useful" ideas—when they help other people take useful action. An idea will probably be talked *about* and argued for in a report or proposal, but a good idea becomes a usable idea when it is turned into a set of directions, a set of procedures, or a handbook for an audience of end users.

On the surface, these texts can take many forms, from a simple check list to a detailed troubleshooting manual or staff handbook. What these texts have in common is that the writers must see a situation from a reader's point

Answers: 1. False. 2. True. 3. False. 4. True. 5. False. 6 False. 7 True

INTRODUCTION

This handbook provides information that is particularly relevant to single women who have recently graduated from college. It is organized in six sections:

- Budgeting
- Establishing Credit
- Buying Insurance
- Saving
- Investing
- Planning Long-Range Economic Security

EXAMPLE 14,
continued

of view. They translate their research into accessible information written to help someone with an activity.

Guidelines for Writing Directions, Procedures and Handbooks

- *Shared purposes and problems.* Guides need to start with the questions, problems, and purposes of the reader (which may be different from those of the writer). They may even be organized with a question/answer format or use questions as headings. Focusing on reader's needs not only motivates readers, it helps you decide what information to include.

- *Steps and "how-to" plans.* These texts convert goals and ideas (e.g., increasing sales or having a fair hiring procedure) into procedures that lead to that goal. The problem is that even supposedly straightforward procedures, such as using a computer, get complicated. The ideal text would know where the reader is starting and carry on a dialogue that answers questions such as "what next," or "but what do I do if . . ." Therefore, many guides are built around "what if" scenarios or combine general strategies with more detailed discussion of special conditions. That is, they state the conditions for and qualify their guidance; they anticipate alternatives and possibilities.

- *Inventive visual and verbal design.* These texts often need to perform the role of a literal guide, standing at the reader's shoulder saying: start here; do the following; notice that; oh, if that happens, stop and try this. Guides have to be memorable if you hope to influence what people really do. But many handbooks are also reference tools designed so readers can find specific information quickly. In short, because these texts have to *function* in so many ways, they encourage writers to design the text with a variety of visual and verbal cues from bold key words and sections, to formatting cues (e.g., headings, lists, white space), to varied type faces, to multiple kinds of graphics. Because these design features are still only cues—signals that you hope the reader will read the way you intended—it is important to test such texts on users to see how readers in fact interpreted your cues.

Example Informative Guide

When Irene Etzkorn was about to graduate and take a job with a large design firm in New York she began seeking advice on managing her personal finances. Although she found a "score of magazine articles and dozens of books" on the subject, none addressed her situation as a recently graduated, unmarried woman. The placement office and alumni services center offered no help either, even though Irene knew from her own experience and the problems of friends that it was needed. So for her professional writing course (and to develop her own portfolio) she wrote a low-cost proposal to the Alumni Center to offer the following handbook (Example 14, page 321) to graduating women and recent alumni. (Irene, by the way, stayed in New York and is now Executive Vice President of her company.)

Example Emergency Handbook

In 1987 two offices of the State of California signed a contract with the Applied Technology Council (ATC)—a nonprofit consulting group. ATC's job was to develop guidelines for evaluating the safety of buildings after earthquakes and to train nonengineers to do emergency evaluations. As the publications consultant to this project, Dr. Joann Dennett knew they needed to make technical information immediately understandable, in a form that would lead to good decisions and quick action in time of great stress. (In later projects, for instance, the audience would be Post Office employees and other civil officials.) In addition to a 152-page final report on *Procedures for Postearthquake Safety Evaluation of Buildings,* they produced a pocket-sized 4″ × 7″ field manual (Example 15) that used a wide array of text conventions to translate ideas and information into actions.[2]

Question heading

Uses a "so what" question to motivate the guide

Answers the reader's "how to" questions

Anticipates problems with another level of "how to" steps and alternative strategies

EXAMPLE 14,
continued

BUDGETING

Why is a written budget a good idea?

A written budget makes you more conscious of how you spend your money and allows you to plan, because you know how much of your income goes for each of your expenses. It also helps you control spending and spot "leaks" in your finances. For example, you may discover that your entertainment expenses are twice the size of your food expenses. It also has a psychological benefit; you feel in control of your money rather than bewildered by the monthly disappearance of your paycheck. And it helps you determine how much of your income you can *regularly* deposit to savings.

The real key to sticking to a budget is to have a goal. It can be long-term, such as buying an antique shop in ten years, or short-term, such as saving for a vacation. Either way, the goal makes the restrictions of the budget worthwhile.

How do I develop a realistic budget?

GMAC, the General Motors financing division, has developed a formula for calculating your "discretionary income." Simply stated, your discretionary income is the amount of money you have left after you pay all your monthly commitments, such as rent, food, transportation, etc. To find this figure, total your net monthly income (after taxes) and subtract all of your monthly expenses. If you've never determined this figure, you aren't really aware of what you can afford to spend, save, or borrow.

Determining your monthly expenses is more difficult than it may sound at first, because it is very difficult to remember all your expenses, particularly those that only occur once or twice a year. Go through last year's checks to make sure you don't forget expenses. Or if this year is radically different from last, sit down with someone to brainstorm a list of all possible expenses, then see which apply to you. Last, try carrying a pocket pad for a month and jotting down expenses as they occur. The following list may help you.

Switches to list format

Monthly Expenses

Housing
Rent
Gas/Electric/Oil
Water
Garbage Removal
Telephone
Renters' Insurance

Transportation
Public transit
Gas
Auto Insurance
Car loan payments
Car Maintenance/Repairs

Savings

Food
Groceries
Eating out and Entertaining

Miscellaneous
Gifts
Recreation/ Vacations
Membership Fees
Papers/Magazines/Books
Laundry
Lessons

Medical
Doctor/Dentist
Health & Life Insurance
Pharmaceuticals

After you've determined what you actually spend, examine your priorities. Do your spending patterns reflect these priorities or do you need a budget to help you achieve your financial goals?

ESTABLISHING CREDIT

Who needs credit?

Question format

Establishes the need for the section

Everyone, no matter what their financial situation, needs good credit. The number of Americans who will make every purchase during their lifetime without credit is so small, it can almost be disregarded.

EXAMPLE 14,
continued

Starts with where reader "is" now and what reader needs to do

When should you seek credit?

Are you waiting until you make a major purchase, such as a car, to seek credit? If the answer is yes, you may want to reconsider. Without a past history to indicate how reliable you are at paying your debts, lenders are reluctant to give you a loan. They may insist on a co-signer to ensure that they will receive their money. It is wise to establish credit before you actually need to borrow money, so that it is available when you do.

What does the law say?

Congress passed the Equal Credit Opportunity Act in 1975. What you need to know about the law is that it means:

Information that may contradict common assumptions.

Women can obtain credit in their own names and single women can not lose their credit ratings when they marry.

You have the right to know why you were refused credit. At your request, the lender must state in writing, within 60 days of rejection, the reason you were denied credit.

If you were denied credit because of information supplied by a credit bureau report, the creditor must tell you its name and address. There is no charge for seeing your file at the credit bureau, if you have been denied credit on the contents of its report.

How do you get a credit rating?

Practical steps, and "what if" answers

You may be unsure about whether or not you already have a credit rating. To find out, contact your local credit bureau, listed under "Credit Bureau" in the white pages of the phone book. They will charge a small fee (about $5) to provide you with copies of your file. If you have started to pay back a student loan, this should be noted in your file. However, merely having the loan before you start to repay does not constitute a credit reference.

What does a lender look for?

Here is the next question a reader actually looking for credit might have-- and an answer that qualifies common assumptions

Basically, a lender looks at a prospective borrower's ability to pay and their willingness to pay. To measure ability to pay, creditors will examine the amount of your salary, how regularly you receive it, and how much you owe other creditors. To determine your willingness to pay, they will investigate your repayment record for other debts and your stability, i.e., how long you have been at your present job or residence. Thus, a substantial balance in your savings account will not impress a creditor more than having worked at a company for a long time.

EXAMPLE 14,

continued

The Table of Contents is presented as a flow chart that says:

1) if you are doing this kind of inspection, and

2) if you see this, then

3) do this.

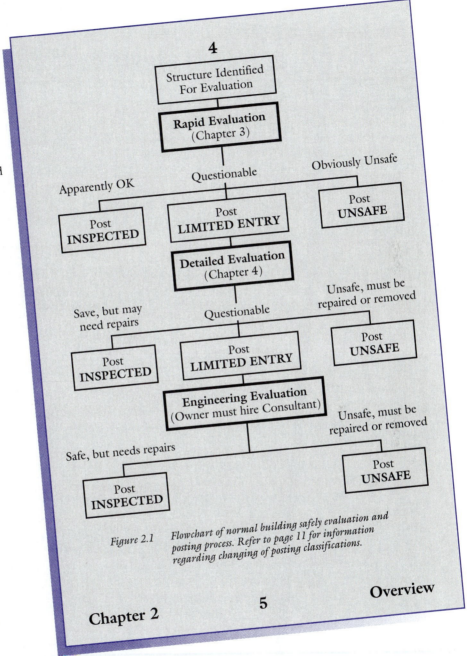

4

Structure Identified
For Evaluation

Rapid Evaluation
(Chapter 3)

Apparently OK   Questionable   Obviously Unsafe

Post
INSPECTED

Post
LIMITED ENTRY

Post
UNSAFE

Detailed Evaluation
(Chapter 4)

Save, but may   Questionable   Unsafe, must be
need repairs   repaired or removed

Post
INSPECTED

Post
LIMITED ENTRY

Post
UNSAFE

Engineering Evaluation
(Owner must hire Consultant)

Safe, but needs repairs   Unsafe, must be
                                 repaired or removed

Post
INSPECTED

Post
UNSAFE

Figure 2.1   Flowchart of normal building safely evaluation and posting process. Refer to page 11 for information regarding changing of posting classifications.

Chapter 2   5   **Overview**

EXAMPLE 15

An Emergency
Handbook

Rapid Evaluation is an emergency measure designed to protect people in areas where aftershocks and further collapse are possible.
So the text is short and sweet.

After its problem/purpose statement, it tells the reader to take 6 steps, followed by an "if/then" paragraph with special conditions. Note how each paragraph points to other parts of the text

The essential "how to" information is presented in a table as "condition/action" pairs.

The pages that follow contain a black and white photo of each condition.

To back up the table, readers can then flip to a more detailed, 1-page procedure. This is followed by a copy of a Rapid Evaluation Safety Assessment Form--a one page form designed as a check list for recording major decisions with a place to add comments if desired

EXAMPLE 15,
continued

3   Rapid Evaluation Method

Rapid Evaluation Criteria

The objective of Rapid Evaluation is to quickly inspect and evaluate buildings in the damaged area. It is performed by evaluating a building for six basic screening criteria (Table 3.1). These are primarily externally observable conditions that, individually or collectively, are sufficient to warrant use of the AREA UNSAFE or in the case of falling or other hazards, the AREA UNSAFE postings. See page 19 for the Rapid Evaluation inspection procedure.

If a building is found to have none of the conditions listed in Table 3.1, and there is no other hazard, it is apparently safe and should be posted INSPECTED. If the situation is doubtful and requires a more extensive review, the building should be posted LIMITED ENTRY and given a subsequent Detailed Evaluation.

Examples of conditions that illustrate each of the six Rapid Evaluation criteria are illustrated in Figure 3.1

Table 3.1   Rapid Evaluation Criteria

Condition	Posting
1. Building has collapsed, partially collapsed, or moved off its foundation	UNSAFE
2. Building or any story is significantly out of plumb	UNSAFE
3. Obvious severe damage to primary structural members, severe racking of walls, or other signs of severe distress are present	UNSAFE
4. Obvious parapet, chimney, or other falling hazard present	AREA UNSAFE

But instead of a table or photos, the writers use hand-drawn figures that reduce detail to key feature the inspector needs to look for.

The "key" for reading the figure (the arrow) is prominent.

And technical terms such as "coupled shear wall" are attached to a graphic image of such structures that says: "Look here!"

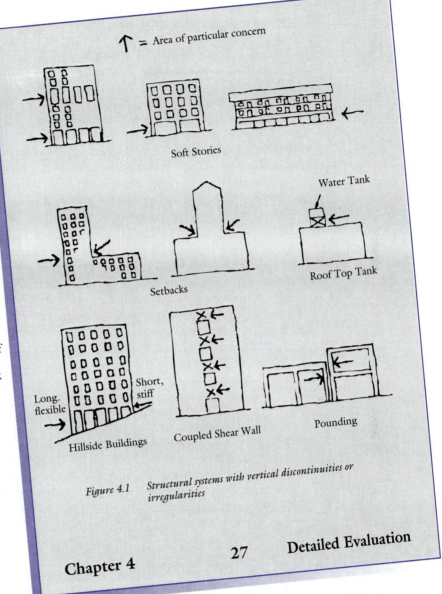

↑ = Area of particular concern

Soft Stories

Setbacks

Water Tank

Roof Top Tank

Long. flexible

Short, stiff

Hillside Buildings

Coupled Shear Wall

Pounding

Figure 4.1   *Structural systems with vertical discontinuities or irregularities*

Chapter 4   27   **Detailed Evaluation**

EXAMPLE 15,
continued

Example Procedural Manual

One of the most common—and most frustrating—kinds of procedural instruction is the computer documentation we face every time we have to learn a new program or do something extra with ones we know. Since computers themselves operate with what are known as "condition/action rules," it is not surprising that good documentation helps readers learn not just what to do but when to do it.

See the two versions of a computer instruction manual on pages 144-45. They not only contrast two ways to organize a manual, but introduce the text convention of numbering (2.1; 2.2) to show hierarchy of information. Notice also the use of type fonts in the "After" example. Write your own annotations for this example, naming for yourself the sets of features, conventions, and cues to the reader each version uses.

Summary

- **Short correspondence** (memos and letters) maintain the "conversation" of business, but become a permanent record of agreements and decisions.
- **Reports** in business are designed to be "used" and their different parts, from executive summary to closing matter, are organized to serve special functions for various primary and secondary audiences of the report.
- Writing an effective unsolicited **proposal** depends on reading the context and building a good argument. Writing a solicited proposal adds another constraint—paying close attention to the Request for Proposal.
- Although textbooks can show you generic models and formats for different kinds of reports and proposals, in practice you will find great variability. The key is in adapting a generic format and designing a model to fit your rhetorical situation.
- One way to make your proposal or recommendation operational—that is, usable—is to write your own guide for how to turn those ideas into action.
- **Direction, procedures,** and **handbooks** are unique forms of business communication because they provide information that is put to direct use. Writing them requires that you know how they will be read and for what specific purpose.

References

1. Anderson, P. (1984). "What Survey Research Tells Us about Writing at Work." In L. Odell and D. Goswami (Eds.), *Writing in Non-academic Settings*. New York: Guilford (3–76). Redish, J. (1985). "Writing in Organizations." In L. Odell & D. Goswami (Eds.), *Writing in Nonacademic Settings*. New York: Guilford (97–124).
2. The ATC's *Procedures for Postearthquake Safety Evaluation of Buildings ATC 20 and ATC 20-1* was funded by State of California's Office of Emergency Services and Office of Statewide Health Planning and Development and by the Federal Emergency Management Agency.

8
Tools for Writers

THIS CHAPTER is a resource for writers, a quick-access "tool-kit," with guidelines and information for special jobs and circumstances. All of these tools assume that you have read a rhetorical situation, and that you have thought carefully about how and to whom you are to write or speak. And now you need additional resources.

 TOOL 1. Document Design
  Design documents to make them visually appealing and easy to read.

 TOOL 2. Graphic Design
  Develop and integrate graphics into your writing.

 TOOL 3. Formal Oral Presentations
  Organize and present orally, using visual aids.

 TOOL 4. Informal Presentations: Conversation and Active Listening
  Participate in informal oral presentations.

 TOOL 5. Information-Gathering Interviews
  Ask questions and make sense of what you learn.

 TOOL 6. Writer's Block
  Ways to respond and act when a writer cannot write

8
Tools for Writers

Writers on various occasions need specific information to solve specific problems. Perhaps they need to know how to ask a series of questions to learn more about a rhetorical situation, how to refine a solid draft to make it visually appealing, or how to take the gist of a document and create an oral presentation. All of these occasions are important, and we wrote this text to argue that writing is a broad activity that encompasses speaking, designing texts, and working with people successfully. Here we provide a quick access, a series of *tools,* to key activities for writers and speakers. For our purposes, a *tool* is a collection of strategies and guidelines that help you solve a specific problem.

This chapter assumes that a writer is immersed in a rhetorical situation and is acting strategically—or that a writer has acted on a plan and produced an acceptable text, the goal now being to make that text visually effective or turn it into a spoken exchange. Thus, the first four tools help you to design a page and graphic aids to enhance your writing or to prepare for formal and informal oral presentations. The remaining two tools help you to ask questions—either to gather information, prepare for a reader review, or job interview—or to get un-stuck as a writer. In each tool section, we offer strategies which function as general principles on which to act and guidelines which are more specific directions for successful communication.

TOOL 1: DOCUMENT DESIGN

All written texts send graphic messages. Many writers think of "graphics" as a special set of graphs, tables, and illustrations that augment printed text, and we present those graphic devices in the next tool section. **Document design** refers to all of the devices and strategies that writers use to communicate visually through a printed page. Document design is important for writers because every printed message conveys not only information but an image of the writer or the organization represented. Recall the two letters we used to introduce the rhetorical situation in Chapter One. The Bill Collection Letter (Figure 1–2) used document design techniques to invoke a serious tone in addition to the words on the page that demanded payment.

STRATEGIES

Design each page as a grid for a balanced and visually appealing **page lay-out,** *so that the eye can easily move down the page and so that the reader is drawn to the essential information.*

Reading is a physical act as well as an mental process; therefore the more res-olution (degree of sharpness) that can be designed with **whitespace, margins,** and **highlighting techiques** *the better.*

Page layout and document design, like other features in written texts, send messages about ideas and their organization. Choose **headings, introduc-tions,** and **indexing techniques** *that announce the structure of your writing.*

Try for simplicity and consistency and avoid cluttering your pages because your design reflects an **image** *of you or your organization. Study the paper trail and survey the rhetorical situation, if you are writing in an organization or a discourse community.*

Guideline 1. Page Layout and the Grid. Design your page around blocks of visual information, so that each component on a page has consis-tent margins and is balanced. As Figure 8–1 illustrates, margins are defined on a page by horizontal and vertical dimensions.

Try either to balance sections on the page horizontally or to counterbal-ance white space with blocks of printed text or graphics.

Guideline 2. Whitespace and Margins. Whitespace is all the area on a page that is not devoted to print or ink: the spaces defined by margins, tabs, or spaces between lines and graphics. Design your page so that the whitespace balances and enhances the print and other visual aids:

- Tabs or indentions must be consistent and draw the reader toward the point or section.
- Indent numbered or bulleted lists to pull embedded information out of paragraphs, just as you would a lengthy quotation or example.
- Use single-spaced pages with double-spacing between paragraphs.
- Triple-spacing may be used to set off major sections.
- Consider using a single-spaced paragraph for a critical point.
- Use columns (i.e., newsprint format) to highlight comparisons or levels and types of information.
- Use standard margins, 1″ to 1.5″ on all sides.
- Avoid artificial justification, i.e., use flush left margins and ragged-right margins. Some computer programs will produce an oddly spaced justified line to accommodate flush-right margins.
- Do not leave one or two lines on a final page.

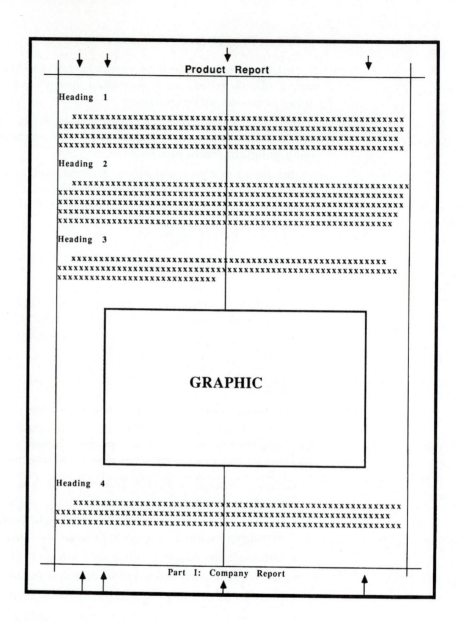

FIGURE 8–1

Example Grid for a
Short Report

- Avoid paragraphs that dominate the page (these usually signal other organizational problems or poor attention to the reader's needs).
- Do not end a page in mid-list or with a heading.

Guideline 3. Highlighting Techniques. Because of the computer's versatility, there are a number of highlighting techniques available that can quickly draw attention to an idea or organization. Use highlighting techniques sparingly, however, to avoid clutter on the page.

- Vary fonts to draw attention to words, ideas, or sections.
- Use **bold,** *italics,* <u>underline</u>, outline, and shadowing to accentuate headings and to reinforce key terms or ideas, qualifiers ("a <u>break</u> from tradition"), or quoted material.
- Avoid cluttering a page or an item with *too many techniques.* The effect is a gaudy and less formal page.
- Boxes, lines, arrows and other highlighting devices may also be used—again avoiding overuse that complicates the page.

- Carefully choose type style and size. The computer now offers a range of fonts and font sizes. Unless you are designing overheads or special printed materials, stick with standard fonts (e.g., Times Roman, Helvetica) in standard sizes (8–12 point types). You may, of course choose to vary fonts and their size as a highlighting technique. Note that some fonts on the computer dramatically vary in point sizes.
- Vary upper- and lower-case letters. Use upper- and lower-case letters together to enhance the resolution on a page, avoiding all-UPPERCASE letters unless they are part of headings and page layout. Lines, sections, or documents written entirely in uppercase are difficult to read because they confound the horizontal resolution (that is, the difference in height that makes letters easy to distinguish quickly).
- Check line length. Although you may vary paragraph size and use white space to draw attention to print or graphics, try to use standard line lengths (6–7 inch).
- Check printer and ribbon quality. Unless you are sharing a draft or using your writing to plan or draft, use a letter-quality printer or a typewriter with a good ribbon. Obviously, you may choose to balance cost with attractiveness, but avoid dot matrix printing or other printing where the resolution fades or is inconsistent. Do not submit erasures.
- Use quality paper. Use bond paper that is heavy enough for printing

and photocopying. Letterhead looks more professional. Do not submit paper with perforated tracking fringe.

- Use appropriate cover pages, clips, jackets, and binders. These coverings may enhance your delivered product, but make sure they convey the level of formality you seek and that they are invited or required by your reader.

Guideline 4. Headings, Introductions, Indexing Techniques. Include design features that link the visual design of your texts to the structure of your ideas and arguments. These design techniques should closely connect with the outline, plans, or models you used to build a draft. For example, if you used a topical issue tree to plan or common text moves to arrange your ideas, those topics may be the words and phrases you now highlight in your heading, introductions, and indexes.

- Organize your information. If you planned well and used strategies and text moves for developing your ideas and argument, your text may come organized so that a reader can quickly access or recognize your key points or information. Check to see if your sentences and paragraphs appear to be logically organized.

- Use context-setting introductions. As we described in Chapter Five, make sure you provide cues to the reader, especially by announcing in your introduction or front material the main ideas that will follow. This move not only prepares your reader for your message, it introduces the graphic organization that enhances it.

- Use headings to bring your ideas and organization forward. Reinforce your division of ideas and information and provide easier access for your reader by using consistent, standard subdivisions and highlighting techniques to accentuate the divisions. For example,

- Revise generic labels or vague topics, such as "SOLUTION #3," into reader-centered topics and questions. For example,

  How experienced writers respond

  Can anyone learn how to solve problems?

- Match your headings with your table of contents and accompanying outlines.

- Build an accurate table of contents. In longer documents, a table of contents can pull the major headings, subheadings, and divisions out of the text and preview them for the readers. In constructing a table of contents, decide if the text requires one (because of length or access). Some writers will include a basic table of contents up-front and then include local tables at the start of major sections, so that readers can reference from that point on in the text. Use high-lighting techniques, indentions, margins, and tabs to produce a clean table.

Table of Contents

- Add an index or glossary to help your reader with details and special terms. Similarly, you may include an index at the end of your manu-script, organized either by section or alphabetically. Glossaries, usu-ally placed in the back, provide a dictionary of your special terms or concepts, and they highlight key words or phrases for readers.

Guideline 4. Matching the Design to the Image. With so many doc-ument design options available, the key will be to select and orchestrate them to enhance what you are trying to say. Overuse or misuse can send a message contrary to your intentions. For instance, when students combine whitespace and double spacing to stretch a paper, often readers judge it to be thin on content or even disrespectful. When writers in professional settings fail to consider design as part of their rhetorical strategy, they miss the opportunity to enhance what they are trying to say with words.

To conclude this tool section, here is a letter from an insurance company that uses many document design devices (Figure 8–2). Are they used well? What message is sent along with the printed message, and how might this letter be revised?

Here is the same letter revised to bring the message forward and to make the message easier to read (Figure 8–3). We kept the heading the same and only concentrated on the printed text and how it fits on the page. Do any of these changes reflect good document design strategies?

TOOL 2: GRAPHIC DESIGN

The need for quality graphics and illustrations has grown over the last few decades for two reasons. First, more and more professions and businesses rely on graphic information as part of their decision and development processes and as a way to represent efficiently the technical information in their organization or discourse community. And second, well-designed and integrated graphics do save space and words. When the pace of business quickens, graphics are used to present complex ideas efficiently.

STRATEGIES

The basic principles for graphic design, presented here, come from Edward R. Tufte's *The Visual Display of Quantitative Information*, one of the best references we have found that illustrates how graphics can honestly and accurately communicate complex sets of numbers and ideas.[1] Graphic design attends to all of the standard graphic devices such as line and bar graphs, tables, charts, and illustrations, and to how these devices are accurately and ethically integrated into printed texts.

Choose the **graphic device** that fits your information and rhetorical plan, and follow the basics guidelines for each particular device.

Integrate the graphic into the larger text, making sure it fits the rhetorical and informational purpose of the writer—to describe, illustrate, compare, refute, exemplify.

Accurately and ethically reveal all relevant data, whether they are numbers or words or images. The quality of the graphic is only as good as the data or model captured.

DONEGAL MUTUAL
Insurance Company

P.O. BOX 302
MARIETTA, PENNSYLVANIA 17547
(717) 426-1931

ALFRED BEACHEM
1894 TREATCHER AVENUE
BINGHAM CITY, UT 84105

POLICY NUMBER
DXL013486104

DEAR POLICY HOLDER

ACT 86 ACT OF JULY 3, 1986, P.L. 396, NO. 86 , REQUIRES THAT
EACH POLICY OF INSURANCE COVERING COMMERCIAL
PROPERTY OR CASUALTY RISKS IN THE COMMONWEALTH OF
PENNSYLVANIA SHALL PROVIDE FOR NOT LESS THAN 60 DAYS
NOTICE OF INTENT TO INCREASE AN INSURED S RENEWAL
PREMIUM. RECENTLY IT HAS BEEN DETERMINED THAT
DWELLING POLICIES INSURING RENTAL PROPERTIES ARE TO
BE CONSIDERED COMMERCIAL PROPERTY RISKS.

NOT ALL OF OUR POLICY PREMIUMS WILL INCREASE AT
RENEWAL. IN FACT, SOME POLICY PREMIUMS WILL DECREASE.
SOME OF THE FACTORS WHICH MAY AFFECT YOUR POLICY
PREMIUM ARE AN INCREASE IN THE AMOUNT OF INSURANCE,
CHANGE IN DEDUCTIBLE, A COMPANY RATE INCREASE OR
DECREASE, A POLICY UPGRADED FOR ADDITIONAL PERILS
INSURED AGAINST, ETC.

THE RENEWAL PREMIUM FOR YOUR POLICY HAS NOT YET BEEN
DETERMINED. HOWEVER, IN COMPLIANCE WITH ACT 86, WE
ARE HEREBY NOTIFYING YOU THAT YOUR PREMIUM COULD
POSSIBLY INCREASE AT RENEWAL.

IN ORDER TO FURTHER COMPLY WITH THE ABOVE
MENTIONED ACT, APPROXIMATELY 30 DAYS PRIOR TO THE
EFFECTIVE DATE OF YOUR RENEWAL POLICY, YOU WILL
RECEIVE EITHER THE ACTUAL RENEWAL POLICY WITH A
BILLING NOTICE OR A SEPARATE NOTICE ADVISING YOU OF
THE ESTIMATED RENEWAL PREMIUM.

SINCERELY YOURS,

PERSONAL LINES DEPARTMENT

FIGURE 8–2
Donegal Insurance
Letter

Policy Number
DXL013486104

Alfred Beachem
1894 Treatcher Avenue
Bingham City, UT 84105

Dear Policy Holder:

Act 86 of July 3, 1986, P.L. 396, No. 86, requires that each policy of insurance covering commercial property or casualty risks in the commonwealth of Pennsylvania shall provide for not less than 60 days notice of intent to increase an insured S renewal premium. Recently it has been determined that dwelling policies insuring rental properties are to be considered commercial property risks.

Not all of our policy premiums will increase at renewal. In fact, some policy premiums will decrease. Some of the factors which may affect your policy premium are an increase in the amount of insurance, change in deductible, a company rate increase or decrease, a policy upgraded for additional perils insured against, etc.

The renewal premium for your policy has not yet been determined. However, in compliance with Act 86, *we are hereby notifying you that your premium could possibly increase at renewal.*

In order to further comply with the above mentioned act, approximately 30 days prior to the effective date of your renewal policy, you will receive either the actual renewal policy with a billing notice or a separate notice advising you of the estimated renewal premium.

Sincerely,

Personal Lines Department

FIGURE 8–3

The Donegal Letter
with Alternative
Design Techniques

Guideline 1. Basic Graphic Devices. Figure 8–4 holds many of the basic graphic devices. We based the graphs and charts on the same numerical data to show how one device or another presents different features and relationships and supports this progression. Refer to this figure as we describe and provide guidelines for tables, bar charts, line graphs, pie charts, and illustrations. First study the numerical and word tables, because (although excerpted here) they provide the basic information. Then, see if you can tell how each graphic tool alters and re-represents the data before moving on to our descriptions.

Tables. Tables of numbers and words compile large amounts of information, and it is from tables that many other graphic charts and graphs are built. In creating and designing tables, refer to the document design guidelines at the beginning of this chapter and to these additional guidelines:

- Provide adequate whitespace between rows, columns, and numbers.
- Include summary numbers (averages for columns and rows) and category headings (e.g., "region" summarizes the states included).
- Use columns for the most important information.
- Round numbers off whenever possible, and avoid decimal points or numbers longer than two or three places.
- Use tables for professional audiences who understand what the numbers mean, know their origin, or have specific uses for the actual data.
- Prose tables are especially useful for presenting series, parts, or procedures.
- Tables may be used with other graphics to offer the reader a choice and to provide a background and resource for other graphic tools.

Bar Charts. Bar charts present trends and relationships and can focus a finding or discussion. They often compare sizes, amounts, or different items at the same point(s) in time.

- Depending on the size of value, orient the bar chart vertically or horizontally. Note that a horizontal chart may save space on a page and may improve the design and balance of whitespace.
- A comparison of items and time can be combined on a bar chart, creating mini-charts in one larger display.
- Make sure all abbreviations are understood, and that all numbers, color variations, and items are either defined or clearly evident.
- Consider labeling the bars, unless their definition is clear or their value is easily read from an axis (vertical or horizontal).

Gross State Product by State

United States Regions

Southeast	Southwest	Rocky Mts	Far West
Alabama	Arizona	Colorado	Alaska
Arkansas	New Mexico	Idaho	California
Florida	Oklahoma	Montana	Hawaii
Georgia	Texas	Utah	Nevada
Kentucky		Wyoming	Oregon
Louisiana			Washington
Mississippi			
North Carolina			
South Carolina			
Tennessee			
Virginia			
West Virginia			

Source: U.S. Department of Commerce; Bureau of Economic Analysis

Gross State Products in $1000 Increments

Region	1985	1986	1987	1988	1989
New England	225	248	275	301	312
Mideast	761	821	889	972	1026
Great Lakes	661	701	743	802	849
Plains	278	290	305	325	349
Southeast	829	879	946	1025	1092
Southwest	431	419	432	459	482
Rocky Mts	117	117	120	127	135
Far West	668	712	774	845	919
United States	3966	4186	4484	4854	5165

US Gross Product by Region, emphasizing the Great Lakes

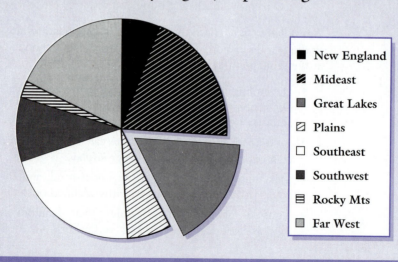

- New England
- Mideast
- Great Lakes
- Plains
- Southeast
- Southwest
- Rocky Mts
- Far West

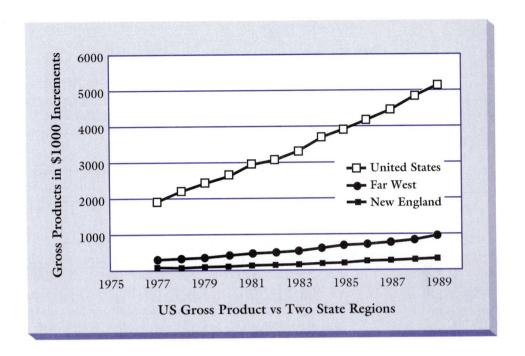

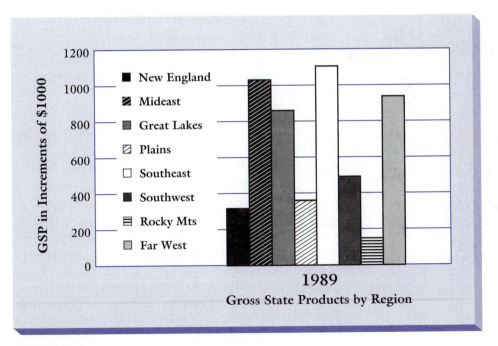

FIGURE 8–4
Basic Graphic Devices

- Pictographs are bar charts on which the bars have been turned into a visual metaphor for the item represented. We could image bar charts presented as stacks of coins for each states gross product.

Line Graphs. Line graphs show how something has changed over time, and they usually compare a time or series of events on one axis and a quality (amount, size, rates, etc.) on another. Line graphs are common because growth or change in business and the sciences is based on time, giving these graphs a strength and accessibility beyond others.

- Make sure the lines are labeled and the lines themselves graphically unique, and that you do not include too many comparisons. Too many lines would have the same effect on a reader's eyes as small print, long lines, and no whitespace.
- Include the actual data points along a line or trend.
- Choose the best time or quality increment for a visually balanced line graph, making sure you do not distort the relationships or changes in trends.
- Although a time sequence or a series of events has good explanatory power, consider whether this incremental progression reveals the relationship you seek—that something has improved, decreased, etc. over the increment of time that matters.
- Consider including more than one element (for example, the profit trend for the three major auto corporations) to show the trend over time for multiple, comparable elements.

Pie Charts. Pie charts present all of the parts that add to a whole, whether that whole is a year's sales figures or the total number of voters in an election. The circle represents 100 percent of whatever is counted and the pie sections contrast the different percentages.

- Arrange and color the sections so that readers can easily tell the rank order.
- Label sections with a legend or by including the exact value or percent.

Photos, Drawings, Illustrations, Diagrams. Pictures can be used either to illustrate a point or convey an image or message. The photographs and sketches that we included at the beginning of "Three Problem-Solving Scenarios (Chapter One) were chosen to make a number of points at once. First, the three buildings represent three quite different sites for business. Then, the pictures help to make the buildings secondary to the people in them. And finally, the texts remind us what the people have as their business at hand. We have used drawings and sketches throughout this book to illustrate a relationship, or just to offer a second representation of a key point.

Diagrams are sketches arranged either along a timeline or to capture some kind of hierarchical order. A common use of timeline diagrams is in project planning. As we saw in Chapter Six, planners begin with tasks and sketch them from first to last using a flow chart. Those tasks and flowcharts can then be further refined by using a Gantt chart which turns the flowchart into a modified bar graph, with tasks on one axis and time on the other.

The other common diagram in business is an organizational chart, arranged by employee roles or organizational divisions. Figure 8–5 offers an example of the corporate organization at Pacific Telesis Group.

Notice how a fairly simple graphic flowchart with shading enhances what is essentially an outline. All illustrations must be integrated into the text around them, and they must not detract from the rhetorical goals of the writer. Pictures and illustrations sometimes capture too much of a reader's attention, or they are reproduced so poorly that readers ignore them.

Guideline 2. Integrating Graphic and Text. This second guideline is one of the most important and is often overlooked by writers who believe that pictures replace words or assume that their graphics are as understandable to others as they are to them. In other words, avoid *writer-based graphics* (see Chapter Five for an introduction to writer-based prose) and carefully integrate illustrations into a text, whether you are designing a visual aid for an oral presentation or a graphic to be inserted into a document. Writers integrate their graphics by:

- Announcing and referring to the graphic, so that the reader knows what is coming, where it can be found, how it can be read.
- The graphic should be as close to the reference as possible.
- In the text, instructions should be included that direct the reader to the important details.
- The value or importance of the graphic or its message may then be pointed out in the writing that follows it.

We have tried to integrate the various graphics we have used in this textbook, but a reader review might reveal some problem places. Choose any figure and look for how it is integrated and whether you are given enough direction and information to understand it.

Guideline 3. Accuracy and Ethics in Graphics. Although we began this section by pointing out the demand for quality graphics to replace and augment texts, many people view graphics with the same skepticism they bring to statistical data. Numbers, without interpretation, can lie and often do because designers fail to link the visual image to the message intended.

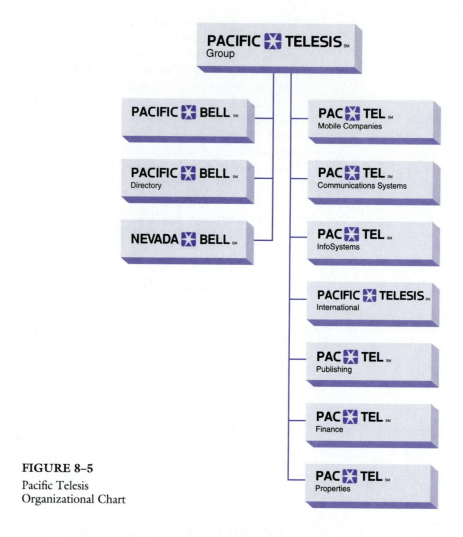

FIGURE 8–5

Pacific Telesis
Organizational Chart

- Accuracy in graphic design can be achieved by a 1 to 1 ratio of data to the ink or visual tools on the page. All graphics have the potential to distort ideas by going too far in trying to visually enhance data. Distortion can be avoided by comparing the surface relationships in a graphic to the actual numbers or values they represent.

- Clear labeling will counter many distortions by making sure the graphic metaphor (a line, bar, wedge, etc.) is linked to its actual value.

- Induce the viewer to think about the substance of the data or ideas and not the graphic itself by avoiding extra embellishments, just as it is possible to overdesign a document.

This line, representing 18 miles per gallon in 1978, is 0.6 inches long

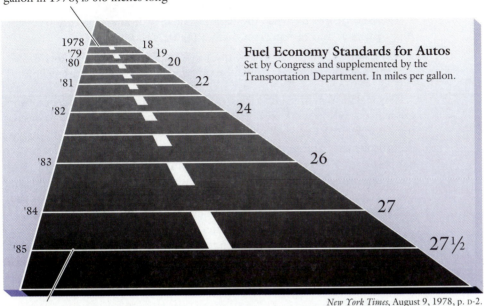

1978
'79
'80
'81
'82
'83
'84
'85

18 19 20 22 24 26 27 27½

Fuel Economy Standards for Autos
Set by Congress and supplemented by the
Transportation Department. In miles per gallon.

New York Times, August 9, 1978, p. D-2.

This line, representing 27.5 miles per gallon in 1985, is 5.3 inches long

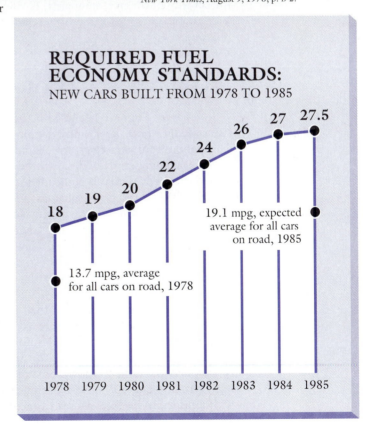

REQUIRED FUEL ECONOMY STANDARDS:
NEW CARS BUILT FROM 1978 TO 1985

18 19 20 22 24 26 27 27.5

19.1 mpg, expected
average for all cars
on road, 1985

13.7 mpg, average
for all cars on road, 1978

1978 1979 1980 1981 1982 1983 1984 1985

FIGURE 8–6

Distortion in a Line Graph:
Two Versions

- Avoid distorting what the data say or reveal, and efficiently reduce large sets and re-represent them accurately.

- Design to direct the eye to the most important details to reveal the data at several levels, from a broad overview to closer relationships.

We realize that the intricacies of graphic design go beyond our simple guidelines. As you work with graphic devices in your writing, try to evaluate them for accuracy and ask whether the impression that you create fits your rhetorical plan. The graphic on the preceding page on auto mileage standards (Figure 8–6) uses the basic line graph but integrates it with the visual metaphor of a highway.[2] This graphic distorts the basic information three ways, as we will discuss. The second graphic reports the same data without distortion, returning to basic graphic devices and guidelines.

Although the actual increase of fuel standards is 53 percent, the increase represented by the lines in the road are much larger. Compare the width of the lines, by year, as they decrease from 27.5 miles per gallon down to 18 mpg. Also, the metaphor of a road going to the horizon usually means that the future is distant. Here that relationship is reversed, exaggerating the severity of the new standards. Finally, the two lines of numbers are not a constant size, distorting the relationship between year and mileage required.

TOOL 3: FORMAL ORAL PRESENTATIONS

In Chapter Four we began with the decision to speak or write, and we acknowledge here that most communication in business is spoken. Throughout our strategies for reading and context, planning, building drafts, evaluating and working with others, we presented writing as a problem-solving activity that is embedded in other conversations. Those conversations could be the goals, agendas, and conflicts that you witness in social interaction; they could be the paper trail that leads to and supports what you write; they could be the ongoing language and expectations in a discourse community. Most of this spoken conversation appears naturally as people talk to interact and do their jobs. Tool 4 presents strategies and guidelines for conversing and listening, the basics of presenting and receiving information orally in less formal settings.

But other occasions require formal preparation, and speaking (like writing) is used to present ideas, debate alternatives, and make decisions. To call an occasion to speak "formal" does not mean that it is stuffy, with the participants dressed in ball gowns and tuxedos. Formal oral presentations are those when a specific purpose and audience are before you—in staff meetings, standing and ad hoc committees, briefing sessions, and presentations with a principle speaker. As with writing, your first steps are to survey the rhetorical situation and read the context for the agendas and conflicts that might guide your composing. If you have done a good job of finding the rhetorical problem, you then can plan and build a draft using the many strategies we presented earlier. However, oral texts introduce some extra problems into the picture: (1) you have to present a concise version, in real time, in front of real people, and (2) they have to comprehend and remember oral information with only one chance to hear it. So you need some *additional* strategies in your problem-solving repertory to meet these additional features of the rhetorical situation.

If you are inexperienced at giving oral presentations, here are some guidelines that let you concentrate on features that can make the biggest difference and on features that often cause trouble. Focusing your attention on these key areas lets you use planning and a little practice to compensate for your lack of experience.

Guideline 1. Make Your Plan Half As Complex and Make Your Cues Twice As Clear As You Would in Writing. Imagine the problem listeners face: Without the visual cues of a text or the opportunity to reread, they have to turn your flow of talk into a mental issue tree that recognizes the key points and sees how the rest of the discussion supports those points. Listeners face the problem of *information overload*. Therefore, in preparing a talk,

- Choose a few key points. Decide what issues are most important given your time frame for speaking, extracting the key gists of written texts if available.

- Use a clear or familiar rhetorical pattern or set of text moves (such as problem-solution) so listeners can predict what is coming.

- Provide some detail and examples—abstractions are hard to remember.

- However, keep tying those details and examples back to your point, or they will tend to float as merely interesting, independent, or irrelevant bits of the talk.

- Use a strong introduction and conclusion. Your introduction should alert the audience to the need to listen (get their attention) and clearly state what purpose, problem or proposal you will discuss in your presentation. Your conclusion should tie together the presentation, either by summarizing, or pointing again to the key issues you have presented.

- Try to create a scenario from which to speak. This could be an opening story or question, something to engage the audience's attention.

- Define any troublesome terms or language that your audience may be unfamiliar with as you first use them.

Guideline 2. Build in Reinforcing Redundancy. In trying to decide what is important to remember, listeners use the repetition of an idea as an important clue to its significance. Be creative: build in this redundancy to reinforce your point in a variety of ways.

- Preview, then emphasize, then summarize the key points in your presentation. The old adage is, "tell them what you are going to tell them; tell them; then tell them what you told them."

- Use visuals to overview key points. Keep them simple, though, or they will simply increase the listeners' information overload and bury your key points.

- Use handouts to summarize what you want people to retain or to show data or examples you want to go over in detail. (But remember, people can end up reading handouts instead of listening.)

Guideline 3. Design Your Speaking Notes to Highlight Your Key Points. Although it may seem tempting to read a word-for-word typescript, only a very experienced speaker can read to an audience without putting them to sleep. Moreover, if you lose your place on the page (or lose page 5) it can be difficult to recover. A typescript restricts you in many ways: your eyes will be glued to the text and the table it is sitting on—you can't hold rattling sheets of paper in your hand.

- Use a combination of an outline, notes and word-for-word text (where needed). Try using large 5 × 7 cards. But whether you talk from cards or paper, use your graphic design skills to format your notes with cues that tell you where you are in the talk and how to deliver it. For example:

- Number your key points and put them in boldface type or underline in red. If you lose your place, are interrupted by a question, or lose your train of thought you can always find your way back to the key points you need to make.

- Indent, block off, or chunk the information that supports your key point. The goal of this formatting is to help keep your top-level idea structure (or issue tree) in your mind's eye and let you know when you have finished a section. You may want to write down your actual words for a difficult part and just use a detailed outline for points you can say without reading.

- Put in cues that will remind you of the logic of your presentation and its rhetorical moves. Use bold headings that introduce the next section as an EXAMPLE, ANECDOTE, STATISTICS, SHOW WHY, WRAP UP, etc. These will let you look up from your notes, look at your audience, and in a regular speaking voice make a relaxed metacomment such as, "And now I want to show you WHY we think this is the best plan."

- Put in cues that remind you of what to do. Write in cues (such as underlining, color, space, or symbols in the margin) that remind you of when to PAUSE (at the end of key points), when to EMPHASIZE key words, when to LOOK UP, when to SHOW OVERHEAD or ASK FOR QUESTIONS. Treat your notes like a musical script that reminds you of the rhythm, emphasis, and the various stage business you intend to use. Remember an effective talk is more than a "talking head" or words on a page, so build the cues to your total plan into your notes.

Figure 8–7 shows a note card for a talk on "Financial Information for Recent Graduates" drawn from the Guidebook illustrated in Chapter Seven. Notice how many different cues this speaker used to help herself look up, pause, and interject friendly and natural asides, such as the comment that begins, "I know, . . ." or the move to look up from her notes and *explain* the GMAC calculation on the overhead.

Guideline 4. Plan To Be Nervous—and Go on Speaking. If public speaking makes you break into a cold sweat, you are not alone. In one survey, Americans listed talking in public as one of their greatest fears. Many people are perfectly at ease in one-to-one situations or even in a class, but when they go to the front of a group their palms begin to sweat, their faces turn beet red, their hands begin to tremble, or their voices begin to break. These are all common physical side effects of feeling nervous. If that happens to you, simply expect it, accept it, and be prepared to perform in spite of what your body is doing. It is quite possible to deliver a very effective argument even if your hands do tremble, because listeners care about what you have to say and are usually very sympathetic to speakers who deliver a well-prepared performance, despite these side effects of nerves.

- The key is to be prepared to carry on. The first few minutes are the worst, so have your beginning well learned and carefully outlined. Practice it (and the entire talk) out loud more than once. The irony of nervousness is that the people who fear public speaking often try to avoid what they fear by procrastinating, *not planning* ahead, and by *not practicing* in the privacy of home or office.
- The best solution is: if you can't stop the side effects, then let them happen, let your body do what it will. Nerves can't stop you. Compensate for comfort by practicing what to do while being nervous, and focus your attention on delivering what you have to say.

But what if you enjoy public speaking and look forward to the chance to present your ideas? Don't assume that self-confidence is a suitable substitute for professional preparation.

- Time your talk to the minute, including your asides and comments on visuals.

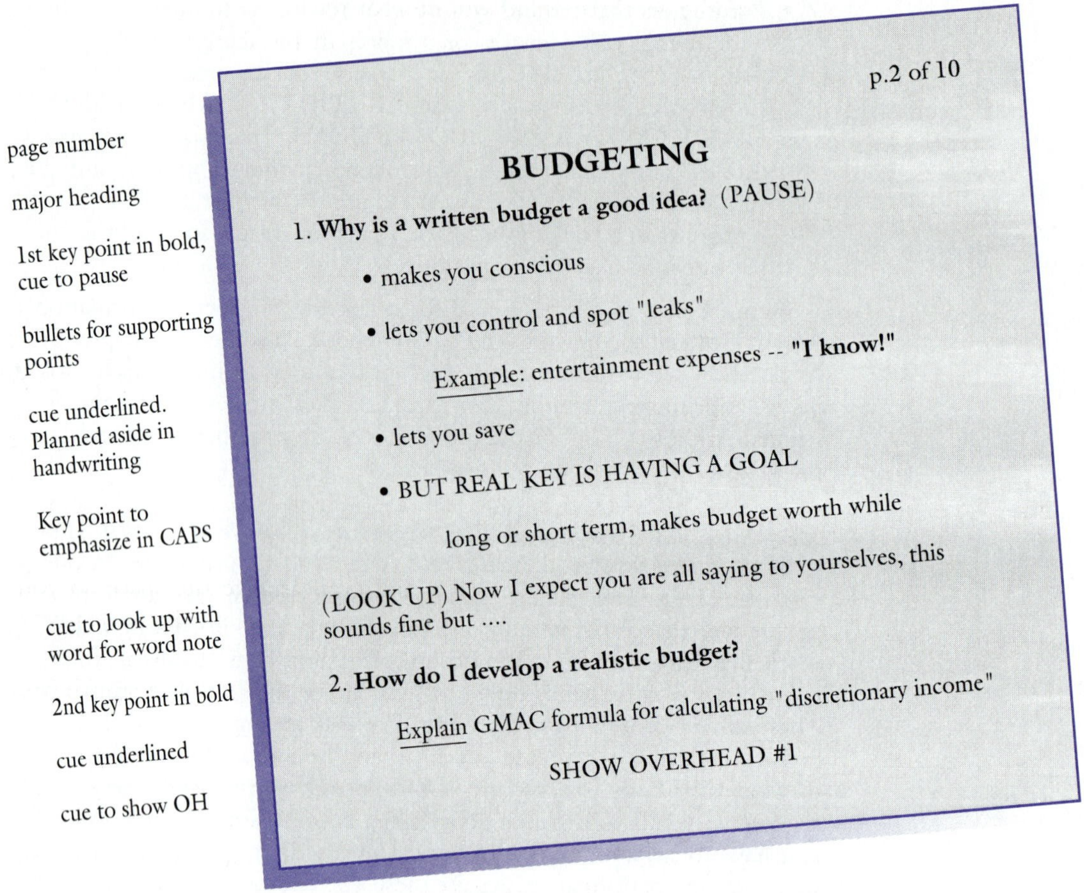

page number

major heading

1st key point in bold,
cue to pause

bullets for supporting
points

cue underlined.
Planned aside in
handwriting

Key point to
emphasize in CAPS

cue to look up with
word for word note

2nd key point in bold

cue underlined

cue to show OH

BUDGETING

1. Why is a written budget a good idea? (PAUSE)

- makes you conscious

- lets you control and spot "leaks"

    <u>Example</u>: entertainment expenses -- **"I know!"**

- lets you save

- BUT REAL KEY IS HAVING A GOAL

    long or short term, makes budget worth while

(LOOK UP) Now I expect you are all saying to yourselves, this
sounds fine but ....

2. How do I develop a realistic budget?

    Explain GMAC formula for calculating <u>"discretionary income"</u>

    SHOW OVERHEAD #1

FIGURE 8–7

A Note Card with Key Points, Word-for-Word Text, and Cues

- Practice out loud, standing up, walking around. Hearing your own
  voice is the best way to develop an auditory memory that lets you
  "know your talk cold," but appear to speak more extemporane-
  ously, in a conversational style and tone.

Guideline 5. Get Set. Take a tip from actors. While you are still in the
wings or waiting to talk, concentrate on your content: Try to picture the
overall structure of your talk and your main points. You can also relax yourself physically in three important ways:

- Breathe deeply to stretch your diaphragm.
- Yawn to get extra oxygen and balance the air flow (this is a little harder to do around a conference table, but very effective).
- Stretch your neck (actually, shoulder rolls in which you lift then drop and roll your shoulders are the most effective, though it is hard to be inconspicuous with shoulder rolls). Both yawning and stretching help by relaxing and stretching the neck, throat, and jaw muscles that become tight from tension. Physical relaxation increases your mental relaxation, and it brings your voice into a resonant, pleasing range.

Guideline 6. Take the Floor. As the speaker, take over the space you are speaking in. Walk up like you owned the front of the room. Pause. Smile. Then, when you have eye contact and everyone's attention, begin your talk. Remember this is your show; so play the part, from the minute the stage or the moment is yours. However, taking the floor also begins well before you start to speak.

- You may need to come early and even arrange the space so you aren't boxed in by tables, chairs, or a tall podium that covers you up. (People lose attention when they can't see the speaker well.) You need to create a clear space which allows you to move and which you as the speaker appear to control.
- The center position is the position with the power to keep people's attention. Speaking from a side position, it is easy to be upstaged by people leaving, entering, rustling paper, or talking.
- Decide on the relation you want to have with the audience: Do you want to sit or stand informally in front of a table, or behind a table or podium? Remember, each new piece of furniture creates another barrier between you and your audience. You may choose to start with a podium and then move out to the side from time to time for more informal discussion.
- Come early to any new setting and visualize your presentation unfolding. Always test any visual displays and equipment beforehand. Give yourself at least 10–15 minutes lead time to run down the missing overhead projection, replace burned out bulbs, or do any of the many "little" things that could have a major impact on your talk.

Guideline 7. Take a Solid Stance or Seat.
- To look balanced and comfortable, stand with your feet about 6 inches apart. Putting one foot slightly in front can prevent rocking.

If you sit on a chair or table, sit down with your weight well back on the object, not on the edge which can make you appear to be precariously perched.

- Sometimes speakers think they will look more at ease if they slouch, lean, or stand casually with hands in pockets, but interestingly enough being off balance has just the opposite effect on an audience. The ideal is to look perfectly balanced. Use a boxer's stance which makes it easy to turn to all sides of the room. And present listeners with what is called a full front figure—an open stance that makes you seem available to the audience. To see what that stance feels like, stand up, do a shoulder roll, put your hands straight up in the air, and then drop them. Notice where they ended up—that is a relaxed, natural position.

Guideline 8. Plan Your Body Language and Watch for "Leakage." The way speakers stand, move, and use their hands conveys a message of its own. Folding your arms across your chest and turning slightly to the side gives the audience a "cold shoulder," while facing people with a full front figure creates a message of openness. Hands used in cutting gestures convey aggressiveness, hands in pockets look rough, open hands can invite people to look at a point. Use gestures and body language as ways to reinforce your message.

- Sometimes body language can tell a story you didn't intend to tell. This phenomenon, called "leakage," occurs when the voice is saying one thing (e.g., "I am glad to be here" or "We listen to customers") and a cold shoulder, defensive or aggressive gestures, or the failure to make eye contact are saying something else. Practicing in front of a mirror can tip you off to some of the unintended messages you may be sending.

- The most positive and powerful body language a speaker has is eye contact. It says to the audience, "I am speaking to *you* and I am interested in your *response*." It also gives you a chance to pause and see how the audience is responding. If maintaining eye contact doesn't come naturally, practice looking to different parts of the room, and put cues in your notes to do so. Some speakers find it more comfortable to actually focus on a spot just above and between the eyes of individuals in the audience. Apparently no one can tell the difference.

Guideline 9. Use Your Voice As an Instrument. Your voice has a great deal of natural power, so try to use its full range of potential.

- Talk to the back of the room—this will let you naturally adjust your volume and pitch to the space. But it helps to practice out loud and listen for two things: variety in your voice and pauses.

- Are you speaking in a monotone—a steady pitch that puts even dedicated listeners to sleep? Practice in a private place, varying the loudness and intensity of your voice at key places. Don't be embarrassed; close the door and speak out. Hearing yourself do it once or twice will make it sound natural and easy to do later. (*Never* assume that after mumbling through a practice, you will do it right or differently when it is time to perform the real thing.)

- Secondly, listen for the length of your pauses. Do you pause in strategic places so the listener can catch up and consolidate what you just said? Do you pause at important or difficult points? Sometimes speakers are so afraid of dead air, they feel the need to fill in every available space with talking. But just for an experiment, practice pausing in your talk and notice how long you can actually remain silent as you establish eye contact or regain your place; and notice how effective silence itself is.

- Because pauses and emphasis are a part of your message, put cues for when to use them on the notes you talk from.

Guideline 10. Support What You Say with Visual Aids. Visual aids are used to augment speaking to offer the audience some of the benefits of writing and graphic devices. Visual aids can be used to underscore a point, involve the audience with a particular issue, exemplify something so that it need not be described, extend by graphic or example what is orally described, organize and sharpen a talk. Visual aids take many forms:

- Handouts which outline or summarize key points, or include graphs, illustrations, or text that is referred to in the talk.
- Outlines, key words, or graphics drawn on marker or chalk boards.
- Overheads, which may be used to present the extracted gists from a written text.
- Displays and demonstrations, slides and videos.

Visual aids must be integrated into a speech in much the same manner as they are integrated in a written text. They should be introduced or previewed and explained so that the audience understands what they are supposed to see. One problem speakers have with graphs, charts, or illustrations is that they "walk the audience through" the visual aid, pointing out totals or relationships, instead of talking *to* the audience.

- Make them large enough and clear enough for the audience to see. This might mean using a 24 to 36 point font or using bold to high-light. Make sure you design your visual aid with the same care that you use to design a graphic device for a text.

- Simplicity is preferred, since speeches usually have a time limit and the audience members do not have the luxury of going over the visual aid at their own pace.

- Speak to the audience, not the visual aid.

- Use the aid to support your main points or to clarify your trouble spots, but do not use them to replace important statements.

- When you are finished with a visual aid, or the various technologies, put them aside or turn them off to return the audience's attention to you. However, it is better to remove the overhead than to switch a projector off and on repeatedly.

- Don't dim the room lights any longer or any more than necessary. In a soothing, darkened room, minds begin to wander—especially if the speaker is not highly visible or illuminated. Try to keep your-self—and your listeners—in the best light you can create.

- Practice for a formal presentation. You may need to learn to run an overhead or know exactly when to walk to the marker board. Mark cues in your script or notes, to remind yourself, or these cues can be used by someone who offers to run an overhead or slide projector.

Guideline 11. Anticipate Some Common Mistakes. If we simply listed these points as good tips, they would seem obvious (Who would spend their entire talk with their back to the audience looking at their slides?). But, in fact, in the heat of the presentation, these are just some of the things that happen to inexperienced speakers. Fortunately, by practicing your talk ahead of time with these things in mind, you can avoid these common mistakes.

- DON'T talk to your slides, your notes, or one small section of the room. DO practice looking up and looking around, maintaining eye contact with each section of the audience.

- DON'T talk with your hands in your pockets, standing on one foot, or engaging in whatever form of nervous "leakage" you are most likely to do (people have individual habits they can learn to look out for—one of us used to torture paper clips into interesting shapes during lectures). DO practice (in front of a mirror) standing up calm, balanced and relaxed so your body remembers what that feels like.

- DON'T assume that the best way to *appear* natural is to start with an informal, spontaneous introduction. Shortly after you begin speaking is when you will be most nervous. So to *appear* natural,

DO rehearse your informal, spontaneous beginning until you know it cold. (Then do a variation if you feel comfortable.) And do the same thing for your ending, right down to the gracious, "thank you," eye contact, and request for questions. In other words, DON'T plan to wing it at the key places—such as the beginning and ending of a talk—that create strong impressions.

- DON'T avoid the hard question: "Does my talk actually fit the time limit?" by failing to time and revise it if necessary. Two things often occur when presenters fail to time talks. Sometimes the speaker is allowed to run over (maybe taking up someone else's time) but creates an impression of discourtesy or unprofessionalism. Or someone in charge asks the speaker to conclude and the speaker, finding it hard to summarize or rewrite the speech "on the fly," leaves out important points and walks off with a bungled, inconclusive ending.

- DON'T assume that the few impromptu comments or asides you might work into your talk "won't take up much time." Many a speaker has been undone to find half her points covered and all her time up. Asides, especially comments on visuals, take up far more time than you think (particularly if you are nervous and, therefore, not perfectly concise). So DO rehearse and time the whole talk, asides and all.

- Finally, DON'T assume that your talk has to sound like a flawless, spontaneous performance, carried out without a pause or hitch. Some speakers assume that they have to keep the talk flowing and their mouths going at all times, so when they lose their train of thought, they just keep on talking—without anything to say. In fact, you will find that listeners appreciate a speaker who has done them the courtesy of being well prepared and who cares about the accuracy of the information he or she has to share. Although they will dismiss speakers who keep referring to their mistakes or spend time making excuses, they will feel quite comfortable with someone who says, "Now let me see where we were" or who stops to review his or her notes and say, "Let me be sure we have covered all the points." Listeners want to be in the hands of a thoughtful speaker who takes them seriously enough to make and follow a plan.

TOOL 4: INFORMAL PRESENTATIONS—CONVERSATION AND ACTIVE LISTENING

Most communication in work settings happens through casual conversation, except that this conversation is anything but casual. Chitchat aside, conversation is the fundamental level at which people negotiate their problems and reach a decision. We know from our experience that some people are good at conversation—not just witty or entertaining—they know how to convey information, learn things, and negotiate even when talking informally. Here are some of their strategies.

Conversation in the world of work is typically about something and often carries hidden agendas. This does not mean that you necessarily have to distrust those around you, but it does mean that you can be strategic and ethical in how you represent yourself and others through informal conversation.

Guideline 1. Sensitive, Effective Conversation.

1. Speak for yourself and recognize when you speak for others. *I propose,* instead of, *It's best for the company,* or *People think that . . .* locates the responsibility and the origin of an idea with you. If you do talk about other people's opinions, beliefs, or ideas, limit what you say or qualify, *You should hear this from them,* or *What I took from Pete's briefing was. . . .*

2. In deciding what to say, respect the confidentiality of others. Negotiation at its best is reproducing information so that all are informed or involved. At worst, it is gossip or political maneuvering, where private truths are made public.

3. Statements about others say as much about the speaker as the person spoken about. Such statements always belie some sort of value system. Good speakers do not hide their values (if they could), but they do monitor the frequency and velocity of value judgements, especially about others.

4. From time to time, summarize or paraphrase what someone says to you, to check your understanding, and to let them know you are listening. Allow the person with whom you are speaking to correct your interpretation.

5. Silence can be misconstrued as either boredom or disapproval. Long pauses from one party are filled in by the other, often with the wrong information or intent.

6. Listen for content and interaction patterns that suggest how you or others perceive and use authority. For example, constant interruptions or filibustering may mean that others believe they have power or that they wish they did. Look for gender and ethnic differences in who speaks loudest, longest, and most often.

7. Good conversationalists can adjust to different styles of turn-taking. Some speakers are uncomfortable with casual, slow talk while others are silenced by quick, aggressive turn-taking.

8. Question your physical presence as you speak. Even in informal settings, sitting, standing, posture, hand gestures are part of the conversational context you create.

9. Remember that, while understandings can be shared through conversation, meanings are individual. What someone takes from a conversation will continue to evolve because it will be based on past experience and other interactions to come. Good conversationalists do not walk away believing issues are settled and further discussion is not necessary.

10. Conversations can last for a few turns, *Hi . . . How'ya been . . . Great presentation* . . . or continue for years. Good speakers strengthen their memory for past conversations and use that recall to make a new interaction feel comfortable.

Meetings can be regularly scheduled, called for a specific purpose and duration such as a task force, or appear out of circumstantial need. Regular meetings are criticized because they waste time and disrupt individual schedules. They need not if the members prepare in advance. The purpose for meeting should tell participants how to prepare: to make decisions, to respond to a plan, to report developments, to brainstorm ideas, to secure agreement for political gains.

Guideline 2. Active Listening. The ability to listen will greatly enhance your ability to speak and write. We prefer to approach listening as method of research: how can I learn the most from this speaker or group so that I can contribute later or further their projects? Active listeners make use of the following strategies.

1. Listen and take note of main ideas or claims, even when the speaker does not preview or highlight them.

2. Try to image or reconstruct an outline or framework for the presentation. By using notes and drawings (arrows, boxes, etc.), a listener can both remember and test what is being heard and keep involved through a lengthy engagement.

3. Take note of questions, and rank their importance if space is provided for questions and answers:
   • conceptual questions that require clarification
   • conceptual questions that are related, interesting, entertaining
   • definitional questions that can be quickly answered
   • confirmational questions, to make sure you understand

4. Look over the physical setting. You may choose to move closer if you cannot see or hear, and where and how you sit will send messages to others in the room as to attentiveness.

5. In informal settings such as planning meetings, make sure you do

indeed listen if someone else has the job of setting the agenda or leading the discussion.

6. As in conversation, listen for cues, turn-taking, and style of talk that mark boundaries of authority, ethnicity, and gender.

TOOL 5: INFORMATION-GATHERING INTERVIEWS

Interviews are basic tools for investigating activities in business and professional contexts. The typical situation for an interview is hiring. Someone asks questions that hopefully elicit enough information to act wisely, and someone answers questions in such a way as to promote his or her attributes. But interviews happen anytime someone needs to know something, and we present guidelines for using interviews to collect information, whether one is preparing for a job interview, surveying a rhetorical situation, or setting up a reader review. We offer guidelines for *deciding on a purpose, choosing the right questions, adapting your questions for your audience, and making sense of what you have learned.*

Guideline 1. Deciding On a Purpose. Interviews are used to hire people, review and promote them, and as part of the on-going research in being a strategic writer. Interviews are structured questions that respond to a need to know something, and interviews can be used to learn about writing and other important activities in an organization or discourse community. First think about the sources of information that will add to or direct your information-gathering interviews. If we were to study writing practices in an organization, we might look at:

- the document(s) provided by writers
- public or prior knowledge about a writer or a team
- our first and ensuing impressions and experiences
- informal and formal observations with the interviews, and
- the interviews themselves

Interviews allow us to pursue in-depth lines of inquiry about a company or corporate culture, common writing practices, or a writer's experience. Interviews can also cover more obvious questions about types of writing or job status. Ground these types of questions in specific texts. **Discourse-based interviews** are a common research tool; the idea is to tap some of the decision-making processes behind a given document, as well as some of the writer's assumptions and tacit knowledge about writing and professional life.

Questions tied to specific text features help to prompt a writer's memory, working backwards from the text through the writer's decisions, biases, motives, constraints, contexts, and assumptions. A discourse-based question may be something like, "Can you tell me why you wrote this?" to "Let me propose a revision and see what you think." Both questions attempt to return the writer to a given moment in the composing process and are more grounded than a question such as, "What is your preferred style?"

Interview-based research is an open-ended process, beginning with preparation and anticipation but proceeding according to what is learned along the way and according to the interests and tolerance of the key players—the interviewers (us) and interviewees. Begin planning for one or a series of interviews by studying the rhetorical situation. Like most research techniques, interviews are not neutral or invisible, and they will leave an imprint on future negotiations and interactions. Plan them as you would plan a dialogue, as the opening act in what might turn into a longer and richer interaction with a client or associate.

Guideline 2. Choosing the Right Questions. In planning *what* to ask, look for broad concerns that can then be narrowed. In research writing and writing processes, we could arrange questions around the writer, documents, the composing process, and the larger context in an organization or community. We might begin with informational questions about job definition, types of writing, experience and training, and company background. Discourse-based interviews can then lead to questions about organizational structure and authority, which may help you draw some inferences about the company culture and ethos of your company. Try to sort the major issues into ones you think you can ask about directly (and get a straightforward answer) and ones involving attitudes, relationships, and consequences of decisions which you will ask only after trust has been established. You may need to think of a number of more indirect questions to get at these issues.

Usually researchers come up with way too many concerns and potential questions. The exercise then is to prune your list until you have focus and order. It may help to think in terms of a progression of two or more interviews, the first consisting of basic information and the remainder building on the first. Here is how a group of students arranged their questions for a series of interviews of writers in an organization (Figure 8–8).

To prepare for this interview, the students first asked what they wanted to learn and then thought about how these issues formed a progression of ideas that might appeal to their interviewee as much as to them.

Guideline 3. Shaping Your Questions to Fit Your Audience. The keys to interviewing are to think about what you want to learn, scrupulously prepare for the interview (i.e., write a script), choose your questions wisely, and pay attention to what you learn as you are giving the interview and afterwards. Try to differentiate *content* questions from *question types*. Content questions seek information about the interviewee's attitudes, knowledge, or demographic facts, such as job title, background, or experience. Three important question types you might use are *open* questions (that invite whatever the interviewee has to say on a topic), *closed* questions (that require yes/no or specific answers), and *scaled* questions (that require the interviewee to place a value or a rank on his or her response, as on a scale of 1 to 5). Script the interview, anticipating answers, and practice if there is time. As you conduct the interview, look for other kinds of information besides the verbal response. If you conduct the interview in pairs, someone can take note of the environment and nonverbal information. Observing is part of the interview process, and the interview ends only after thoughts and impressions about the interview have been recorded.

Expert interviewers learn to consider the interviewer's and the interviewee's roles in the larger context and to consider social and practical constraints on the interviewing process. They pit what they want to learn against who can provide that information and what might motivate someone to share their time and knowledge. They also consider what topics are out of bounds or place an interviewee in an awkward position. All of these concerns can be anticipated by carefully preparing for an interview. Here is a summary of the steps experienced interviewers follow in completing their research.

STEPS IN PREPARING AND COMPLETING AN INTERVIEW

1. Select the interviewee that best fits the purpose of your interview, if that person is not obvious.
2. Make (and double check) arrangements for the interview.
3. Search for existing information on the subject, anything that can be known prior to the interview.
4. Structure the interview questions or script, carefully matching question type to content:

Content:	Attitude	*What is your impression of recent decisions?*
	Knowledge	*What are your main responsibilities?*
	Demographic	*What is your education and training?*
Type:	Open-ended	*Describe your first years here.*
	Closed	*Which of the two technologies suits you best?*
	Scaled	*Rank these training programs from 1 to 7.*

(STEPS CONTINUED ON PAGE 364)

Interviewers: Clark King (Plan to have two interviewers with other group
                members present to observe interview)
Interviewee:
Date:
Time:
Location:
Purpose: Establish rapport and gain a working knowledge of the organization.
We intend to follow up in the second interview with direct references to the
documentation.

Introductions:
            Introduce group members
            Explain purpose and espectation
                        thanks for opportunity
                        pieces of writing
                                    reports, proposals
                        3 to 4 interviews
                        time commitment
                        explain confidentiality
                                    documents, interviews, our reports
                        purpose of today's interview

Background:
            Background in business
                        college past experience
                        specialized training
            Current employer
                        position and tenure
                        job responsibilities
            Explanation of organization
                        structure (model of)
                        where do you fit in this structure

Context:
            Types of writing
                        the organization in general
                        interviewee
                                    Q: How does the interviewee's writing fit into
                                        structural model?

            Time spent writing
            Knowledge about writing
                        courses
                        on the job training
                                    Q: How has your education helped you in your
                                        current writing responsibilities?
            Assessment of personal writing ability
            Obtain documents
                        need for further documents

Conclusion:
            Set up second interview
            Explain purpose and direction of second interview
            THANK YOU

FIGURE 8–8

Interview Questions
for Writers in an
Organization.

For scales questions, use consistent labels for the extremes.

1 ———— 2 ———— 3 ———— 4 ———— 5
very   somewhat   not at all
usable   usable   usable

5. Format and write a draft of the interview script, using the following suggestions for ordering the interview.
   a. Start with the easy, nonthreatening, but necessary questions. Never start with an open question.
   b. Consider putting demographic questions toward the end, since they may be perceived as less essential.
   c. Try to start with the more general questions and move to specifics.
   d. When collecting histories, follow chronological order.
   e. Complete questions on a given topic before starting another.
   f. Use transitions and reminders between sections.
   g. Arrange for variety to avoid set responses.
   h. Filter questions can be used at the beginning of sections to expedite the interview, such as "What type of writing requires most of your time?" (and then proceed with questions directed at that type).
   i. Keep it short by avoiding redundancy and weak questions.
   j. Consider the salience of the questions to your audience. How long will your questions stave off boredom and tedium?

6. *Pilot* the interview script.

7. Revise for order, content, pacing.

8. Run the interview (some are tape recorded): by this point the script should be a guide not a crutch.

9. Transcribe or rewrite notes, *adding any observations or impressions.*

10. Code and analyze the information gathered.

11. Structure the information and write your analysis or conclusions.

If you can, look at someone else's script before going out on your first interview. It may also be helpful to read or listen to a transcript of an interview to get a sense of the timing, pace, and turn-taking. Here are a few procedural questions to ask yourself before you go:

- Who asks the questions? The person who made the initial contact? Someone who knows the client? A new group member each time? There are consequences for all options.

- Are notes and/or a tape recorder used to record the interview? Some clients are nervous about machines; best to approve this in advance.

- Should transcripts be made of recorded interviews? A text of an interview is a marvelous tool for analysis and planning, but it is expensive in time and money.
- Can follow-up interviews transpire over the phone or more informally? Some of the best interview data come from casual conversation or are embedded in another activity such as a committee meeting or a company tour. Work from planned, formal interviews toward spontaneity and coincidence.
- Might there be corroborating interviews to follow, such as with competing companies, other employees, or people with comparable positions or experience?

To help you get a sense of the turn-taking in an interview situation, Figure 8–9 offers the first few pages from the transcript of student interviews with Jim, a writer in a utility company. They may have had a script to work from, but notice how the interview quickly becomes a conversation, with the interviewee directing traffic as much as the students. Can you see questions that could have been phrased differently? Do you see the moments where the interview gathers momentum or lags?

Guideline 4. Making Sense of What You Have Learned. Sometimes, follow-up interviews will come naturally—either you will see that you have just scratched the surface, or new lines of inquiry will open and cohere. But, what happens after you have asked obvious questions about job and company descriptions, years of experience, and types of writing? First, look closely at answers to obvious questions. Recount your interview experience and focus on impressions drawn and evidence to support your conclusions. Working from transcripts (preferably) or notes, study the responses to informational questions. You may not be immediately aware of the shadings and hedging that goes on in conversation or the subtle manipulations that may take place in an interview. Remember that the interviewee conducts the interview as well as you and has an investment in the exchange. Candor may not come quickly or may have to be pursued.

Peers can help you make sense of an interview. Have them interview you, using a "cued recall" technique based on your transcript. This pushes you back into the data and explores your impressions, conclusions, and evidence. Interpreting an oral script may be a different experience for you, but you may find it as rich and provocative as anything else you read. Try to read interview data skeptically, not as a statement of what is true, but merely as data that you can use to support a claim you wish to make. Remember, when you quote interviews as evidence, not everyone will believe an event happens or a statement is true just because your interviewee said so.

(TEXT CONTINUED ON PAGE 372)

Frank: As we mentioned in the letter, we are trying to get an insight to what type of writing takes place in a business environment. In doing that, we've prepared a general set of questions based on the material I got from Alice. They're just general background questions and things like that.

Shane: Basically, that's all I'm going to do at first. Just ask questions to understand the business writing done in your department. We were wondering if you would agree that writing is a "key work activity"? In relation to your other tasks and responsibilities, how would you rate your writing. Would you rate it as very important or...

Jim: Yes, I would rate it as very important. In fact, it's a lot more important than I anticipated for the work I do. Especially with a background in accounting I felt that most of the work I would be doing would involve numbers or reports. Types of things that would be pre formatted. If there was any course that I would recommend that people going into business should take it would be business writing and that would be writing above the technical fields that they would be going into, whether it be engineering, accounting, law or whatever.

Shane: Do you feel you spend a lot of time writing?

Jim: I spend more than most people who are good at it. Like I said, I envy people that can put their thoughts down on paper in a concise, consistent manner very quickly. Most of the time I write a letter through and then I have to rewrite it. Even though the secretary takes a lot of dictation, there are some things that you just have to sit down and think through as you write.

Shane: Do you actually prepare most of your own documents as far as the actual writing down of the information is concerned?

Jim: I do fifty percent of my documents probably. Actually write them down because a lot of the time I generally write those that I have to include details: such as financial information, for example. Letters that don't have technical information in them, I tend to just dictate them. Normal communication correspondence I'll dictate.

FIGURE 8–9
Student Interview
Script.

Frank: With those that contain technical information, do you have Stan Carter do the research for you or use the other sources that are available to you?

Jim: Yeah, it could be anybody. That's a good question, Frank. I have Stan do a lot of the technical work in the department. If it's financial in nature, I'll do it. If I need help in more high level financial information or areas that I'm not accustomed to or that I don't have all the information necessary to compile the documents, I'll have other people send me that information, or if it's legal information, I'll have them send that information from the legal department.

Shane: I noticed in one of the documents you are requesting specific information and later use that information you requested in a later memo. Is this generally how research is done? Do you more or less contract it out?

Jim: Yeah, I guess so. If I don't have the information readily available or if somebody else can do it faster, I request that information from another area and have that area send that information to me and then I compile it the way I want to.

Shane: Do you spend a lot of time doing that or are most of the documents of the nature that the information is readily available?

Jim: That's a tough one to answer. I don't deal with a lot of the same questions and analyses that most departments do. There's not really a lot of redundant reports that come out of this department.

Shane: Is most of the writing solicited or do you do it on your own initiative?

Jim: No. Generally, it's something that I feel needs to be communicated to the rest of the company or with the parent company and I'll just prepare what I need to communicate with them.

FIGURE 8–9,
continued

Shane: Are written communications more important than verbal communications? In several of the documents, you don't include a lot of information but tell the reader to talk to someone else who knows about the subject of the document. Do you feel that the written part is more important or do they both play a part?

Jim: They both play a part. Even if I've communicated something verbally to a department, most of the time I'll write it down and send it in a memo. Either in addition to or opposed to verbal communication.

Shane: Would the purpose of that be to have it in writing as if in a contractual form to prove that it was said?

Jim: I think it helps both parties. It helps them use more of their senses. They can not only hear it but they can also read it and have a hard copy of it.

Frank: When do you decide something is so important that a phone call is just not enough by itself?

Jim: I debate that every time I write anything. Should I just talk to them, make a phone call, or should I write it down? Usually it has to do with short term or long term benefits and ramifications. If it's long term or something that's going to be ongoing, I'll write it down. If we're going to need feedback on it someday or if we're going to need to check out when we started a certain process, then I will write it down.

Frank: So it also gives the target of your letter or memo something to refer back to?

Jim: That's right.

Shane: In an urgent situation, such as "American Express," do you feel that you should tell these people first or do you feel the written document is enough to stand on its own?

FIGURE 8–9,
continued

Jim: I think that can stand on its own. A lot of times I'll write something down when it would be difficult to contact all those involved. In a department as diverse as this, some of the employees involved don't have an office that they sit in all day so you can get in touch with them. A lot of them are out in the field or work in a remote area or another state. A written document serves better in this type of situation .

Shane: How often does writing serve as a social function? There are a lot of letters that express congratulations or thanks rather than an actual business communication. How much of the writing is like this?

Jim: Probably five percent.

Shane: Do you feel that's important? Do you need that type of communication?

Jim: Yeah. In fact I ought to do more of it. I slipped a little into the "utility company mentality" a little bit where you don't congratulate anybody on doing a good job and you don't write anybody a letter and put it in their file or congratulate someone for doing something extra. I could do more of that. I try to do as much as I can. I should be devoting probably ten percent of my time doing that because I believe you can actually improve productivity better that way than to actually give someone better working skills, technical skills. This plays a larger part than most people realize.

Shane: So you don't do that as much as you would like to?

Jim: I don't do it as much as I should and I use the token term that I don't have enough time.

Shane: I noticed that all of the documents are very brief. Is this just due to their nature or...

FIGURE 8–9,
continued

Jim: No, I don't make anything very long. If I can consolidate things, I do. I don't usually clarify myself where I mention a certain subject and in another paragraph mention it in another way and then later on in a different paragraph reverse the language and present it again. The reason that I say that is generally when I receive a memo that is more than three paragraphs long it's not very well read by me. If I can read it quickly and get it off my desk and it just makes one or two key points as the intent, then I'll try to get that right up front. When a memo goes three paragraphs, I start to get nervous because I feel that it has gone on too long. Generally, I'll try to pick it apart and shorten it up even from there. But I'm not one to write lengthy memos and hopefully I never will.

Shane: Do you ever receive any criticisms of your writing?

Jim: No, but I've never really had anybody who I thought was competent in that area review it, which would be a good thing. I think you need that. If I really wanted to improve on my writing, what I should do is have somebody analyze that on a six month or yearly basis. Somebody that really knows writing. Maybe someone who teaches one of these business writing classes. Have them review it and say "you've slipped in this area" or "you use the passive voice here." I use the passive voice in a lot of the documents and I think the reason I do this is because it's a little better accepted with the older generation people that I'm communicating with. As opposed to saying "we need to replace this vehicle's engine because of...", I usually start a memo with "it is necessary to..." That's really poor but it's also, so far, in this company accepted as formal, so I cringe when I write in the passive voice but...

Shane: In your documents, it seems that this is a briefer format that way and lets you communicate your message without going into a lot of detail. Even if it is in the passive voice, it seems like a more brief way to communicate. On the other hand, do you ever comment or critique others?

Jim: No.

Frank: Do you have an editing cycle where others read the documents?

FIGURE 8–9,
continued

Jim: That's a good point. We do edit just about everything that goes out of here. If supervisors are writing anything that goes to anybody but me, that goes to a higher level of management, I'll edit those. And Alice edits everything I write and a lot of times she criticizes my writing. Don't you criticize my writing, Alice? Every once in a while Alice will take a document and recommend a different sentence structure or a different word to replace a group of words and that's helpful. In fact, generally speaking, people doing writing, if they're not going to have a backup or have someone type the document, they really should have an edit process, especially on spelling. People shouldn't really worry about the spelling in the document but should have it checked later, either with an automated system or by Alice.

Frank: I've always heard that Alice was the head of the department.

Jim: That's true. She always has and she maintains that she always will be.

Shane: Is there a lot of training involving writing?

Jim: No. A lot of positions don't require writing and if they do, I try to lend a hand, not from the criticism standpoint, but from the generally accepted standpoint.

Shane: Along those same lines does your company or department have any specific regulations? Is there a general superstructure that you have to follow?

Jim: No.

FIGURE 8–9,
continued

Here are some other tools to help analyze your data.

1. Read your interviews (listen) for a **thematic progression.** You may find, across interviews, that a writer returns to the issue of authority or constraints on his or her writing process, for example. These themes will be easier to see if you have a framework—a theory, prediction, standard, or perhaps a comparison that can guide your analysis.

2. Look for **show stoppers,** by reading back through your notes and transcript to see where an interviewee invests him- or herself. This may take the form of longer comments, nonverbal cues, or explicit statements such as, "that's a good question" or "hmm, I've never thought about that before." You may also read your notes and transcripts for direct questions that provoked indirect answers. Remember that the interviewee shapes the interview as much as the question-asker, and we may find in an answer a gesture toward the more subtle issues of power, authority, gender, personal investment, assumptions, values, ethics, or cultural bias.

3. One tool qualitative researchers use to avoid easy conclusions or being swayed by their own assumptions is consciously to look for *converging evidence,* that is, for evidence on the same point from different perspectives or bodies of data. The following grid represents many of the crossing and corroborating perspectives available in research on writers, process, and contexts. This grid is not to be filled. It only suggests that there are points of overlap; and the more points you find, the stronger position you will be in to interpret and make claims from your data.

    Figure 8–10 has three access points. Along the left-most, vertical axis are three kinds of information from interviews, in this case questions that probed writers, texts, and the context for writing in an organization. Along the top is information from texts: your analysis of models, a reader review, readability (those features that help or cue the reader), graphics, and document design. And along the bottom is information, in the form of observations, impressions, and assumptions that you bring to your research. As the diagram depicts, a convergence that signals stronger evidence can happen when any of these sources of information agrees with another.
    Use this grid to plan for your research or to analyze the information that you have found.

4. A final method for analyzing interview data is to share a transcript or listen to an interview with a group. You will be surprised at what you hear and how others hear differently.

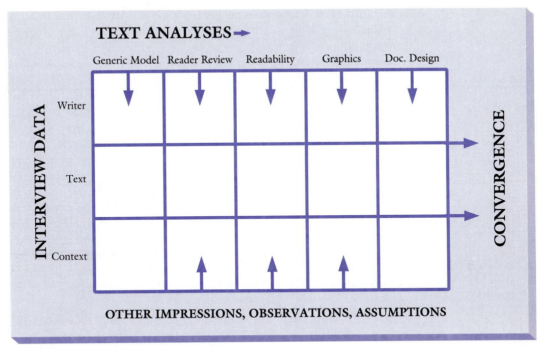

FIGURE 8–10
A Planning Grid for Convergences in Interview Research

 ## TOOL 6: WRITER'S BLOCK

Writer's block is not a tool that fits a specific purpose—people do not decide not to write. But blocking, or freezing up, is a real psychological phenomenon that has made its way into our cultural psyche. Movies portray undiscovered writers tossing page after empty page into a trash can late at night, unable to move beyond trite openings to their breakaway mystery novels—*It was a dark and stormy night . . .* We know of a screenwriter, who sometimes stays up for days, unable to uncork the formulas and twists that define modern television dramas. His solution?—to drive the Los Angeles freeways at 4 A.M. shouting out loud into a tape recorder. And as students, all of us have felt the tortured tick of the clock as we fish for an opening, a thread of an idea, a logical turn into a topic or style of writing unfamiliar to us. And every time we mutter, *never again.*

People block as writers for the same reasons as other personal and social situations build in complexity to the point of frustrated inability. Studies of writing anxiety and apprehension point to a basic contradiction in creative behavior. Composing is a highly creative *and* socially valued process—it demands full attention and a range of skills, ideas, and strategies, and it draws attention to itself. People judge it and we, as creators, know it. Some people still believe that good writers have a given knack instead of earned ability. Writing, more than other creative acts in our culture, tends to be quickly judged as imperfect because we equate good writing or speaking with intelligence, class, and power. Most of us have learned from school and society to judge writing primarily for its grammatical correctness. As readers we seek coherence, "flow," and impressive word choice; and we seek grammatical correctness because schools have overemphasized grammar at the expense of creativity and problem solving. But as writers, the creative demands conflict with our anticipation of critique—when our critical, editor selves override our ability to experiment with words and ideas, we block. The mystery writer is correct in throwing away his trite opening line, except that his timing is awful. More often than not, writers begin with bad prose, stuff that eventually needs to be thrown away—but to silence it prematurely is to deny the possibility of the better writing to come. Every writer starts somewhere.

We could argue that this entire book is our answer to writer's block because we want to help you to be conscious and strategic about how you size up a rhetorical situation, how you plan and craft a statement, and how you revise to the point of sharing with others. Practicing our strategies and yours will help you through many of those moments when writing and preparing a speech are hardest. There are, however, a few other strategies for solving writer's block that have evolved from research and the experiences of writers unknotting themselves.

1. Relax your commitment to rules, correctness, perfection. If you cannot produce, ask yourself why, and you may find that there is a rule (*Never use "I" in persuasive writing* or *Always begin a paragraph with a topic sentence*) that has tangled you up. Reject the rule until you have composed to the point of accomplishment; then return and ask if the rule is a strategy that has merit.

2. Walk away. We have written about incubation as a planning strategy. If you have the time, walking away from a writing dilemma could be a wise strategy. Psychologists have shown how people selectively forget certain details that allow them to reconceive a problem and solution.

3. Shift modalities. If you experience writer's block, go read something or talk to someone. Reading can be especially helpful because reading a paper trail or even reading a different kind of writing can help you hear and visualize the prose you want to write.

4. Accept blocking as part of your process; recognize it and call it something else. Names matter, and if you understand that writer's block may be a natural component of writing (and other kinds of creative behavior) you may become more accepting, less self-critical, and better able to resume sooner.

5. Shift to a different form of writing. Sometimes formal writing can be difficult, with all its models and conventions. Try writing less formally, in a letter form or story.

6. Plan to do. Reconsider the difference between planning to do and say, and shifting your attention away from ideas to your purpose in writing and your intended effect on an audience.

7. Shift the venue. Following the advice of our screenwriter, change the location. Your comfortable office may have turned into a reminder of all the work before you, and the activity of moving to another place may force you to think of something else.

8. Talk through the problem. If you plan collaboratively, you probably will not block because you have a partner to help you through the trouble spots.

9. Move to another part of the text. If you have trouble writing an executive summary, move on to another task. By shifting to tasks such as formatting or working with graphics, you can leave the time you have given to writing with a sense of accomplishment.

10. When the poet William Stafford was asked if he ever blocked, he said, "Of course, routinely, every day of my writing life!" When asked what he did about it, he replied, "I lower my standards!"

Summary

- **Document design** gives you a large body of devices and strategies for communicating visually through a printed page.
- Create a balanced page **layout** or grid that uses **whitespace** and margins for emphasis and clarity and uses **highlighting** techniques to draw the eye.
- Link your **visual design** to the structure of your ideas with devices such as text blocks and headings.
- Integrate your **graphic design** with the text, but make it tell its own clear story. Consider your options: tables, bar charts, line graphs, pie charts, or illustrative figures.
- The accurate and **ethical use** of graphics depends not only on what they say, but how they invite readers to interpret them.
- Develop an **oral presentation** just as you would a text, through planning and testing, but make use of the special conventions speech allows, including visual aids.

- A good communicator starts by being an active **listener** who depends on strategies for both creating and interpreting a dialogue.
- **Interviewing** depends on preparation beforehand that can focus discussion and anticipate the unexpected, and it calls for careful interpretation after the fact.
- If **writer's block** tries to stop you, change strategies.

Projects & Assignments

1. Return to the two letters in Chapter One, the Bill Collection Letter and the Heated Reply. Analyze the document design features that both writers used to augment their message. Itemize the features in these letters (or others that you have discovered) and write a short assessment of the document design approach and its success, given the intended purpose of the letters.
2. Revise the Donegal Mutual letter further for other stylistic features. You probably noted that the insurance firm used legalistic language. Consult Chapter Five for making local and global revisions of this letter. When you have finished, what can you say about how revising for a reader-based approach is complemented by document design?
3. Choose a graphic device out of a newspaper, textbook, magazine, or journal and see if you can reproduce the same data using another device. Often it is relatively easy to move back and forth from table to chart or from chart to table. As you make the switch, what rhetorical power is lost or gained?
4. Find examples of illustrations that are used to augment written text. Try writing the text without the picture to see how or whether words can replace pictures and as a way to practice integrating visuals into written text.
5. If you have written an essay, report, proposal, or critique lately, try to design an oral presentation of what you think are the key themes and examples. Not only choose what to talk about from your text, but use the text to produce visual aids to enhance your presentations. Have someone listen to your talk and read your text to see what was covered or missed in the change of form.

References

1. Tufte, Edward R. (1983). *The Visual Display of Quantitative Information*. Cheshire, CT: Graphics Press.
2. Ibid. p. 57.

Credits and Acknowledgments

Fig. 1.8 "Community Literacy Center Proposal Timeline." Reprinted by Permission of Community Literacy Center: A Community-University Collaborative, Pittsburgh, Pennsylvania.

Fig. 2.4 "Letter to the Editor from Concerned Property Owners and Taxpayers." Fig. 2.5 "County Organizations Back Pine Creek Trail Project." Fig. 2.6 "Letter to the Editor from Roy Fontaine, group chair; David Hafer, outings coordinator; and Gregory Merchant, newsletter editor." Reprinted by Permission of Wellsboro Gazette.

Fig. 2.7 "Proposal for Use of the Railroad Bed in Pine Creek Gorge." Reprinted by Permission of Patrick and Jill Maier, Mountain Trail Horse Center, Inc.

Fig. 3.5 "Investing with the Twentieth Century, an Interview." Reprinted by Permissions of Twentieth Century Investors.

Fig. 3.13 "Oil: The Introduction," and Fig. 3.14 "Oil: The Spice Editor." From "Planning in Writing: The Cognition of a Constructive Process" by Linda Flower, Karen A. Schriver, Linda Carey, Christina Haas and John R. Hayes. A portion of a computer manual written by a computer scientist: The "Before." A Portion of a computer manual written by a professional writer: The "After." A Rhetoric of Doing: Essays on written discourse in honor of James L. Kinneavy, Edited by Stephen P. Witte, Neil Nakadate, and Roger D. Cherry, published by Southern Illinois University Press, Carbondale. Reprinted by Permission of Karen A. Schriver.

Fig. 4.5 "Chairman's Letter to Shareowners." Reprinted by Permission of Pacific Telesis Group.

Fig. 4.12 "Design of corporate office building." Reprinted by permission of Valentiner, Crane, Brunjes, & Onyon Architects.

Fig. 6.5–6.10 "Example of Applications of MAC Project Software." "Example of Applications of MAC Project II Software." Reprinted by Permission of Claris Corporation.

Fig. 7.a–f "Professional correspondence of Rogers & Associates Engineering Corporation." Reprinted by Permission of Michael Rudick, Rogers & Associates.

Fig. 7.7a–d "Information from Jordan School District Finance Committee Report." Reprinted by Permission of C. Devon Sanderson, Jordan School District.

Fig. 7.7a–d "Outline Jordan School District Finance Committee Report." Reprinted by Permission of Brenda W. Weaver.

Fig. 7.14, 7.14b–f "Proposal for Professional Engineering Water system Master Plan and Development Prepared for by Sandy City, Feb. 1991." Reprinted by Permission of James W. Denney, Bush & Gudgell Inc.

Fig. 7.15 "The Recent College Graduate's Handbook of Financial Information with Special Reference to the concerns of Single Women." Reprinted by Permission of Irene Etzkorn, Siegel & Gale.

Fig. 7.17, 7.18 "Rapid Evaluation Method Criteria and Evaluation." from "Procedures for Postearthquake Safety Evaluation of Buildings by Applied Technology Council." Reprinted by Permission of California's Health, Planning, and Development Federal Emergency Management Agency.

Fig. 8.2 "Policyholder Correspondence," Reprinted by Permission of Donegal Mutual Insturance Company.

Fig. 8.8, 8.9a–f "Interview Questions for Writers in an Organization." Reprinted by Permission of Clark King.

Fig. 8.4b Reprinted by Permission of Edward Tufte, Graphics Press.

Fig. 8.6 "Copyright (co) 1978 Fuel Economy Standards for Autos by the New York Times Company. Reprinted by Permission."

Photographs, page 25, top to bottom: © J. Pickerell/The Image Works; Courtesy of International Business Machines Corporation; © Paul Talley.

Index